SOVEREIGNTY, EMERGENCY, LEGALITY

It is widely recognized that times of national emergency put legality to its greatest test. In such times we rely on sovereign power to rescue us, to hold the danger at bay. Yet that power can and often does threaten the values of legality itself. *Sovereignty, Emergency, Legality* examines law's complex relationship to sovereign power and emergency conditions. It puts today's responses to emergency in historical and institutional context, reminding readers of the continuities and discontinuities in the ways emergencies are framed and understood at different times and in different situations. And, in all this, it suggests the need to be less abstract in the way we discuss sovereignty, emergency, and legality. This book concentrates on officials and the choices they make in defining, anticipating, and responding to conditions of emergency as well as the impact of their choices on embodied subjects, whether citizen or stranger.

This book is a product of the University of Alabama School of Law symposia series on "Law, Knowledge & Imagination." This series explores the ways law is known and imagined in a diverse array of disciplines, including political science, history, cultural studies, philosophy, and science. Books produced through the Alabama symposia will explore various conjunctions of law, knowledge, and imagination as they play out in debates about theory and policy and will speak to venerable questions as well as contemporary issues.

Austin Sarat is William Nelson Cromwell Professor of Jurisprudence Political Science at Amherst College and Justice Hugo L. Black Senior Faculty Scholar at the University of Alabama School of Law. He is author or editor of more than seventy books, including *When the State Kills: Capital Punishment and the American Condition*; *Something to Believe In: Politics, Professionalism, and Cause Lawyers* (with Stuart Scheingold); *The Blackwell Companion to Law and Society*; and most recently *The Road to Abolition?: The Future of Capital Punishment in the United States* (with Charles Ogletree Jr.). Sarat is editor of the journal *Law, Culture and the Humanities* and of *Studies in Law, Politics and Society*. In 1997, he received the Harry Kalven Award given by the Law and Society Association for distinguished research on law and society. In 2004, he received the Reginald Heber Smith Award, given biennially to honor the best scholarship on the subject of equal access to justice. In 2006, the Association for the Study of Law, Culture and the Humanities awarded him the James Boyd White Prize for distinguished scholarly achievement in recognition of his "innovative and outstanding" work in the humanistic study of law. In 2009, he received the Stan Wheeler Award from the Law and Society Association for distinguished teaching and mentoring.

Sovereignty, Emergency, Legality

Edited by

Austin Sarat

Amherst College

CAMBRIDGE
UNIVERSITY PRESS

CAMBRIDGE UNIVERSITY PRESS
Cambridge, New York, Melbourne, Madrid, Cape Town, Singapore,
São Paulo, Delhi, Dubai, Tokyo

Cambridge University Press
32 Avenue of the Americas, New York, NY 10013-2473, USA

www.cambridge.org
Information on this title: www.cambridge.org/9780521112239

First published 2010

Printed in the United States of America

A catalog record for this publication is available from the British Library.

Library of Congress Cataloging in Publication data
Sovereignty, emergency, legality / [edited by] Austin Sarat.
p. cm.
Includes index.
ISBN 978-0-521-11223-9 (hardback)
1. Sovereignty. 2. War and emergency legislation. 3. Rule of law.
4. Milligan, Lambdin P. 5. Constitutional law. 6. Democracy.
I. Sarat, Austin. II. Title.
K3344.S68 2010
342′.062–dc22 2009047103

ISBN 978-0-521-11223-9 Hardback

To Stephanie, Lauren, Emily, and Ben

Contents

Contributors

Debra Lyn Bassett, Professor of Law, Southwestern Law School

Sumi Cho, Professor of Law, DePaul University

J. Shahar Dillbary, Assistant Professor of Law, University of Alabama

David Dyzenhaus, Professor of Law and Philosophy and Associate Dean, Graduate Studies, Faculty of Law, University of Toronto and Fellow of the Royal Society of Canada

Leonard C. Feldman, Associate Professor of Political Science, University of Oregon

Tony A. Freyer, University Research Professor of History and Law, University of Alabama

Gil Gott, Associate Professor of International Studies, DePaul University

Patrick O. Gudridge, Professor of Law, University of Miami School of Law

Paul Horwitz, Associate Professor of Law, University of Alabama

James Leonard, Associate Dean for Legal Information Services and Professor of Law, University of Alabama

Michel Rosenfeld, Justice Sydney L. Robins Professor of Human Rights and Director, Security, Democracy, and the Rule of Law, Cardozo Law School

Austin Sarat, William Nelson Cromwell Professor of Jurisprudence and Political Science, Amherst College, and Hugo Black Senior Faculty Scholar, University of Alabama School of Law

Acknowledgments

This volume is the product of a symposium held at the University of Alabama School of Law on October 17, 2008. I want to thank the colleagues, students, and staff who helped make that such a successful event. I am grateful for the financial support of the University of Alabama Law School Foundation. A special word of thanks to Dean Ken Randall for his unstinting support, for sharing the vision of legal scholarship reflected in these pages, and for making me feel so at home at the law school.

Introduction: Toward New Conceptions of the Relationship of Law and Sovereignty under Conditions of Emergency

Austin Sarat

It is widely recognized today that times of national emergency put legality to its greatest test.[1] In such times we rely on political leaders, using sovereign prerogative, to act in the national interest. John Locke famously defined that prerogative as the "power to act according to discretion, for the public good, without the prescription of the Law, and sometimes even against it. … [T]here is a latitude left to the Executive power, to do many things of choice, which the Laws do not prescribe."[2]

Yet, political leaders may go too far, threatening the values that define our national identity. Thus, in June 2004 the United States Supreme Court sharply rejected George W. Bush's assertions that he had unchecked unilateral authority to lock up indefinitely any person he declared an "enemy combatant" in the global "war on terrorism." Writing for the Court, Justice Sandra Day O'Connor declared that a "state of war is not a blank check for the President."[3] And more recently, the Supreme Court ruled that foreign nationals held at Guantanamo Bay have a right to pursue habeas challenges to their detention.[4] Justice Anthony M. Kennedy, writing for the majority in *Boumediene v. Bush* and *Al Odah v. U.S.*, wrote that the Constitution's Suspension Clause "protects the rights of the detained by a means consistent with the essential design of the Constitution. It ensures that, except

1 David Dyzenhaus, *Legality and Legitimacy: Carl Schmitt, Hans Kelsen and Hermann Heller in Weimar*. New York: Oxford University Press, 1999. Also John Yoo, *The Powers of War and Peace: The Constitution and Foreign Affairs After 9/11*, Chicago: University of Chicago Press, 2005.

2 John Locke, *Second Treatise on Civil Government*, C. B. Macpherson, ed., Indianapolis, IN: Hackett Publishing, 1980, sections 159–160.

3 See *Hamdi v. Rumsfeld*, 542 U.S. 507, 521 (2004).

4 *Boumediene v. Bush/Al Odah v. U.S.*, 553 U.S. (2008).

during periods of formal suspension, the Judiciary will have a time-tested device, the writ, to maintain the 'delicate balance of governance' that is itself the surest safeguard of liberty."[5]

Nevertheless, the tensions between sovereignty and legality that arise in times of emergency seem hardly to be put to rest even by such decisions. While scholars such as Bruce Ackerman have tried to identify ways to reconcile the demands of emergency and the procedures of legality,[6] in the aftermath of 9/11 most scholars have suggested that the United States faced a rather stark choice – between the prerogatives of sovereignty to respond to conditions of emergency and strict adherence to the rule of law.[7] Drawing on theorists such as Carl Schmitt and Giorgio Agamben, many have recently articulated tensions between sovereignty and legality that conditions of emergency bring to the fore.[8]

Agamben suggests that sovereignty is the power to decide on an exception and remove a subject from the purview of "regular" law. In the use of such terminology, of course, Agamben draws on Schmitt's famous definition: "the sovereign is he who decides on the state of exception."[9] This definition reflects Schmitt's interest in the personal element of the decision and in the agonistic and borderline relation of exception and norm. Schmitt, who was a prominent legal and political theorist of Weimar and Nazi Germany, understood the exception in relation to a state of emergency, a situation of economic and political crisis that imperils the state and would require the suspension of regular law and rules to resolve.[10]

Both capture "the essence of the state's sovereignty, which must be juridically defined correctly, not as the monopoly to coerce or to rule, but as the monopoly to decide."[11] At its core, Schmitt insists sovereignty embodies a conception of power that is decisionist. Sovereignty cannot, of course, live

[5] *Id.*, at 574.

[6] Bruce Ackerman, "The Emergency Constitution," *Yale Law Journal* 113 (2004), 1029.

[7] See Laurence Tribe and Patrick O. Gudridge, "The Anti-Emergency Constitution," *Yale Law Journal* 113 (2004), 1801.

[8] See Carl Schmitt, *Political Theology: Four Chapters on the Concept of Sovereignty*, 2nd ed., George Schwab trans. Cambridge, MA: MIT Press, 1932, 1985; Also Giorgio Agamben, *Homo Sacer: Sovereign Power and Bare Life*, Daniel Heller-Roazen, trans. Stanford: Stanford University Press, 1998.

[9] Schmitt, *Political Theology*, 5.

[10] See Nasser Hussain, "Thresholds: Sovereignty and the Sacred," *Law and Society Review* 34 no. 2 (2000), 495.

[11] Schmitt, *Political Theology*, 13.

without the concept of norm that it subtends and is parasitical upon, but that only leaves the matter more relational and agonistic.

The sovereign exception is, as Agamben puts it, "a kind of exclusion," and, as if recapitulating the distinction between law and equity, he says that "What is excluded from the general rule is an individual case. … [W]hat is excluded … is not, on account of being excluded, absolutely without relation to the rule. On the contrary, what is excluded in the exception maintains itself in relation to the rule in the form of the rule's suspension. The rule applies to the exception in no longer applying, in withdrawing from it."[12] As Jill Stauffer explains, "Agamben traces Schmitt's argument about sovereignty: the sovereign decides on the state of exception such that what the sovereign declares exceptional is still legal. A state of emergency is a 'zone of indistinction' between exception and rule – it is both and neither. Of course, Schmitt aimed to justify that form of sovereign power while Agamben's analysis instead teases out its lasting implications."[13]

Agamben's *Homo Sacer* points to the formative and continuing influence of a vision of sovereignty that is by no means completely extinguished by electoral democracy or the rule of law. However, he is distinctly less useful in understanding the historical mutations and contemporary arrangements of sovereign power under these conditions. Indeed, it may be that existing scholarship is so caught up in the Schmitt/Agamben opposition of sovereignty and law that we have been inattentive to the myriad of ways in which law imagines, anticipates, and responds to emergencies, ways in which sovereign prerogative is either irrelevant or operates within the terrain of ordinary legal procedures.[14] As Paul Kahn puts it, "The sovereign power is not just at the border of law, but deep within the law as well."[15]

One way of beginning to break through those binary conceptions is to recognize that, in the Hobbesian social contract tradition, law itself issues from emergency or, if not emergency, then a slightly lesser kind of urgency. In its most influential iteration, in Hobbes' *Leviathan*, the liberal account describes a state of disorder from which all prudent reasoning persons seek

[12] Agamben, *Homo Sacer*, 17–18.

[13] Jill Stauffer, "The Thought of Freedom: A Possible Coming Sovereignty," unpublished ms., 10.

[14] See Cass Sunstein, *Laws of Fear: Beyond the Precautionary Principle*, Cambridge: Cambridge University Press, 2005.

[15] Paul Kahn, "The Question of Sovereignty," *Stanford Journal of International Law* 40 (2004), 63.

to flee.[16] Recall, for Hobbes the state of nature does *not* refer to a historical condition; in this regard, he parts company with Locke who believed that all societies evolved out of such a state. For Hobbes, the state of nature, is an *analytic* condition: it is the state that societies always threaten to revert back to given the right set of conditions.

Seen in this light, law is constituted in the effort to escape an impending state of emergency; indeed, law is what makes possible the defeat of catastrophic disorder and violence. In this reckoning, then, emergency is both jurisgenerative[17] – it is the ever-present threat of chaos that creates the need for law – and the very antithesis or negation of law – it is the uncontrollable force that threatens to extirpate law's ordering effects on social life. Once law has been established to maintain social order, emergency remains as law's nemesis, the unruly force that would overturn the rules and regimes so carefully constructed by the principles and practices of legality. In this picture, the specter of emergency plays a crucial role in law's justificatory logic; law appears as the bulwark between civilization and its breakdown.

Another way to get beyond the oppositional logic that animates many discussions of sovereignty, emergency, and legality is to examine the quotidian, or ordinary, modes through which political authorities anticipate and respond to emergency and to attend to their distributional effects. Thus anticipating emergency and responding to it may be embedded within an existing regulatory apparatus. Administrative agencies are often charged with articulating and enforcing rules that attempt to anticipate and prevent emergencies.[18] For example, the Transportation Security Administration is responsible for regulating passenger and freight transportation in the United States in a manner that will safeguard against catastrophic accidents and attacks.

Yet regulatory agencies and administrations do not occupy the entire field of law's response to emergency. Thus criminal law's response has been

[16] Thomas Hobbes, *Leviathan*, Cambridge: Cambridge University Press, 2002.

[17] See Robert Cover, "Nomos and Narrative," in *Narrative, Violence, and the Law*, Martha Minow, Michael Ryan, and Austin Sarat, eds., Ann Arbor: University of Michigan Press, 1995.

[18] William Petak, "Emergency Management: A Challenge for Public Administration," *Public Administration Review* 45 (1985), 3. Also Bonnie Honig, "Bound by Law? Alien Rights, Administrative Discretion, and the Politics of Technicality: Lessons from Louis Post and the First Red Scare," in *The Limits of Law*, Austin Sarat, Lawrence Douglas, and Martha Merrill Umphrey, eds., Stanford: Stanford University Press, 2005.

preoccupied with two kinds of emergency threats: those posed by states and those posed by terrorist groups. Under the former, we think of trials of perpetrators of state-sponsored atrocities, such as genocide and crimes against humanity.[19]

In the case of terrorist threats, the law's response *has* clearly been aimed at anticipation and prevention – though this itself has emerged as a subject of intense controversy.[20] Indeed, the most pressing constitutional issues of the day now involve questions such as the following: Does the executive branch enjoy inherent powers to order wiretaps of alleged terrorist suspects in the absence of congressional authorization or judicial warrants? Does the executive have inherent powers to authorize the use of "unorthodox" interrogation techniques for terrorist suspects? Should terrorist suspects be entitled to the full panoply of rights and procedures that come with trials before Article III courts? And how can we characterize the powers claimed by the executive branch? Are they either legal or illegal, or is it important to use another characterization altogether such as "extralegal"? These controversies raise the larger question of how we should go about striking the proper balance between civil liberties and collective security in an age of terrorism.

At the most basic level, then, the need to anticipate and prevent terrorist-sponsored catastrophes has raised foundational questions about the substance and procedures of the criminal law.[21] Predictably enough, the answers to these questions often fall back on classic Hobbesian arguments: that in the face of catastrophic violence, the interests of security trump all. And yet this logic is peculiarly self-defeating: the law's draconian efforts to anticipate and prevent terrorism threaten to erode its distinctive status as a *normative* tool of social order.

As we shift our attention to the civil law, strategies for anticipating and preventing emergencies are perhaps still less controversial. In the world of civil law, emergencies originate not in Al Qaeda plots but, for example, in corporate malfeasance. The paradigmatic instance remains the Bhopal disaster, and the paradigmatic response involves the assignment of risk: the

19 See Lawrence Douglas, *The Memory of Judgment: Making Law and History in the Trials of the Holocaust*, New Haven, CT: Yale University Press, 2001.

20 See James Renwick and Gregory F. Treverton, *The Challenges of Trying Terrorists as Criminals*, Santa Monica, CA: Rand Corporation, 2008.

21 *Id.*

law shifts risk to the party best able to assess and manage it.[22] In the case of emergency, the costs of amelioration are so staggeringly high, that emphasis must be on prevention. This also is a central argument of Judge Richard Posner's *Catastrophe: Risk and Response.*[23] For Posner, the law often falters in response to emergencies as a result of the "bafflement that most people feel when they try to think about events that have an extremely low probability of occurring even if they will inflict enormous harm if they do occur."[24]

What all this suggests is the need to think beyond the drama of the sovereign suspension of legality to appreciate the more ordinary ways through which law anticipates and responds to emergency. It suggests the need to put today's responses to emergency in historical and institutional context, to remind ourselves of continuities and discontinuities in the ways emergencies are framed and understood at different times and in different institutions. And, in all this, it suggests the need to be less abstract in the way we discuss sovereignty, emergency, and legality. Instead, we need to concentrate on officials and the choices they make in defining, anticipating, and responding to conditions of emergency as well as the impact of their choices on embodied subjects, whether citizen or stranger.

The chapters in *Sovereignty, Emergency, Legality* take up these challenges. Indeed in one sense *Sovereignty, Emergency, Legality* might be accurately described as engaging the work of a second generation of post-9/11 scholarship, one that seeks to get beyond binary conceptions to explore new analytic possibilities. This book begins with a chapter of historical exegesis, examining the roots of legal restrictions on emergency power and a chapter examining the institutional practices of courts, especially their use of the so called "collateral bar" rule in situations of emergency. Subsequent chapters re-theorize the relationship of sovereignty, emergency, and legality, moving away from Schmitt and Agamben toward new understandings.

Sovereignty, Emergency, Legality is the product of an integrated series of symposia at School of Law at the University of Alabama. These symposia bring leading scholars into colloquy with faculty at the law school on

22 William Bogard, *The Bhopal Tragedy: Language, Logic, and Politics in the Production of a Hazard*, Westview, CT: Westview Press, 1989. Also Paul Shrivastava, *Bhopal: Anatomy of a Crisis*, Cambridge: Ballinger, 1987.

23 Richard Posner, *Catastrophe: Risk and Response.* New York: Oxford University Press, 2004.

24 *Id.*, 9.

subjects at the cutting edge of interdisciplinary inquiry in law. That colloquy is represented here in the commentaries that accompany each chapter.

This book opens with a chapter by David Dyzenhaus which applies what A.V. Dicey wrote about martial law in a common law constitutional legal order to America's constitutional system. Dyzenhaus considers not only Dicey's writings, but also compares the Supreme Court rulings in *Ex Parte Milligan* (1866) and *Boumediene v. Bush* (2008). Dicey appears to agree with the Court's holding in *Milligan* that military tribunals established by the executive or the legislature may not try civilians as long as ordinary courts of law are open. As Dicey puts it, "'martial law' ... is unknown to the law of England." However, as Dyzenhaus points out, Dicey took for granted the supremacy of Parliament; because he believed that judges must defer to statutes passed by Parliament, judges could find themselves having to sign off on the establishment of martial law, were Parliament to pass a statute demanding it.

But, as Dyzenhaus emphasizes, there is a difference between power and authority; while Parliament may have the power to do anything it pleases, it does not possess the authority to do so. In his words, "authority is lost when any institution of legal order, no matter its place in the hierarchy, exercises its power in a way that subverts instead of maintaining or enhancing the general project of legality to which all institutions of a legal order are committed."

According to Dyzenhaus, the United States today possesses a "Realist" legal system, meaning that many in the legal academy believe that the history of emergency law reveals that, for all intents and purposes, either executive unilateralism (radical Realism) or legislative unilateralism (moderate Realism) has reigned during emergencies. For Dyzenhaus, however, where the sovereign power is ultimately located is not as important as the quality of the legal order – whether "government exercises its power in accordance with law, in accordance, that is, with the rule of law or legality."

As Dyzenhaus notes, it is easiest to understand this in the context of a common law legal order like Dicey's England. While Parliament is sovereign, it "is constrained in so far as that if it wishes to speak as a *legal* sovereign, it has to speak in the language of the law." In order to overrule common law in a period of emergency, Parliament must pass new laws explicitly stating what the government can do. In this way, the rule of law is preserved, rather than suspended.

Dyzenhaus applies this idea of legal sovereignty to a reading of the *Milligan* decision, in which the U.S. government argued that the executor of martial law had the power to do whatever it deemed necessary. In response, Milligan's counsel argued that, on the contrary, "the President has no authority but that which he gets from law." A five-justice majority sided with Milligan, asserting that neither the executive nor the legislature had the power to establish military tribunals to try civilians unless normal courts were actually closed.

According to Dyzenhaus, "U.S. Supreme Court jurisprudence since 9/11 has tended to reproduce a shuttle between judicial unilateralism and legislative unilateralism, with the latter containing the same dangerous tendency to endorse executive unilateralism, as long as it can claim a statutory warrant." The first Supreme Court decisions following 9/11 were largely consistent with an "institutional process-based approach." However, as Dyzenhaus points out, the *Boumediene* decision did not follow this approach; despite the fact that Congress had passed the Military Commissions Act at the president's request, the Supreme Court ruled that portions of it were unconstitutional.

Justice Scalia picked up on this point in his dissent. He pointed out the inconsistencies between four of the justices' positions in *Hamdan* (that the military commissions were unconstitutional only because Congress had not approved them) and their position in *Boumediene* (that the Combat Status Review Tribunals, CSRTs, established by Congress were not an adequate substitute for habeas corpus). The four justices to whom Justice Scalia refers essentially moved from supporting a form of legislative unilateralism to supporting a form of judicial unilateralism. As Dyzenhaus observes, the majority in *Boumediene* believed that it matters very little which branch of government has the final say; the quality of the power matters far more. Thus, that Congress had authorized the CSRTs could not make up for the fact that they were a wholly inadequate substitute for the writ of habeas corpus in the first place.

As Dyzenhaus explains, even in a common law system in which Parliament is supreme, Parliament cannot throw out the rule of law. Instead, it can explicitly alter it for the duration of an emergency. Thus, parliamentary supremacy "makes the rule of law possible, since it provides the basis for accountability of the executive to law." In considering how sovereignty is affected by emergency, then, Dyzenhaus emphasizes, contra Schmitt and Agamben, that we must consider more than simply who can make the final decision. More importantly, we must make sure that the sovereign's actions remain within both the state's positive laws and its commitment to the rule of law.

The next chapter, by Patrick O. Gudridge, takes up the question of how conditions of emergency affect judges' understandings of their roles. He is particularly interested in the extent to which in such conditions judges insist that citizens strictly adhere to legality's forms and procedures. Gudridge presents an intriguing analysis of the famous case of *Walker v. City of Birmingham*, a case in which the Supreme Court refused to reach the merits of a constitutional claim on the grounds that the petitioners had not abided by an arguably unconstitutional injunction. The Court did so by invoking the so called "collateral bar rule." That rule provides that a party may not violate an order and raise the issue of its unconstitutionality collaterally as a defense in a criminal contempt proceeding.

Justice Felix Frankfurter provided vigorous defense of the collateral bar rule in *United States v. United Mineworkers*. The Mineworker's leadership had set in motion a dramatic nationwide strike, flouting a judicial order enjoining that strike. It simply did not matter, Justice Frankfurter thought, whether the judge who issued that injunction initially acted rightly or wrongly. Knowing disregard of the judicial order was contempt. To protect "legal process," judges – especially Supreme Court Justices – are duty-bound to ignore legal substance in bringing to bear legal force. Judges too, Gudridge contends sometimes act as "soldiers" who are "authorized legally to act forcefully independently of ordinarily applicable legal norms."

In *Walker*, the collateral bar rule was again brought to bear. As Gudrigde notes "Justice Stewart's majority opinion agreed that the ordinance and the order were constitutionally questionable. However, respect for the '[j] udicial process... is a small price to pay for the civilizing hand of law,' the means to 'give abiding meaning to constitutional freedom.'"

Gudridge asks "Why was it so important, in cases of such obvious significance on the merits to wield judicial prerogative so emphatically?" Here he turns his attention to another case, *Korematsu v. United States*. Fred Korematsu was prosecuted for violating a military order during World War II directing him to report to a relocation center. He disobeyed the order and sued. The Supreme Court reached the merits of his claim and upheld the validity of the order. Thus Gudridge asks, "Why was Korematsu permitted to challenge the validity of the order he disobeyed when Martin Luther King (and John L. Lewis and the Mine Workers) were not?"

The answer to this question, Gudridge contends, suggests that in times of emergency the law emphasizes and protects its own authority as the touchstone of any decision. As he puts it, "Insubordination vis a vis the military in time of war did not pose a crisis; disregard of judicial orders did." In the analysis of the complex relationships of sovereignty, emergency, and legality, Gudridge argues, "the pertinent sense of emergency must be strongly keyed to institutional perspective." He cautions against decontextualized treatments of states of emergency. Careful examination of judicial responses to emergencies suggests "Judges may not perceive emergencies that other actors are quite sure are at hand; but judges – perhaps unexpectedly from other points of view – may experience crises of their own."

In "The Banality of Emergency" Leonard Feldman attempts to reorient the ways scholars investigate the politics of the emergency. He argues that this field has been too narrowly focused on the theories of Schmitt and Giorgio Agamben, with the result that even scholars critical of these approaches become entangled in Schmitt's outlines of the inside and outside of law. A newer approach, which Feldman's chapter elaborates emphasizes the "prosaic politics of emergency" rather than the extraordinary "state of exception" and recognizes that the true state of exception, a state of unlimited authority for the sovereign, is not created by every extraordinary or emergency measure. Since emergency powers are mainly employed in circumstances less extraordinary than total emergencies, this new approach, Feldman contends, may prove more helpful than Schmitt's model.

Feldman discusses two areas in which the legacy of Schmitt has distorted the discourse on emergency powers. First, he describes the focus on the spatial relationship between sovereign exceptionalism and the ordinary legal order. Contemporary debates often work within this framework, as "extra-legalists" or "neo-Lockeans" argue that emergency powers exist outside of the law and the jurisdiction of courts, and "institutional reformers" attempt to create a legal basis for emergency powers by making them subject to legal checks.

Schmitt himself, Feldman argues, held the more nuanced position that the sovereign exists both inside and outside of the law, but he still focused on the spatial aspect of this relationship. This conception presents problems for scholars attempting to identify as either inside or outside of the law the sovereign actions of American presidents or the prerogative power of Locke's prince. Feldman asserts that this emphasis on a spatial model neglects the temporal aspects of political processes. In a temporal understanding, emergency actions are within the law so long as they are accepted by the public and official institutions and outside the law when the public and institutions begin to resist them. The focus on spatiality also narrows the field of inquiry to the extraordinary while ignoring the routine violence of the law, such as prison violence and warrantless searches.

Schmitt's influence is also felt in the analogy he proposed between the exception and the miracle. The exception is analogous to the miracle in two ways. First, the exception does not exist within preformed outlines, but is created by the decision of the sovereign as a kind of performative speech. Secondly, the sovereign's suspension of positive law in the exception parallels God's suspension of natural laws in the performance of miracles. Schmitt's other representation of the exception is that of real life erupting into the legal machine. With the rise of popular sovereignty the role of the sovereign has been minimized so that the machine runs itself until it is necessary for the sovereign to break into the bureaucratic machine and redeem the political order. Against these formulations Feldman juxtaposes Foucault's ideas about governmentality based on pastoral power claiming that it is more helpful than Schmitt in examining the intersection between religion and politics.

Feldman next takes up everyday emergencies involving police actions. For Agamben, the sovereign exception extends to the police when they decide how much violence to use in a situation. Police authority allows for a great deal of discretion, especially when the action can be placed under the heading of "community care taking" rather than law enforcement. Community care taking is understandable as a form of princely prerogative power in a liberal order, acting outside of the law for the public good. Feldman argues that this power is best understood as discretion rather than sovereignty and offers evidence for the frequent blurring of the line between law enforcement and community care taking leading to many suspensions of the Fourth Amendment.

Feldman concludes by arguing that the debate about emergency powers needs to recognize the coexistence of multiple legal orders. In this framework, the exception can be understood as belonging to a different body of laws rather than as a departure from all laws.

Feldman claims that in the study of emergency we should, like Schmitt himself, insist on the difference between a true state of exception and "lesser" emergencies in order to establish the redemptive and generative power of a state of exception. We should take up this difference as a way to gain better insight into the prosaic (and perhaps more insidious) politics of emergency in the life of constitutional democracies.

In the next chapter, Sumi Cho and Gill Gott also take up Schmitt's conceptions of sovereignty, emergency, and legality and join Feldman in rejecting his binary approach to separating sovereignty and legality. They focus their critique on the lack of attention that proponents of Schmittean theories have devoted to the racial aspects of the political and legal systems underlying Schmitt's model. Schmittean "decisions on the exception" by sovereign holders of state power, while seen by Schmitt as revealing the fundamental weakness of legal liberalism, may, they argue, "also be taken in the current US context as instances of socially-inflected, identity/ideology-driven exercises of imperially-oriented legalism, liberal or otherwise."

The racial basis of sovereignty can be seen, they argue, in particular instances in which the race of Barack Obama was explicitly or implicitly introduced into the 2008 presidential campaign. As the election grew nearer and the Republican nominees sought to overcome losses in the debates and in poll numbers, they and their supporters increasingly brought up Senator Obama's race, Arab-sounding name, and alleged connection to domestic terrorism. For example, Governor Palin cited a *New York Times* article in tying Senator Obama to Bill Ayers at a rally in Florida, allowing comments from the audience such as "Kill him!" to pass unaddressed. While she did not explicitly mention Senator Obama's race or use language that was directly racial, Cho and Gott argue that some aspects of her remarks invoke common racialized themes of this country: a white female launching unsubstantiated charges against a black man, the implication that the black man is somehow dangerous to the mainly white audience, and the shouts from the crowd for vigilante justice. Similar strategies of invoking race can be seen in previous presidential elections as well, with the Republican Party's "southern strategy" of deliberately attracting racist whites during Nixon's campaign, Reagan placing his campaign kick-off in Philadelphia, Mississippi, famous for local complaisance toward the race-based murder of civil rights workers, and the Willie Horton attack ad on Governor Dukakis as some of the most obvious examples.

These events illustrate underlying racial prerequisites in our conception of sovereignty, whether physical – being white – or ideological – presenting an image of an appropriate level of whiteness – that persist even in these times of "formal equality." Traditional discourses setting emergency against legality and civil liberties against security are flawed, Cho and Gott argue, because they neglect the racial components of security and the social nature of the sovereign. Recognizing these facts leads to an analysis of the state of exception as a racialized and politicized event.

Courts, Cho and Gott note, historically affirmed the "racial dictatorship" of whites, in part by developing foundational legal principles, such as the definitions of "citizen" and "national security," that reinforced racial stratifications. In addressing questions of native sovereignty, for example, Supreme Court Justice John Marshall contradicted European and early American customs of recognizing the sovereignty of Native Americans over their land. As American expansionism and military strength led to increased conflicts with natives, Marshall sought, in cases like *Johnson v. M'Intosh*, to reconcile the need to grant natives enough sovereignty to legitimize the treaties they signed ceding land to the United States but not enough that they could enforce the terms of those treaties. Marshall's decision in *Johnson* invoked the European Doctrine of Discovery, British Rights of Conquest, and the "Might Makes Right" philosophy, all based on the endorsement of white racial supremacy over the "fierce," "savage," "uncivilized" natives who do not meet the anthropological threshold of inclusion under the law.

Cho and Gott link this historical argument with an examination of the concept of whiteness as security. Security is not a pre-existing concept, they argue, but gains meaning only through social, cultural, and institutional practices as those who are involved in defining security interests invest them with racial meaning. This is apparent in *Korematsu* and in modern times on such issues as Guantanamo Bay detainees and Immigration and Customs Enforcement (I.C.E.) raids in Latino communities.

Cho and Gott conclude by advocating that more attention be paid to the social reality behind both Schmittean and liberal formulations of sovereignty, emergency, and legality. The most important aspects of these concepts, they suggest, are their roles in the racial subordination of certain groups.

Like Feldman, Michel Rosenfeld worries about the traditional divide between times of normalcy and times of emergency. Modern problems like terrorism, religious fundamentalism, and globalization require a third category, he contends, that of "stress," which is less severe, less intense, and more durable than a time of crisis. Periods of stress are conceptually located between normalcy, in which political rights are protected to their fullest, and emergency, in which the sovereign may suspend rights. But Rosenfeld argues that rather than a curtailment of political rights between these extremes, the appropriate reaction in times of stress is often the reinforcement of these rights.

All contemporary constitutional democracies are pluralistic, meaning that members hold different conceptions of the good. Rights in pluralist societies therefore deal with mediating conflicts between competing conceptions of the good. The state must choose one conception of the good to pursue, and Rosenfeld focuses on what he calls "comprehensive pluralism," in which societies that are pluralist-in-fact pursue the good of promoting pluralism as a norm. This involves the eradication of all entrenched institutional support for one good over another and the reintegration of disparate conceptions of the good in a manner that accommodates as many conceptions as possible while simultaneously providing equal opportunity for each to flourish. Comprehensive pluralism, here, is a conception of the good that differs from all others because it depends on them for its own existence.

In comprehensive pluralist polities, the norms of pluralism are second-order, and the norms of other conceptions of the good are first-order. The second-order pluralist norms provide the framework for the constitution. This constitution may resemble liberal ones by incorporating the rule of law and the protection of rights, but pluralist constitutions will be different, for example, by protecting greater freedom of expression and group as well as individual rights. The primary tasks of the polity are to decide how to set up the government and to decide what subjects fall under the purview of constitutional politics and what under ordinary politics. Both of these tasks are to be addressed based on an evaluation of the circumstances of the particular polity.

During ordinary times, the conflicts between self and other are resolved within the political framework and do not threaten the unity of the polity. Claimants generally see the resolutions as fair and just. In periods of crisis, however, when the polity itself is in peril, different conceptions of the good are not accommodated and citizens often perceive resolutions as unfair. Between these extremes, during times of stress, there is some diminished accommodation of different conceptions of the good.

State actions in the ongoing war on terror may limit political rights of association and political participation for some citizens. Rather than completely suspending fundamental rights, Rosenfeld contends, the state should engage in a "re-calibration" of the balancing of rights that gives greater than normal weight to state security interests. In all instances of stress, Rosenfeld argues, the goal of the state should be to strengthen, or at least to prevent weakening of the bonds between selves and others. The appropriate response may be to reinforce, readjust, or weaken certain rights. The specific circumstances of any situation of stress determine the best course to follow.

Taken together the essays collected here point the direction for an historically and contextually rooted understanding of the relationship of sovereignty, emergency, and legality. They urge scholars to break with binary, "spatial" conceptions in which sovereign responses to emergency must be either lawful or not. They highlight the importance of moving beyond abstractions to consider the social relations and social dynamics that emergencies depend on and bring into being. And, in the end, they dramatically expand the range of normative responses that our society can and should consider in times of stress, urgency, or emergency.

1

The "Organic Law" of *Ex Parte Milligan*

David Dyzenhaus*

Introduction

In 1866 the Supreme Court of the United States of America decided *Ex Parte Milligan*,[1] a landmark constitutional decision on the question of the relationship between sovereignty, emergency, and legality. The Supreme Court decided, against the wishes of President Lincoln and his Secretary of War, that military tribunals established by executive proclamation may not try civilians as long as the ordinary courts are open. In addition, the majority held that the constitutional prohibition on the executive extended to Congress.

In 1885 Albert Venn Dicey, Vinerian Professor of English Law at the University of Oxford, published the first edition of his great book, *An Introduction to the Study of the Law of the Constitution*.[2] In this and

* Professor of Law and Philosophy, University of Toronto. I thank Pooja Asnani and Rayner Thwaites for excellent research assistance and comments on drafts, and the participants in the symposium on "Sovereignty, Emergency, Legality" as well as David Golove and Rick Pildes for illuminating discussions.

1 *Ex Parte Milligan*, 71 U.S. 2 (1866).

2 AV Dicey, *Introduction to the Study of the Law of the Constitution*, 8th ed. (London: MacMillan, 1924). I use this edition, hereafter "Dicey," because it is the last to contain Dicey's Note X on "Martial Law in England During Time of War or Insurrection," 538–55. Dicey took his book on constitutional theory through eight editions himself, the last appearing in 1914 on the eve of the First World War, an event that along with the political issue of female suffrage provoked a jingoistic and chauvinistic preface from Dicey. But while Dicey made significant organizational changes to the book in the third edition, and significant substantive changes to the text especially in regard to his initial treatment of the French system of administrative law, he changed almost nothing in regard to his treatment of the themes of sovereignty, martial law, and the rule of law, other than to add the Note on Martial Law in the appendix to the sixth edition of 1902. The Note reacted to *Ex parte DF Marais* (1902) AC 109 a decision by the Privy Council, the final court of appeal for the colonies, about martial law in a case that arose during the Boer War.

subsequent editions, Dicey grappled with the same themes. More precisely, the issue for Dicey, as for the Supreme Court, was the relationship between sovereignty, martial law, and the fundamental commitment of a constitutional order to the rule of law. Dicey said, echoing the Supreme Court some twenty years before: "'Martial law' in the proper sense of that term, in which it means the suspension of ordinary law and the temporary government of a country or parts of it by military tribunals, is unknown to the law of England."[3] This, in his view, was "unmistakable proof of the permanent supremacy of the law under our constitution."[4]

As we will see in more detail later, Dicey was writing in a context in which he conceded Parliament was sovereign. By this he understood that Parliament had absolute legislative supremacy – the ability to make any law it liked. Judges could and should interpret Parliament's statutes in accordance with their understanding of the principles of the common law constitution – the principles protective of individual interests articulated by judges over time in their decisions. But they had to defer to any clearly expressed intention of Parliament. Thus it seems that Parliament could, if it so chose, establish martial law simply by stating clearly in a statute that this was its intention, just as Dicey also conceded it could override any principle of the common law constitution. Put differently, the hallmark of common law constitutionalism is, somewhat counterintuitively, that Parliament has the last word on what the law is, including the law of the constitution.

Marais was a civilian who had been arrested without warrant in one town in South Africa and then detained in another. Both towns were in areas where martial law had been proclaimed but in both the ordinary courts were open. His lawyers argued, relying in part on *Milligan*, that the civil courts were still exercising uninterrupted jurisdiction, which went to show that the "ordinary course of law could be and was being maintained," thus a state of war did not exist and martial law could not be applied to civilians. The Privy Council rejected this argument. The decision was considered momentous enough for the *Law Quarterly Review*, then as now the leading law journal in the common law world, to publish in 1902 a four article symposium on it, which is no doubt why Dicey felt compelled to respond: W. S. Holdsworth, "Martial Law Historically Considered," *Law Quarterly Review* 18 (1902): 117; Cyril Dodd, "The Case of Marais," *Law Quarterly Review* 18 (1902): 143; H. Erle Richards, "Martial Law," *Law Quarterly Review* 18 (1902): 133; W. S. Pollock, "What Is Martial Law?" *Law Quarterly Review* 18 (1902): 152. See further Richard A Cosgrove, "The Boer War and the Modernization of British Martial Law," *Military Affairs* 44 (1980): 124. I discuss *Marais* and these articles in more detail in "The Puzzle of Martial Law," *University of Toronto Law Journal* 59 (2008): 1. My discussion of Dicey in this chapter both relies on that article and takes its argument forward.

3 Dicey, *Law of the Constitution*, 283–84, footnotes omitted.

4 Ibid.

I will argue later that this claim is true in one sense – Parliament does have the power in a common law legal order to override the most fundamental principles of the constitution. But I will also argue that we must be careful not to equate Parliament's power with its authority. Authority is lost when any institution of legal order, no matter its place in the hierarchy, exercises its power in a way that subverts instead of maintaining or enhancing the general project of legality to which all institutions of a legal order are committed. So the claim is in another sense false – as a claim about what Parliament may *legally* do. Armed with this distinction, we are better equipped to understand not only *Milligan*, but also important decisions of the U.S. Supreme Court after 9/11.

Put differently, common law constitutionalism may facilitate an understanding of sovereignty, emergency, and legality in a legal order in which there is an entrenched bill of rights. Indeed, an interesting feature of the argument put by counsel for Milligan and of the reasoning in the majority opinion of the Supreme Court is that these lawyers and judges regarded U.S. constitutional law on these matters as an inheritance from England's common law constitution, though one enhanced both by the fact that an entrenched bill of rights not only gives definitive articulation to the principles of the constitution, but also protects those principles against legislative override by giving judges the authority to resist the legislature.

Nowhere is this thought more strikingly illustrated than in the passage from which my title is adapted. One of Milligan's lawyers, speaking of the founding fathers of the U.S. Constitution, said that they threw away not "an atom" of the "great rights" already won in England:

> They went over the *Magna Charta*, the *Petition of Right*, the *Bill of Rights*, and the rules of the *common law*, and whatever was found there to favor individual liberty they carefully inserted into their own system, improved by clearer expression, strengthened by heavier sanctions, and extended by a more universal application. They put all these provisions into the organic law, so that neither tyranny in the executive, nor party rage in the legislature, could change them without destroying the government itself.[5]

However, even if it is granted that *Milligan* is of a piece with common law constitutionalism, the decision might seem both quaint and irrelevant

[5] *Milligan*, 67.

to the post-9/11 world just because of that fact. While *Milligan* is often thought by civil libertarians to be, as in Charles Warren's line, "recognized by all men as the palladium of the rights of the individual,"[6] others – I will call them *Realists* – have regarded it as irrelevant or worse to the practice of sovereignty, legality, emergency.

Realism is, of course, the dominant mode of thought within the U.S. legal academy, and comes in many different varieties. In its most radical version, Realism is the position of those who wish to understand law purely as a matter of the play of political and social forces. Law, they say, is not an autonomous constraint on actions but a constraint which those with political power will accept or not depending on their relative strength. The rule of law tradition in Western thought is, in their view, a romantic and naïve attempt to obscure the fact that legal considerations are but one of a number of, and far from the most important, considerations, when one is seeking to understand the constraints on the state.

In seeking to debunk legal theory and refocus our concerns on political and social forces, such Realists ask us to give up on the aspiration that the rule of law replaces the arbitrary rule of men. Theirs is an account of the dynamics of power that tries to cut the ground from under an account of legal authority. Realists consider the state of emergency to prove their general debunking claim since they take the history of legal responses to such states to show that the executive asserts its sovereignty during the emergency. In other words, the state of emergency demonstrates the truth of the position we can call *executive unilateralism*, the position that the executive is the legal sovereign because in times of stress the executive will as a matter of fact exercise sovereignty.

For example, Edward S. Corwin said of the *Milligan* majority's reasoning that it would be "difficult to uncover a more evident piece of arrant hypocrisy. … To suppose that such fustian would be of greater influence in determining presidential procedure in a future great emergency than precedents backed by the monumental reputation of Lincoln would be merely childish."[7] This opinion is supported by Clinton L. Rossiter in his

[6] Charles Warren, *The Supreme Court in United States History: Volume Three, 1856–1918* (Boston: Little, Brown and Company, 1924), 154.

[7] Edwin S. Corwin, *The President: Office and Powers: History and Analysis of Practice and Opinion* (New York: New York University Press, 1940) 165–66. See further the study by Mark E. Neely Jr. *The Fate of Liberty: Abraham Lincoln and Civil Liberties* (New York: Oxford University Press, 1991), who titles his chapter on the case "The Irrelevance of *Milligan*."

classic study of presidential power during states of emergency, when he concludes that *Milligan* is "sound doctrine in forbidding the presidential establishment of military commissions for the trial of civilians in areas where the civil courts are open – but it is little else. . . . Here again the law of the Constitution is what Lincoln did in the crisis, not what the Court said later."[8]

More recently, in a book written to address the problem of the "infancy" of case law on these themes in the contemporary world, Judge Richard A. Posner deplores the "thralldom to precedent" of American lawyers, and remarks of *Milligan* that the "idea that a case almost a century old should guide us in dealing with Al-Qaeda is ridiculous, as I think most of the Supreme Court justices would acknowledge, at least sotto voce."[9] He goes on: "Not that hauling U.S. civilians before military tribunals isn't something to worry about. But we don't need an ancient case to tell us that. Would the civil libertarians fold their tents if the Supreme Court had allowed Milligan to be executed?"[10] In another recent book, Eric A. Posner and Adrian Vermeule declare that *Milligan* is irrelevant to one of the central questions that has faced U.S. courts since 9/11 – the detention and trial by military tribunals of individuals who fall within the category created by the Bush administration of "enemy combatants."[11]

That the Realists may be wrong about *Milligan's* relevance is indicated by the majority opinion in *Boumediene v. Bush* (2008),[12] which found that constitutional habeas corpus protection extends to noncitizens detained at Guantanamo Bay and that the procedures accorded to these detainees for

8 Clinton L. Rossiter, *The Supreme Court and the Commander in Chief* (Ithaca: Cornell University Press, 1976, expanded edition with an introduction and additional text by Richard P. Longaker), 39. Note that even Warren tempered his claim about *Milligan* as the "palladium of the rights of the individual" by agreeing with the minority that the majority should not have ventured any opinion on the question of congressional power, lest that venture, in the words of Chief Justice Davis, "cripple the constitutional powers of government and . . . augment the public dangers in times of invasion and rebellion". Warren, *The Supreme Court in United States History*, 162.

9 Richard A. Posner, *Not a Suicide Pact: The Constitution in a Time of National Emergency* (Oxford: Oxford University Press, 2006), 28.

10 Ibid.

11 Eric A. Posner and Adrian Vermeule, *Terror in the Balance: Security, Liberty, and the Courts* (Oxford: Oxford University Press, 2007), 252.

12 *Boumediene v. Bush*, 553 U.S. (2008), 128 S. Ct. 2229 (2008). *Milligan* was also important to the first major post-9/11 decision by the Supreme Court, *Hamdi v. Rumsfeld*, 542 U.S. 507, 518 (2004), but, as I will point out below, it was distinguished by the plurality and relied on only by Justice Scalia in dissent.

contesting their detentions are an inadequate substitute for habeas corpus. As I will show in more detail later, there is a direct lineage from *Milligan* to *Boumediene* some 130 years later, one which is only hinted at in the majority's citation in *Boumediene* of *Milligan* for the proposition that martial rule is appropriate only when, because there is a foreign invasion or war, "the courts are actually closed, and it is ... impossible to administer criminal justice according to law."[13]

Relevance does not, however, demonstrate correctness and the dissenters to *Boumediene* complained about the majority in that case for the same reasons that we will see drove the minority in *Milligan* and the adverse public reaction to that decision. For example, in *Boumediene*, Chief Justice Roberts said that the majority had substituted the "rule of lawyers" for the rule of law, thus giving the judges "a greater role than military and intelligence officials in shaping policy for military aliens" with the result that the American people "today lose a bit more control over the conduct of this Nation's foreign policy to unelected, politically unaccountable judges."[14] And Justice Scalia said that what "drives today's decision is neither the meaning of the Suspension Clause, nor the principles of our precedents, but rather an inflated notion of judicial supremacy."[15]

On their face, as we will see in more detail later, these comments do not support the executive unilateralism of radical Realism. Rather, they (and perhaps Rossiter and Justice Posner as well) support a kind of *legislative unilateralism* – the position that the legislature is the ultimate arbiter of the most fundamental questions of legality because it is the body that most appropriately decides such questions.

Legislative unilateralism in the U.S. context is a more moderate form of Realism. It too reacts against an alleged romanticism and naivety of the rule of law tradition, in particular against the way that tradition manifested itself in *Lochner*-era jurisprudence. It thus opposes *judicial unilateralism* – the position that makes judges the ultimate arbiter of the most fundamental questions of legality. It is realist in that it wishes to strip away what it sees as a judicial attempt to cover a process of political decision making with

13 *Boumediene*, 2274, quoting *Milligan*, 127.

14 *Boumediene*, 2293. And see 2302, "One cannot help but think, after surveying the modest practical results of the majority's ambitious opinion, that this decision is not really about the detainees at all, but about control of federal policy regarding enemy combatants."

15 Ibid.

the rhetoric of legality. But it is moderate in that it does not stake its claim solely on the sheer facts of power. It also makes a normative claim that in a democracy the legislature is the best placed body to make decisions about fundamental questions of legality, so that judges should defer to its interpretations of the law and the executive may act only when it can show a legal warrant in some piece of legislation.[16]

Now it might seem that Dicey on this account is a legislative unilateralist because, as least in the English common law constitutional order, he thinks we have to recognize that, as a matter of fact, the legislature is sovereign. However, as I will argue, unilateralist understandings of sovereignty, wherever they locate ultimate sovereign power, draw the wrong conclusion from the fact that legal orders will differ structurally from each other in regard to the way they answer the question, "Who ultimately decides fundamental issues of legality?" As Dicey showed, and as the majorities in both *Milligan* and *Boumediene* attest, the crucial feature of legal order is not the location of this power, but its quality as a legal order, an order in which government exercises its power in accordance with law, in accordance, that is, with the rule of law or legality.

This point is best appreciated in the context of a common law legal order, one in which Parliament is given the last word, precisely because in such an order constitutional principles are vulnerable to legislative override. The common law context is far from demonstrating that Parliament has sovereignty in the way suggested by unilateralist understandings of sovereignty. Rather, it shows that Parliament is constrained in so far as that if it wishes to speak as a *legal* sovereign, it has to speak in the language of the law, which means that it must speak in accordance with the rules of a normative grammar, rules that also discipline the speech of other institutional actors. Moreover, in seeing this, we will also see why executive unilateralism is not even a plausible understanding of sovereignty. Judicial and legislative

[16] As I will show later, executive unilateralists also seem to make, at least implicitly, a claim about why the executive should exercise this role. Note that in a legal order where there is a written constitution, the executive may and will seek to show that it has a constitutional warrant when it lacks a clear legislative warrant. However, things are no different where there is no written constitution, as attested by both the history of legal thought and the history of political thought (e.g., Locke's account of the prerogative). Legislative unilateralism, perhaps more than executive unilateralism, cannot really make sense of an entrenched bill of rights since such a bill is what I have called in other work an "institutional mistake," that is, a mistake in the design of legal order. See generally my *The Constitution of Law: Legality in a Time of Emergency* (Cambridge: Cambridge University Press, 2007).

unilateralism do capture important structural differences in the way in which a legal order may maintain its quality as such, and do so in a way that attempts to maintain this normative discipline. But executive unilateralism is a challenge to the very project of legal order since it asserts that the executive may break free of that discipline.

In the next section, I will explore *Milligan*, focusing on the division between the majority and the minority on the question whether the constitutional prohibition on setting up military commissions to try civilians when the ordinary courts are open applies beyond the executive to Congress. I will then analyze *Boumediene* to prepare the way for showing that the majority was right in *Milligan* that the kind of theory for which the minority opinion is taken to stand is not viable. That task is accomplished in the final sections, where I set out Dicey's common law constitutional position on the themes of sovereignty, legality, and emergency.

Milligan

Lambdin P. Milligan was a U.S. citizen and a civilian resident of Indiana, a state not embroiled in the Civil War.[17] He was, however, a "Peace Democrat," who wanted Confederate independence conceded and the fighting stopped. Moreover, he was a member of a secret society of the Peace Democrats, a military branch that planned to free Confederate prisoners and stage an uprising. With others, he was charged in 1864 with various crimes, all punishable by statute and before the federal courts. However, a political decision was made to have the matter decided by a military commission. Such commissions owed their existence to a proclamation of President Lincoln of September 24, 1862, which established military commissions and courts-martial to punish in accordance with martial law "all persons discouraging volunteer enlistments, resisting militia drafts, or guilty of any disloyal practice affording aid and comfort to rebels against the authority of the United States." [18] The proclamation also suspended

[17] I rely for the background on Charles Fairman, *History of the Supreme Court of the United States: Volume VI, Part One: Reconstruction and Reunion, 1864–88* (New York: MacMillan, 1971), chapter 5, "The *Milligan* and *Test Oath* Cases", 182–252; Neely, *The Fate of Liberty*, 160–84; Rossiter, *The Supreme Court and the Commander in Chief*, 26–46; Warren, *The Supreme Court in United States History*, chapter 29, "The Milligan Case," 140–76.

[18] See Rossiter, *The Supreme Court and the Commander in Chief*, 26–27, for the full text.

habeas corpus in respect of all persons arrested or detained by the military. Milligan was convicted and sentenced to death. As it happened, Lincoln had decided not to have Milligan and the others executed, but after his assassination his successor, President Johnson, determined that the executions should go ahead.

Milligan petitioned the Circuit Court of the United States for Indiana, asking that he be brought before the court and then either turned over to a civil tribunal to be proceeded against according to the law of the land or discharged from custody.[19] The judges of that court disagreed about how to answer that question and it was subsequently certified for the Supreme Court.

Counsel for the U.S. government argued that the military commission was operating under conditions of martial law, and that the officer executing martial law

> is at the same time supreme legislator, supreme judge, and supreme executive. As necessity makes his will the law, he only can define and declare it; and whether or not it is infringed, and of the extent of the infraction, he alone can judge; and his sole order punishes or acquits the alleged offender.[20]

Its authority so to act stemmed from Lincoln's proclamation of September 24, 1862 and Lincoln's authority was vested in the president, in virtue of his power to wage war under the Constitution, and thus did not need any legislative sanction. But counsel was clear that this constitutional authority simply recognized an authority in the executive branch of all civilized nations;[21] and was derived, so it was claimed, from the constitutional order of England – the "mother country."[22]

To the extent that provisions of the Constitution seemed inconsistent with this interpretation, it had to be understood that these parts of the Constitution were "peace provisions" and "like all other conventional and legislative laws and enactments, are silent amidst arms, and when the

19 I will not discuss the preliminary procedural objection with which the Supreme Court had to deal – whether the fact that the circuit court had not issued the writ meant that there was no "cause" for the court to adjudicate.

20 *Milligan*, 14.

21 Ibid., 10–11.

22 Ibid., 42.

safety of the people becomes the supreme law."[23] That Congress had in 1863 enacted a statute that permitted the president to suspend habeas corpus and provided express due process protections to those detained as "state or political offenders" was not relevant, as Milligan was taken as a prisoner of war.[24]

In response, Milligan's counsel argued that the president has no authority but that which he gets from law.[25] There was further no such thing as martial law, only military law and the law of nations that governs warfare. In fact "martial law" was a misnomer for "martial rule," which abolishes "all law."[26] They took the history of the struggle in England to establish the writ of habeas corpus and the principle that only Parliament could suspend it as the relevant background for the assertion that only Congress could authorize suspension.[27] They also relied extensively on the idea that the common law constitution does not know martial law, only the defense of necessity.[28] Thus they argued that either the commissioners had complete jurisdiction or none, which led to the conclusion, that "there is no middle ground on which to stand."[29]

The Supreme Court found that a writ of habeas corpus ought to be issued, that Milligan ought to be discharged from custody, and that, on the facts as stated in the petition, the military commission had no jurisdiction to try and sentence Milligan. But the Supreme Court divided 5–4 on the question whether the constitutional prohibition on the executive extended to Congress.

The opinion of the majority of the Supreme Court was delivered by Mr. Justice Davis. In his view, the importance of the question before the court could not "be overstated; for it involves the very framework of the government and the fundamental principles of American liberty."[30] He noted that Lincoln had in effect suspended habeas corpus by detaining people in custody without trial and, when his authority so to act was questioned, had secured from Congress in March of 1863 the statute that gave him the

23 Ibid., 20.
24 Ibid., 21.
25 Ibid., 30.
26 Ibid., 36.
27 Ibid., 38–40.
28 Ibid., 47.
29 Ibid., 61.
30 Ibid., 109.

authority to suspend habeas corpus when he judged this necessary. He had then relied on this authority in his proclamation of September 1863.[31] But Justice Davis pointed out, the "suspension of the writ does not authorize the arrest of any one, but simply denies to one arrested the privilege of the writ in order to obtain his liberty."[32] Moreover, the statute also provided that no person so detained could be detained beyond a certain fixed period unless judicial proceedings "known to the common law" were commenced against him.[33] So the question for the Supreme Court was whether the military tribunal had "*legal* power" to try and punish Milligan[34]:

> No graver question was ever considered by this court, nor one which more nearly concerns the rights of the whole people; for it is the birthright of every American citizen when charged with crime, to be tried and punished according to law. . . . By the protection of the law human rights are secured; withdraw that protection, and they are at the mercy of wicked rulers, or the clamor of an excited people. If there was law to justify this military trial, it is not our province to interfere; if there was not, it is our duty to declare the nullity of the whole proceedings.[35]
>
> The Constitution of the United States is a law for rulers and people, equally in war and in peace, and covers with the shield of its protection all classes of men, at all times, and under all circumstances. No doctrine, involving more pernicious consequences, was ever invented by the wit of man than that any of its provisions can be suspended during any of the great exigencies of government.[36]

Thus Justice Davis reasoned not only that the president lacks constitutional authority to set up military commissions to exercise a judicial power over civilians, but also that "Congress could grant no such power; and to the honor of our national legislature be it said, it has never been provoked by the state of the country to attempt its exercise."[37] In general, the majority reasoned, there is nothing to the claim that martial law permits the military to act as it sees fit, subject only to internal controls and the president's authority.[38]

[31] Ibid.
[32] Ibid., 115.
[33] Ibid.
[34] Ibid., emphasis in the original.
[35] Ibid., 119.
[36] Ibid.
[37] Ibid., 122.
[38] Ibid., 126.

> The statement of this proposition shows its importance; for, if true, republican government is a failure, and there is an end of liberty regulated by law. The only constitutional safeguard that the President can disturb is the writ of *habeas corpus* and the Constitution does not say that once the writ is denied, that a citizen shall be tried otherwise than by the course of the common law.[39]

In other words, the majority wished to emphasize that all congressional suspension of the writ can secure is the inability of a court to order the release of the detainee. It does not make the arrest of the individual or any other proceeding against him legal.

The majority did recognize that there might be occasions when martial law could properly be applied.[40] During a foreign invasion or civil war, only if the courts were actually closed so that it was impossible to administer criminal justice according to law, would there be a "necessity to furnish a substitute for the civil authority. ..." Thus the majority emphasized that "martial rule can never exist where the courts are open, and in the proper and unobstructed exercise of their jurisdiction."[41]

Here the majority joined a long tradition in the jurisprudence on martial law that sees a fundamental challenge to the rule of law in any executive or legislative bid to establish military tribunals with the power to detain and/or try civilians. It is important to recall that in English constitutional history the statutes that solidified the place of habeas corpus in the constitution – the Petition of Right, as well as the various Habeas Corpus statutes that followed it – were events in a political struggle over legal order waged not primarily between the courts and the executive but between Parliament and the executive.[42] Moreover, the main focus of that struggle was not the acts of the military in times of stress in responding to particular threats, or in authorizing military actions such as forcible billeting of soldiers, but on the claim of the military to be able to set up a system of courts parallel to the civil courts.[43]

39 Ibid., 124.

40 Ibid., 127.

41 Ibid.

42 See Edward Jenks, "The Story of the *Habeas Corpus*," *Law Quarterly Review* 18 (1902): 64; and Lindsay Boynton, "Martial Law and the Petition of Right," *The Historical Review* 79 (1964): 255.

43 See in particular, Holdsworth, "Martial Law Historically Considered."

However, the Chief Justice and others expressed their strong disagreement on the question whether Congress could have authorized the military commissions. If Congress could not, they said, it might "be thought to follow, that Congress has no power to indemnify the officers who composed the commission against liability in civil courts for acting as members of it."[44] So the minority judges entered two reservations: in their view, "when the writ is suspended, the Executive is authorized to arrest as well as detain"; and there are "cases in which, the privilege of the writ being suspended, trial and punishment by military commission, in states where civil courts are open, may be authorized by Congress, as well as arrest and detention."[45] They said:

> It was for Congress to determine the question of expediency. And Congress did determine it. That body did not see fit to authorize trials by military commission in Indiana, but by the strongest implication prohibited them. With that prohibition we are satisfied, and should have remained silent if the answers to the questions certified had been put on that ground, without denial of the existence of a power which we believe to be constitutional and important to the public safety, – a denial which, as we have already suggested, seems to draw in question the power of Congress to protect from prosecution the members of military commissions who acted in obedience to their superior officers, and whose action, whether warranted by law or not, was approved by that upright and patriotic President under whose administration the Republic was rescued from threatened destruction.[46]

In regard to martial law, the minority recognized, as did the majority, the existence of military law – the law that governs the armed forces. But it also recognized two further categories that the majority denied existed, at least in so far as these categories allow for trial by military tribunals of civilians at a time when and where the courts are open, and in the proper and unobstructed exercise of their jurisdiction. According to the minority, there is "MILITARY GOVERNMENT," "superseding, as far as may be deemed expedient, the local law, and exercised by the military commander under direction of the President, with the express or implied sanction of

[44] *Milligan*, 136.
[45] Ibid., 137.
[46] Ibid., 141.

Congress."[47] And there is "martial law proper,"[48] "called into action by Congress, or temporarily, when the action of Congress cannot be invited, and in the case of justifying or excusing peril, by the President, in times of insurrection or invasion, or of civil or foreign war, within districts or localities where ordinary law no longer adequately secures public safety and private rights."[49]

In a perceptive analysis of the division, Samuel Issacharoff and Richard H. Pildes strongly support the Chief Justice's minority opinion, as it exemplifies their preferred approach to emergency situations, one that steers a path between judicial and executive unilateralism by setting out a "process-based, institutionally focused approach."[50] According to them, the majority erred in framing the issue as a clash between executive power and the rights of individuals, a frame that they contend entails the irrelevance of the congressional response to Lincoln's proclamation of martial law. The minority, in contrast, took the "dynamic political process" seriously and thus framed the issue as one that turned on the relationship between Congress and the president. "The fatal flaw of Lincoln's administration" was "that the president had exercised power beyond the domain in which *Congress* had authorized him to act."[51] In other words, the minority made the issue turn on the question whether Congress had explicitly or implicitly authorized the action of the executive, and so did not have to reach the issue of whether the Constitution permitted Congress to issue that authorization. In this way, the minority rejected the majority's "absolutist, nonpragmatic vision of constitutional law," one that required the majority to "transform a challenge to executive authority into a challenge to legislative authority."[52]

Issacharoff and Pildes note the public outrage that followed the decision, occasioned not so much by the conclusion that the military commission lacked authority to try Milligan, but by the fact that the majority had expressed its views on Congress's inability to institute trial by military

47 Ibid., 142.

48 Ibid.

49 Ibid.

50 Samuel Issacharoff and Richard H. Pildes, "Between Civil Libertarianism and Executive Unilateralism: An Institutional Process Approach to Rights during Wartime", in *The Constitution in Wartime*, ed. Mark Tushnet, 161, 162–63 (Durham: Duke University Press, 2005), their emphasis. They use "civil libertarianism" for the approach I call judicial unilateralism.

51 Ibid., 167; their emphasis.

52 Ibid., 168.

tribunal. This outrage was stoked by the fact that the public saw the court as claiming a role in resolving the conflicts that would ensue between claims of right and national power as the country entered the period of reconstruction. And so the majority's reasoning was viewed as akin to the infamous decision in *Dred Scott*, in which the majority of the court some ten years earlier found that Congress was constitutionally precluded from interfering with the institution of slavery in federal territories.[53] The judges, in Issacharoff's and Pildes's view, quickly recognized the point of the outrage because two years later in *Ex parte McCardle*, the court upheld a statute that took away the courts' jurisdiction over a trial by the military authorities of a newspaper editor.[54]

However, it is important to keep in mind that the court did not divide on the issue of congressional power alone. There was also the division on whether, to use Dicey's formulation, martial law is "known" to the Constitution. In this context, the minority assumes that martial law is known to the Constitution, since it is committed to the view that Congress is entitled to authorize the president to proclaim martial law. Its view differs from executive unilateralism only in that it denies that the president has an inherent authority to make such a proclamation. Hence, the minority's approach turns out not to be purely procedural, since it presupposes the substantive conclusion that martial law is known to the Constitution, in that the legislative branch may authorize its proclamation.

One has to be a little cautious here. Issacharoff and Pildes's process-based approach rejects the view that there is generally a determinate constitutional meaning available on this or any other fundamental legal question. In line with the general Realism of the U.S. legal academy, their view is that because the law is likely indeterminate on the kinds of questions that get to appellate courts, law should be rendered determinate by the body that is best placed to do so. Further, Congress is from both a normative and a pragmatic perspective the best placed body when it comes to the kinds of fundamental questions that arise in the emergency context. In sum, their approach may more accurately be described not as a procedural approach, but as a kind of legislative unilateralism, one that says that the legislature

[53] Ibid., 169; *Dred Scott v. Sandford*, 60 U.S. 393 (1856). See Warren, *The Supreme Court in United States History*, 149–65 for extracts from comments of the time that manifest the outrage.

[54] *Ex parte McCardle*, 74 U.S. 506 (1868).

must have the last word on any fundamental issue of legality, with judicial and executive interpretations serving as a kind of advice to the legislature, which it is free to reject.

But that is not quite the *Milligan* minority's view. As we have seen, the minority seemed rather to argue that, as a matter of fact, the Constitution does permit Congress to bring martial law into operation, with the issue of indeterminacy being not about that matter, but about whether the president's judgment is justified in any particular context where the circumstances do in fact require martial law. Perhaps then the minority's reasoning is not really exemplary of the process-based approach. Indeed, Pildes and Issacharoff do not wholly endorse the minority's reasoning, since they say that it involved a "perhaps strained, pro-liberty reading of the statute suspending habeas corpus."[55] That is, they seem to suggest that since Congress had authorized the president to proclaim martial law, it had also authorized the president to set up military commissions to try civilians.

Issacharoff and Pildes are right in so far as the minority's position on martial law is in tension with the pro-liberty reading, as is revealed in one of the minority's reasons for rejecting the majority's position – that "when the writ is suspended, the Executive is authorized to arrest as well as detain."[56] The minority's view of suspension thus amounts to what Trevor Morrison has recently called the model of "suspension-as-legalization."[57] On this model, suspension provides more than an explicit grant of authority to detain; it also displaces any constitutional or other legal objections to the detention.[58] Suspension thus creates a "lawless void, a legal black hole, in which the state acts unconstrained by law."[59]

Recall in this regard that the minority adduced in support of their view the claim that if Congress could not authorize martial law, it might "be thought to follow, that Congress has no power to indemnify the officers who composed the commission against liability in civil courts for acting as members

[55] Issacharoff and Pildes, "Between Civil Libertarianism Libertarianism and Executive Unilateralism," 168.

[56] *Milligan*, 137.

[57] Trevor W. Morrison, "Suspension and the Extrajudicial Constitution" *Columbia Law Review* 107 (2007): 1533, 1539.

[58] Ibid.

[59] Ibid., quoting from David Dyzenhaus, "Schmitt v. Dicey: Are States of Emergency Inside or Outside the Legal Order?" *Cardozo Law Review* 27 (2006): 2005, 2006.

of it."[60] That is, from the fact that Congress is entitled retrospectively to indemnify officials against liability for illegal acts, the minority judges reasoned that Congress must prospectively have authority to authorize officials to do acts which would otherwise be illegal. Their legislative unilateralism thus risks endorsing a stance that allows for executive unilateralism, as long as the executive has or can claim the blessing of the legislature.

As I will now show in an analysis of *Boumediene*, U.S. Supreme Court jurisprudence since 9/11 has tended to reproduce a shuttle between judicial unilateralism and legislative unilateralism, with the latter containing the same dangerous tendency to endorse executive unilateralism, as long as it can claim a statutory warrant. This is in part because in the first major post-9/11 decision, the court refused to face up to the fact that it was faced with a situation quite similar to an executive proclamation of martial law.[61] Such reproduction might give one cause to think that the shuttle and its dangerous tendency are inevitable. But I will argue in the final two sections that Dicey's account of the relationship between sovereignty, legality, and emergency, may show us a way forward.

Boumediene

Boumediene arose out of a provision in the Military Commissions Act of 2006 (MCA), §7 that stripped the federal courts of jurisdiction in regard to habeas actions by detained aliens detained at Guantanamo Bay who had been determined to be "enemy combatants." This provision, as we will see, purported to protect from the federal courts' general habeas jurisdiction two different processes – first, the process of determination by a military tribunal, a Combatant Status Review Tribunal (CSRT), that an individual was an "enemy combatant"; second, the criminal trial by a military commission of such an individual.

In *Boumediene*, the Supreme Court was faced with a challenge to the protection from habeas jurisdiction of the CSRT process. It held 5–4 that aliens detained at Guantanamo Bay have the constitutional privilege of habeas corpus, which thus could not be withdrawn except in conformance with

60 *Milligan*, 136.

61 As David Golove has pointed out to me, the legal ambiguities in the situation do not stop here. There is also the issue whether the laws of war govern or domestic law.

the Suspension Clause of the Constitution. It held further that the CSRT procedures for review of the detainees' status were not an "adequate and effective substitute for habeas corpus," from which it followed that the jurisdiction-stripping provision was an unconstitutional suspension of the writ.[62]

The context for this jurisdiction-stripping provision grew out of a series of legal events after 9/11, the first being the congressional resolution – the Authorization for Use of Military Force (AUMF)[63] – empowering the president to "use all necessary and appropriate force against those ... he determines planned, authorized, committed, or aided the terrorist attacks ... on September 11, 2001."[64]

The second event was *Hamdi v. Rumsfeld*, where a plurality of the Supreme Court (Justice O'Connor, joined by the Chief Justice, Justice Kennedy, and Justice Breyer), held that the AUMF authorized the detention of enemy combatants, since detention of individuals for the duration of the conflict was "so fundamental and accepted an incident to war as to be an exercise of the 'necessary and appropriate force' Congress has authorized the President to use."[65] The plurality also held that the detainees were entitled to contest their detention orders before an independent tribunal.[66] Finally, the plurality indicated that a military tribunal would be an appropriate forum for the contest to take place with its procedures determined in accordance with a cost-benefit calculation, that is, one that weighs security and rights considerations together, and that it would be appropriate for the detainee to have to rebut a presumption – established through the process of the initial military decision to detain – that he is an enemy combatant.[67]

Hamdi was an American citizen held on U.S. territory, which left open the possibility that alien detainees held outside the sovereign territory were not within the scope of its ruling. But in *Rasul* v. *Bush*,[68] the majority of the Supreme Court rejected the argument that since the naval station at

62 *Boumediene*, 2237.
63 Authorization for Use of Military Force, Pub L. No. 107–40, 115 Stat. 224 (2001).
64 Ibid., § 2(a).
65 *Hamdi*, 518.
66 Ibid., 533.
67 Ibid., 538.
68 *Rasul v. Bush*, 542 U.S. 466 (2004).

Guantanamo Bay is outside the sovereign territory of the United States, habeas corpus jurisdiction did not extend there.[69] In response, the government established the CSRTs to determine whether individuals were "enemy combatants" and Congress enacted the Detainee Treatment Act of 2005 (DTA) which both stripped the federal courts of jurisdiction in regard to habeas actions by detained aliens who had been determined to be enemy combatants and provided that the Court of Appeals for the District of Columbia Circuit would have "exclusive jurisdiction" to review decisions of CSRTs.[70]

Hamdan v. Rumsfeld[71] concerned a different body set up by executive order – the military commissions that are given the task of trying criminal offenses in respect of those who have been determined by CSRTs to be enemy combatants. The Supreme Court held that the jurisdiction-stripping provision in the DTA did not apply to cases like the petitioners that were pending when the DTA was enacted.[72] It held further that the military commissions to try enemy combatants were not authorized by the text or history of the congressional resolution, and that their procedures violated the Uniform Code of Military Justice and Common Article 3 of the Third Geneva Convention.[73] Subsequently, the MCA both authorized the setting up of such commissions and made it plain that the petitioners' cases were included in an amended jurisdiction-stripping provision.

One way of understanding these legal events is as a clear illustration of the kind of process-based approach advocated by Issacharoff and Pildes working its way through the problems posed for a constitutional democracy in the aftermath of 9/11. The court is less deferential or not deferential at all to the executive when the executive claims constitutional authority, but cannot rely on congressional authorization, or at least cannot adduce even an ambiguous authorization. However, the court defers when there is congressional authorization, especially when Congress responds directly

[69] The Supreme Court relied on statutory not constitutional protection of habeas corpus, which allowed it to avoid the question of constitutional jurisdiction until *Boumediene*. This kind of constitutional avoidance seems generally admired by U.S. constitutional scholars, but for well-founded doubts about the wisdom of this approach, see Owen Fiss, "The Perils of Minimalism," *Theoretical Inquiries in Law* 9 (2008): 643.

[70] See Detainee Treatment Act of 2005, Pub. L. No. 109–48, tit. X § 1005 (e)(2)(A), 119 Stat. 2863 (2005).

[71] *Hamdan v. Rumsfeld*, 548 U.S. 557 (2006).

[72] Ibid., 584.

[73] Ibid., 567.

to a judicial finding that there was no authorization by issuing a clear statement that it intended the executive to act as it had previously done. On this understanding, the Supreme Court in *Boumediene* was faced in the MCA with a clear response to its findings in both *Hamdi* and *Hamdan*, despite the fact that the decisions pertained to different tribunals.

In response both to the finding in *Hamdi* that detention of enemy combatants was authorized by the AUMF and to the plurality of the Supreme Court's indications of appropriate due process, the executive had set up the system of CSRTs. In response to the finding in *Hamdan* that the jurisdiction-stripping provision of the DTA did not include cases that were pending at the time of the DTA's enactment, the MCA made it clear that Congress did intend such cases to be included. Thus, given that the executive was now acting in accordance with Congress's altogether explicit authorization, as well, it should be added, in accordance with the plurality of the *Hamdi* Supreme Court's advance indications of appropriate due process, it was time for the court to defer. Moreover, whether or not the CSRTs had followed their prescribed procedures in making the determination that someone was an enemy combatant was reviewable by the Court of Appeals for the District of Columbia, thus ensuring that independent judges had a role in the process.[74]

Indeed, this was one important strand in the reasoning of the dissenting judges in *Boumediene*. As Justice Scalia pointed out in his dissent, in *Hamdan* four members of the five-Justice majority in *Boumediene* had said that nothing prevented the president from seeking authority from Congress for the criminal trials by military commissions that he had tried to set up by executive order.[75] And Justice Breyer in his concurring opinion in *Hamdan* had seemed to suggest that were Congress to decide that the president should have such authority, the Supreme Court would for democratic reasons defer.[76] Since the majority in *Boumediene* subsequently declined to defer to what Congress had decided, Justice Scalia's

[74] Note that this Supreme Court was also given jurisdiction to test the constitutionality of the CSRT's procedures.

[75] *Boumediene*, 2295.

[76] Ibid., 2296 quoting from *Hamdan*, 636, "Where, as here, no emergency prevents consultation with Congress, judicial insistence upon that consultation does not weaken our Nation's ability to determine – through democratic means – how best to do so. The Constitution places its faith in those democratic means."

comment on their posture in *Hamdan was:* "Turns out they were just kidding."[77]

In other words, Justice Scalia took the *Hamdan* majority to espouse the kind of legislative unilateralism I have argued was the stance of the minority in *Milligan*. But, when their commitment to that stance was tested in *Boumediene*, that same group of judges reneged in favor of judicial unilateralism. There is something to this charge.[78] But one can as easily retort that the dissenters think that the judges, including the Supreme Court can debate, after which the political branches will decide. In short, whatever the rhetoric, the majority and the dissenters appear to be in a standoff between judicial and legislative unilateralism.

In my view, the standoff arises because of difficulties arising from *Hamdi*.[79] In his dissent in that case, Justice Scalia, joined by Justice Stevens, held that *Hamdi*, a U.S. citizen held on U.S. soil, was entitled to a writ of habeas corpus because the AUMF did not *explicitly* suspend the writ as required by the Suspension Clause of the Constitution. He supported this holding by a lengthy discussion of the common and constitutional law history of the writ, including the decision in *Milligan*.[80] In his dissent, Justice Thomas found that the executive was justified in acting as it did as a matter of executive unilateralism, and both constitutional and congressional authorization.[81]

Justice Souter in a minority opinion, joined by Justice Ginsburg, concurred in the judgment of the plurality in order to give it practical effect, but did not agree that the AUMF authorized detention and also expressed

77 *Boumediene*, 2296. He also accused the majority of "striking a pose of faux deference to Congress and the President," commenting that what the Supreme Court "apparently means is that the political branches can debate, after which the Third Branch will decide"; ibid., note 1.

78 See *Boumediene*, 2243. "If the Supreme Court invokes a clear statement rule to advise that certain statutory interpretations are favored in order to avoid constitutional difficulties, Congress can make an informed legislative choice either to amend the statute or to retain its existing text. If Congress amends, its intent must be respected even if a difficult constitutional question is presented. The usual presumption is that members of Congress, in accord with their oath of office, considered the constitutional issue and determined the amended statute to be a lawful one; and the judiciary, in light of that determination, proceeds to its own independent judgment on the constitutional question when required to do so in a proper case."

79 See Chief Justice Roberts in *Boumediene*, 2285, "*Hamdi* merits scant attention from the Court – a remarkable omission, as *Hamdi* bears directly on the issues before us. … *Hamdi* was all about the scope of habeas review in the context of enemy combatant detentions."

80 *Hamdi*, 555–77 and 566–69.

81 Ibid., 579.

doubts about the kind of truncated due process that the plurality seemed to endorse.[82] He too cited *Milligan* for the proposition that martial law is justified only by "present and actual necessity," as is the case when there is a "genuine invasion that closes civilian courts," and followed this citation with the claim that the judges, in "insisting on the careful scrutiny of emergency claims … are heirs to a tradition given voice 800 years ago by Magna Carta, which, on the barons' insistence, confined executive power by the 'law of the land.'"[83] The plurality, however, distinguished *Milligan* on the basis that Milligan was a resident of Indiana, arrested while at home there, whereas *Hamdi* was alleged to have taken up arms on the battlefield during the U.S. invasion of Afghanistan.[84] In addition, the plurality relied on *Ex parte Quirin*,[85] for the proposition that the military may try American civilians for wartime offenses.[86]

In *Boumediene*, the majority seems to be seeking to find its way back to *Milligan*. It firmly endorsed the common law constitutional understanding of the centrality of the individual interest in liberty, and thus of the writ of habeas corpus, to a regime of legality.[87] It also rejected the government's attempts to place its alleged enemies in the "war on terror" beyond the reach of the rule of law by creating new legal categories such as "enemy combatant," by invoking distinctions between citizen and alien, and by holding individuals in areas where it exercises total control but which it deems to be extra-territorial.[88] The political branches, the majority said, do not have the

[82] Ibid., 539–40.
[83] Ibid., 552.
[84] Ibid., 507.
[85] *Ex Parte Quirin*, 317 U.S. 1 (1942).
[86] *Hamdi*, 522–23.
[87] The majority pointed out that constitutional protection for habeas corpus preceded the Bill of Rights and thus for the framers of the Constitution, the writ of habeas corpus "had a centrality that must inform proper interpretation of the Suspension Clause"; *Boumediene*, 2235. The common law history of habeas corpus, the combination judgment and legislative interventions such as the Petition of Right and the Habeas Corpus Acts was thus highly relevant to any understanding of habeas corpus within the U.S. constitutional context; ibid., 2244–46. "This history, they said, was known to the Framers"; ibid., 2246. It no doubt confirmed their view that pendular swings to and away from individual liberty were endemic to undivided, uncontrolled power. The Framers' inherent distrust of governmental power was the driving force behind the constitutional plan that allocated powers among three independent branches. This design serves not only to make government accountable but also to secure individual liberty. Ibid. And from that history, though they admitted that there was controversy on this point, they concluded that the writ was both not confined to citizens and that it did have extra-territorial reach; ibid.
[88] Ibid., 2236.

power "to switch the Constitution on or off at will."[89] Finally, the majority rejected the claim that in times of stress security concerns have to be balanced against liberty concerns, with the executive being the best placed branch of government to strike the balance.[90]

However, *Hamdi* and *Hamdan* undermine these rejections and create further difficulties for the future.[91] In regard to *Hamdi*, the majority in *Boumediene* at times asserted that it did not find the due process signaled by the plurality in *Hamdi* inadequate, only the truncated form of judicial review mandated by the MCA.[92] At other times, the majority in *Boumediene* suggested that the MCA was a poor interpretation of what the plurality had in mind in *Hamdi*, that the MCA in any case had not been endorsed by the majority of the *Hamdi* court, and that the real problem was that the Court of Appeals, which was given jurisdiction by the DTA, was not able to consider evidence tendered after the CSRT hearing.[93] In regard to *Hamdan*, the majority in *Boumediene* said that "[t]he authority to which the concurring opinion [in *Hamdan*] referred was the authority to 'create military commissions of the kind at issue' in the case. ... Nothing in that opinion can be construed as an invitation for Congress to suspend the writ."[94] This is strictly speaking right, but does not speak to the problem sketched above of the combination of *Hamdi* and *Hamdan* – that together these two decisions support a stance of legislative unilateralism

In addition, there is a tension between the endorsement by the majority in *Boumediene* of both *Hamdi* and Lord Shaw's dissent in the House of Lord's decision during World War I, *Rex v. Halliday*.[95] In an issue in *Halliday* was

89 Ibid.

90 "Security depends upon a sophisticated intelligence apparatus and the ability of our Armed Forces to act and to interdict. There are further considerations, however. Security subsists, too, in fidelity to freedom's first principles. Chief among these are freedom from arbitrary and unlawful restraints and the personal liberty that is secured by adherence to the separation of powers. It is from these principles that the judicial authority to consider petitions for habeas corpus relief derives." Ibid., 2277. "Our opinion does not undermine the executive's powers as commander in chief. On the contrary, the exercise of those powers is vindicated, not eroded, when confirmed by the Judicial Branch. Within the Constitution's separation-of-powers structure, few exercises of judicial power are as legitimate or as necessary as the responsibility to hear challenges to the authority of the Executive Branch to imprison a person." Ibid., 69.

91 See further Fiss, "The Perils of Minimalism."

92 *Boumediene*, 2237–38.

93 Ibid., 2270–71.

94 Ibid., 2242.

95 *Rex v. Halliday* [1917] AC 260, cited in *Boumediene*, 2247.

the question whether the Defence of the Realm Consolidation Act 1914 authorized by implication the regime set up to deal with perceived threats to national security, when it gave very wide powers to the executive to deal with the situation of wartime emergency, but did not explicitly authorize the setting up of a detention regime by regulation. The majority of the House of Lords, like the plurality in *Hamdi*, held that in times of stress such an authorization had to be taken to be implicit.

In dissent, Lord Shaw started with the assumption that Parliament must be taken to intend that its delegates act in accordance with the rule of law, which meant that it had explicitly to authorize any departures from the rule of law. As Lord Shaw puts it, the judicial stance should be that "if Parliament had intended to make this colossal delegation of power it would have done so plainly and courageously and not under cover of words about regulations for safety and defence."[96] For judges to allow the right to be abridged is to revolutionize the constitution, perhaps, more accurately to undertake a counterrevolution. It amounts to what he called a "constructive repeal of habeas corpus,"[97] a repeal by the executive that is then ratified by judges. He would, he said, have come to his conclusion even though the language of the statute "had been much more plain and definite than it is."[98] It followed that the regulation that brought the detention regime into play was invalid.

Not only did the plurality in *Hamdi* ratify just such a constructive repeal, but, as we have seen, they went on to signal to the executive and to Congress that, when it came to checking the legality of the detention of enemy combatants, the court would be satisfied in the future with a rather minimal form of executive-devised due process, presided over by a military tribunal. Had the Supreme Court followed the common law constitutional path, it would have required of Congress that it either suspend habeas corpus, as recommended by Justice Scalia's dissent, or put in place a legislative scheme for detention of enemy combatants that would prescribe procedures and substantive criteria in a way that reflected Congress's understanding of its obligation of fidelity to the Constitution. The latter option, which I take to be the *Hamdi* minority opinion's preference, would reflect Congress's understanding of a set of procedures and criteria that provided

96 *Halliday*, 292–93.
97 Ibid., 294.
98 Ibid., 293.

an adequate regime of legality, one to which the court should, if the scheme were challenged, defer.

Given the time – a period of three years after 9/11 in which there had been no attack on the United States – and the firm sense that the conflict would be indefinite, the latter option was, from the perspective of a commitment to legality, by far the better choice. Congress would have been required to devise a comprehensive regime for arrest and detention and probably, given the inevitability of some criminal trials, for prosecution as well. Because that did not happen, CSRTs are operating without any legislative authorization,[99] are not according to recent lower court decisions following their own procedures,[100] and the procedures themselves are under increasing critique (a problem at which the Supreme Court could only vaguely gesture.)[101] There is also, following *Bouemdiene*, now an uneasy relationship between habeas corpus review and the operation of the CSRTs. This mess is in large part *Hamdi's* legacy.

Moreover, had the Supreme Court followed this option suggested by the *Hamdi* minority, it would have done so in a context in which the court had firmly repudiated executive unilateralism, thus perhaps emboldening Congress to exercise more constitutional discipline over the executive. The problem with *Hamdi* is that it is a fudge between accepting executive unilateralism and repudiating it, an inevitable consequence of not requiring express authorizations, that is, clear statements, when it comes to infringements of fundamental interests. However, it is important to see that *Hamdi* does still answer, albeit ambiguously, to what I have called in other work the compulsion of legality – the compulsion to justify all acts of state as having a legal warrant, the authority of law.[102]

As *Hamdi* illustrates, the compulsion of legality can provoke two very different cycles of legality. In one *virtuous* cycle, the institutions of legal order cooperate in devising controls on public actors which ensure that their decisions comply with the principle of legality, understood as a substantive

[99] Though they have of course been mentioned by reference in post–*Rasul* legislation.

[100] See *Parhat v. Gates*, 532 F.3d 834 (D.C. Cir. 2008) and *Al-Marri v. Pucciarelli*, 534 F.3d 213 (4th Cir. 2008).

[101] See Julian Davis Mortenson, "What Comes Next?" http://opiniojuris.org/author/julian-davis-mortenson/.

[102] See my "The Compulsion of Legality" in *Emergencies and the Limits of Legality*, ed. Victor Ramraj, 33 (Cambridge: Cambridge University Press, 2008); and my "Cycles of Legality in Emergency Times," *Public Law Review* 18 (2007): 165.

conception of the rule of law. In the other, *empty* cycle, the content of legality is understood in an evermore formal or empty manner. Government is said to exercise its power according to law, but there is little or no law in place against which to test that claim and, in addition, the ability to test it before an independent court is either removed, whittled down, or made very difficult. In this case, the compulsion of legality may result in the subversion of constitutionalism, since it subverts the ideal of government in accordance with the rule of law. Indeed, as I will soon argue, the very requirement that all acts of public power have a legal authorization might become counterproductive when the kind of power sought is of a kind that is legally unjustifiable.

Justice Thomas's dissent in *Hamdi* is at the end of the continuum where legality is maintained only through emptying it of any content by deeming anything the executive sees fit to do as legal. It is, as least in the context of claims about the appropriate responses to emergencies, executive unilateralism writ large – the position that the executive is the supreme interpreter of what is legally required. Justice Scalia's dissent requires express legislative intervention, so is a little bit further away from vacuity and executive unilateralism. But after the legislature has intervened to suspend, the executive is authorized to act as it likes, so in substance executive unilateralism is enabled. The plurality's fudge in *Hamdi* is still further away from emptiness, far enough along to provide some traction for a virtuous cycle of legality to get a grip at a later point, but not itself far enough along to be part of that cycle. Indeed, at the same time as it provides traction it also makes it difficult for the virtuous cycle to get a proper grip. It is this feature that explains why in *Boumediene* the dissenters have some basis for portraying themselves as the virtuous deferrers to an appropriate regime of legality, that is, as legislative unilateralists, and the majority as judicial unilateralists.

It might seem that this kind of mess is inevitable, given that one has to choose between the judiciary, the executive and the legislature as the final decision-maker, with other participants reduced to the role of giving advice to the real decision-maker. Moreover, in any context in which the executive has effective control over the legislature, a choice for the legislature will turn out to be a choice for disguised executive unilateralism. I will now show how Dicey offers us a way out of this conundrum, a way that is revealed precisely because his understanding of constitutionalism is elaborated in a common law context, in which constitutional principles seem utterly vulnerable to legislative override.

Common Law Constitutionalism

Dicey's position on martial law replicated that stated by the majority in *Milligan*. As we have already seen, in his view, "'[m]artial law' in the proper sense of that term, in which it means the suspension of ordinary law and the temporary government of a country or parts of it by military tribunals, is unknown to the law of England."[103] "This" was, he claimed, "unmistakable proof of the permanent supremacy of the law under our constitution."[104] According to him, the English Constitution recognizes martial law only in two other, very different senses. There is the law that governs the military both in war and in peace, and there is the common law defense of necessity, which can be invoked by any citizen who responds appropriately to an immediate threat to peace and order. When it comes to the defense of necessity, the question of whether the response was appropriate, and therefore not illegal, is one for the courts to decide according to established common law criteria.

One practical consequence of Dicey's position is that any trial of an individual who is not subject to martial law in the first sense, that is, anyone who is not a member of the military forces, must be conducted by the ordinary civil courts. So trial of civilians by military tribunals during times of stress is constitutionally precluded and the idea that such individuals could be tried by such tribunals on capital offenses at a time when they posed no immediate threat is an even greater constitutional abomination.

Dicey, however, was writing in a constitutional context in which, as he put it, the "sovereignty of Parliament is (from a legal point of view) the dominant characteristic of our political institutions."[105] He understood by this that "Parliament ... has, under the English constitution, the right to make or unmake any law whatever; and, further, that no person or body is recognised as having a right to override or set aside the legislation of Parliament."[106]

[103] Dicey, *Law of the Constitution*, 283–84, footnotes omitted.
[104] Ibid.
[105] Ibid., 38.
[106] Ibid.

This makes his position rather more puzzling than that taken by the majority in *Milligan*, which could rely on the fact of an entrenched bill of rights. So if, as Dicey thought, English judges have no option but to defer to the explicit content of statutes, even statutes that override constitutional principles, they must defer to legislative will when a valid statute legislates martial law into operation.

However, the possibility of statutory installation of martial law helps to show that what might seem to be the common law constitution's vulnerability – its susceptibility to legislative override by the absolutely sovereign legislature – in fact makes it easier to understand why martial law is unknown to the common law constitution. Indeed, it may help to show why martial law is in general unconstitutional, so that executive unilateralism is unconstitutional, whether as a claim about inherent legal authority or whether as a claim about the ability of the legislature explicitly or implicitly to delegate equivalent authority to the executive.

According to Dicey, the sovereignty of Parliament is but one of the two features of English political institutions, the other being the rule of law.[107] Dicey took the rule of law to include three "distinct though kindred conceptions."[108] First, the rule of law means that

> no man is punishable or can be lawfully made to suffer in body or goods except for a distinct breach of law established in the ordinary legal manner before the ordinary Courts of the land. In this sense the rule of law is contrasted with every system of government based on the exercise by persons in authority of wide, arbitrary, or discretionary powers of constraint.[109]

Secondly, the rule of law means not only that "no man is above the law" but also "a different thing" that "every man, whatever be his rank or condition, is subject to the ordinary law of the realm and amenable to the jurisdiction of the ordinary tribunals."[110] This Dicey termed the "idea of legal equality, or of the universal subjection of all classes to one law administered by the ordinary Courts."[111]

[107] Ibid., 179.
[108] Dicey, *Law of the Constitution*, 183.
[109] Ibid., 183–84.
[110] Ibid., 189.
[111] Ibid.

The third meaning is rather more ephemeral, the rule of law understood as "the predominance of the legal spirit [that] may be described as a special attribute of English legal institutions":

> We may say that the constitution is pervaded by the rule of law on the ground that the general principles of the constitution (as for example the right to personal liberty, or the right of a public meeting) are with us the result of judicial decisions determining the rights of private persons in particular cases brought before the Courts; ... whereas under many foreign constitutions the security (such as it is) given to the rights of individuals results, or appears to result, from the general principles of the constitution.[112]

This last claim may seem to make Dicey's theory more puzzling, especially when we note that he also asserted that a "judge-made" or common law constitution is superior to a written constitution. He argued that in the former the rights are part of the ordinary law and do not "depend upon the constitution" since the "law of the constitution is little else than a generalisation of the rights which the Courts secure to individuals." With a written constitution, Dicey elaborates, the general rights it guarantees are "something extraneous to and independent of the ordinary course of law," hence subject to suspension.[113] In contrast, if the right to individual freedom is "part of the constitution because it is inherent in the ordinary law of the land, the right is one which can hardly be destroyed without a thorough revolution in the institutions and manners of the nation."[114]

However, Dicey also provides us with the clue to solving the puzzle in his discussion of martial law, in particular in his account of the relationship between Habeas Corpus Suspension Acts and Acts of Indemnity. Recall that the minority in *Milligan* adduced in support of their view the claim that if Congress could not authorize martial law, it might "be thought to follow, that Congress has no power to indemnify the officers who composed the commission against liability in civil courts for acting as members of it."[115] That is, from the fact that Congress is entitled retrospectively to indemnify officials against liability for illegal acts, they reasoned that Congress must

[112] Ibid., 191, footnote omitted.
[113] Ibid., 196.
[114] Ibid., 197.
[115] *Milligan*, 136.

prospectively have authority to authorize officials to do acts that would otherwise be illegal.

Dicey explains why this view is fallacious. He recognizes that there might be legitimate recourse by officials to illegality in times of emergency, that is, to actions that cannot be justified by the defense of necessity. It is this category of morally justified but illegal acts that an Act of Indemnity, properly so called, is meant to cover. But the fact that such a statute, one which retrospectively grants criminal and civil immunity to officials for their acts, amounts (in Dicey's words) to the "legalisation of illegality,"[116] vindicates the claim that the English Constitution does not know martial law.

In order to appreciate how this vindication works, recall the difference between executive unilateralism and legislative unilateralism when it comes to emergency powers. Executive unilateralism holds that the executive has an inherent authority to decide both that there is an emergency and what measures are appropriate in responding to it. Neither decision is subject to the checks of either of the two other branches of government. On this theory, an Act of Indemnity is superfluous since whatever the executive did during the time of emergency is by definition legal. In contrast, legislative unilateralism holds that the legislature has the authority which executive unilateralism claims for the executive. The legislature can thus authorize prospectively whatever it can authorize retrospectively. Hence, if it can legalize illegality retrospectively, it can authorize illegality prospectively. For legislative unilateralism then, Acts of Indemnity are not superfluous because the executive may act to deal with a perceived emergency before there is time for the legislature to authorize it so to act, and so there will be a point to the legislature retrospectively authorizing whatever it deems appropriate.

However, legislative unilateralism fails to notice the distinctions between three classes of acts that are candidates for retrospective authorization. First, there are those acts that would be justified by the defense of necessity if an official were called to account before a court of law. Such acts are legally justified on a test amenable to judicial evaluation and thus, strictly speaking, there is no need for retrospective legalization, though an Indemnity Act may serve the purpose of economy in preempting actions against officials, which would otherwise have to be decided one by one. Second, there

[116] Dicey, *Law of the Constitution*, 233.

are those acts, which while not legally justified, are justifiable in that they were done in good faith and reasonable in the circumstances. In respect of this class of acts, an Act of Indemnity is required, both because the officials might otherwise be vulnerable to legal sanctions and for the sake of legality, with the latter, as I will shortly show, being the more important reason. Finally, there are those acts that are never legally justifiable because they cannot comply with legality, whether or not these requirements are formally entrenched.

Now as a matter of practice, it might be that the third class of acts is more likely to attract criminal prosecutions than the second, as it is more likely to occasion individual and public outrage. In practice, that is, the second class might not require an Act of Indemnity, at least not to the same extent as the third. But for Dicey, on my interpretation, even if the officials will not in practice be called to account for illegalities in the second class, the legal order needs to repair itself for the sake of legality, as is revealed in the following passage:

> An Act of Indemnity … though it is the legalisation of illegality, is also … itself a law. It is something in its essential character, therefore, very different from the proclamation of martial law, the establishment of a state of siege, or any other proceeding by which the executive government at its own will suspends the law of the land. It is no doubt an exercise of arbitrary sovereign power; but where the legal sovereign is a Parliamentary assembly, even acts of state assume the form of regular legislation, and this fact of itself maintains in no small degree the real no less than the apparent supremacy of law."[117]

This is the more important reason for an Act of Indemnity. In its absence the legal order undermines its commitment to legality – to the principle that all official acts must be able to display a legal warrant, especially acts that infringe the most fundamental of individual interests; most prominently in the emergency context, the interest in liberty protected by habeas corpus.

In the passage above, Dicey acknowledges that a retrospectively bestowed legal warrant is arbitrary, since it is itself not controlled by law; yet, he wants to claim, it is qualitatively significant since it asserts the supremacy of law. As I will now show, from Dicey's analysis of Habeas Corpus Suspension Acts

[117] Ibid., 233.

and Acts of Indemnity, we can extract the thought that all that is wrong with these executive acts is that they are arbitrary in the sense that they were both unjustifiable by the defense of necessity and not authorized in advance. They are, to use my own term, *legalizable* – that is, they are acts fit to be governed by a prospective regime of legality in contrast to acts in the third class – acts that are *unlegalizable* in that they are not only legally unjustified, but legally unjustifiable.

When it comes to the writ of habeas corpus, Dicey thought that the Habeas Corpus Suspension Acts that were familiar to him from English constitutional history were consistent with legality. He noted that the Acts typically did not suspend habeas corpus as such, but rather "made it impossible for any person imprisoned under a warrant signed by a Secretary of State on a charge of high treason, or on suspicion of high treason, to insist upon being either discharged or put on trial."[118] While, as he said, such an act was a "serious measure," he emphasized that it "falls very far short of what its popular name seems to imply … [being] not, in reality, more than a suspension of one particular remedy for the protection of personal freedom." He went on:

> The *Habeas Corpus* Act may be suspended and yet Englishmen may enjoy almost all the rights of citizens. The constitution being based on the rule of law, the suspension of the constitution, as far as such a thing can be conceived possible, would mean with us nothing less than a revolution.[119]

Dicey was of course aware that a statute could go well beyond granting this limited authority to the executive. But his point was that a Suspension Act does not grant the executive any authority beyond its limited terms, and was usually followed by an Act of Indemnity just because these limited terms might not cover all those things that had to be done in order to deal with the emergency.[120] Dicey was similarly aware that an Act of Indemnity could go far beyond what he considered to be its proper "moderate" scope – covering acts that were done in good faith and reasonably.[121] But it is clear that for him official acts that fall into the third class, the class

[118] Ibid.
[119] Ibid.
[120] See his discussion of a statute that gave wide powers to the Irish executive in 1881, ibid., 227–28.
[121] Ibid., 230–33.

of legally unjustifiable or unlegalizable acts, are not the proper subjects of either a Suspension Act or an Act of Indemnity, or some combination of the two.

Legislative unilateralism, as I have suggested, does not distinguish between these three classes of acts. The difference between it and executive unilateralism in this regard is only the question whether the executive requires legislative authorization, whether prospective or retrospective. But Dicey's theory entails that there is a difference, despite the fact that the legislature can, whether prospectively or retrospectively, grant criminal and civil immunity to officials in respect of the third class. Acts within that class can be declared beyond the reach of criminal prosecution and civil suit, but, because they are unlegalizable, they will have to be explicitly individuated in the statute.

It does not suffice, for example, to say in advance that the executive may do "all acts it considers necessary to deal with the emergency" in order to authorize it to make a detention regulation that allows it to detain. Such a regulation has to be explicitly authorized. And if the legislature wishes to give a power to make a detention regulation that is not subject to due process, it must also specify exactly what aspects of due process are to be sacrificed. Similarly, it does not suffice for a statute to indemnify retrospectively "all acts done by the executive in the course of dealing with the emergency" for it to cover acts done in bad faith or unreasonably. Rather, the statute has to say "all acts, including acts done in bad faith or unreasonably" and even such a wide-ranging authorization would not be taken to include, for example, the authority to torture.

The point is that the suspension of any principle will be limited to the strict terms of the suspension, which is why the minority in *Milligan* did not engage, as Issacharoff and Pildes suggested, in a "perhaps strained, pro-liberty reading of the statute suspending habeas corpus."[122] Rather, the minority interpreted the statute in exactly the way that common law constitutionalism recommends. It is true that the common law constitutionalism that underpins this part of the minority's opinion is in tension with their legislative unilateralism. But, as I will now argue, the way to resolve that tension is by rejecting all three kinds of unilateralism.

[122] Issacharoff and Pildes, "Between Civil Libertarianism and Executive Unilateralism," 168.

This claim is best appreciated in a common law context just because there legislative unilateralism may appear to be the constitutional *Grundnorm*, as it appears Dicey acknowledges in his description of Parliamentary sovereignty. Indeed, Dicey could be said to go even further. He argues that Parliament can abdicate its sovereignty altogether, by employing a statute that either dissolves itself and leaves no means "whereby a subsequent Parliament could be legally summoned" or that transfers sovereign authority to some other person or body of persons.[123] Given this, it might seem that a statute that establishes martial rule is no big deal.

However, the abdicating statute is less problematic from the perspective of legality than a martial rule statute in one important respect. The abdicating statute does away with Parliamentary sovereignty and the rule of law together, while the martial rule statute purports to maintain Parliamentary sovereignty while doing away only with the rule of law. Put differently, it purports to maintain legality in the sense of rule by law (Parliament's law), while only doing away with the rule of law (the principles of legality over which independent judges have an important guardianship role). The martial rule statute differs from the abdicating statute, then, because it installs a contradiction in legal order, rather than presenting a wholesale challenge to the very project of legality and constitutionalism. Moreover, it operates by stealth, in purporting to maintain legality while in fact deeply undermining it.

In other words, Dicey's theory of the rule of law requires the category of an unconstitutional but valid statute, though this requirement is somewhat obscured by his insistence both on the centrality of remedies to common law constitutionalism and that "constitutional law" is the law that courts can enforce since law properly so called is those rules and norms that "are enforced by the courts."[124] This understanding of law requires Dicey to distinguish between "constitutional law" and "constitutional morality,"[125] with the apparent result that a statute that overrides constitutional principle is both itself constitutional and changes the constitution.

But notice the difference between an overriding statute and a suspending statute. An authentic suspension statute does not purport to override

[123] Dicey, *Law of the Constitution*, 65–66n3.

[124] Morrison, "Suspension and the Extrajudicial Constitution," 1578, referring to and quoting from Dicey, 10th edition, 23–24 (23 in the 8th edition).

[125] Dicey, *Law of the Constitution*, 23.

any principle. Rather, it simply makes the principle temporarily and in a limited respect unenforceable. In contrast, the overriding statute seeks to oust the principle from legal order. I say "seeks" because the statute has to be interpreted by judges whose constitutional duty it is to try to minimize disruption to the rule of law. In addition, the judges must seek to interpret all statutes in accordance with what they take as the legislature's and the executive's shared commitment to upholding the rule of law. As we have already seen, this means that an overriding statute has to be both precise and very explicit about its intended effects.

By way of illustration consider the United Kingdom's Human Rights Act (1998), which gives to judges two different roles when it comes to interpreting in light of the human rights commitments in the act. Section 3 of the act requires judges to try to interpret statutes so that they do conform to the act. Section 4 of the act tells judges that when they cannot reach a rights-conforming interpretation, they must declare the offending provision incompatible with the act. Such a declaration does not affect the validity of the provision but merely raises explicitly the possibility of either legislative or executive amendment to produce conformity.

Hence, a question arises about how to understand the statute from a constitutional perspective. As Tom Hickman has suggested, the best answer to this question is to view a declaration of incompatibility "as a device that allows courts to vent their scorn on a piece of rights defying legislation, thus excluding it from the integrity of law."[126]

The exclusion is not without institutional effect. The very fact that using the declaration is an explicit duty and that avenues for amendment are explicitly set out, including the rather unusual authorization to the executive to amend, raises formally the expectation that amending legislation will follow. That expectation is bolstered as a matter of its place in a context where the United Kingdom has ratified the European Convention on Human Rights. The convention is the source of the rights listed in the Human Rights Act, and so failure to conform to those rights will bring admonition from the European Court of Human Rights, whose judgments are not binding on the U.K. government, but are ignorable only on pain of

126 Tom R. Hickman, "Constitutional Dialogue, Constitutional Theories and the Human Rights Act 1998" [2005] *Public Law*, 327.

signaling to the world that it does not regard itself as a member of that rights-respecting community.

It is thus unsurprising that prior to 1998, just as the U.K. government responded positively to adverse judgments of the European Court of Human Rights, so after 1998 it responds positively to declarations of incompatibility by the House of Lords. From this we can see that a statute may be valid and unconstitutional, in that its result is one that makes it such that it cannot fit into the scheme of constitutional principle of the legal order. It cannot, as Hickman suggests, be shown to fit with the "integrity of law," or, as Dicey would say, it is "unknowable" as law.

In my view, in a pure common law legal order, structurally things are not very different. Judges are under the interpretive obligation, set out by Section 3, to try to interpret all statutes in a rights-conforming manner and when they are unable to do so, they should in virtue of the same obligation issue an informal declaration of incompatibility, a statement that the statute while valid is nevertheless unconstitutional in the relevant sense.[127] And such a statement will in any rights-respecting society require the government to consider the political costs of not initiating legislative amendment. Of course, the formalization of this obligation as well as the enumeration of many of the fundamental constitutional principles might well enhance the informal sometimes implicit culture of common law constitutionalism. But the point I want to drive home is that an analogy with the more formal constitutional culture of the United Kingdom after 1998 can help us to understand the Diceyan idea that a statute can in a common law constitutional order be both valid and unconstitutional in the relevant sense. Moreover, as long as the constitutional culture of the society is maintained, an overriding statute will stick out like a sore thumb, limited to a parsimonious understanding of the scope of the statute, until such time as the statute is repealed, amended, or becomes obsolescent.

Of course, there is another possible scenario. That statute is joined in the legal landscape by other overriding statutes. Consequently, judges are not only overly deferential to the executive's generous understanding of the authority it has from the statutes, but also even begin to find that they should more generally interpret the law as if particular statutes were

[127] The best treatment of this issue remains Murray Hunt, *Using Human Rights Law in English Courts* (Oxford: Hart Publishing, 1997).

intended to override constitutional principles, even when no such intention was explicit in the particular statute. This is the kind of interpretive approach adopted by the plurality in *Hamdi*.

But that scenario fully unfolded does not amount to the installation of a new set of constitutional principles as the basis of legal order. Rather, it produces through the cooperative efforts of the legislature and the judiciary a legal facade over an executive unilateralist regime, a kind of silent constitutional revolution. That the plurality in *Hamdi* seemed for a time to risk setting American constitutional jurisprudence on this revolutionary path, a problem that *Boumediene* does not fully resolve, helps to make a further point.

Judges in a legal order with an entrenched bill of rights have a much more powerful means of safeguarding constitutional rights than either the formal or informal declaration of incompatibility, in that their authority to grant remedies equivalent to declaring unconstitutional statutes invalid can secure coincidence between the categories of legality and validity. However, this authority is in no way a guarantee that they will act appropriately to preserve the constitutional order.[128] Moreover, when judges fail to exercise this

[128] This point was fully appreciated by Justice Davis as he tried to weather the storm of disapproval that greeted his opinion in *Milligan*. In a letter to his brother-in-law, he argued that the constitutional prohibition on executive establishment of military tribunals to try civilians and the prohibition on Congress were of a piece:

> We held that the provisions of the Constitution were irrepealable and could not be suspended. Did it not logically follow, that Congress could not repeal. Believing as we did, that the whole thing was fundamental, wd it not have been unmanly, & unworthy a court, to have confined the denial to the Executive, and wd it not at once have been claimed, that we admitted Congress could do it. ... These [provisions of the Constitution] we had therefore to interpret, & we interpreted them, as binding on all, for ever. The opinion wd have been worth nothing for future time, if we had cowardly toadied to the prevalent idea, that the legislative dept of the govt can override everything. Cowardice of all sorts is mean, but judicial cowardice is the meanest of all. Not a word is said in the opinion about reconstruction & the power is conceded in the insurrectionary States, & yet the Republican press every where has denounced the opinion as a second Dred Scott opinion, when the Dred Scott opinion was in the interest of Slavery, & the Milligan opinion in the interest of liberty.

He went on:

> Congress claims omnipotent power like the British Constitution. Why then a written Constitution. Majorities don't need any. Our ancestors were not willing like Chief Justice Chase to trust the virtue and intelligence of the people. They believed in the necessity of written, irrepealable guaranties to protect minorities against the aggressions of majorities.

Quoted from the extracts reproduced in Fairman, *History of the Supreme Court of the United States*, 232–33.

authority, they perforce end up endorsing substantive claims about what the Constitution in fact requires, for example, as we saw with the *Milligan* minority, the claim that the Constitution does know martial law.

Conclusion

For Dicey, as we have seen, rule by law and rule of law are the two sides of the same coin, as is proved by the unknowability of martial law. Here the crucial point is the one made by counsel for Milligan that martial law is a misnomer for "martial rule," which abolishes "all law."[129] The issue here is both normative and epistemological: normative because of the stakes for liberty; epistemological because there is an interesting sense in which martial rule is quite literally unknowable as law.

On Dicey's understanding, one that is shared by the majorities in *Milligan* and *Boumediene*, the statutes that solidified the place of habeas corpus in the English Constitution (the Petition of Right and the various Habeas Corpus statutes that followed it) were events in a political struggle over legal order waged not primarily between the courts and the executive but between Parliament and the executive.[130] The main focus of that struggle was not the acts of the military in times of stress in responding to particular threats, but the claim of the military to be able to set up a system of courts parallel to the civil courts.[131]

The immediate consequence of Parliament's victory was the other main feature Dicey identified of English political institutions, the "undisputed supremacy throughout the whole country of the central government," an authority that had once belonged to the king as "the source of law," but which had passed into the "supremacy of Parliament."[132] As we have seen, this feature can and has been seen as threatening as the rule of law, since Parliament's supremacy makes possible parliamentary abolition of the rule of law. However, in order for this possibility to arise, the rule of law has itself to be brought into existence. That requires the establishment of the supremacy of law over the executive, which involves creating a centralized

129 *Milligan*, 21–22.

130 See Edward Jenks, "The Story of the *Habeas Corpus*," *Law Quarterly Review* 18 (1902): 64; and Lindsay Boynton, "Martial Law and the Petition of Right," *The Historical Review* 79 (1964): 255.

131 See in particular, Holdsworth, "Martial Law Historically Considered."

132 Dicey, *Law of the Constitution*, 179.

body for adjudication of disputes about law's limits, a body that is independent of the officials who claim to act in the name of the law. In other words, Dicey's genius and the solution to the puzzle of martial law lie in the insight that parliamentary supremacy also makes the rule of law possible, since it provides the basis for accountability of the executive to law.

Dicey then rejects unilateralism of all sorts.[133] In his constitutional theory, both Parliament and the judges are required to work in a cooperative relationship if executive accountability to law is to be secured. The common law constitution is, on his view, as much the product of legislation as it is of judicial decisions, although to call it a product is only to acknowledge what Dicey himself was at pains to point out – that the project of the rule of law requires creativity on the part of both Parliament and judges.[134] At the same time, Dicey, like others working in the common law tradition, understands this project as one that must work with the idea that participants in it are engaged in a process of articulating and thus rendering explicit the normative commitments that are already implicit in the practices that make up the project.

Both judicial unilateralism and legislative unilateralism are then inadequate conceptions of that constitutional project. But at least they are conceptions whereas executive unilateralism is not a conception, but an attempt to establish a rival project, what Ernst Fraenkel called the "dual state" – a state in which officials have the authority to displace legal controls whenever they think this appropriate.[135] Fraenkel regarded Carl Schmit as the preeminent theorist of that state and it thus unsurprising that Eric A. Posner and Adrian Vermeule, two of the most prominent supporters of executive unilateralism in the United States, find Schmitt's legal theory, more accurately, his "anti-legal" theory congenial.[136]

Schmitt's theory is anti-legal because he wishes to show that the executive and not the legislature is the sovereign, a position that entails that the

[133] See Murray Hunt, "Sovereignty's Blight: Why Contemporary Public Law Needs the Concept of 'Due Deference'," *Public Law in a Multi-Layered Constitution*, eds. Nicholas Bamforth and Peter Leyland, 337 (Oxford: Hart Publishing, 2003).

[134] See Hickman, "Constitutional Dialogue, Constitutional Theories and the Human Rights Act 1998," 323–26, exploring the important contribution of Dicey's analysis of these issues in his underappreciated work, *Lectures on the Relation between Law and Public Opinion in England during the Nineteenth Century* (London: MacMillan, 1905).

[135] Ernst Fraenkel, *The Dual State: A Contribution to the Theory of Dictatorship* (New York: Oxford University Press, 1941).

[136] Posner and Vermeule, *Terror in the Balance*, 38–39.

executive stands above the law. Posner and Vermeule follow him in arguing that legalism is a set of cloaks of varying thickness that governments don and shed according to an instrumental calculation of how to maximize political support in societies "that have a general interest in security but tolerate normal political opposition."[137] In contrast to legislative unilateralism, executive unilateralism does not envisage a cycle of legality, but only a series of events in a contest over power.

It is instructive to note that Schmitt relied heavily in his arguments on the way in which Hobbes starkly posed the question to which the various kinds of unilateralism seem a response: "Who will decide?" Schmitt took that question and dramatized it in the context of states of emergency in the twentieth century, as Posner and Vermeule now do for the twenty-first century. But what Schmitt failed to appreciate is that Hobbes is firmly in the tradition of rule of law thought, in that for him the sovereign is not a person or group of persons, but an artificial creation within civil society. Hobbes's sovereign, no less than Dicey's, can only articulate his commands through law, which entails that the commands must be interpretable in accordance with the laws of nature – Hobbes's detailed list of the presuppositions of the project of legality.

Hobbes does think that in any legal order there has to be an answer to the question, "Who ultimately decides?" and that sovereignty is located in the artificial person of the ultimate decider. As is well known, his own preference is that a monarch can occupy that role. But this is not a preference for executive unilateralism since the monarch, while he will have the first and the last word about the content of the positive law, has still to speak in the language of the law, that is, in ways that respect what we might think of as the normative grammar of legality, a conversation in which the monarch's judges have a distinct and necessary part. There is thus no difference between Hobbes's position, on the one hand, and the positions of Dicey and the U.S. constitutional order, on the other, in respect of the fundamentals of legality. Where these positions differ is simply on where, as a matter of fact or normative argument, ultimate decision authority is located. Put differently, for them the decision to have legal order is of far more importance than the decision as to which body will have ultimate decision-making authority within legal order. Moreover, that the positions are a complex blend of fact and normative argument is significant.

[137] Ibid., 228.

Realism, whether in its radical, executive unilateralist or its moderate, legislative unilateralist version, claims to shift our focus productively from the rhetoric of legality to facts about power, from, as it were, claims about who should decide to who does in fact decide. But, as the division between the two versions shows, claims about the facts of power underdetermine the conclusion as to where power lies, since the radicals claim that it lies with the executive and the moderates with the legislature. Indeed, to the Realist charge that the rule of law tradition disguises the facts of power with a normative rhetoric of legality, the rule of law sorts can respond that Realism disguises its normative claims with a supposedly objective rhetoric from social science. At base, that is in both the radical and the moderate versions of Realism is a normative claim about where power should lie.[138] Moreover, the line of reasoning from *Milligan* to *Boumediene* illustrates that any engagement with the rhetoric of legality requires taking substantive positions on the interpretation of the law of the constitution. There is no procedural or normatively neutral ground from which to survey the jurisprudential contest.

Finally, that contest has to be one in which it is appreciated that there is an "organic law" around the protection of individual liberty. The centrality of the writ of habeas corpus to common law constitutionalism comes about because of the individual interest in liberty.[139] But the right to have executive interferences with liberty justified by the display of a legal warrant would be empty if there were not law that provided the basis for a test for the congruence of official action.[140] "Law" here includes the positive law

[138] See Dyzenhaus, "The Compulsion of Legality."

[139] Habeas corpus was not originally about the individual interest in liberty but about the monarch's control of legal process. But, as Dicey remarked, *Law of the Constitution*, vii: "The possible weakness at any rate of the historical method as applied to the growth of institutions, is that it may induce men to think so much of the way in which an institution has come to be what it is that they cease to consider with sufficient care what it is that an institution has become." That is, even if the project of legality started off as mainly one about the centralization of power – the use of law as an instrument for enhancing the ruler's ability to rule by law – that historical fact is hardly conclusive of the normative question of how best to understand that project. Moreover, it is plausible to argue that the commitments implicit in even the centralization-of-law/rule-by-law project tend to turn that project into the rule-of-law/liberty-preserving project. This point may be exactly what Lon L. Fuller was after in his parable of King Rex – Lon L. Fuller, *The Morality of Law* (New Haven: Yale University Press, 1969, Revised Edition), chapter 2.

[140] Lon L. Fuller's eighth principle of the internal morality of law; ibid., 81–91. Note that for Dicey, constitutional law "in the proper sense of the term" consists of "the rules which (whether written or unwritten, whether enacted by statute or derived from the mass of custom, tradition, or

to be found in statutes governing detention regimes and executive regulations made under appropriate authority. It also includes the constitutional principles that are taken to be entwined with the protection of the interest in liberty, that is, the principles associated with the idea of due process, and may include principles from other legal orders, as in the reliance of the Supreme Court on the history of common law constitutionalism, or of international law. In the last case, this may come about as a matter of constitutional culture or through the formal accession to human rights treaties, which require fidelity to the principles in such treaties. In emergencies, it may also require procedures such as explicit derogation from rights commitments, which will be reviewable on proportionality grounds and subject to some degree of international supervision. To use (or perhaps abuse) Kelsenian terminology, we might say that around the *formal* conditions of constitutionalism, the criteria of legality that makes sense only as criteria that serve the interests of the individual legal subject, will perforce be clustered *material* conditions that include both positive law and constitutional principles that serve those same interests. The requirement of congruence thus presupposes that there is an "organic law" protective of individual liberty. A legal order that observed the formal criteria of legality but which contained no positive law or other material protections of liberty would be a very odd thing, so odd that even its formal claim to be a legal order would be doubtful.[141]

judge-made maxims known as the Common Law) are enforced by the Courts"; Dicey, *Law of the Constitution*, 23. Martial law does not however consist of rules since it is an absence of law. There is nothing, in other words, for official action to be congruent with.

[141] It follows that Justice Davis's claim in note 128 above is justified that *Milligan* should not be compared to *Dred Scott* because that opinion "was in the interest of Slavery, & the Milligan opinion in the interest of liberty."

Comment on Chapter 1

David Dyzenhaus, "The 'Organic Law' of *Ex Parte Milligan*"

Tony A. Freyer

The war on terror threatened the interdependency between nation-state sovereignty and the rule of law. Parliamentary democracies like Great Britain and the United States generally maintained their legitimacy by claiming that law rules over particular leaders or interests. Victorian jurist Albert Venn Dicey articulated a distinctive rule of law, in part to defend British imperialism. Dicey's rule of law derived from the English unwritten constitution and common law heritage. In America the rule of law was inseparable from what legal historian Willard Hurst called the constitutional ideal that all power should be accountable to power outside of itself. Whatever its constitutional form, the rule of law was vulnerable during wartime emergencies as nation-state authorities demanded unilateral power.[1] Professor David Dyzenhaus's fine paper explores the tension between the rule of law and emergency war powers mobilized to preserve national survival, the ultimate test of constitutional sovereignty. Dyzenhaus employs the U.S. Supreme Court's Civil War-era decision of *Ex parte Milligan* and Dicey's rule of law to address this tension in controversial U.S. cases arising from the Bush administration's war on terror.[2]

In several historical contexts Dyzenhaus offers *Milligan* as the source for a legal theory defending the rule of law. He frames the discussion of

1 Richard A. Cosgrove, *The Rule of Law: Albert Venn Dicey, Victorian Jurist* (Chapel Hill: North Carolina Press, 1980); James Willard Hurst, *Law and Markets in the United States: Different Modes of Bargaining among Interests* (Madison: University of Wisconsin Press, 1982), 97–98; Joseph Margulies, *Guantánamo and the Abuses of Presidential Power* (New York: Simon & Schuster, 2006); Harold H. Bruff, *Bad Advice: The President's Lawyers in the War on Terrorism* (Lawrence, KS: University Press of Kansas, 2009).

2 Quotes below cited to Draft text Professor Dyzenhaus read at the conference, "The 'Organic Law' of *Ex Parte Milligan*." Case cite: 71 U.S. 2 (1866).

Milligan relying primarily on the facts involving the president's assertion of extraordinary war powers in post–Civil War Indiana. His discussion of Dicey includes passing reference to an imperial "small war" the British fought against South African Boers during the turn of the nineteenth to the twentieth century. President George W. Bush's conduct of the war on terror receives the least historical context. Dyzenhaus employs these selective historical contexts in order to enrich the very insightful "organic" legal theory he extracts from *Milligan* and Dicey. He thereby skillfully reveals alternative constructions of the Supreme Court's controversial war-on-terror decisions.[3] The following critique broadens the historical perspective, reconsidering the scope of changing constitutional sovereignty in historically distinct wartime emergencies. The critique puts the historical context first; it thus expands upon Dyzenhaus' argument that cooperation among constitutional branches of government rather than unilateral action by one better preserves liberty and security.[4]

The Conflicted Images of *Milligan*

Dyzenhaus affirms *Milligan* in defense of liberty during wartime emergency. He weighs the venerable precedent against statements of American legal commentators identified with "Realist" legal theories that, he asserts, dominate contemporary American legal and constitutional discourse. He quotes U.S. Court of Appeals Judge Richard A. Posner forcefully rejecting *Milligan* because it purportedly epitomizes American lawyers gripped by the "thralldom to precedent." Indeed, Posner finds "ridiculous" the "idea that a case" so "old should guide us in dealing with al-Qaeda." Posner declares further that while "hauling U.S. civilians before military tribunals" raises legitimate policy concerns, "we don't need an ancient case to tell us that." Dyzenhaus notes other American commentators similarly dismissing

[3] In response to comments Professor Dyzenhaus indicated that his historical contextualization of legal theory was in part motivated by a critical reading of R. W. Kostal, *A Jurisprudence of Power Victorian Empire and the Rule of Law* (Oxford: Clarendon, 2005). His critique was being published in an issue of the *University of Toronto Law Journal* (forthcoming 2009) and was not available for use in this comment.

[4] For the method of historical contextualization of constitutional doctrine employed in this comment see Tony A. Freyer, *Little Rock on Trial Cooper v. Aaron and School Desegregation* (Lawrence, KS: University Press of Kansas, 2007).

Milligan during World War II, the Cold War, and its aftermath. Such commentators advocate a sovereignty of raw power based on nation-state absolutism during wartime emergencies. Dyzenhaus, however, identifies in *Milligan* an "organic law" refuting extreme Realists' assumptions defending unilateral executive action. Yet he defends the fundamental doctrine of liberty within a selective historical context focusing on the conflict the doctrine engendered.[5]

The "organic" law inherent in *Milligan*, Dyzenhaus argues, is consistent with "principles of the common law constitution." While these principles were "protective of individual interests articulated by judges over time in their decisions," they also assume that judges "had to defer to any clearly expressed intention of Parliament." Dyzenhaus acknowledges, "it also seems that Parliament could, if it so chose, establish martial law simply by stating clearly in a statute that this was its intention, just as (as Dicey also conceded) it could override any principle of the common law constitution. Put differently, the hallmark of common law constitutionalism is, somewhat counter-intuitively, that Parliament has the last word on what the law is, including the law of the constitution." Regarding wartime emergency both the U.S. written and the English customary or "unwritten" constitutions constitute a common law constitution. Under the common law constitution unilateral action by the executive, the legislature, or the judiciary may legitimate wartime necessity. According to Dyzenhaus, hard-line Realists endorse executive unilateralism, "the position that the executive is the legal sovereign because in times of stress the executive will as a matter of fact exercise sovereignty."[6]

The majority and concurring opinions in *Milligan* affirmed, respectively, judicial and legislative authority as the final arbiters of the common law constitution. According to Dyzenhaus, although the common law constitution reflects "a common law legal order" that assumes legislative supremacy, Parliament or Congress "is constrained" to the point that "if it wishes to speak as a *legal* sovereign, it has to speak in the language of the law, which means that it must speak in accordance with the rules of a normative grammar, rules which also discipline the speech of other institutional actors," including legislators, judges, and the executive. By contrast, "executive

[5] "Organic Law," as quoted, at 5.

[6] Ibid., 2.

unilateralism is a challenge to the very project of legal order since it asserts that the executive may break free from that discipline [imposed by the 'normative grammar' of legal rules]."[7] Dyzenhaus applies these standards to the facts and decision of *Milligan*. During the Civil War Lambdin P. Milligan was an Indiana "Peace Democrat" working overtly for a Confederate victory; with others, he also covertly planned active resistance, including the liberation of Confederate prisoners. Upon his arrest by Union authorities, the state's federal courts were open for trial; but a military commission sentenced him to death.[8]

Lincoln's September 24, 1864 proclamation authorized military commissions, even in places distant from an active war zone. These commissions applied military justice to civilians such as Milligan accused and convicted of "traitorous" conduct. The availability of federal courts nonetheless suggested a legal condition of sufficient ambiguity that Lincoln intended to save Milligan from execution. Following Lincoln's assassination, Andrew Johnson ordered the execution to proceed, then relented and commuted the sentence to life imprisonment at hard labor. War having passed into the uncertain constitutional era of Reconstruction, Milligan's petition for release under a writ of habeas corpus divided the judges of Indiana's U.S. Circuit Court. Upon appeal the Supreme Court unanimously upheld Milligan's release yet split over the reasons for that result. The majority affirmed the broad principle that in peacetime as long as the civil courts remained open, military tribunals lacked jurisdiction over civilians. Chief Justice Salmon P. Chase's concurring opinion argued, however, that Congress could authorize such jurisdiction during wartime. Applying the "normative grammar" of common law legality, Dyzenhaus concludes that both opinions refuted executive unilateralism.[9]

[7] Ibid., 7–8 (italics in original text).

[8] For the history of *Milligan* Dyzenhaus cites in note 18 primarily the works of leading authorities Charles Fairman, Mark E. Neely Jr., Charles Warren, and Clinton L. Rossiter.

[9] For the transition from war to "peacetime" Reconstruction during 1865–66 see Harold M. Hyman and William M. Wiecek, *Equal Justice Under Law Constitutional Development 1835–1875* (New York: Harper Torchbooks, 1986), 232–385; Stuart Streichler, *Justice Curtis in the Civil War Era at the Crossroads of American Constitutionalism* (Charlottesville: University of Virginia Press, 2005), 151–71. On Milligan's Civil War actions culminating in the treasonous conduct that resulted in his trial before the military commission see Allan Nevins, "The Case of the Copperhead Conspirator," in *Quarrels That Have Shaped the Constitution*, ed. John A Garrety, 90–108 (New York: Harper Colophon Books, 1966).

Historical Contexts in *Milligan*

Additional historical context highlights that Lincoln's martial law program, including suspension of habeas corpus, relied on implied constitutional authority. Chief Justice Roger Taney and other Democrats claimed that such implied powers were contrary to a strict reading of the Constitution. Whig and former Justice Benjamin Curtis – whose famous dissent denied the constitutionality of Taney's notorious *Dred Scott* decision – also objected to Lincoln's theory of implied powers. Amid such criticisms, Lincoln accepted the Habeas Corpus Act of 1863. Thus, Lincoln endorsed congressional authority retroactively to impose constitutional limitations on the martial law program. Chief Justice Salmon P. Chase's concurring opinion in *Milligan* argued that during wartime the act permitted some form of military commissions even if civil courts were open. Moreover, one reason for Andrew Johnson's impeachment was that he resisted congressional authorization of military commissions used to enforce Reconstruction against terrorists and their supporters. Chase's concurrence thus was consistent with congressional Republicans' support for Reconstruction programs that endorsed military commissions amid the southern terrorist campaign.[10]

Further considerations suggest a still more complex story. By 1862 the status of habeas corpus and the related issues of military authority against civilian combatants were enmeshed in questions about the scope of the Emancipation Proclamation. Based on the implied war powers theory, the Proclamation not only freed slaves in Confederate territory but it also encouraged their enlistment in the Union's military forces. Curtis' criticism of the Proclamation included the demand that federal troops and authorities should be indemnified against slaver holders' damage claims. The Habeas Corpus Act reconciled the Emancipation Proclamation and the implied powers with such criticisms; it included, for example, Curtis' indemnity principle. Undoubtedly, one reason Lincoln accepted the Habeas Corpus Act was that it followed the comprehensive constitutional defense articulated by War Department lawyer William Whiting. From 1862 to 1864, Whiting published at least eight editions of a manual addressing the war powers of the president, military arrests, and Reconstruction. The theories of Whiting and Curtis influenced Justice David Davis's majority and

10 Hyman and Wiecek, *Equal Justice Under Law*, 234–42, 259–62, 314–34, 380–85, 455–59.

Chief Justice Chase's concurring opinions in *Milligan*. Davis and Curtis exchanged correspondence concerning the decision.[11]

Reconsidering *Milligan* in light of this wider context suggests several points. First, Milligan's and his fellow conspirators' conduct clearly constituted treason as Whiting and Curtis defined it. Moreover, while the regular federal courts were open when military authorities arrested Milligan, there had been isolated Confederate raids in Indiana that enhanced perceptions of military threat when the commission sentenced the conspirators.[12] Next, the proceedings Milligan initiated in the U.S. Circuit Court occurred *after* both Robert E. Lee's surrender at Appomattox and Lincoln's assassination. The appeal and decision of the case occurred between May 1865 and April 1866 by which point the clash over Reconstruction was underway between congressional Republicans and Johnson.[13] Thus, the Supreme Court was addressing an issue that had arisen under Lincoln's reliance upon wartime necessity; the new president, however, claimed war powers during a conflicted peace. Davis denied that the opinion touched Reconstruction. Nevertheless, Chase's concern that the Davis's opinion could be read as aiding Johnson's position surely influenced the Chief Justice's opinion defending congressional authority in *Milligan*.[14]

This historical contextualization suggests in turn a broader reading of *Milligan*. Cleary Davis declared to be "false" any "theory of necessity" that justified suspending constitutional guarantees solely because of a declared national emergency. He also affirmed that the Constitution allocated to the government "all the powers granted to it, which are necessary to preserve its existence." In addition, Congress had imposed criminal penalties that provided the basis for trying Milligan's conduct *during wartime* in federal court, including the Habeas Corpus Act of 1863. Davis's narrow constitutional holding thus was that martial law imposed by a military commission did not supersede ordinary federal law enforceable in federal courts

[11] Ibid., 234, 246, 257, 267, 270, 323, 337; Streichler, *Justice Curtis*, 156–71; and compare editions of William Whiting, *The War Powers of the President, and the Legislative Powers of Congress in Relation to Rebellion, Treason, and Slavery* (Boston: J. L. Shorey, 1862); *The Powers of the President, Military Arrests, and Reconstruction of the Union* (Boston: J. L. Shorey, 1864).

[12] Ibid.; Lester V. Horwitz, *The Longest Raid of the Civil War: Little-Known & Untold Stories of Morgan's Raid into Kentucky, Indiana, and Ohio* (Cincinnati: Farmcourt Publishers, 1999).

[13] *Ex parte Milligan* 71 U.S. 2, 6–8 (December, 1866); Hyman and Wiecek, *Equal Justice Under Law*, 325–26.

[14] Streichler, *Justice Curtis*, 168–69.

during peacetime conditions. The context sketched above links Milligan's treasonable conduct to actions potentially harmful to Union troops before Appomattox. Moreover, Davis noted, martial law was appropriate "in the theatre of active military operations, where war really prevails," even if the regular courts were open. Indeed, after April 1865 this very situation increasingly prevailed under Reconstruction, where Davis informed Curtis, the "power [to impose martial law while courts remain open] is conceded in insurrectionary States."[15]

Davis's majority opinion thus prescribed the Supreme Court as the ultimate arbiter of how, when, and why martial law and ordinary federal civil law operated. By early 1867 Davis clearly felt the Republican criticism of *Milligan* amid Johnson's defiant affirmation of the unilateral executive. He urged Curtis to publish a reasoned constitutional argument supporting the majority opinion. Though Curtis never did so, he wrote Davis, "I do not think an elaborate defense of your opinion either necessary or expedient." He nonetheless understood that the opinion calls for "a *clear & solid* statement of the part which the judiciary has in the gov[ernment] of the U.S. not only from the express provisions of the constitution but from the very nature of the government & the necessities of our condition, in all times, both bad and good." The ambiguity over judicial authority Curtis recognized was consistent with Chase's concurring opinion arguing that Congress also possessed power to address the issues arising from martial and civil law coexisting. Both members of the Supreme Court, as well as Whiting and Curtis rejected, however, the unilateral executive authority Johnson declared in defiance of congressional Reconstruction.[16]

Dicey's Common Law Constitution and British Imperialism

This alternative context of *Milligan* suggests a reconsideration of Dicey's common law constitution within the British Empire. The shifting war-to-peace context in *Milligan* accentuated issues of shared deference among the U.S. government's three branches. During the Civil War military authorities' arrested, detained, and punished civilian combatants in

[15] 71 U.S., 121, 127; Davis as quoted, Hyman and Wiecek, *Equal Justice Under Law*, 383. In text italic emphasis added.

[16] Exchange between Davis and Curtis as quoted in Streichler, *Justice Curtis*, 169.

Union states where the civilian courts remained open. More often than not northern public opinion and Union officials deferred to Lincoln's lenient treatment.[17] These results were consistent with the constitutional theories of implied wartime emergency powers William Whiting developed in defense of Lincoln's "adequacy constitutionalism." These theories affirmed reciprocity among the executive, judiciary, and Congress. Accordingly, Lincoln accepted both judicial tests and retroactive legislative prescriptions defining executive war powers where civil-military authority coexisted. Johnson's defiance amid ambiguous peacetime Reconstruction, however, garnered the Supreme Court's and congressional rejection.[18] This changing U.S. context contrasted with Dicey's support for British imperial policy in the Boer War, highlighting differences between the British and American common law constitutions.[19]

While Dyzenhaus examines in another article the British imperial context, the Boer War receives passing note in the piece under review. He cites the Privy Council case, *Ex parte DF Marais* (1902). Marais' lawyers argued that as a civilian his arrest without warrant in one South African community and detention in another – both under martial law – were illegal because the civil courts remained in operation. As an authority for their claim, Marais' lawyers cited *Milligan*. For purposes of the present review, the paper's limited consideration of Dicey's views toward the Boer War highlights the value of fuller context.[20] The ferocity of the Boer's insurrection and the British ruler's ruthless response aroused sharp defense and criticism within and without Britain. Dicey defended vigorously the Empire, declaring "a nation which means to win must be prepared to fight a perfectly indefinite time." Moreover, he wrote Oliver Wendell Holmes Jr., "I believe the war myself to be as just as it is necessary & to bear a curious resemblance to the conflict with Secession." His priorities were straightforward: "There seems to be considerable risk that humane feeling about the sufferings of women & children may lead people to do a good deal of injustice to the Army, the Government, & the nation."[21]

17 Hyman and Wiecek, *Equal Justice Under Law*, 241.
18 Note 11.
19 Cosgrove, *Rule of Law*, 199–201.
20 "Organic Law," 45n13; *Ex parte DF Marais* [1902] AC 109.
21 Cosgrove, *Rule of Law*, as quoted 200–201.

Dicey's privately expressed support for British policy in the Boer War was consistent with the Privy Council's decision in the *Marais* case. The Judicial Committee held that the availability of civil courts had no direct legal bearing on Marais' arrest and detention. A commentator in *The Law Quarterly Review* quoted the stated reasons for the decision: "The truth is that no doubt has ever existed that where war actually prevails the ordinary courts have no jurisdiction over the action of military authorities. Doubtless cases of difficulty arise when the fact of a state of rebellion or insurrection is not clearly established." The potential application of the decision nonetheless aroused, the same commentator noted, "some criticism even from those whose legal vision is not coloured by their political sympathies." Indeed, another commentator in the *Review* disputed these reasons, though others agreed that in some form the defense of necessity justified the military's actions. The last commentator, Frederick Pollock, stated reasons that were consistent with Dicey's general defense of British policy: the "only point" the *Marais* opinion "really decided . . . was that the absence of visible disorder and continuing sitting of the courts are not conclusive evidence of a state of peace."[22]

Pollock's narrow legal analysis suggested the principle underlying Dicey's defense of British policy toward the Boers. The central point was that in order to be lawful, executive emergency action must be subject to judicial review and Parliament's possible indemnification. "So-called 'martial law,' as distinct from military law, is an unlucky name for the jurisdiction by the common law of acts done by necessity for the defence of the Commonwealth when there is war within the realm," wrote Pollock. The "jurisdiction of any particular act done in a state of war is ultimately examinable in the ordinary courts, and the prior question whether there was a state of war at the given time and place is a question of fact." In light of the "modern conditions of warfare and means of communication," the government may declare "a state of war at any place where aid and comfort can be effectively given to the enemy." Moreover, Parliament may as a "measure of indemnity and grace" pass "[a]n Act of Indemnity." Pollock concluded that "[i]f any one suggests a danger of this doctrine of necessity being extended

22 W. S. Holdsworth, "Martial Law Historically Considered"; H. Erle Richards, "Martial Law"; Cyril Dodd, "The Case of Marais"; Frederick Pollock, "What Is Martial Law?," *Law Quarterly Review* 18 (April, 1902): 117–32, 133–42, as quoted at 140, 143–51, 152–58, quoted at 157. See also Kostal, *Jurisprudence of Power*, 458–59.

without limit, the answer ... is that courts of justice must conclusively presume the ordinary process and remedies of law to be sufficient in time of peace."[23]

Pollock's confident assessment of *Marais* suggested tension between Dicey's common law constitution and the *Milligan* decision. Dyzenhaus is surely correct that Dicey's rule of law rejected executive unilateralism within the common law constitution. Nevertheless, Dicey's vigorous defense of the government's ruthless suppression of the Boer's harsh resistance exposed how little judicial review checked imperial policy in cases like *Marais*. Indeed, Pollock declared, the Privy Council's "decision is not binding on any English Court, and probably not binding on the Judicial Committee itself on any future occasion." Parliament had final authority, of course, but it promoted British imperial policy.[24] The broadened war-to-peace context of *Milligan* revealed, by contrast, Lincoln's restraint in applying Whiting's wartime emergency theory of implied reciprocity. Consistent with the American constitutional ideal that all power should be held accountable to power beyond itself, the Supreme Court and Congress deferred to Lincoln because in principle he formally deferred to them. The court and Congress reaffirmed the ideal, however, against Johnson's defiant claim of executive unilateralism. These considerations give new perspective to the court's war-on-terror cases.[25]

The Bush Administration's War-on-Terror Cases in Historical Context

Dyzenhaus makes a significant contribution to the growing analysis of cases arising from the 9/11 terrorist attacks.[26] His analytical categories of executive, legislative, and judicial unilateralism deepen theoretical understandings of a divided U.S. Supreme Court's plurality opinions since 2004. The tripartite categorization clarifies these opinions' overlapping yet competing

23 Pollock, "What Is Martial Law?" *Law Quarterly Review* 18 (April, 1902): 157–58.

24 Ibid., 158.

25 Note 11.

26 Craig Green, "Wiley Rutledge, Executive Detention, and Judicial Conscience at War," *Washington University Law Review* 84 (2006): 99–177; Jay Alan Bauer, "Detainees Under Review: Striking the Right Constitutional Balance between the Executive's War Powers and Judicial Review," *Alabama Law Review* 57 (Summer 2006): 1081–1103; Margulies, *Guantánamo*; Bruff, *President's Lawyers*.

assertions of executive, legislative, or judicial supremacy. Given space limitations, this review will assume without restating Dyzenhaus' theoretical analysis in each case. What requires emphasis is his point that "Dicey then rejects unilateralism of all sorts. In his constitutional theory, both Parliament and the judges are required to work in a cooperative relationship if executive accountability is to be secured. The common law constitution is, on his view, as much the product of legislation as it is of judicial decisions ... [and] the project of the rule of law requires creativity on the part of both Parliament and judges."[27] An extended historical context supports this point through Justice David Souter's analysis of the notorious wartime emergency decision, *Korematsu v. United States* (1944) in *Hamdi v. Rumsfeld* (2004).[28]

This extended historical context includes more diverse legal theories than the Realism Dyzenhaus describes. By the late twentieth century efficiency theories associated with public choice exercised enormous influence. These theories gave much weight to images of motivation and conduct grounded on rationally self-interested choices freely competing for dominance in political and judicial markets. Proponents of public choice conceived of law as an instrument of authority relying on rational incentives to shape and maintain its own accountability and individual's behavior. Dyzenhaus' account of the Supreme Court's plurality opinions in *Hamdi* notes that the justices employed a "cost-benefit calculation" to decide that "a military tribunal" was an appropriate "forum" for trying "enemy combatants." The "calculation" undoubtedly owed more to public choice than Realist theorizing. Also relying on public choice theories were self-described conservative lawyers within the Bush administration who developed the constitutional theories justifying the unilateral executive as the basis for fighting the war on terror. Public choice theories thus equipped President Bush with what his lawyers believed to be "rational" war powers.[29]

Competing versions of Legal Realism also were discernable in the *Hamdi* litigation. True to Dyzenhaus' characterization of "Realism," the Solicitor

27 "Organic Law," 40–41.

28 *Korematsu v. U.S.*, 323 U.S. 214 (1944); *Hamdi v. Rumsfeld*, 542 U.S. 507 (2004); extended commentary on Souter's concurring opinion in the latter case, Green, "Executive Detention," 140–51.

29 Reza R. Dibadj, *Rescuing Regulation* (Albany: State University of New York Press, 2006), 17, 21–23, 38, 43, 57–65, 100, 104, 107, 116; "Organic Law," 19; Margulies, *Guantánamo*, 45–59, 89–95, 104–9; Bruff, *Bad Advice*.

General's brief argued that a decision by the Supreme Court overturning the Bush administration's suspension of habeas corpus and denial of ordinary criminal proceeding would be "constitutionally intolerable." Justice Antonin Scalia addressed squarely the complex constitutional issues this claim raised. His position was consistent with a tradition of pragmatic Legal Realism identified with Thurman Arnold. Though strongly affiliated with Legal Realism, Arnold supported a pragmatic approach he shared with William O. Douglas. These Realists generally accepted that an emotional logic of psychological and sociological motivations influenced legal conduct; Arnold's approach endorsed fundamental trial and appellate procedures as a way to discipline irrationalism. These lawyers were confident that truly fair procedures promoted effective advocacy on behalf of any client, however, weak, unpopular, dangerous, or stigmatized by popular prejudice. Scalia's willingness to reach constitutional questions inferentially sanctioned such process over raw power.[30]

Like Arnold's Realism, Justice David Souter's *Hamdi* plurality opinion affirmed the need to adhere to "notice, fair rebuttal, a neutral decision-maker, and counsel," though he did not go as far as a federal judge would require under the Constitution's Article III. More forcefully, Souter urged wide-ranging analysis of precedent, especially the notorious internment of Japanese American citizens the Supreme Court upheld in *Korematsu*. Souter undoubtedly knew of the findings published in the 1980s revealing that after Pearl Harbor the U.S. government had suppressed evidence proving the Japanese Americans' loyalty. Souter's opinion stated that "for the purpose of avoiding another *Korematsu*" Congress in 1950 passed legislation demonstrating that it "meant to require a Congressional enactment that [more] clearly authorized detention or imprisonment" when the executive claimed wartime emergency powers. Thus, Souter said: "For reasons of inescapable human nature the [Executive] branch of Government ... is not the branch on which to rest the nation's entire reliance in striking the balance between the will to win and the cost in liberty on the way to victory. ... Hence the need for an assessment by Congress before citizens

[30] Brief for Respondent's, *Hamdi v. Rumsfeld*, 542 U.S. 507 (2004) (No. 03–6696) 2004 WL 724020, 46; *Hamdi*, 542 U.S., 554 (Scalia, J. dissenting). For "pragmatic realism" compare Karl N. Llewellyn, *Jurisprudence Realism in Theory and Practice* (New Brunswick: Transaction Publishers, 2008), 65–66, 159–63; Thurman W. Arnold, *Fair Fights and Foul: A Dissenting Lawyer's Life* (New York: Harcourt, Brace, and World, 1965), 54–70.

are subject to lockup, and likewise the need for a clearly expressed congressional resolution of the competing claims."[31]

Souter's analysis of *Korematsu* suggested that self-interested psychologies could engender "manipulated facts and risk assessment in wartime." The president's lawyers advocated the unilateral executive at least partially to shield from public scrutiny the problematic, often tragic, policies such as torture American authorities employed to prosecute the war on terror. Conscious of government authorities' past abuses, Souter was more sensitive than other members of the Supreme Court that meaningful legislative oversight was necessary. In *Hamdi*, observed Craig Green, the "plurality seemed not even to recognize such possibilities' existence. Souter called historically grounded risks firmly to mind and took strong steps to prevent them from repeating. By requiring a clear congressional statement before citizens are detained without charges, and by recalling what may happen when presidential detention authority is not carefully supervised," Souter offered "just the sort of calm, normatively grounded analysis" that enable the Supreme Court to avoid a "mistake" that recalled *Korematsu*. As the abuses derived from Bush administration's theory of unilateral executive became public knowledge, Souter's historical contextualization of precedent in *Hamdi* proved to be prophetic.[32]

Conclusion

Dyzenhaus rejects all unilateralism following the Supreme Court's belated affirmation of judicial supremacy in *Boumediene v. Bush* (2008). Dyzenhaus is probably correct that – after acquiescing to executive unilateralism and congressional laxity in *Hamdi* – the court finally reconsiders the spirit of liberty *Milligan* embodies.[33] Even though only Scalia's dissent formally relied on *Milligan*, the court's tenuous denial of legislative and executive unilateralism in *Boumediene* provides grounds for the theory of intra-governmental cooperation Dyzenhaus extracts from Dicey. Yet, expanded historical

[31] Compare sources to Arnold and Llewellyn cited n. 30 to Souter's legal philosophy, Tinsley E. Yarbrough, *David Hackett Souter, Traditional Republican on the Rehnquist Court* (New York: Oxford University Press, 2005), 40–41, 70–74, 131–37, 186–87, 198, 219–20, 240–42; Green, "Executive Detention," 146–48, quote at 149; *Hamdi*, 542 U.S. at 543, 545 (Souter, J. concurring in judgment).

[32] Green, "Executive Detention," 149–50; note 28 above.

[33] 553 U.S. (2008), 128 S. Ct. 2229 (2008): "Organic Law," 20–21, 47.

context reveals how readily Dicey accommodated his theory of liberty to British imperialism. By contrast, reconsidering *Milligan* within a broader context suggests that the Supreme Court embraced the intra-governmental reciprocity Lincoln sanctioned even as he exercised expansive implied wartime emergency powers. The court checked, however, Johnson's assertion that those same powers persisted during Reconstruction. Similarly, notwithstanding the court's excessive deference in *Hamdi,* Souter deploys *Korematsu* for the purpose of historical warning. Wider historical examples thus strengthen the theory of liberty Dyzenhaus mounts against the Bush administration's claims of unchecked power.[34]

[34] Notes 11, 21–24, 28.

2

Emergency, Legality, Sovereignty: Birmingham, 1963

Patrick O. Gudridge

Emergency, it is often thought, challenges sovereignty. Usual agendas, distributions of responsibilities – the ordinary patterns of government – are put in question. Extraordinary schemes prompt new assignments of authority, new claims to power. Precisely because these claims mark departures, they unsettle. Ultimate authority, it may be said, rests with whoever seizes the moment, successfully characterizes the right response to emergency, redefines the organization of government, inevitably thereby fixing limits on the reach of previously settled arrangements. Legality, within this account, is secondary: elaborates and reinforces the ordinary regime, or within the state of emergency *reboots* (we might say), elaborating and reinforcing the new order.

There is also another account.[1] Legality – its working accumulation of instruments, norms, and institutions – constructs sovereignty, establishes authority, throughout the course of its ramifications. Emergencies, like ordinary matters, are occasions for construction, occasions for bringing to bear legal resources, become parts therefore of the overall project, perhaps peripheral but sometimes perhaps central or paradigmatic. *Emergency, Legality, Sovereignty*.

In *Law in Times of Crisis*, writing with characteristic verve, Oren Gross and Fionnuala Ni Aolain name this way of thinking "Business as Usual":

> In times of danger and peril, as in normal times of quiet and calm, the laws (and the powers vested in the government) remain the same.

1 This essay takes as one point of departure ideas developed in Laurence H. Tribe and Patrick O. Gudridge, "The Anti-Emergency Constitution," *Yale Law Journal* (2004): 1801. Readers here will no doubt note the absence of the insights and good judgment of my co-author there.

> Ordinary legal rules and norms continue to be followed strictly and adhered to with no substantive change or modification. This approach offers a unitary vision of the constitutional order. While the occurrence of emergencies and acute crises is acknowledged, such events are of no constitutional significance because no distinct legal emergency regime is recognized under the constitution. We may think of this model as "Ordinary/Ordinary": Ordinary rules apply not only in times of peace but also in times of emergency.[2]

Gross and Ni Aolain worry much and rightly about the dangers of "normalization." "[T]he previously unthinkable may transform into the thinkable."[3] "Business as usual," they think, risks "detachment from reality," becomes vulnerable to challenge, demands that the constitutional order explicitly "accommodate the necessities of the situation," and as a result "may lead to adjustments to the system that are made in ways that are less transparent."[4] They prefer, readers may conclude, that the "distinction between the spheres of normalcy and emergency" be drawn openly, that the "mechanisms of separation" appear as well-defined.[5]

American constitutional law, I think, *almost* fits the Gross and Ni Aolain model. It does not consist of only "rules and norms," "following" is a noticeably sometime thing even in cases addressing "ordinary" settings, "emergencies" and "crises" of various sorts present themselves with surprising frequency, and the "regime" (it appears) often supplies substantial resources *both* to defend and to criticize the particular efforts its participants undertake. This considerable complexity, as often useful as problematic, comes into being precisely because constitutional law as it stands is, along side its "rules and norms," also a grab bag of models, structures, and either outrageous or exemplary paradigms.

In this essay, I test this alternate characterization by considering the civil rights demonstrations in Birmingham, Alabama, in the spring of 1963. These efforts and their aftermaths are famous, of course. But "Birmingham" – the event, the sequence of occurrences considered whole – is not ordinarily discussed as though it were either an especially significant moment

[2] Oren Gross and Fionnuala Ni Aolain, *Law in Times of Crisis* (New York: Cambridge University, 2006), 88.

[3] Id. at 228.

[4] Id. at 173.

[5] Id. at 174.

constitutionally – or as an "emergency," as an extraordinary event prompting distinctive governmental response. I think that we can learn much about the crisis resources of ordinary constitutional law, both critical and affirmative, by reading carefully the principal documents pertinent to constitutional law written during and about the Birmingham sequence. In particular, I take as points of departure Martin Luther King's "Letter From a Birmingham Jail," John F. Kennedy's "Radio and Television Report to the American People on Civil Rights," and two decisions of the United States Supreme Court: *Walker v. City of Birmingham* and *Shuttlesworth v. City of Birmingham.*[6] In the process, discussion ranges much more widely.

I. "Birmingham"

The efforts of the Southern Christian Leadership Conference (SCLC) in support of a locally organized antisegregation boycott in Birmingham, Alabama, in the spring of 1963 had at least three notable consequences.

- First, Martin Luther King and other SCLC leaders were jailed, early on, for contempt of court after violating a judicial injunction prohibiting parading without a municipally issued permit. This injunction and the ensuing contempt sanction became the occasion for the United States Supreme Court decision in *Walker v. City of Birmingham.* King used his incarceration (about a week) to write – famously, in the margins of scraps of newspapers – his "Letter From a Birmingham Jail," a now-classic contribution to the literature of American political argument.
- Second, the marches and other demonstrations following the release of King and his colleagues culminated in a dramatic series of confrontations involving (at various stages) civil rights supporters, local and state police, crowds, and terrorist bombers.
- Third, the accumulating incidents were almost immediately understood as a great victory for the SCLC. Birmingham business leaders

[6] For rightly celebrated discussion of King's Letter" and *Walker*, see David Luban, "Difference Made Legal: The Court and Dr. King," *Michigan Law Review* 87 (1989): 2152. This essay flies at a lower attitude: I do not, for example, challenge Martin Luther King's readings of Christian scripture. Like Professor Luban, I do read *Walker* closely and critically (here our arguments overlap somewhat), but I proceed in large part by juxtaposing *Walker* with other Supreme Court opinions, ultimately most importantly *Shuttlesworth*.

agreed to desegregate. Nationally and internationally "Birmingham" was perceived as marking a sea change.

The SCLC undertakings in Birmingham plausibly constitute "a historical event" in the strict sense in which William Sewell uses the term – "a chain of occurrences that durably transforms previous structures and practices."[7] Why was this the case? There is something important to be learned, I think, by first looking closely at King's "Letter" as though it were a guide to understanding the sequence that unfolded in Birmingham, and also as one key to decoding the subsequent significance of "Birmingham" the event.

Political Theology

On April 12, 1963, at the outset of the SCLC efforts, eight prominent Birmingham clergymen – Protestant bishops and ministers, a Catholic bishop, and a rabbi (all white) – published a joint statement.[8] The same group, following George Wallace's inauguration as Alabama governor in January that year, had previously set themselves up in opposition to Wallace. "[D]efiance is neither the right answer nor the solution." "[H]atred and violence have no sanction in our religious and political traditions." Instead, "[w]e respectfully urge those who strongly oppose desegregation to pursue their convictions in the courts, and in the meantime peacefully to abide by the decisions of those same courts."[9] The April statement sounded much the same themes. "We ... strongly urge our own negro community to withdraw support from these demonstrations. ..." "When rights are consistently denied," the eight signers declared, "a cause should be pressed in the courts and in negotiations among local leaders, and not in the streets." Public protest actions "incite to hatred and violence, however technically peaceful those actions may be." "We appeal to both our white and negro citizenry to observe the principles of law and order and common sense."[10]

[7] William H. Sewell Jr., *Logics of History* (Chicago: University of Chicago, 2005), 227.

[8] The statement is reprinted in S. Jonathan Bass, *Blessed Are the Peacemakers* (Baton Rouge: Louisiana State University, 2001), 235–36. Much of Bass's melancholy book reconstructs the careers of the eight clergy – and their thinking about race and civil rights "before and after."

[9] Bass, *Blessed Are the Peacemakers*, 233, 234.

[10] Id. at 236.

Martin Luther King's "Letter" takes the April 12 statement of the eight clergy as its point of departure.[11] King begins and ends with elaborate collegial courtesies: "My dear Fellow Clergymen" – "If I have said anything in this letter that is an overstatement of the truth and is indicative of an unreasonable impatience, I beg you to forgive me." "Yours for the cause of Peace and Brotherhood. . . ."[12]

It is obvious, however, reading the main body of the text, that the "Letter" means to deny the authors of the April 12 statement the position they implicitly claimed as arbiters, central and superior figures judging immediate participants in a dispute. King took over this pose himself, assumed the role of minister, addressed his "fellow clergymen" as though they were congregants in need of counseling:

> We have to repent in this generation not merely for the vitriolic words and actions of the bad people, but for the appalling silence of the good people. We must come to see that human progress never rolls in on wheels of inevitability. It comes through the tireless efforts and persistent work of men willing to be co-workers with God, and without this hard work time itself becomes an ally of the forces of local stagnation. We must use time creatively, and forever realize that the time is always ripe to do right.[13]

Religiously, he declared, the role of "extremist" that the eight deplored, was precisely the right status to embrace – politically so, as well:

> Was not Jesus an extremist in love. . . . Was not Amos an extremist for justice. . . . Was not Paul an extremist for the gospel of Jesus Christ. . . . Was not Martin Luther an extremist. . . . Was not John Bunyan an extremist. . . . Was not Abraham Lincoln an extremist. . . . Was not Thomas Jefferson an extremist. . . .? So the question is not whether we will be extremist but what kind of extremist we will be. Will we be extremists for hate or will we be extremists for love? Will we be extremists for the preservation of injustice – or will we be extremists for the preservation of justice?[14]

[11] Martin Luther King, Jr., "Letter from Birmingham City Jail," in *A Testament of Hope: The Essential Writings and Speeches of Martin Luther King, Jr.*, ed. James M. Washington, 289–302 (New York: HarperCollins, 1986).

[12] Id. at 289, 302.

[13] Id. at 296.

[14] Id. at 297–98.

Religiously, King also concluded, "our willingness to break the law" regarding parade permits in Birmingham was neither wrong nor inconsistent with "diligently urg[ing] people to obey the Supreme Court."[15]

> I would agree with Saint Augustine that "An unjust law is no law at all." … To put it in the terms of Saint Thomas Aquinas, an unjust law is a human law that is not rooted in eternal and natural law. … Any law that degrades human personality is unjust. All segregation statutes are unjust because segregation distorts the soul and damages the personality. It gives the segregator a false sense of superiority, and the segregated a false sense of inferiority. To use the words of Martin Buber, the great Jewish philosopher, segregation substitutes an "I-it" relationship for the "I-thou" relationship. … So segregation is not only politically, economically and sociologically unsound, but it is morally wrong and sinful. Paul Tillich has said that sin is separation.[16]

The "Letter" agrees with the statement of the eight clergy that nonviolent, civilly disobedient demonstrations of the sort that the SCLC was staging in Birmingham might "incite to hatred and violence." This was, in a sense, precisely the idea:

> [W]e who engage in nonviolent direct actions are not the creators of tension. We merely bring to the surface the hidden tension that is already alive. We bring it out in the open where it can be seen and dealt with. … [I]njustice must be exposed, with all of the tension its exposing creates, to the light of human conscience and the air of national opinion before it can be cured.[17]

There was – again, simultaneously as a matter of religious and political morality – nothing wrong in "actions, even though peaceful," which "precipitate violence."[18]

[15] Id. at 293.

[16] Id. at 293–94. This is, of course, an utterly breathtaking passage: In the course of one paragraph King groups early Christian (Augustine), high medieval Catholic (Aquinas), and modern Jewish (Buber) and Protestant (Tillich) thinking – all, he makes it seem, an effortless and obvious gloss on the central (and to some, controversial) assertion of *Brown v. Board of Education*, which therefore becomes, it seems, itself a kind of religious text. See also Luban, "Difference Made Legal," 2206.

[17] King, "Letter," 295.

[18] Id.

> Isn't this like condemning the robbed man because his possession of money precipitated the evil act of robbery? ... Isn't this like the condemning Jesus because his unique God-consciousness and never-ceasing devotion to his will precipitated the evil act of crucifixion? We must come to see, as federal courts have consistently affirmed, that it is immoral to urge an individual to withdraw his efforts to gain his basic constitutional rights because the quest precipitates violence. Society must protect the robbed and punish the robber.[19]

Radical polarization: a fraternal punch to the stomach – most of King's readers would have recalled the antecedent: "He that is not with me is against me."[20]

In the Street

"[T]he hidden tension" that Martin Luther King posited surfaced dramatically after he and other SCLC leaders left jail.[21]

The incarcerations themselves did not stimulate increased participation in marches and other demonstrations by the Birmingham black community at large. The disappointing results of efforts to mobilize substantial local participation in civil disobedience exercises, and consequent declining press coverage – the means to obtaining public support nationally – threatened the SCLC campaign with outright failure. James Bevel, who had taken charge of efforts to work with teenagers and children, persuaded other SCLC leaders to allow volunteers ordinarily thought to be too young to join in the Birmingham demonstrations. King – troubled by the dangers that participation posed for young volunteers – did not agree but also did not try to stop the new effort. Thousands of high school students skipped or simply left school, climbing walls where necessary, to converge on churches used as SCLC meeting points. The students, exuberantly idealistic, welcoming arrest, marched – wave after wave – directly toward police as crowds of watchers accumulated. Directed by the volatile, openly-racist Bull Connor,

19 Id. at 295–96.

20 Matthew 12:30.

21 The abbreviated account here is not much more than a cartoon. There is much good history already written. I draw chiefly on Glenn T. Eskew, *But for Birmingham* (Chapel Hill: University of North Carolina, 1997), 217–322; Taylor Branch, *Parting the Waters* (New York: Simon and Schuster, 1988), 725–809. See also David B. Oppenheimer, Kennedy, King, Shuttlesworth and Walker: The Events Leading to the Introduction of the Civil Rights Act of 1964, 29 University of San Francisco Law Review 645 (1995).

police arrested great numbers but also, again on Connor's order, responded in force, deploying fire houses, water cannon, dogs, and the like.

These tactics, like the triggering demonstrations, were largely ignored or downplayed by local media, but become the focus of national and international coverage, as well as increasingly intense public reaction – perhaps in large part because of the vivid photographs and television transmissions that the police actions readily inspired.[22] Within the Birmingham black community, adult support for the demonstrations burgeoned – especially noticeably encompassing on-looker responses (not organized by the SCLC) protesting police conduct. Elementary school students joined the marches; teenage participants were deployed in small groups initially seeking to out-flank police and launch demonstrations in other parts of Birmingham. Police use of force persisted. Teenage groups made their way quietly to the downtown retail business district and suddenly surfaced, protesting segregation of stores and restaurants, precisely in the midst of white shoppers. Downtown merchants and SCLC leaders, in part working through federal intermediary Burke Marshall, negotiated a compromise settlement of desegregation demands.

The arrangement provoked criticism from Fred Shuttlesworth, the Birmingham minister whose long-time, fierce work in opposition to segregation had initially occasioned SCLC support. It also provoked white outrage and bombings of the home of Martin Luther King's brother and the motel that had served as the SCLC headquarters. Police arriving on scene confronted angry black onlookers and an extended series of violent skirmishes ensued. State forces, ordered in by Governor Wallace, introduced additional, brutal and largely-undisciplined violence. President Kennedy raised the possibility of federal military intervention and also committed his administration to proposing legislation that – after Kennedy's death later in 1963 – would be enacted as the Civil Rights Act of 1964.

The Birmingham incidents accelerated efforts to organize the long-proposed march on Washington, culminating in Martin Luther King's famous speech.[23] King would win the Nobel Peace Prize. A horrifying

22 For press perspective, see Gene Roberts and Hank Klibanoff, *The Race Beat* (New York: Knopf, 2006), 304–24.

23 "Only half-joking, Bayard Rustin told Thomas Gentile, one of the March's first historians, that its real organizers were 'Bull Connor, his police dogs and his fire hoses.'" Eric J. Sundquist, *King's Dream* (New Haven: Yale, 2009), 40–41.

bombing in Birmingham of one of the churches used as a staging site for demonstrations killed several very young girls. After passage of the Civil Rights Act, voting rights campaigners, now joined by King and other SCLC leaders, organized a march to Selma, Alabama – set against the backdrop of murders of black and white voting rights workers in several states – that triggered violent police responses plainly of a piece with Birmingham excesses. The Voting Rights Act of 1965 followed.

In the White House

What happened? The sequence of incidents was a complex mix of idealism, provocation, initially measured police responses giving way to increasingly disproportionate force, angry and sometimes violent crowds, terrorist violence, local compromise, and competing state and federal attempts at intervention. Amid all of this, what prompted – suggested as the right reaction – the landmark legal, political, and cultural changes that followed?[24]

In his "Letter," Martin Luther King described what he wanted to have happen: "Like a boil that can never be cured as long as it is covered up but must be opened with all its pus-flowing ugliness to the natural medicine of air and light, injustice must likewise be exposed. …"[25] The "ugliness" that the Birmingham demonstrators brought to the surface was and is easy to recognize – but what counted as "the natural medicine of air and light"? After the Selma march King evoked another, quintessentially Cold War image:

> Confrontation of good and evil compressed in the tiny community of Selma generated the massive power to turn the whole nation to a new course. A president born in the South had the sensitivity to feel the will of the country, and in an address that will live in history as one of the most passionate pleas for human rights ever made by a president of our nation, he pledged the might of the federal government to cast off the

[24] I do not mean to suggest that the sequence of incidents in Birmingham was, without more, the only or plainly most important factor prompting enactment of the Civil Rights Act of 1964 and the Voting Rights Act of 1965. There does seem to be a generally held understanding, however, that "Birmingham" was an important catalyst of much that followed, including the two great statutes. There were other important factors: for example, President Kennedy's assassination and President Johnson's responses to his own ascendancy certainly mattered much. There are also still other considerations that would figure in an exhaustive account.

[25] King, "Letter," 295.

> centuries-old blight. President Johnson rightly praised the courage of the Negro for awakening the conscience of the nation.[26]

The Selma march was a well-shaped explosion, the moral equivalent of an atomic bomb, a release of "massive power," forcing a "new course," presidential redirection of "the might of the federal government." Birmingham would have been the first such blast. The imagery changes. "[N]atural medicine" becomes weapon design. But what precisely happened? King concludes that "the courage of the Negro ... awaken[ed] the conscience of the nation." What conscience?

Accounting for "Birmingham," we might think, is something like trying to explain the import of the storming of the Bastille, the ostensible start of the revolutionary phase of the French Revolution. William Sewell, studying the Bastille incident as a prototypical historical "event," notes that the Paris crowd could have easily been characterized as a mob, and their acts therefore akin to a riot – not new in European urban history, usually of limited political significance, often condition precedent for repressive responses. After the Bastille guards surrendered, the guard leaders were torn to pieces by the crowd, with their heads displayed on pikes. An incident of this sort appeared to be some distance removed from acts of "the people of France" conceived – usually rather less concretely, as it were – as a sovereign entity. Members of the National Assembly, Sewell observes, were initially quite cautious in their comments concerning the Paris happenings. Louis XVI, however, famously treated the capture of the Bastille and its weapons as politically significant, traveling to Paris with members of the National Assembly to assent to establishment of a new Parisian government and national guard.

> It was not until July 20 that the Assembly spelled out ... a conception of the taking of the Bastille as a legitimate popular revolution. The Assembly was driven to this elaboration not by sheer gratitude, but by a practical need to distinguish the just violence of the sovereign people from the unacceptable violence of the dangerous mob.[27]

The Birmingham and Bastille events do not entirely match up, of course. The SCLC demonstrations and their aftermaths nonetheless did

[26] Martin Luther King Jr., "Our God Is Marching On!" in Washington (ed.), *A Testament of Hope*, 228.

[27] Sewell, *Logistics of History*, 240. For development of the argument in full, see id. at 225–70.

accomplish something akin to "rupture and . . . rearticulation" (in Sewell's terms). The Birmingham incidents were much more than "a brute physical occurrence," possessed a distinctively "theatrical character," and appeared to occasion a "novel code switch politically and culturally."[28] King's comments about Selma concerning the importance of President Johnson's actions also underscore a theorem Sewell extracts from his own study: "To become definitive, rearticulations of structures must gain authoritative sanction."[29]

Stressing the importance of "Birmingham," Jeffrey Alexander reaches a conclusion much like King's and consistent with Sewell's assertion. Alexander's extended discussion of the civil rights movement is a centerpiece of *The Civil Sphere*, his grandly ambitious sociology of public culture. He singles out in particular President Kennedy's televised speech following in the wake of the Birmingham demonstrations:

> Kennedy . . . not only announced his identification with the spirit and goals of the black dissenting movement, but became the spokesman for the movement inside the state. . . . [H]is official and public commitment to civil repair set off a chain reaction that would have been impossible without this decisive and unprecedented act. With the submission of the Kennedy civil rights bill, the symbolic space of communicative mobilization had become transformed into the concrete details of law and organization. . . .[30]

What prompted President Kennedy?

> In 1966, . . . Robert Kennedy . . . told an interviewer, "What aroused people generally in the country and aroused the press was the Birmingham riots in May of 1963." . . . Kennedy gestured to Birmingham's communicative success, its ability to reach over local boundaries and to mobilize a symbolic extension and psychological identification among whites in the North. . . . The effect of this dramatic deepening of identification of northern whites with protesting southern blacks, and the profound

28 Sewell, *Logistics of History*, 244, 245, 252, 265.

29 Id. at 257.

30 Jeffrey C. Alexander, *The Civil Sphere* (New York: Oxford, 2006), 363. For the central chapters in Alexander's consideration of the civil rights movement, see id. at 293–391. The Birmingham demonstrations and their significance are discussed at id. at 347–58. Professor Alexander writes within a vocabulary evoking the impressive theoretical structure he assembles elsewhere in *The Civil Sphere*.

> arousal of civil consciousness that both triggered and reflected it, was to push the elected representatives of the civil sphere decisively in the direction of regulatory reform.[31]

But why did Senator Kennedy refer to the SCLC demonstrations and their aftermath as "riots"? Why depict Birmingham as seemingly of a piece with the 1964 and 1965 Rochester, Philadelphia, and Los Angeles (Watts) disturbances, large-scale instances of racially-specific crowd violence and police and military responses? John Walton Cotman assembled public statements, interviews, and transcripts of recordings President Kennedy made of Oval Office conversations.[32] Cotman's powerfully presented collage depicts White House perceptions in 1963 that are surprisingly consistent, we might think, with Robert Kennedy's later word use. Three themes are especially evident:

First, there is a preoccupation with "no-jurisdiction." "[I]n the context of Birmingham and our conversations with the President at the time, my conversation with Bob Kennedy, was always in the context of not having any solution under law to this problem. And that was *the* problem in Birmingham."[33] "'Why don't you do something? What is President Kennedy doing?' ... That's the great problem. Whether we have an excuse for doing something today."[34]

Second, there is ongoing worry about violence, black against white, more so white against black, escalating out of control. "An injured, maimed or dead child is a price that none of us can afford to pay."[35] "A number of the policemen were badly hurt. And I guess ... a number of the Negroes were badly hurt. And it was very close to becoming complete chaos. During the course of it a couple of buildings were set on fire."[36] "[The downtown merchants] want Birmingham to look like Atlanta. And they want it to solve its

31 Alexander, *Civil Sphere*, 360, 361.

32 John Walton Cotman, *Birmingham, JFK and the Civil Rights Act of 1963* (New York: Peter Lang, 1989). See also Jonathan Rosenberg and Zachary Karabell, *Kennedy, Johnson, and the Quest For Justice: The Civil Rights Tapes* (New York: W. W. Norton, 2003).

33 Cotman, *Birmingham*, 56 (Burke Marshall). Marshall was Assistant Attorney General and the principal representative of the Kennedy Administration, often on the scene, in discussions with groups caught up – from several different perspectives – in the Birmingham melee. Professor Cotman took Marshall's observations from an interview conducted by Anthony Lewis in 1964. See id. at 210.

34 Cotman, *Birmingham*, 83 (Robert F. Kennedy).

35 Cotman, *Birmingham*, 30 (Robert F. Kennedy).

36 Cotman, *Birmingham*, 73–74 (Robert F. Kennedy).

own problems.... So they wouldn't like [the introduction of federal troops]. ... [T]hey might rather have [troops] than have a racial war down there. If those are the alternatives and they understand them clearly as they did last week."[37] "[O]ne of the things would be to control the Negro mob. ... What we've got is to, is to provide an atmosphere [in] which this agreement can be carried out, and in the meanwhile prevent the Negroes from rioting and therefore prevent the whites from taking reactions against them. I think that's our purpose."[38] "The Negroes gathered, several thousands when the police came and the fire department came with the fire hoses. They threw rocks and stones, brought out their knives and they got out of hand. ... Then the Governor sent his people. ...So then they started clubbing people and beating them and then the situation got completely out of control. ... Well, the Negroes then felt that they had been betrayed. And ... they indicated quite clearly that, that night you were going to have a real war in Birmingham. Some of them were armed. They had knives. They had guns. And they were going after these people. ..."[39]

Third, there is a working hypothesis that the problems of jurisdiction and violence are inter-related. "[E]verybody's mind was turned to the future and they thought that this pattern of Birmingham had been established, that it would recur in many other places. ... [T]he President wanted to know what he should do ... to deal with what was clearly an explosion in the racial problem that could not, would not go away, that he had not only to face up to himself, but somehow bring the country to face up to and resolve. ... [T]hat's what led to the legislation [the proposed Civil Rights Act]."[40] "[T]he President ... wanted to have a legal solution, as he said ... then and he said constantly. He wanted to bring this problem under law."[41] "Our argument ought to be that these people who object to mob action and unreasonable demonstrations and so on, the problem is today there is no other remedy. This would give another remedy in law and therefore. ..."[42] "We couldn't go into Birmingham. ... We can't go into any of these other communities. The result is that you have street demonstrations. The result of that it that

[37] Cotman, *Birmingham*, 79 (Burke Marshall).
[38] Cotman, *Birmingham*, 80 (John F. Kennedy).
[39] Cotman, *Birmingham*, 129–30 (Robert F. Kennedy). See Luban, "Difference Made Legal," 2213.
[40] Cotman, *Birmingham*, 52 (Burke Marshall).
[41] Cotman, *Birmingham*, 59 (Burke Marshall).
[42] Cotman, *Birmingham*, 118 (John F. Kennedy).

someone is very likely to get hurt. ... What this will do is get this into the court and out of the street."[43]

President Kennedy's radio and television address of June 11, 1963, indeed included eloquent appeals precisely evoking the processes of identification and solidarity that Professor Alexander emphasizes.[44] "I hope that every American ... will stop and examine his conscience. ..." "[E]very American ought to have the right to be treated as he would wish to be treated, as one would wish his children to be treated. But this is not the case." There was, however, also a second, intertwined line of thought. "The events in Birmingham and elsewhere have so increased the cries for equality that no city or State or legislative body can prudently choose to ignore them." "The old code of equity under which we live commands for every wrong a remedy, but in too many communities, in too many parts of the country, wrongs are inflicted on Negro citizens and there are no remedies at law. Unless the Congress acts, their only remedy is the streets." "[A] rising tide of discontent ... threatens the public safety." "It is better to settle these matters in the courts than on the streets." Kennedy pulled the two sequences together. "[N]ew laws are needed at every level, but law alone cannot make men see right." "We are confronted primarily with a moral issue. It is as old as the scriptures and is as clear as the American Constitution."[45]

Someone – President Kennedy? Robert Kennedy? – had read Martin Luther King's "Letter" or in any event came to understand the moment in much the way that King wanted it to be understood. Kennedy administration officials reacted as much or more to the *aftermath* of the SCLC marches, perceiving "Birmingham" as incipient chaos, perceiving "the streets" and therefore demonstrations as potentially explosive. In the process, they learned to appreciate and put to work a very old constitutional logic. The governmental crisis of sovereignty come up short, of incomplete jurisdiction

[43] Cotman, *Birmingham*, 147 (Robert F. Kennedy).

[44] I take the passages quoted in this paragraph from John F. Kennedy, "Radio and Television Report to the American People on Civil Rights," June 11, 1963, John F. Kennedy Presidential Library and Museum, Historical Resources, http://www.jfklibrary.org/Historical+Resources/Archives/Reference+Desk/Speeches/JFK/003POF03CivilRights06111963.htm (accessed January 31, 2009).

[45] "The fires of frustration and discord are burning in every city, North and South, where legal remedies are not at hand. Redress is sought in the streets, in demonstrations, parades, and protests which create tensions and threaten violence and threaten lives. We face, therefore, a moral crisis as a country and as a people." Kennedy, "Radio and Television Report."

and agency, was also understood as a problem of protection, of inability to act in aid of persons in crisis, persons therefore immediately at risk. It is as though we have reentered the constitutional universe of the early Middle Ages, the era of pledges of protection deployed as assertions of authority.[46] Emergency becomes the occasion for extension of jurisdiction in the form of legal action: initially, proposal of the Civil Rights Act of 1963; eventually, through granting power to courts to address issues individuals could otherwise confront only in dangerous streets. *Emergency, legality, sovereignty.*

There really is no surprise, therefore, in finding a complex interplay of reason of state and recognition of individual rights in the Kennedy administration response to the Birmingham sequence of incidents. And there is no reason to try to assign priority to one or the other driving concern. Each informs the other, as President Kennedy's address shows. Nonetheless, this structural doubling may suggest that the ideas of "identification" and "solidarity" that Jeffrey Alexander reads as resonating so strongly in the Kennedy speech risk overstatement. Alexander manages this hazard within his own larger project chiefly through recurring emphasis on the only incompletely-established status of the civil sphere, conceived as always in competition with other modes of social interaction, all registering each other's distinctive projections.[47] At the level of particular choices, however, complexity therefore ordinarily carries a negative case. "The autonomy of civil society is continually compromised and consistently reduced."[48]

Alexander himself stresses possibilities for "civil repair" and "incremental but real integration of formerly excluded groups"[49] – this is, indeed, the starting point for his study of social movements generally and the civil rights movement in particular. We may think, however, that there is also an alternative formulation, not inconsistent, but a more apt starting point for considering responses to particular crises like President Kennedy's. The idea of "acknowledgement," sketched by Stanley Cavell[50] and stressed by Patchen Markell,[51] marks as "[w]hat matters" "*what we do*," "avowal, " "coming to terms."[52]

[46] See Barbara H. Rosenwein, *Negotiating Space: Power, Restraint, and Privileges of Immunity in Early Medieval Europe* (Ithaca: Cornell, 1999), 99–134.

[47] See Alexander, *Civil Sphere*, 193–209.

[48] Alexander, *Civil Sphere*, 194.

[49] Alexander, *Civil Sphere*, 205, 209.

[50] Stanely Cavell, *The Claim of Reason* (New York: Oxford, 1979), 428–40.

[51] Patchen Markell, *Bound by Recognition* (Princeton: Princeton University, 2003), 9–38, 177–89.

[52] Markell, *Bound by Recognition*, 34, 36, 38.

It seeks out "a pattern of mutual and interlocking relations," "equitably distributing the sacrifices inevitably produced by political decisions."[53] This vocabulary, it appears, catches the promise Kennedy made and also underlines the risk. "[E]xisting relations of injustice will be preserved or ... reinforced, albeit cloaked in a superficial layer of reform."[54] (I will make much of the idea of acknowledgement later on.)

II. Walker *Inter Alia*

The Warren Court's first consideration of the Birmingham demonstrations was off-puttingly complex – at best, many readers conclude. *Walker v. City of Birmingham*[55] addressed contempt of court punishment imposed upon Martin Luther King and other SCLC and local leaders of the initial civil rights marches that had proceeded without permits required by a Birmingham ordinance and notwithstanding an injunction issued by a local judge. The Supreme Court, Justice Stewart writing for the majority, upheld the contempt sanctions, in the process denying civil rights leaders any opportunity to raise directly a free speech challenge to the constitutionality of the ordinance and injunction the contempt proceeding treated as its predicate. Stewart's analysis is, on first reading, a rote, mechanical application of the "collateral bar" rule.[56] In at least one respect, however, his opinion is obliquely ambitious. It attempts, without saying so right out, to frame an alternative to judicial approaches developed in prior cases, cases of great moment themselves. In the process, Justice Stewart and his colleagues in the majority also appear to be trying to acknowledge the extraordinary dimensions of the case at hand while still insisting upon the value of the ordinary workings of legal institutions.

The Strangeness of Justice Stewart's Opinion

The Supreme Court announced *Walker* on June 12, 1967.[57] The extraordinary events that followed the contempt jailings in the case had by then

[53] Markell, *Bound by Recognition*, 188.

[54] Markell, *Bound by Recognition*, 188.

[55] 388 U.S. 307 (1967).

[56] "[B]egged, and begged to its depths": Luban, "Difference Made Legal," 2179. To be sure, there are also readers – for example, Chief Justice Rehnquist – who have read *Walker* positively, as an important vindication of "the orderly process of law." *Celotex Corp. v. Edwards*, 514 U.S. 300, 313 (1995).

[57] See *Walker*, 388 U.S., 307.

become inescapable facts of modern American history. There was almost no acknowledgement of this in Justice Stewart's opinion – except for a terse, tense, and cryptic concluding paragraph:

> The rule of law that Alabama followed in this case reflects a belief that in the fair administration of justice no man can be judge in his own case, however exalted his station, however righteous his motives, and irrespective of his race, color, politics, or religion. This Court cannot hold that the petitioners were constitutionally free to ignore all the procedures of the law and carry their battle to the streets. One may sympathize with the petitioners' impatient commitment to their cause. But respect for judicial process is a small price to pay for the civilizing hand of law, which alone can give abiding meaning to constitutional freedom.[58]

The Supreme Court acknowledges the "exalted ... station" and "righteous ... motives" of King and his colleagues. But Justice Stewart also cites *Kasper v. Brittain* – in which a federal district judge enforced an ex parte restraining order against a white agitator "'from somewhere in the East'" who had denied the validity of the order in the course of urging resistance to a school desegregation decree.[59] Obliquely, Stewart suggests a version of the point Hugo Black also made: The civil rights movement did not just need the support of courts generally – but the assistance in particular of the "rule of law" enforced in *Walker*.[60] There was more implicit in this paragraph,

58 *Walker*, 320–21.

59 *Walker*, 321n16, summarizing and quoting *Kasper v. Brittain*, 245 F.2d 92, 94 (6th Cir. 1957), cert. denied, 355 U.S. 834 (1957).

60 Justice Black joined Justice Stewart's opinion in *Walker*. Black had previously dissented in part in *Cox v. Louisiana*, addressing a conviction for demonstrating too close to a courthouse. He included a passage plainly foreshadowing the *Walker* conclusion:

> [C]onstitutional and statutory rights have to be protected by the courts, which must be kept free from intimidation and coercive pressures of any kind. Government under law as ordained by our Constitution is too precious, too sacred, to be jeopardized by subjecting the courts to intimidatory practices that have been fatal to individual liberty and minority rights wherever and whenever such practices have been allowed to poison the streams of justice. I would be wholly unwilling to join in moving this country a single step in that direction.

Cox v. Louisiana, 379 U.S. 536, 584 (1965) (Black, J., dissenting in part). See also Roger K. Newman, *Hugo Black*, 2nd ed. (New York: Fordham University, 1997), 543:

> Black felt that King's practice of civil disobedience could result in anarchy across the nation. "Marches lead to violence," he said, "and are not the way our system is supposed to work." Time and again he argued that the state had authority to take over an area. He knew

however, than *realpolitik*. The final sentence seems to claim an "exalted . . . station" for "judicial process" too: "the civilizing hand of law," "alone" giving "abiding meaning to constitutional freedom." Oslo envy?

The Body of the Walker Majority Opinion Discloses other Obscurities

Justice Stewart depicts the Alabama Supreme Court, affirming the Birmingham trial judge's contempt ruling, as relying on *Howat v. Kansas*,[61] a 1922 United States Supreme Court decision.[62] The state supreme court, however, also reproduced at considerable length an excerpt from a more recent United States Supreme Court decision in *United States v. United Mine Workers*, which itself drew from *Howat*, but notably gave substantial attention to *United States v. Shipp*, work of Justice Holmes well prior to *Howat*.[63] Stewart peripherally cites *United Mine Workers* and *Shipp*. [64] Why stress *Howat*? This is the extract Stewart uses:

> An injunction duly issuing out of a court of general jurisdiction with equity powers, upon pleadings properly invoking its action, and served upon persons made party therein and within the jurisdiction, must be obeyed by them, however erroneous the action of the court may be, even if the error be in the assumption of the validity of a seeming, but void law going to the merits of the case. It is for the court of first instance to determine the question of the validity of the law, and until its decision is reversed for error by orderly review, either by itself or by a higher court, its orders based on its decision are to be respected, and disobedience of them is contempt of its lawful authority, to be punished.[65]

the southern temperament. . . . He had seen mob violence at first hand in the Klan. He had predicted it would happen after *Brown* and he urgently wanted to thwart it now."

61 258 U.S. 181 (1922).

62 See *Walker*, 388 U.S., 312–13, quoting *Walker v. City of Birmingham*, 181 So. 2d 493, 500, 502 (Ala. 1966).

63 See *Walker*, 181 So. 2d at 500–502, quoting *United States v. United Mine Workers*, 330 U.S. 258, 290–95 (1947), discussing *Howat v. Kansas*, supra, and *United States v. Shipp*, 203 U.S. 563 (1906).

64 *Walker* includes both *Mine Workers* and *Shipp* at the end of the very long string citation associating *Howat* with "the rule of law followed by the federal courts." *Walker*, 388 U.S. 314 and n15. Whatever the reason he chose *Howat*, why did Justice Stewart include and emphasize in the *Walker* opinion *Howat* language the Alabama Supreme Court did not quote or cite below (*Mine Workers* had made use of a different excerpt)? Compare id. at 314, with *Walker*, 181 So. 2d 502.

65 *Howat*, 258 U.S. 280–81, quoted in *Walker*, 388 U.S. 314.

Is this language in any way controversial?

The *Walker* majority concluded that the injunction in the case at hand was defensible (to the point, at least, of establishing no justification for excusing failure to comply.) Early in the opinion Justice Stewart described a demonstration that took place after the SCLC leadership announced that they would not comply with the injunction:

> On Easter Sunday, April 14, a crowd of between 1,500 and 2,000 people congregated in the midafternoon in the vicinity of Seventh Avenue and Eleventh Street North in Birmingham. One of the petitioners was seen organizing members of the crowd in formation. A group of about 50, headed by three other petitioners, started down the sidewalk two abreast. At least one other petitioner was among the marchers. Some 300 or 400 people from among the onlookers followed in a crowd that occupied the entire width of the street and overflowed onto the sidewalks. Violence occurred. Members of the crowd threw rocks that injured a newspaperman and damaged a police motorcycle.[66]

This recitation anticipated the discussion later in the *Walker* opinion of the considerations Stewart thought sufficed to establish the injunction as binding:

> [T]his is not a case where the injunction was transparently invalid or had only a frivolous pretense to validity. We have consistently recognized the strong interest of state and local governments in regulating the use of their streets and other public places. ... When protest takes the form of mass demonstrations, parades, or picketing on public streets and sidewalks, the free passage of traffic and the prevention of public disorder and violence become important objects of legitimate state concern.[67]

Howat required "[a]n injunction duly issuing out of a court of general jurisdiction with equity powers." But in *Walker* Stewart also demands that the injunction at issue – if obedience to it is to be a necessary precondition to challenge – not be "transparently invalid or ... frivolous" in its claim to validity. The *Walker* opinion, it seems, does not mean to intimate that free speech rights simply give way in the face of the catalogued concerns. Justice Stewart himself would write the majority opinion in *Shuttlesworth*

[66] *Walker*, 311.

[67] *Walker*, 315–16, quoting *Cox v. Louisiana*, 379 U.S. 536, 555 (1965).

v. Birmingham[68] two years later, holding that the ordinance that the *Walker* injunction enforced was unconstitutional on free speech grounds. Why would it be sufficient, therefore, to write in *Walker almost* just like the Court in *Howat*, calling attention to considerations warranting regulation but not considerations suggesting limits to regulation?

Implications of the Missing Cases

Three prominent previous opinions of the Supreme Court reveal a complex backdrop.

In re Debs,[69] famously (or infamously) upholding a federal injunction breaking the Pullman strike, concluded by affirming the contempt convictions of Eugene V. Debs and his associates: "[T]he Circuit Court, having full jurisdiction in the premises, its finding of the fact of disobedience is not open to review on habeas corpus in this or any other court."[70] The great bulk of the opinion addressed subject matter jurisdiction. Because the Supreme Court was reluctant to rely on the federal antitrust statute[71] and other congressional enactments apparently did not grant the requisite authorization,[72] the standing of the Attorney General needed to be derived directly from the Constitution, in terms evocative of equity jurisdiction. Justice Brewer brought to bear the idea of nuisance:

> The strong arm of the national government may be put forth to brush away all obstructions to the freedom of interstate commerce or the transportation of the mails. If the emergency arises, the army of the Nation, and all its militia, are at the service of the Nation to compel obedience to its laws. ... Is the army the only instrument by which rights of the public can be enforced and the peace of the nation preserved? ... Every government, entrusted, by the very terms of its being, with powers and duties to be exercised and discharged for the general welfare, has a right to apply to its own courts for any proper assistance in the exercise of the one and the discharge of the other, and it is no sufficient answer to its appeal ... that it has no pecuniary interest in the matter.[73]

[68] 394 U.S. 147 (1969).
[69] 158 U.S. 564 (1895).
[70] *Debs*, 600.
[71] See id.
[72] See id. at 579–81.
[73] Id. at 582, 584. Justice Brewer generalized to extend to all three branches of the federal government a power already recognized as held by Congress: "Every right, created by, arising under, or dependent upon the Constitution, may be protected and enforced by such means and in such

The extraordinary sweep and confident ambition of Justice Brewer's overall opinion underscores the narrowness of the terms within which it addresses the *Walker* question as such. The question denied review was not the question of the legality of the injunction as a matter of equity or constitutional law, only a question as to "the fact of disobedience," with review improper (apparently) just because of limits on habeas corpus jurisdiction.[74] Constitutionality and jurisdiction intertwine throughout much of his analysis. Brewer cites *Ex parte Yarbrough*: "If the law which defines the offense and prescribes its punishment is void, the court was without jurisdiction, and the prisoners must be discharged."[75]

The Supreme Court proceeded much more peremptorily addressing a jurisdictional challenge to sanctions in *United States v. Shipp*.[76] Joseph Shipp, a Tennessee county sheriff, was charged with contempt of the Supreme Court itself, after allegedly acquiescing in the mob lynching of Ed Johnson, a black prisoner – convicted in a state court of raping a white woman – whose execution had been stayed by the Court pending argument (itself ordered by the Court) regarding his appeal from a federal circuit court decision denying habeas corpus.[77] Shipp contended that, because no nonfrivolous constitutional question (and thus no federal matter) grounded the prisoner's habeas petition, neither the circuit court nor the Supreme Court possessed jurisdiction. He was therefore free to ignore the stay. Justice Holmes wrote for the Court:

> [E]ven if the circuit court had no jurisdiction to entertain Johnson's petition, and if this court had no jurisdiction of the appeal, this court, and this court alone, could decide that such was the law. It and it alone

manner as Congress, in the exercise of the correlative duty of protection, or of the legislative powers conferred upon by the Constitution, may in its discretion deem most eligible and best adapted to attain the object." *In re Quarles*, 158 U.S. 532, 535 (1895).

74 See *Debs*, 600. Brewer would write a few years later: "Habeas corpus is not treated as a writ of error, and while it may be issued by one court to inquire into the action of a court of co-ordinate jurisdiction, yet the inquiry is only whether the action of the court in imposing punishment was within its jurisdiction." *Bessette v. W. B. Conkey Co.*, 194 U.S. 324, 336 (1904).

75 *Ex parte Yarbrough*, 110 U.S. 651, 654 (1884); see *Debs*,158 U.S. 600. See also *In re Swan*, 150 U.S. 637, 649 (1893) (constitutional considerations preclude construing state statute as authorizing warrantless search and thus statute does not authorize challenged official acts), cited in *Debs*, supra.

76 203 U.S. 563 (1906).

77 For extended discussion of the case, see Mark Curriden and Leroy Phillips Jr., *Contempt of Court* (New York: Anchor, 2001).

> necessarily had jurisdiction to decide whether the case was properly before it. ... Until its judgment declining jurisdiction should be announced, it had authority, from the necessity of the case, to make orders to preserve the existing conditions ..., just as the state court was bound to refrain from further proceedings until the same time. ... The fact that petitioner [Johnson] was entitled to argue his case shows what needs no proof, that the law contemplates the possibility of a decision either way, and therefore must provide for it.[78]

A faint echo of *Debs*? Holmes also, however, moved past jurisdiction as such to the merits of the case – at least preliminarily. Shipp's declaration under oath was not enough to establish that he had nothing to do with Johnson's horrific murder,[79] and thus the acts charged could indeed constitute contempt.[80]

The *Shipp* opinion figured prominently in *United States v. United Mine Workers*,[81] decided some forty years later. The Secretary of the Interior, exercising congressionally granted power, temporarily took control over ("seized") "the major portion of the country's bituminous coal minds" in 1946, entering into agreement with John L. Lewis, president of the Mine Workers, favorable to the miners, carrying forward wartime arrangements.[82] The union, evidently with an eye to putting in place terms that would govern after mine owners reacquired control, sought to renegotiate the agreement with the Secretary, and threatened a work stoppage if no new deal were reached. The United States persuaded a federal district judge, in an ex parte proceeding, to issue a temporary restraining order, the Mine Workers struck nonetheless, shutting down coal mines nationally, and the federal judge held the union (and John L. Lewis) to be in contempt of

78 "The murder of the petitioner has made it impossible to decide that case. ... Therefore we shall say no more than it does not appear to us clear that the subject-matter of the petition was beyond the jurisdiction of the circuit court, and that, in our opinion, the facts that might have been found would have required the gravest and most anxious consideration before the petition could have been denied." *Shipp*, 203 U.S. 573–74; see id. at 563 (summarizing habeas petition).

79 See *Shipp*, 574–75.

80 "It may be found that what created the mob and led to the crime was the unwillingness of its members to submit to the delay required for the trial of the appeal. From that to the intent to prevent that delay and the hearing of the appeal is a short step." *Shipp*, 575. For the no longer unanimous Supreme Court's subsequent decision finding that Shipp had aided and abetted the lynching, see *United States v. Shipp*, 214 U.S. 386 (1909).

81 330 U.S. 258 (1947).

82 *United Mine Workers*, 262, 262–63.

court, levying heavy fines – all notwithstanding the union argument that the Norris-LaGuardia Act denied federal district courts jurisdiction to issue injunctions regarding labor disputes and thus contempt sanctions were unwarranted.[83] The Supreme Court ruled that sanctions were proper but the fines were excessive. The Justices, however, disagreed elaborately and complicatedly among themselves.

Chief Justice Vinson wrote the lead opinion, arguing that the Norris-LaGuardia Act did not apply given the government's involvement, and that, even if this argument was wrong, the union could not challenge contempt punishment because it had violated the temporary restraining order. This second, "alternative" part of the opinion relied heavily on *Shipp*, quoting Holmes at length.[84] Vinson noted that "a different result would follow were the question of jurisdiction frivolous and not substantial."[85] He also invoked *Howat*: "[W]e find impressive authority for the proposition that an order issued by a court with jurisdiction over the subject matter ... must be obeyed ... until it is reversed. ... This is true without regard even for the constitutionality of the Act under which the order is issued."[86]

Justice Frankfurter defended *Shipp*:

> No one, no matter how exalted his public office or how righteous his private motive, can be judge in his own case. That is what courts are for.[87]
>
> Only when a court is so obviously traveling outside its orbit as to be merely usurping judicial forms and facilities, may an order issued by a court be disobeyed and treated as though it were a letter to a newspaper.[88]
>
> There can be no free society without law administered through an independent judiciary. If one man can be allowed to determine for himself what is law, every man can. That means first chaos, then tyranny. Legal process is an essential part of the democratic process. ... [T]his Court, beyond any other organ of society, is the trustee of law and charged with the duty of securing obedience to it.[89]

[83] See id. at 264–69.
[84] Id. at 289; see id. at 290–92.
[85] Id. at 293.
[86] Id. at 293; see id. at 293–94 (quoting *Howat*).
[87] Id. at 308–9 (Frankfurter, J., concurring in the judgment).
[88] Id. at 309–10.
[89] Id. at 312.

But Justice Rutledge would have limited *Shipp* to its facts:

> The force of such a rule, making the party act on pain of certain punishment regardless of the validity of the order violated or the court's jurisdiction to enter it as determined finally upon review, would be not only to compel submission. It would be also in practical effect for many cases to terminate the litigation, foreclosing the substantive rights involved without any possibility for their effective appellate review and determination. . . . The First Amendment liberties especially would be vulnerable to nullification by such control. . . . These and other constitutional rights would be nullified by the force of invalid orders issue in flat violation of the constitutional provisions securing them, and void for that reason.[90]

Justice Stewart, it appears, read *Mine Workers* quite closely. His phrasing in *Walker*'s last paragraph – "no man can be judge in his own case, however exalted his station, however righteous his motives" – obviously recalls Justice Frankfurter.[91] Frankfurter feared "first chaos, then tyranny." Stewart stressed "the civilizing hand of law." But unlike Frankfurter, Stewart did not treat "the possibility of a decision either way" as to jurisdiction as the governing question, as a conclusion sufficient to ground judicial imposition of contempt sanctions in all instances except those in which "a court is so obviously traveling outside its orbit as to be merely usurping judicial forms and facilities." Indeed Stewart waved off jurisdiction in *Walker* – treated it as an essentially irrelevant issue in the case at hand. "Without question the state court that issued the injunction had, as a court of equity, jurisdiction over the petitioners and over the subject matter of the controversy." He did not stop there, however, as Frankfurter and also Chief Justice Vinson would have. "And this is not a case where the injunction was transparently invalid or had only a frivolous pretense to validity." "*And*" – This is the *Shipp* glancing consideration of "possibility," we now see, now put to use to introduce and organize a separate inquiry, the question that does concern Justice Stewart: whether the Supreme Court's free speech cases recognized counter-concerns that might warrant constitutionally the *Walker* injunction.

Perhaps Justice Stewart took to heart Justice Rutledge's dissent in *Mine Workers*. Alternately, Stewart might be thought to work within a framework

90 Id. at 351–52 (Rutledge, J., dissenting); see id. at 357–61.

91 See Luban, "Difference Made Legal," 2169–70.

something like the one that Justice Brewer set up in *In re Debs*. Or perhaps he took his cue from Justice Holmes's brief glance at substance in *Shipp*. The project in *Walker*, however, was not determining directly whether the injunction at issue fell inside or outside the domain of Birmingham's municipal authority, on the model of Brewer's depiction of the nuisance-based need to regulate interstate commerce. Instead, the *Walker* majority recognized, after the fashion of the opinion that Justice Miller wrote in the *Yarbrough* case cited in *Debs*, that injunctions transgressing constitutional rights might be ultra vires independently of the question of municipal power per se. "If the law which defines the offense and prescribes its punishment is void, the court was without jurisdiction, and the prisoners must be discharged."

Justice Stewart and Professor Chafee

Zechariah Chafee published his immediately classic *Some Problems of Equity* just a few years after the Supreme Court decided *Mine Workers*, developing his own reaction to the contempt sanctions at issue in the case in the last two chapters of the book, both entitled "Lack of Power and Mistaken Use of Power."[92] He took as his starting point this proposition: "The test of lack of power ... is whether the law has withdrawn this kind of dispute altogether from this court. ... Thus true lack of power exists only when the court ought to stop short and refuse to make a decision either way."[93] As a result, "jurisdiction over the person and the subject matter are the sole requisites of power."[94] Subject matter jurisdiction should be understood broadly – not tied to the application of principles of equity jurisdiction or legislation addressing the availability of particular remedies in particular cases otherwise falling within the general jurisdiction of courts. "If a court is bound to come to some conclusion, it has jurisdiction."[95] "[A]n injunction or other equity decree which the court has power to render may not be disregarded on the ground that it is erroneous. ... Any person who violated

[92] Zechariah Chafee Jr., *Some Problems of Equity* (Ann Arbor: University of Michigan, 1950), 298–380.

[93] Chafee, *Some Problems of Equity*, 308.

[94] Id. at 379.

[95] Id. at 308.

the order is punishable for criminal contempt, even though the order was eventually set aside as erroneous."[96]

Given his overall approach, Professor Chafee took a strong stand on the question of whether constitutional errors excused ignoring an injunction.

> How can a judge have power to do what the Constitution forbids to be done? ... When a judge passes on constitutional questions, as when he passes on any other issues in a case, the proposition of Judge Noyes ... holds good, that "the power to hear and determine a cause ... includes power to decide wrong as well as right." If a court is asked to enjoin a libel and soundly refuses to do so, it has jurisdiction over the case. So it must also have jurisdiction when it grants the injunction, although its action is mistaken. It is only a question of violating sound principles of decision, whether those principles are a laid down by a statute, or by a mass of appellate decisions, or by a constitutional provision as interpreted by the court of last resort.[97]

The *Walker* majority opinion does not agree, it appears. Stewart takes notice of at least some considerations evidently pertinent to constitutional law – an utterly unnecessary exercise from Chafee's perspective.

But Chafee also declared: "So long as a good procedure for rapid review is available, I see no necessity for encouraging unions or any other private persons to take the law into their own hands."[98] He suggested that at least some of the decisions blocking contempt sanctions for violations of unconstitutional injunctions might be explained by the absence of "rapid review." "[I]nsofar as the results of these cases were just, they can best be rested on the ground that the court was groping its way toward a summary method of review and toward relieving the defendant from the oppressiveness of protracted obedience to a decree which was probably wrong."[99] Perhaps we ought to read *Walker* in this light.[100] Justice Stewart indeed insisted that "rapid review" might have been possible in the case at hand:

> There was an interim of two days between the issuance of the injunction and the [first] march. The petitioners give absolutely no

[96] Id. at 296–97.
[97] Id. at 348.
[98] Id. at 374.
[99] Id. at 349.
[100] For thoughtful recent development of this perspective, see John R.B. Palmer, Note, Collateral Bar and Contempt: Challenging a Court Order After Disobeying It, *Cornell Law Review*, 88 (2002): 215.

> explanation of why they did not make some application to the state court during that period. The injunction had issued ex parte; if the court had been presented with the petitioners' contentions, it might well have dissolved or at least modified its order in some respects. If it had not done so, Alabama procedure would have provided for an expedited process of appellate review.[101]

Professor Chafee notwithstanding, it is nonetheless evident that Stewart – glancing at the organization of free speech law – also undertook something like an improvised "summary ... review," however one-sided, to determine whether the decree at issue was one "which was probably wrong."

III. *Shuttlesworth* As Against *Walker*

Zechariah Chafee thought that the idea of a "void" law was silly. "[I]t is about as unprofitable to speculate about the duty to obey a void decree as it would be to do research on the question whether a railroad has a duty to carry a centaur in the passenger car on a regular ticket or in a freight car at the rates charged for horses."[102] But just two years after *Walker*, with Justice Stewart again writing the majority opinion, the Supreme Court held in *Shuttlesworth v. City of Birmingham*[103] that the municipal ordinance requiring a license before conducting a "demonstration" on city streets was unconstitutional on its face – the ordinance that had supplied the substantive ground for the injunction at issue in *Walker*. Remarkably – given *Walker* – Stewart noted: "[O]ur decisions have made clear that a person faced with such an unconstitutional licensing law may ignore it and engage with impunity in the exercise of the right of free expression for which the law purports to require a license."[104]

The *Walker* majority opinion had acknowledged that "[t]he generality of the language contained in the Birmingham parade ordinance ... would unquestionably raise substantial constitutional issues. ..."[105] Chief Justice Warren, dissenting in *Walker*, thought so too and thought that Birmingham

[101] *Walker*, 388 U.S. 318–19; see *United States v. Ryan*, 402 U.S. 530, 534n4 (1971) (Brennan, J.) ("Our holding [in *Walker*] that the claims there sought to be asserted were not open on review ... was based upon the availability or review of those claims at an earlier stage").

[102] Chafee, *Some Problems of Equity*, 374.

[103] 394 U.S. 147 (1969).

[104] *Shuttlesworth*, 394 U.S. 151.

[105] *Walker*, 388 U.S. at 316.

officials had thought similarly: "In point of fact there is only one apparent reason why the city sought this injunction and why the court issued it: to make it possible to punish petitioners for contempt rather than for violating the ordinance, and thus to immunize the unconstitutional statute and its unconstitutional application from any attack."[106] Justice Stewart had stressed there that "petitioners ... did not even attempt to apply to the Alabama courts for an authoritative construction of the ordinance. Had they done so, those courts might have given the licensing authority granted in the ordinance a narrow and precise scope. ..."[107] But in *Shuttlesworth*, a criminal prosecution of the principal Birmingham civil rights leader with whom the SCLC had worked the Alabama Supreme Court had reviewed the conviction before the United States Supreme Court took jurisdiction. The state justices had indeed read the ordinance – whatever it seemed to say – to grant only "a narrow and precise" authority.[108] In *Shuttlesworth* Stewart thought that the exercise was irrelevant. The facts in *Walker*, he observed, "make it indisputably clear ... that in April of 1963 ... the city authorities thought that the ordinance meant exactly what it said. The petitioner was clearly given to understand that under no circumstances would he and his group be permitted to demonstrate. ..."[109]

In *Walker*, Justice Stewart also acknowledged that "[t]he breadth and vagueness of the injunction itself would also unquestionably be subject to substantial constitutional question."[110] Why not follow *Shuttlesworth*, as it were? It is important to understand more precisely the analysis that Stewart undertook in 1969, the second time around:

> It is argued, however, that what was involved here was not "pure speech," but the use of public streets and sidewalks, over which a municipality must rightfully exercise a great deal of control in the interest of traffic regulation and public safety. That, of course, is true. ... But our decisions have also made clear that picketing and parading may nonetheless constitute methods of expression, entitled to First Amendment protection. ... Even when the use of its public streets and sidewalks is involved, therefore, a municipality may not empower its licensing officials to roam essentially at will, dispensing or withholding

[106] *Walker*, 334 (Warren, C.J., dissenting).
[107] *Walker*, 316–17.
[108] See *Shuttlesworth*, 394 U.S. at 153–54.
[109] *Shuttlesworth*, 394 U.S. at 158.
[110] *Walker*, 388 U.S. at 317.

> permission to speak, assemble, picket, or parade according to their own opinions regarding the potential effect of the activity in question on the "welfare," "decency," or "morals" of the community...."[111]

"[A] municipality may not empower its licensing officials to roam essentially at will...." Justice Stewart now cheerfully metaphorically equates officials and demonstrators. The ordinance did not attempt to organize its own application – did not acknowledge constitutionally protected interests as well as pertinent municipal concerns, did not supply a framework within which officials might assess whether free speech interests and safety or traffic worries, for example, were really in conflict or might be readily reconciled. The ordinance did not meaningfully incorporate within its own terms constitutional considerations as well as local government agendas: It was itself, as written, *aconstitutional* and therefore open to criticism as unconstitutional, as overbroad.[112] But notably just like the Birmingham ordinance it enforced, the *Walker* injunction made no effort to define free speech protections and public order requirements vis a vis each other. It simply and blankly inserted the word "unlawful" over and over.[113] Judicial work, obviously, is subject to the same constitutional scrutiny as legislative efforts. In one of the earliest of the rulings akin to *Shuttlesworth*, *Near v. Minnesota*,[114] the Supreme Court struck down an injunction. Just a few years before *Walker* the Supreme Court had brought the overbreadth inquiry to bear in considering the content of Alabama common law in another case growing out of civil rights efforts – *New York Times v. Sullivan*.[115] It is not easy to explain why the *Walker* injunction was constitutionally different from the *Shuttlesworth* ordinance.

We might wonder whether *Shipp* – on its facts – suggests a point of difference. The mob killed Ed Johnson because the Supreme Court had intervened. Sheriff Shipp, a senior and distinguished figure in the community, not only obviously failed to exercise any leadership whatsoever, abdicating responsibility, but also literally voiced his contempt of court, his asserted view that Johnson's death was the result of the irresponsibility of

[111] *Shuttlesworth*, 394 U.S. at 152–53, 151.

[112] Supreme Court use of approaches of this sort, of course, was already well-established within the court's work by the time of *Walker* and *Shuttlesworth*. See *Shuttlesworth*, 394 U.S. at 151 n. 2.

[113] See *Walker*, 388 U.S. at 322.

[114] 283 U.S. 697 (1931).

[115] 376 U.S. 254 (1964).

the Supreme Court itself.[116] Chief Justice Fuller, ultimately explaining why Shipp should be punished, essentially agreed with the sheriff:

> [T]his lamentable riot was the direct result of opposition to the administration of the law by this court. It was not only in defiance of our mandate, but was understood to be such. The Supreme Court of the United States was called upon to abdicate its functions and decline to enter such orders as the occasion, in its judgment, demanded, because of the danger of their defeat by an outbreak of lawless violence. … [I]f the life of anyone in the custody of the law is at the mercy of a mob, the administration of justice becomes a mockery. When this court granted a stay of execution on Johnson's application it became its duty to protect him until his case should be disposed of. And when its mandate, issued for his protection, was defied, punishment … must be awarded.[117]

Fuller, we can see, anticipated Justice Frankfurter in *Mine Workers*: "[T]his Court, beyond any other organ of society, is the trustee of law and charged with the duty of securing obedience to it."

But aren't all courts – all judges, state as well as federal – trustees of the law? Aren't all judges supposed to be understood as standing outside the immediate moment, above the battle in some important sense, obliged to bring law to bear – federal as well as state, constitutional law along with all the rest? If so it might have been possible to think that the conclusory language of the injunction at issue in *Walker* did not bar a readily accessible judge from revisiting constitutional questions at the behest of SCLC leaders proposing particularized and concrete marching strategies. The injunction had shifted the initiative away not only from the SCLC but – if the injunction were respected – from Bull Connor and angry whites as well. Judges were different – "the civilizing hand of law," they could be assumed to appreciate constitutional concerns: the face of the order, absent affirmative contrary indication, might count for less. Protecting distinctively judicial authority, in any event, might be a useful long-run strategy – a step toward assuring "abiding meaning" for constitutional understandings. Justice Stewart, it is easy to conclude, wrote within the same overall perspective

[116] See *United States v. Shipp*, 214 U.S. 386, 418 (1909).

[117] *Shipp*, 425. have their free cours.

President Kennedy's thinking disclosed in 1963. "It is better to settle these matters in the courts than in the streets."

IV. Ordinary Emergency

Even so, shouldn't *Walker* have followed *Shuttlesworth*?

Consider: Ignoring an injunction treats the issuing court as irrelevant, as though the court had not acted at all, as though the court had not been available to the parties seeking the injunction – in the language of *Ex parte Milligan*, "effectually closes the courts."[118] Ignoring injunctions denies courts "the proper and unobstructed exercise of their jurisdiction," occasions circumstances in which "ordinary law no longer adequately secures public safety and private rights."[119] Cases like *Debs*, *Shipp*, and *United Mine Workers* arose against the backdrop of obvious states of emergency outside court – national strikes, lynch mobs. But they, like *Walker* it appears, also address states of emergency for courts themselves – in the *Milligan* sense. Why cannot judges take matters into their own hands to deal with emergency, act to restore judicial process "unobstructed," so that "the laws can have their free course"?[120] Enforcing the collateral bar rule becomes an emergency measure classically conceived, marking an extra-legal or pre-legal act, forcible seizure (or reseizure) of authority *simplicter*: necessarily inarticulate, able to be put in question only if the jurisdiction purportedly reclaimed was itself inarticulable.[121] *Walker*, Robert Cover wrote, "justifies official violence by the very act of resistance to it. The court ... need never commit itself" to any "particular interpretation" of pertinent law that would explain its exercise of force. "It is the regime of obedience – of state superiority – that warrants the violence."[122]

Cover, we remember, stressed the significance of the "field of pain and death" in which "[l]egal interpretation takes place," but he also recognized the duality of "violence and the word." "Neither legal interpretation nor the violence it occasions may be properly understood apart from the other."[123] Any reading of *Walker* that depicts the assertion and exercise of jurisdiction

[118] *Ex parte Milligan*, 71 U.S. 2, 127 (1866).
[119] *Milligan*, 127; id. at 142 (Chase, C.J., concurring).
[120] Id. at 121, 127.
[121] Cf. *Ex parte McCardle*, 74 U.S. 506 (1869).
[122] Robert M. Cover, "Nomos and Narrative," *Harvard Law Review* 97 (1983): 4, 55.
[123] Robert M. Cover, "Violence and the Word," *Yale Law Journal* 95 (1986): 1601.

as just the exercise of force, we might think, is incomplete. Taking jurisdiction is always also elaboration. It is "the province" – and it only thereupon follows – "the duty" of the judge "to say what the law is."[124] In *Shipp*, for example, Justice Holmes plainly treated jurisdiction not as a matter of blank assertion – rather, as itself an *exercise*,[125] an act precisely taking the form of scrutiny and interpretation of pertinent legal materials.

> [E]ven if the circuit court had no jurisdiction of the appeal, this court, and this court alone, could decide that such was the law. It and it alone necessarily had jurisdiction to decide whether the case was properly before it. On that question, at least, it was its duty to permit argument, and to take the time required for such consideration as it might need.[126]

Adjudicative authority presupposes legislative jurisdiction, obviously enough: courts cannot act absent pertinent substantive law to bring to bear. The assertion and exercise of jurisdiction, therefore, to some extent necessarily involves perusal of whatever legal materials go to substance in any particular case, including (it could not be otherwise) constitutional dictates addressing the applicability of other materials. This overlap, we have already seen, was quite clear in *Debs*. However conclusorily, Justice Holmes repeatedly alludes to the outlines of substantive law in *Shipp*.[127]

In *Walker*, as we have also already seen, Justice Stewart invokes – albeit in notably truncated fashion – judicial understandings of constitutional free speech guarantees in the course of justifying application of the collateral bar rule. *Walker* is nonetheless disquieting. Stewart identifies possible justifications for the initial injunction and points out, even if quite briefly, possible constitutional difficulties the Birmingham ordinance – the injunction's predicate – might face (we know did indeed face.) The Supreme Court's majority, however, is unfazed by these troubles, or any cognate difficulties the language of the injunction itself might trigger. The court more or less closed its own doors, we might think: simply acquiescing, once it concluded that the initial injunction was not issued entirely without explanation, and that the contempt proceeding was therefore not bootless. *Inter armia leges silent?*

[124] *Marbury v. Madison*, 5 U.S. 137 (1803).
[125] Cf. Pierre Hadot, *Philosophy as a Way of Life* (Cambridge, MA: Blackwell, 1995), 79–144.
[126] *United States v. Shipp*, 203 U.S. 563, 573 (1906).
[127] *Shipp*, 574–75.

Emergency Inside Overbreadth Scrutiny

Would the *Shuttlesworth* approach – the overbreadth inquiry – have afforded a way to acknowledge the emergency state of affairs and assess its constitutional significance? *Shuttlesworth* itself was not an emergency case. The license requirement that the Birmingham ordinance imposed applied regardless of circumstances, and the prosecution that the Supreme Court ultimately reviewed proceeded in ordinary course. But both before and after *Shuttlesworth*, overbreadth scrutiny figures prominently in cases in which circumstances present emergency or otherwise extraordinary aspects – and the form of the inquiry is no different in those settings. The free speech overbreadth decisions are well-known.[128] For present purposes, uses of the analysis in other constitutional settings are especially provocative (and remind us that the form is generally available.[129])

Home Building & Loan Association v. Blaisdell[130] is archetypical. Defenders of a Minnesota mortgage moratorium law suspending creditor rights sought to sidestep the Contracts Clause by stressing that economic circumstances – the depths of the Great Depression – could quite plausibly be deemed a state of emergency. Famously, Chief Justice Hughes dismissed the argument out of hand. "Emergency does not create power. Emergency does not increase granted power or remove or diminish the restrictions imposed upon power granted or reserved."[131] But he also noted that, even if "emergency does not create power, emergency may furnish the occasion for the exercise of power."[132] "[T]he state ... continues to possess authority to safeguard the vital interests of its people."[133] Hughes declared:

> [T]he reservation of essential attributes of sovereign power is ... read into contracts as a postulate of the legal order. The policy of protecting contracts against impairment presupposes the maintenance of a government by virtue of which contractual relations are worthwhile, a

[128] For discussion of the use of the free speech overbreadth analysis in Cold War cases not too dissimilar from emergency cases per se, see Tribe and Gudridge, "Anti-Emergency ..." 1851–66.

[129] See, e.g., Gillian E. Metzger, "Facial Challenges and Federalism," *Columbia Law Review* 105 (2005): 873.

[130] 290 U.S. 398 (1934).

[131] *Blaisdell*, 425.

[132] Id.

[133] Id. at 434.

> government which retains adequate authority to secure the peace and good order of society.[134]

The possibility of limitation of contract rights was present – precisely as a possibility – from the beginning. Hughes, however, did not treat reservation as in and of itself grounding the conclusion in *Blaisdell*. He instead derived this formula: "The reserved power cannot be construed so as to destroy the limitation, nor is the limitation to be construed to destroy the reserved power in its essential aspects. They must be construed in harmony with each other."[135] The Minnesota legislation was, on its face, carefully qualified – limited in duration, acknowledging creditor rights, providing interim protections. It was, for this reason, constitutional. A series of subsequent Supreme Court decisions judged other Depression-era debtor relief laws, finding the required efforts at accommodation present in some statutory schemes, but not in others.[136]

Justice O'Connor's plurality opinion in *Hamdi v. Rumsfeld*[137] is surprisingly of a piece with *Blaisdell*. *Hamdi* took up several important questions. The pertinent issue for present purposes had to do with the content of the procedures constitutionally required to be afforded an American citizen alleged to have acted as an enemy combatant in Afghanistan in the hearing to be held to determine whether he was in fact a combatant. Government officials contended that, "in light of the extraordinary constitutional interests at stake," grounded in wartime understandings of separation of powers appropriate in a time of "ongoing conflict," the hearing should properly "eliminate entirely any individual process, restricting the courts" to determining "whether legal authorization exists for the broader detention scheme," or at most reviewing the initial military conclusion as to Hamdi's status "under a very deferential 'some evidence' standard."[138] Justice O'Connor, however,

[134] Id. at 435.

[135] Id. at 439.

[136] E.g., *Wright v. Union Central Life Ins. Co.*, 304 U.S. 502, 516 (1938) ("The rights of the purchaser are preserved, the possibility of enjoyment is merely delayed"); *Wright v. Vinton Branch of Mountain Trust Bank*, 300 U.S. 440, 458 (1937) ("In drafting the new Frazier-Lemke Act, its framers sought to preserve to the mortgagee all of these rights so far as essential to the enjoyment of his security"); *W. B. Worthen Co. v. Kavanaugh*, 295 U.S. 56, 60 (1935) ("studied indifference to the interests of the mortgagee or to his appropriate protection "); *W. B. Worthen Co. v. Thomas*, 292 U.S. 426, 434 (1934) ("no limitations as to time, amount, circumstances, or need").

[137] 542 U.S. 507 (2004).

[138] *Hamdi*, 527.

brought to the case "[t]he ordinary mechanism that we use for balancing . . . serious competing interests, and for determining the procedures that are necessary" – "the test that we articulated in *Mathews v. Eldridge*. . . ."[139] She concluded:

> [W]hile the full protections that accompany challenges to detentions in other settings may prove unworkable and inappropriate in the enemy-combatant setting, the threats to military operations posed by a basic system of independent review are not so weighty as to trump a citizen's core rights to challenge meaningfully the Government's case and to be heard by an impartial adjudicator.[140]

This is the *Mathews* formula as Justice Powell originally stated it:

> [I]dentification of the specific dictates of due process generally requires consideration of three distinct factors: First, the private interest that will be affected by the official action; second, the risk of an erroneous deprivation of such interest through the procedures used, and the probable value, if any, of additional or substitute procedural safeguards; and finally, the Government's interest, including the function involved and the fiscal and administrative burdens that the additional or substitute procedural requirement would entail.[141]

The case itself considered whether the possibility that Social Security disability benefits might have been mistakenly denied to an individual required, as a matter of due process of law, that the individual be given a hearing before benefits were disallowed, or whether the statutorily-afforded review, available only after the fact, was constitutionally satisfactory. "[S]triking the appropriate due process balance," Justice Powell seems to have thought, involved bringing together a notably skeptical assessment of the individual's immediate need for the benefits at stake[142] and an equally pronounced judicial appreciation of administrative concerns and deference to administrative determinations: "In assessing what process is due . . ., substantial weight must be given to the good-faith judgments of the

139 Id. 528–29.

140 Id. at 535.

141 *Mathews v. Eldridge*, 424 U.S. 319, 335 (1976). See generally Jerry L. Mashaw, The Supreme Court's Due Process Calculus for Administrative Adjudication in Mathews v. Eldridge: Three Factors in Search of a Theory of Value, *University of Chicago Law Review* 44 (1977): 28, 41–45.

142 *Mathews*, 342–43.

individuals charged by Congress with the administration of social welfare programs that the procedures they have provided assure fair consideration of the entitlement claims of individuals."[143] Powell's opinion itself, it is not hard to conclude, closely approximated the "very deferential" standard that the government urged in *Hamdi*.

The *Hamdi* plurality understood *Mathews v. Eldridge* much differently. "Striking the ... balance" did not mean, as it seemingly did for Justice Powell, recognizing (or reading in) a clear-cut difference in the credibility of the opposing parties' claims to concern. Justice O'Connor started from the proposition that "substantial interests lie on both sides of the scale in this case."[144] Hamdi asserted "the most elemental of liberty interests"; "[o]n the other side of the scale are the weighty and sensitive government interests in ensuring that those who have in fact fought against the enemy ... do not return to battle."[145] O'Connor sought – as though acrobatically – to maintain "the proper constitutional balance."[146] She framed a standard for procedure-building demanding "due recognition of ... competing concerns."[147]

> [A] citizen-detainee seeking to challenge his classification as an enemy combatant must receive notice of the factual basis for his classification, and a fair opportunity to rebut the Government's factual assertions before a neutral decisionmaker. ... These essential constitutional promises may not be eroded.
>
> At the same time, the exigencies of the circumstances may demand that, aside from these core elements, enemy-combatant proceedings may be tailored to alleviate their uncommon potential to burden the Executive at a time of ongoing military conflict.[148]

Like *Blaisdell*, *Mathews* and *Hamdi* are plainly overbreadth cases. Neither turned on the particular circumstances of the individuals who were dealing and in disagreement with the government; both opinions

143 Id. at 349; see id. at 343–47, 348–49.

144 *Hamdi*, 529.

145 Id. at 531.

146 Id. at 532. "[W]e consider the interest of the *erroneously* detained individual." Id. at 530 (emphasis in original). "Because we live in a society in which '[m]ere public intolerance or animosity cannot constitutionally justify the deprivation of a person's physical liberty,' ... our ... analysis is unaltered by the allegations surrounding the particular detainee or the organizations with which he is alleged to have associated." Id. at 531, quoting *O'Connor v. Donaldson*, 422 U.S. 563, 575 (1975).

147 *Hamdi*, 532.

148 Id. at 533.

address procedures in use or to be put to use generally. The difference in the cases, as overbreadth analyses, lies in the different conclusions that Justices Powell and O'Connor reach about what "due recognition" requires – about the background constitutional acknowledgments that need to be evident on the face of procedural arrangements. Powell, it appears, sees little or nothing of constitutional significance (and therefore procedural importance) in the individual's interest in livelihood; O'Connor judges "the interest in being free from physical detention by one's own government"[149] to be a "core right[]."[150] "At the same time," she writes, it would be entirely proper if proceedings were "tailored to alleviate their uncommon potential to burden the Executive" – it is enough that procedures put in place not "give short shrift to the values that this country holds dear."[151] Neither rights nor powers are trumps – *both* must receive "due recognition." *Blaisdell* redux.

Writing a year after *Hamdi* in *Wilkinson v. Austin*,[152] Justice Kennedy deployed the *Mathews* formula, largely as Justice O'Connor had understood it, in an even more extreme setting. Ohio had adopted procedures to determine which inmates ought to be confined in the state "supermax" prison. The prison regime was dramatic: "[I]nmates are deprived of almost any environmental or sensory stimuli and of almost all human contact. … [P]lacement … is for an indefinite time, limited only by an inmate's sentence."[153] The assignment procedure was largely bureaucratic. After official preparation of an initial report recommending "supermax" incarceration of a particular inmate, the individual was given notice, supplied the report, and offered the opportunity to be heard by a three-member committee – without, however, any opportunity to call witnesses, even if "supermax" assignment were predicated on "specified conduct, *e.g.*, lead[ing] a prison gang."[154] If the committee recommended assignment, its report would be reviewed by the warden of the prison in which the individual was presently confined, whose assent to the reassignment was required.[155]

149 Id. at 529.
150 Id. at 535.
151 Id. at 532–33.
152 545 U.S. 209 (2005).
153 *Wilkinson*, 214–15.
154 Id. at 216.
155 Id. at 217.

Another, overarching committee reviewed the matter after the warden had reported.[156]

Justice Kennedy, writing within the *Mathews* framework,[157] upheld the procedural setup. Inmates, he concluded, could assert a constitutionally pertinent liberty interest. "[A]ssignment ... imposes an atypical and significant hardship under any plausible baseline."[158] Given Ohio prison conditions, the state provided "a sufficient level of process."[159] Ordinary prisons had apparently become Hobbesian hellholes, "imperiled by the brutal reality of prison gangs."[160]

> Clandestine, organized, fueled by race-based hostility, and committed to fear and violence as a means of disciplining their own members and their rivals, gangs seek nothing less than to control prison life and to extend their power outside prison walls. ... Murder of an inmate, a guard, or one of their family members on the outside is a common form of gang discipline and control. ... Testifying against, or otherwise informing on, gang activities can invite one's own death sentence. ... [F]or prison gang members serving life sentences, some without possibility of parole, the deterrent effects of ordinary criminal punishment may be substantially diminished.[161]

Circumstances therefore put in question the usefulness of witness testimony: "[N]othing in the record indicates simple mechanisms exist to determine when witnesses may be called without fear of reprisal." Prison gangs had effectively closed administrative access to adjudicative processes. Kennedy stressed the evident care with which state officials had designed bureaucratic routines to address the risk of mistaken assignment. "Ohio provides multiple levels of review for any decision recommending ... placement, with power to overturn the recommendation at each level. ... Ohio further reduces the risk ... by providing for a placement review within 30 days of an inmate's initial assignment."[162] The inmate's "more than

[156] See id.
[157] See *Wilkinson*, 224, 228.
[158] Id. at 223–24.
[159] Id. at 225.
[160] Id. at 227.
[161] Id.
[162] Id. at 227. "Where the inquiry draws more on the experience of prison administrators, and where the State's interest implicates the safety of other inmates and prison personnel, ... informal, nonadversary procedures ... provide the appropriate model." Id. at 228–29.

minimal" liberty interest was subject to "adequate . . . safeguard" – the Ohio arrangement "strikes a constitutionally permissible balance."[163] The *Hamdi* parallel is evident.

Wilkinson contrasts interestingly with *City of Chicago v. Morales*[164] Chicago city officials concluded, quite plausibly it appears, that gang activity in municipal parks and streets – even if literally nothing more than gathering in groups – contributed (given gang histories of violence and illegal drug dealing, for example) to an atmosphere of terror, in some neighborhoods "relegating [residents] to the status of prisoners in their own homes."[165] The city council enacted an ordinance designed to address the problem, authorizing police to order dispersal of persons an officer "reasonably believes to be a criminal street gang member," or "one or more other persons" in the company of a gang member, if the officer observes" the individuals "loitering in any public place."[166] Failure to comply with a dispersal order became a crime punished by fine and up to six months imprisonment. During the adoption process, law enforcement officials recommended to the city commission that limits on police discretion be developed through police policy rather than through including limits in the language of the ordinance itself.[167] After enactment, Chicago police adopted internal guidelines restricting enforcement of the ordinance to police officers trained in anti-gang work, providing detailed criteria defining gangs and gang membership, and limiting enforcement only to areas designated by police commanders. But the city did not release the list of these areas to the public. Police made heavy use of the ordinance, but eleven of the thirteen trial judges reviewing its constitutionality declared the measure to be invalid.[168]

The Supreme Court also ruled against the ordinance. Justice Stevens, joined only by Justices Souter and Ginsburg, concluded that Chicago could not "conceivably have meant to criminalize each instance a citizen stands in public with a gang member," but left too uncertain "what

[163] Id. at 225, 228, 230.

[164] 527 U.S. 41 (1999). For an especially good discussion of *Morales*, its context, and implications, see Debra Livingston, "Gang Loitering, the Court, and Some Realism about Police Patrol," *Supreme Court Review* (1999): 141.

[165] *Morales*, 99 (Thomas, J., dissenting).

[166] The ordinance is reproduced at *Morales*, 47n2.

[167] See id. at 48–49 and n. 3.

[168] See id. at 49–50.

loitering is covered by the ordinance and what is not."[169] Justice Thomas responded: "There is nothing 'vague' about an order to disperse."[170] Chief Justice Rehnquist and Justice Scalia agreed. Justices O'Connor, Kennedy, and Breyer took no position.[171] These last three Justices, however, concurred in another argument the Stevens plurality put forward.[172] "[T]he ordinance does not provide sufficiently specific limits on the enforcement discretion of the police...."[173] "Chicago's ... ordinance is unconstitutionally vague because it lacks sufficient minimal standards to guide law enforcement officers."[174] "[E]very application of the ordinance represents an exercise of unlimited discretion."[175]

What about the elaborate guidelines that the Chicago police had put in place to structure their discretion?[176] Justice Stevens dismissed this question without much real discussion.[177] Justices O'Connor and Breyer ignored it. This group shrug should be taken seriously. We might think that "void for vagueness" worries about fair notice and police discretion are – sometimes anyway – proxies: in particular, another way of signaling overbreadth concerns.[178] The *Morales* ordinance – because it is put so generally, the city commission seemingly quite purposefully leaving limits to the police – includes in its text no working acknowledgment of constitutional concerns, no "due recognition" or struck "balance." Justice Stevens began his opinion by mapping constitutional liberty. "[A]n individual's decision to remain in a public place of his choice is as much a part of his liberty as the freedom of movement inside frontiers ... or the right to move 'to whatsoever place one's own inclination may direct' identified in Blackstone's Commentaries."[179] The failure of the ordinance, as written, to take notice of the constitutional

[169] Id. at 57.

[170] Id. at 112.

[171] Justice Kennedy stated that he "share[d] many of the concerns" Justice Stevens expressed with regard to fair notice, but did not join that part of the Stevens opinion. *Morales*, 69–70 (Kennedy, J., concurring).

[172] Id. at 45.

[173] Id. at 64.

[174] Id. at 65–66 (O'Connor, J., concurring).

[175] Id. (Breyer, J., concurring).

[176] *See* Livingston, "Gang Loitering," 187–90.

[177] See *Morales*, 63–64.

[178] See Anthony Amsterdam, Note, "The Void-for-Vagueness Doctrine in the Supreme Court," *University of Pennsylvania Law Review* 109 (1960): 67.

[179] *Morales*, 54; see also Erin Murphy, "Paradigms of Restraint," *Duke Law Journal* 57 (2008): 1321, 1403–4.

supposition marks this legislative effort as sharply differing from the procedures required in *Hamdi* and the bureaucratic routines organized in *Wilkinson*. Legislative jurisdiction – like adjudicative jurisdiction – is an exercise of responsibility, constitutionally achieved only if legislation reproduces constitutional commitments (in some way or another) within the substance of the law made, in cases (at least) in which constitutional commitments might be plausibly understood to impinge. The opacity of the *Morales* ordinance – its blank generality – therefore becomes the sign of its invalidity, another version of unconstitutional overbreadth.[180]

*****

Korematsu *as CounterpointKorematsu v. United States*[181] was not an emergency case in the *Milligan* sense. The prosecution was brought in a federal district court under usual rules of criminal procedure.

Fred Korematsu had unabashedly violated the military order to present himself at a processing center: in this sense, his case was like *Walker*. But he had no difficulty raising his challenge to the constitutionality of the order. Korematsu had obstructed executive efforts, at least in his own case, but he had not blocked judicial process. He was convicted regardless, of course. Notably, Justice Black's majority opinion on review treated the government's invocation of wartime necessity quite gingerly, as close kin (at least) to a claim of emergency, seemingly undertaking the most minimal sort of scrutiny, in this regard approximated *Walker* therefore. The organization of analysis in Black's opinion is nonetheless worth considering here. It is a revealing reverse negative (as it were) of the overbreadth frameworks the preceding discussions depict.

Black began with this well-known paragraph:

> [A]ll legal restrictions which curtail the civil rights of a single racial group are immediately suspect. That is not to say that all such restrictions are unconstitutional. It is to say that courts must subject them to the most rigid scrutiny. Pressing public necessity may sometimes justify the existence of such restrictions; racial antagonism never can.[182]

In what way does the *Korematsu* declaration actually disagree with the sequence of propositions the United States asserted in its notably Orwellian brief?

[180] Cf. *Romer v. Evans*, 517 U.S. 620 (1996).
[181] 323 U.S. 214 (1944).
[182] *Korematsu*, 216.

> Measures coming within the war power do not violate the Fifth Amendment, whether or not they could be sustained in normal times, although that Amendment must be considered in determining the validity of a particular exercise of the war power under the circumstances which evoke it. As is true with respect to other governmental powers the limitations imposed by due process upon the war power mark the boundaries of the power itself. … To call in question the exclusion program under the Fifth Amendment is, therefore, to challenge in another way the sufficiency of the war power to support the action taken by the President and Congress and by the military authorities.[183]

If "pressing public necessity" is the decisive question, Justice Black might be read as committing his opinion solely to an exploration of the relevance of "the war power." But it might also be the case that, as with "other governmental powers," it is the concern underlying "due process" in the *Korematsu* setting that actually "mark[s] the boundaries of the power itself." If this concern originates in the interests of individuals – Korematsu and the others subject to the challenged order – then the analysis that the opinion ultimately develops ought to be preoccupied in some way with assessing how the order addresses those interests. This would, of course, be the approach we have noticed in the overbreadth cases. But Black's own last sentence distinguishes "[p]ressing public necessity" from "racial antagonism." If we are to understand the individual interest as an interest in living free from government action in some sense prompted by "racial antagonism," it might be enough to show that the order at issue is plausibly understood as an exercise of "war power" and the definition of "war power" becomes – again – the opinion's primary preoccupation.

Against this backdrop, two passages in the *Korematsu* opinion especially stand out:

> All citizens alike, both in and out of uniform, feel the impact of war in greater or lesser measure. Citizenship has its responsibilities as well as its privileges, and in time of war the burden is always heavier. Compulsory exclusion of large groups of citizens from their homes, except under circumstances of direct emergency and peril,

[183] *Korematsu v. United States*, Brief for the United States, p. 24, reprinted in 42; Philip B. Kurland and Gerhard Casper (eds.), *Landmark Briefs and Arguments of the Supreme Court of the United States: Constitutional Law* (Arlington: University Publications, 1975), 226.

> is inconsistent with our basic governmental institutions. But when under conditions of modern warfare our shores are threatened by hostile forces, the power to protect must be commensurate with the threatened danger.[184]
>
> Korematsu was not excluded … because of hostility to him or his race. He *was* excluded because we are at war with the Japanese Empire, because the properly constituted military authorities feared an invasion of our West Coast and felt constrained to take proper security measures, because they decided that the military urgency of the situation demanded that all citizens of Japanese ancestry be segregated from the West Coast temporarily, and, finally, because Congress, reposing its confidence in this time of war in our military leaders – as inevitably it must – determined that they should have the power to do just this.[185]

We have seen this progression before. Justice Black follows the model of Justice Powell in *Mathews v. Eldridge* (and also Justice Stewart in *Walker v. Birmingham*) Individual interests – if noted at all – are skeptically characterized, official concerns are accorded deference. It might be possible to justify the asymmetry, of course, if the individual interests are of no particular constitutional concern, and governmental authority is constitutionally acknowledged. Black indeed depicts the individual interests as secondary. But he does so precisely by pushing to the foreground – marking as the test of significance – the state of war, the war that also precisely justifies deference to military beliefs, what officials "feared," "felt," "decided." This is essentially the approach urged in the United States brief. *Korematsu* plainly does not share the premises of overbreadth inquiry. There is no or not much interest in the terms of the governing documents – General DeWitt's order, the authorizing Executive Order, or the authorizing congressional legislation. The focus, rather, is on institutions or more precisely officials charged with responsibility, with whether they have attempted to carry out their duties. It is easy to conclude that possibility – merely – becomes the test of constitutional fidelity and not, as in Justice O'Connor's opinion in *Hamdi*, "due recognition … of competing concerns."

[184] *Korematsu*, 219–20.
[185] Id. at 223.

V. Not Schmittian

The overbreadth framework, I should note, is not free from difficulty.[186] Sometimes, for example, questions arise at the threshold regarding the precise content of challenged statutes or other legal instruments – as a result, difficult assessments need to be made concerning the possibility of glosses or severing edits that would moot constitutional inquiry.[187] Sometimes, it seems, the implications of provisions at issue appear to be discernible primarily through consideration of a series of hypothetical scenarios. Critics argue that exercises of this sort draw courts away from their constitutional responsibility to adjudicate only concrete cases and controversies. It also becomes less than clear, if judges proceed by pursuing thought experiments, whether the unconstitutional component of a challenged provision (whatever it is) is itself insubstantial – rarely manifest in the real world. These hard cases, though, coexist with cases in which the overbreadth framework comes into play – now, as in decades past – in full form. To be sure, in some circumstances statutes at issue in the end are understood to sufficiently recognize and address constitutional concerns.[188] Sometimes constitutional provisions, it is held, do not require attention to matters litigants assert warrant accommodation.[189] These conclusions may be controversial in some cases.[190] But it appears – across a wide range of constitutional topics – that a common premise governs. Overbreadth analysis originates in the idea, Henry Monaghan wrote in 1981, that litigants have a right "to be judged in accordance with a constitutionally valid rule of law."[191]

This formula, seemingly "self-evidently correct," in fact poses an important question.[192] Overbreadth inquiries make a distinctive assumption. In cases implicating constitutionally-acknowledged interests, the "valid rule of law" should somehow evidence "due recognition … of competing concerns." Why so?

[186] For a more elaborate discussion, expanding the set of challenging issues, see Richard H. Fallon Jr., "Making Sense of Overbreadth," *Yale Law Journal* 100 (1991): 853.

[187] See Michael C. Dorf, "Fallback Law," *Columbia Law Review* 107 (2007): 303.

[188] E.g., *United States v. Williams*, 128 S. Ct. 1830 (2008).

[189] E.g., *United States v. Grubbs*, 547 U.S. 90, 97–98 (2006) (no constitutional requirement that search warrant specify triggering conditions)

[190] E.g., *Gonzales v. Carhart*, 550 U.S. 124 (2007).

[191] Henry Monaghan, "Overbreadth," *Supreme Court Review* (1981): 1, 3.

[192] Fallon, "Making Sense of Overbreadth," 874. For Professor Fallon's own criticisms of Monaghan's proposition, see id. at 871–74.

Carl Schmitt, in *Constitutional Theory*, first published in 1928, draws a distinction between "constitutions" and "constitutional laws."[193] A constitution is the result of an exercise of constitution-making power, an act of "political will" by an entity "capable of making the concrete, comprehensive decision over the type and form of its own political existence."[194] "In a democracy, more specifically, this is a decision by the people. ..."[195] "The constitution is valid by virtue of the existing political will of that which establishes it. Every type of legal norm, even constitutional law, presupposes that such a *will* already exists."[196] Constitutional laws, in contrast, "are valid first on the basis of the constitution and presuppose a constitution."[197] "[C]onstitutional law ... needs a political decision that is prior to it, a decision that is reached by a power or authority that exists politically."[198] Otherwise, conceived independently, written constitutions in particular are at risk. "The complete unity of a constitutional codification dissolves itself into a set containing numerous individual constitutional provisions."[199] "The concept of *the* constitution is lost in the concept of individual constitutional law."[200] It follows, for Schmitt, that constitutional laws "can be suspended during the state of exception and be violated by measures of the state of exception."[201] On the other hand, "[e]very genuine constitutional conflict" or "gap in the constitution" may "only be decided through the will of the constitution-making power itself."[202] "The natural form of the direct expression of a people's will is the assembled multitude's declaration of their consent or disapproval, the *acclamation*."[203]

The United States Constitution is not Schmittian. The Constitution is first a text, not first the act of already politically capable, unified people. There is, really, no originating moment as such – no acclamation. The 1787 document, we know, is as much critical as affirmative, a reaction to

[193] Carl Schmitt, *Constitutional Theory*, ed. and trans. Jeffrey Seitzer (Durham: Duke University, 2008), 75.
[194] Id. at 125.
[195] Id. at 77.
[196] Id. at 76.
[197] Id. at 78.
[198] Id. at 76.
[199] Id. at 70.
[200] Id. at 71.
[201] Id. at 80.
[202] Id. at 126.
[203] Id. at 131.

the perceived workings of the preceding state constitutions. Ratification revealed a tense and divided politics, prompting a substantial revision of the Constitution, the drafting and adoption of the Bill of Rights. The most radical change of all, following a half century or so later, might be thought to illustrate Schmitt. Slavery was recognized, protected, and to some extent regulated in the 1787 text – it was clear, however, that slavery as an institution preceded the text: figured as a constitutional given, an already-reached political choice (even if as much a matter of acquiescence or compromise as acclamation.) And, of course, abolition was the result (chiefly) of civil war. Constitutional rewriting followed after the fact.

But the overlay of politics and text was more complex than Schmitt's model supposes. We all know that the constitutional changes did not encode an already won new political unity, notwithstanding Abraham Lincoln's eloquent efforts of articulation and imagination. The amendments themselves instead provided points of departure for a renewed struggle, substantively revised to be sure (slavery as such was understood on all sides to have been abolished.) This struggle organized, inter alia, a new politics within which insurgent terror asserted itself with considerable success, followed in turn by an extended period of de facto political partition (again, to be sure, amid some overarching assertions of national unity) – partition itself reciprocally influencing legal and political understandings of the amendments adopted following the Civil War. This, we all know, was the scene within which and against which the civil rights movements of the mid-twentieth century played out. The constitutional text – or rather, the constitutional accumulation of texts – coexists with, is both shaped by and shapes, an ongoing politics of conflict, compromise, and sometimes resolution rarely easily characterized as coherent expression of political will.

The United States Constitution is first of all a complex of texts, specifications subject to interpretation and changes, an ongoing accumulation of documents, and *therefore* understandings, however seemingly wide-ranging.[204] This is its characteristic form. Documentary accumulation establishes a distinctively layered (or laminate) space within which conflicts can

[204] [M]ost of the modes of reasoning to the contents of the invisible Constitution involve arguing in one form or another from its visible text (but not in a way that could be considered "mere logical inference"). At the same time, the Constitution's "dark matter" may be seen to animate and undergird significant portions of its visible text. And in some cases . . ., it is the invisible constitutional principles that all but dictate the remaining widely ascribed to the visible text.

Laurence H. Tribe, *The Invisible Constitution* (New York: Oxford, 2008), 38.

leave marks, in the process becoming manifest and therefore potentially constitutional subjects – to be added to or incorporated in the ongoing agenda. The changing inquiries that over time have figured within elaboration of the idea of "the equal protection of the laws," for example, identify and address systems of classification that come into law, as it were, from the overall culture – and also concerns that various constitutional propositions or other legal commitments themselves mark as significant with regard to questioned differences in treatment. Documentary accumulation is, we can see, the starting point for overbreadth inquiry as well. The investigations and conclusions overbreadth scrutiny organizes search out and demand attention to conflicts picked up in the constitutional accumulation and taken to be themselves part of the Constitution's constitution, conjunctions of several constitutionally acknowledged endeavors. This scrutiny is precisely expressive – emblematic – of overall constitutional structure. "[D]ue recognition ... of competing concerns" is therefore not surprisingly understood to be a hallmark of "a constitutionally valid rule of law."

All of this suggests that the *Walker* effort to reinforce judicial independence – to defend the idea of an autonomous judiciary, unified across federal and state lines, equally expounding and enforcing both federal and state law – was (however worthy a project) founded on a mistaken synecdoche. Legal processes are part of the constitutional accumulation – indeed crucial in the construction of the accumulation – but only a part. The "people out of doors" are another. Complex economic, social, and cultural conflicts are – this is the constitutional expectation structurally expressed – in the main registered, considered, and addressed: framed somehow within the constitutional mix, whether in tension or in harmony with other constituents. The gist of the constitutional project is lost, therefore, if judges close themselves off – prompted by perceptions of emergency – in the process of protecting their jurisdiction. (We ought to realize that the *Milligan* characterization of states of emergency applies as aptly in criticizing courts themselves.) The inquiry that *Shuttlesworth* undertakes, in contrast, asserts and therefore defends jurisdiction in the very process of exploring and criticizing the premises of judicial action.

There is an obvious irony in this conclusion. Absent judicial refusal to consider the overbreadth of either the ordinance enforced or the text of the injunction itself, would the SCLC efforts in Birmingham have achieved as much? If the SCLC were free to march, what would have happened next? We cannot answer these questions, of course. It is more important, I think, to note forward-looking implications. Emergency is ordinary: circumstances that might be plausibly labeled as crises appear in court, as it were, often enough. Judges, it is apparent, have access to means that both recognize extraordinary dimensions and make available methods of critical evaluation. To do this work, judges do not have to become ostriches, denying that they are confronting anything other than banality. They are, rather, put in position to recognize that constitutional materials are capable of assembly in ways that make possible close – perhaps therefore often difficult – testing of whether responses to emergency reflected constitutional consideration within their own formulations. Judges may not want to do this work. But constitutional accumulations disclose bases for criticism if they do not.

Comment on Chapter 2

"Order" in the Court

Paul Horwitz*

Introduction

When and why do courts insist that the parties before them insist on "following the rules," despite the evident frailty of those rules or the terrible consequences that following the rules might entail? Why should citizens follow what they, and we, might conclude are patently bad laws – and why should courts insist that they do?

This is an age-old jurisprudential question, of course. It raises questions that have long been with us concerning the scope and legitimacy of civil disobedience, the nature of legal authority, and the proper relationship between law and morality.[1] These questions are ultimately as intractable as they are fundamental.

In his contribution to this collection, Patrick Gudridge helpfully takes a narrower cut at some of these questions.[2] He asks how we ought to think about "constitutional analysis framing contemplation of emergencies, crises, or other unruly events."[3] The overlap between that narrower question and the broader question when and why courts should insist on obedience to the law is considerable. Emergencies and other "unruly events" are often the moments at which the justification for departing from "orderly ways" is at its

* Associate Professor, University of Alabama School of Law. Thank you to Martha Rogers for her assistance on this paper.

1 See, e.g., Kent Greenawalt, *Conflicts of Law and Morality* (Oxford University Press, 1986); Tom R. Tyler, *Why People Obey the Law* (Yale University Press, 1990).

2 See Patrick O. Gudridge, "Emergency, Legality, Sovereignty: Birmingham, 1963," in this volume at pp. 72–119.

3 Id.

most compelling. These moments thus place in stark relief the immanent conflict between doing the "right" thing and doing the "orderly" thing.

More specifically, Professor Gudridge presents us with what he suggests is an anomaly in Supreme Court jurisprudence. Although he builds on whole sequences of cases, he focuses on two in particular. In *Walker v. City of Birmingham*,[4] the Supreme Court confronted a host of civil rights leaders, including the Rev. Martin Luther King, Jr., who were jailed for contempt of court for violating a judicial injunction prohibiting a civil rights march in Birmingham, Alabama. A closely divided Court upheld the contempt orders. It did so notwithstanding its suspicion, which the Court confirmed only a couple of years later, that the underlying statute on which the injunction was based was facially unconstitutional. [5] It refused to evaluate the merits of the underlying statute, which had not been directly challenged by the contemnors. It justified its decision with the stark statement that "respect for judicial process is a small price to pay for the civilizing hand of law, which alone can give abiding meaning to constitutional freedom."[6] Professor Gudridge contrasts *Walker* with the court's infamous decision in *Korematsu v. United States*,[7] upholding the conviction of Fred Korematsu for remaining in San Leandro, California, in violation of a military order excluding all persons of Japanese ancestry from the area. What is striking, he suggests, is that the Supreme Court did not hesitate to reach the merits of the case.[8]

Professor Gudridge shares the popular consensus that both cases were wrongly decided, but offers the novel argument that the two cases share common failings, and that these failings say something about the courts' treatment of emergency situations.[9] The link between the two, as I understand his argument, is their shared focus on "institutions or more precisely officials charged with responsibility, with whether they have attempted to carry out their duties."[10] In such an approach, he suggests, "[o]fficial good faith becomes the test of constitutional fidelity and not . . .

[4] 388 U.S. 307 (1967).

[5] See *Shuttlesworth v. Birmingham*, 394 U.S. 147 (1969).

[6] *Walker*, 388 U.S. at 321.

[7] 323 U.S. 214 (1944).

[8] See Gudridge, "Emergency, Legality, Sovereignty: Birmingham, 1963," p. 112.

[9] See id. at 73.

[10] Id. at 114.

'due recognition . . . of competing concerns.'"[11] This conclusion leads us back to our starting point: the conflict between good "law" and a functioning legal "order."

Although Professor Gudridge's effort to draw a connection between *Walker* and *Korematsu* is novel, certainly both cases have always been disfavored by the legal academic community. *Korematsu* has been described as a "disaster" almost since its birth.[12] And *Walker*, on which I will focus more closely in this commentary, has similarly, if to a lesser degree, suffered the whips of scorn for many years. *Walker* has been variously described as blind, or unduly harsh, or as an act of judicial insecurity or legerdemain.[13] In terms that are not too dissimilar from Professor Gudridge's, Robert Cover described *Walker* as a "jurispathic" act, one that conceals itself "through the judge's elaboration of the institutional privilege of force – that is, jurisdiction."[14]

What, then, can we say about the Court's refusal to reach the underlying merits in *Walker* and its willingness to do so, however unavailing it proved for the petitioners, in *Korematsu*? And what can we say about what Professor Gudridge perceives as the common tie between the cases – that both focus on the officials charged with enforcing the contested actions? Can we say anything more charitable about the Court's decisions in these cases, at least in the sense that it explains their decisions without wholly condemning them?

In what follows, I attempt to do so. Although I focus primarily on *Walker*, some or much of what I say here may apply to *Korematsu* as well, and it will ultimately be folded back into the discussion. Notwithstanding the common criticism of *Walker* for failing to give voice to Dr. King's perspective,[15] I will focus on the case from the judicial perspective.

[11] Id. (quoting *Hamdi v. Rumsfeld*, 124 S. Ct. 2633, 2648 [2004]).

[12] See Eugene Rostow, "The Japanese American Cases – A Disaster," *Yale Law Journal* 54 (1945): 489.

[13] For particularly striking criticisms of the decision, see, e.g., David Luban, "Difference Made Legal: The Court and Dr. King," *Michigan Law Review* 87 (1989): 2152; Stephen L. Carter, *The Dissent of the Governed: A Meditation on Law, Religion, and Loyalty* (Harvard University Press, 1999), 105–14. The decision has relatively few defenders, but for an early defense of *Walker*, see Sheldon Tefft, "Neither Above the Law Nor Below It: A Note on *Walker v. Birmingham*," *Supreme Court Review* (1967): 181.

[14] Robert M. Cover, "Foreword – Nomos and Narrative," *Harvard Law Review* 97 (1983): 4, 54.

[15] See, e.g., Carter, *Dissent of the Governed*, 109–10. Similarly, Professor Gudridge observes in his paper that there is "almost no acknowledgement . . . in Justice Stewart's opinion" of the

From that perspective, what has been described as an act of judicial blindness or insecurity might be reframed as touching on deep issues concerning the nature of judicial authority and duty. In particular, I want to discuss the relationship between two questions that have both been the subject of substantial discussion, but that are rarely discussed together: the nature of the judicial oath, and the nature of judicial deference.[16] Thinking about the relationship between these two subjects may provide a somewhat different perspective on why the Court acted as it did in *Walker*, *Korematsu*, and many of the other cases Professor Gudridge discusses. This perspective does not amount to an absolute defense of those decisions; it frankly acknowledges that there is much unexplored territory outside the borders of judicial authority and duty. But it may nonetheless lead to a milder view of what the Court did in those cases – and it may speak beyond that to the question of what constitutes legal "order," during emergencies and routine times alike.

I.

Federal judges are twice-bound by oath. In common with all other federal officers, they swear or affirm to "support and defend the Constitution of the United States."[17] In addition, federal judges swear or affirm an oath to "administer justice without respect to persons, and to equal right to the poor and to the rich, and [to] . . . faithfully and impartially discharge and perform all the duties incumbent upon me . . . under the Constitution and laws of the United States."[18]

It is easy enough today to view these oaths as mere parchment barriers of relatively little significance. But their words, and the promise they made,

"extraordinary events that followed the contempt jailings in the case." Gudridge, "Emergency, Legality, Sovereignty: Birmingham, 1963," pp. 87–88.

16 Elsewhere, I have discussed these issues more or less separately. On deference, see Paul Horwitz, "Three Faces of Deference," *Notre Dame Law Review* 83 (2008): 1061 [*Deference*]. On the nature of oaths, see Paul Horwitz, "Religious Tests in the Mirror: The Constitutional Law and Constitutional Etiquette of Religion in Judicial Nominations," *William & Mary Bill of Rights Journal* 15 (2006): 75 [*Religious Tests*]; Paul Horwitz, "Honor's Constitutional Moment: The Oath and Presidential Transitions," *Northwestern University Law Review Colloquy* 103 (2008): 259 [*Honor's Constitutional Moment*]. These projects stem in part from ongoing work on the history and nature of the federal judicial oath. Professor Gudridge himself has written an illuminating article on the oath. See Patrick O. Gudridge, "The Office of the Oath," *Constitutional Commentary* 20 (2003): 387.

17 5 U.S.C. § 3331.

18 28 U.S.C. § 453.

once would have been viewed as solemn, profound, and binding. This has much to do, of course, with the religious significance of the oath, which both bound the oath-taker and called on God to witness the promise.[19]

Beyond this, however, it has much to do with the relationship between the oath and honor.[20] In the founding era, the oath served to tie the performance of public office closely to "human honor and obligation."[21] Honor was all the more important in a new nation "lacking an established aristocracy," in which the display of public virtue and trustworthiness was one of the few "proving ground[s]" available, "a source of stability in [a] contested political [and social] landscape."[22] Honor, as students of this trait have noted,[23] was emphatically not simply a private virtue; to the contrary, it depended on its public nature. Honor was "determined before the eyes of the world; it did not exist unless bestowed by others. Indeed, a man of honor was defined by the respect that he received in public."[24]

The oath thus tied the office-holder's personal honor to the conscientious performance of his duties – linking him, in Alexander Hamilton's words, to "the restraints of public opinion" and "the jealousy and watchfulness of the people."[25] In so doing, as Professor Gudridge has observed elsewhere, the oath served to internalize the values of the Constitution, and judicial reputations could live or die according to how honorably the oath-taker lived up to its terms.[26]

One natural reading of the judge's obligations under the judicial and constitutional oaths simply denies the usefulness or applicability of the concept of an "emergency" that alters or enlarges the judge's duty. On this view, the

19 For more on the religious significance of the oath in the founding generation, see Horwitz, *Religious Tests*, 106–8.

20 Portions of the following two paragraphs appear in somewhat different form in Horwitz, *Honor's Constitutional Moment*, 259.

21 Michael Stokes Paulsen, "The Constitution of Necessity," *Notre Dame Law Review* 79 (2004): 1257, 1263 n. 13.

22 Joanne B. Freeman, *Affairs of Honor: National Politics in the New Republic* (Yale University Press, 2001), xix.

23 See, e.g., Frank Henderson Stewart, *Honor* (University of Chicago Press, 1994).

24 Freeman, *Affairs of Honor*, xvi.

25 *The Federalist No.* 70 at 477–79 (Alexander Hamilton) (Jacob E. Cooke ed., 1961). Hamilton here is referring specifically to the presidential oath.

26 See generally Gudridge, "The Office of the Oath." In a recent book, Professor Philip Hamburger offers a rich description of the relationship between the oath and judicial duty in England well before the American Revolution. See Philip Hamburger, *Law and Judicial Duty* (Harvard University Press, 2008), 106–16.

judge is committed to support and defend the *Constitution*, and to discharge his duties under that document, and nothing more. If the Constitution expressly or impliedly makes special allowance for emergencies, then the judge may – indeed, must – act accordingly. But the Constitution is rather limited in this respect, at least with respect to the judicial office. To the extent that the traditional access to the writ of habeas corpus can be abrogated, for example, such a decision rests within the political branches alone, and then only "when in cases of Rebellion or Invasion the public Safety may require it."[27] But the Constitution does not alter the obligations of the judiciary depending on the emergency circumstances involved. To the contrary, the only mention Article III of the Constitution makes of what we might call emergency situations is to erect high barriers against convictions for the crime of treason.[28]

We might thus conclude that judges are absolutely required to interpret the Constitution as they always have, even in cases of emergency. The Constitution cannot be "waived in some exigency."[29] Judges must simply decide cases under the Constitution, in an absolute and unwavering fashion.

But a world of uncertainties lies within this seemingly simple understanding of judicial duty. First, uncertainties may arise over the oath itself. What does it mean to support and defend the Constitution, or to faithfully discharge one's duties under the Constitution? Perhaps it does indeed mean that judges must rule on their own vision of the Constitution; but perhaps it means little more than that they should enforce duly enacted statutes, leaving it to the legislature to decide any substantive constitutional questions.[30]

Leaving this aside, another uncertainty exists, one that may be less monumental but is certainly more common: uncertainty over facts. However

[27] U.S. Const., Art. I, s. 9, cl. 2. Although the text is not perfectly clear on the question of whether suspension may be affected by Congress only or by the president as well, the placement of the Suspension Clause within Article I has lent itself to the traditional understanding that the suspension power is legislative, not executive. See, e.g., *Ex parte Merryman*, 17 F. Cas. 144 (C.C.D. Md. 1861).

[28] See U.S. Const., Art. III, s. 3 (requiring a confession in open court or the testimony of two witnesses for a treason conviction).

[29] Saikrishna Prakash, "The Constitution as Suicide Pact," *Notre Dame Law Review* 79 (2004): 1299, 1320.

[30] See, e.g., Richard A. Posner, "Modesty and Power," *The New Republic* (Dec. 31, 2008): 38, 40, "Marshall and his colleagues might have decided that Congress like Parliament was a kind of 'court' whose 'decisions' (namely the laws that Congress enacted) could not be overturned by judges."

clear judicial duty under the oath may seem in the abstract, it may easily founder or grow more complicated as judges wrestle with the application of their understanding of the law to particular facts. To take a simple example drawn from the context of emergencies, suppose that Congress in fact suspended the writ of habeas corpus. As we have seen, in those circumstances a court that faced a petition for such a writ would be required to deny it. But it would first be required to decide whether the enacting legislation in fact involved a rebellion or invasion, and if so whether the public safety required the suspension. The Constitution supplies no gloss on what is required to meet these conditions, and ordinary judicial experience offers no ready guide for answering the question. So the faithful execution of the judicial oath may depend on a raft of factual questions whose answers – if there are any answers at all – may prove taxing or intractable.

The final consideration that faces judges under the oath is related to the factual question, but it also raises deeper questions about authority. For judges are only one subset of the countless government officials, federal and state, who are equally bound by oath to support and defend the Constitution. In *Marbury v. Madison*, one of the key struts on which Chief Justice Marshall rested the power and duty of judicial review was the fact that judges take oaths to support the Constitution, and must perforce authoritatively interpret it. But for almost as many years, the retort has come that the very lawmakers whose acts are under question when legislation is judicially reviewed take the same oath.[31] That judges have a duty under the oath thus does not answer the question how they should honor that oath in a system of coordinate oath-takers, each seemingly charged with the same obligation to interpret the Constitution.

In short, as simple as the judges' obligation under their constitutional oaths may seem at first glance, it quickly runs into deeper questions of both epistemic and legal authority. What are they do to in such circumstances? The answer, in short, lies in deference.[32] When they defer, judges follow

[31] For a relatively contemporary version of this criticism, see *Eakin v. Raub*, 12 Serg. and Rawle 330, 352 (Pa. 1825) (Gibson, J., dissenting), "The oath to support the constitution is not peculiar to the judges, but is taken indiscriminately by every officer of the government. …" For modern versions, see, e.g., Alexander Bickel, *The Least Dangerous Branch: The Supreme Court at the Bar of Politics*, 2nd ed. (Yale University Press, 1986), 7–10; William W. Van Alstyne, "A Critical Guide to *Marbury v. Madison*," *Duke Law Journal* 1 (1969): 20–21, 25–26.

[32] For more on deference, and on its relationship to epistemic and legal authority, see Horwitz, "Three Faces of Deference," 1061.

the determination of some other decision-maker that they might not have reached independently.[33] They do so for reasons relating to both epistemic and legal authority: they defer because some other decision-maker might have more expertise on the factual or legal matters at hand, and because it might be vested with greater or more immediate legal authority to decide the question.

To observe that there is a relationship between the oath and judicial deference is not to say that there is not also a deep tension between the two. As we have seen, the judges' oath can plausibly be read to require them to exercise absolute independence in determining what the Constitution demands in the case at hand. This understanding does not seem to leave much room, if any, for deference. And yet, the questions of epistemic and legal authority that haunt the oath also seem to demand some room for listening to and respecting the decisions of other oath-takers. Thus does deference make the burden of the oath, and its equal application to other officials, bearable. Deference and the oath are conjoined twins, uncomfortably but inextricably linked together, at least so long as we exist in a legal system of shared authority and imperfect wisdom.

It is also important to note that deference has its limits. Deference ultimately speaks to what Laurence Tribe once referred to as an "allocation of competencies,"[34] to which we might add that it also speaks to an allocation of authority. When judges defer to other decision-makers, they can at least expect and demand that the other decision-maker is acting "within the proper scope of its legal authority."[35] They can also expect that the deferred-to party is acting within the scope of its epistemic expertise. And they can expect and demand that the decision-maker acts in good faith in reaching a decision to which the courts will defer.[36] A coordinate authority that is not acting within these boundaries does not deserve deference. But within the perhaps broad bounds of these requirements, judges may honor their oath while still deferring to the decision of a coordinate legal authority.

[33] Id. at 1072.

[34] Laurence H. Tribe, "Foreword: Toward a Model of Rules in the Due Process of Life and Law," *Harvard Law Review* 87 (1973): 1, 10–14.

[35] Horwitz, "Three Faces of Deference," 1102.

[36] See id. at 1101–2; see also Philip Soper, *The Ethics of Deference: Learning From Law's Morals* (Cambridge University Press, 2002), 182; Frederick Schauer, "Deferring," *Michigan Law Review* 103 (2005): 1567, 1574 (reviewing Soper, *Ethics of Deference*).

II.

What does this have to do with *Walker v. Birmingham* and *Korematsu v. United States*? Ultimately, I will suggest, both cases, and the other cases Professor Gudridge sees as contributing to a tension in the law, can be understood as a manifestation of the relationship between the judicial duty spelled out in the oath and the necessity of judicial deference.

First, consider *Walker v. Birmingham*. Professor Gudridge notes the peroration of the Court's opinion in that case. Having refused to disturb the petitioners' conviction for contempt of court, Justice Stewart, while conceding some sympathy for "the petitioners' impatient commitment to their cause," writes: "But respect for judicial process is a small price to pay for the civilizing hand of law, which alone can give abiding meaning to constitutional freedom."[37] In the circumstances, this seems almost to echo Anatole France's sardonic celebration of "[t]he majestic equality of the la[w], [which] forbids rich and poor alike to sleep under bridges, to beg in the streets, and to steal their bread."[38] More puzzling still, as Professor Gudridge observes, is the fact that Stewart's opinion *also* made clear that *Walker* was "not a case where the injunction was transparently invalid or had only a frivolous pretense to validity."[39] If the collateral bar rule is a necessary element of "the civilizing hand of law," what relevance can the "transparent invalidity" or not of the injunction have, and why did the Court not dig deeper into the validity of the injunction here?

The answer, I suggest, lies in the relationship between the oath and deference. Judges are called upon to apply the law in accordance with their oaths – even-handedly, treating the rich and poor alike, and absolutely. On that foundation rests both the rule of law, and judicial duty properly understood. But they do not act alone. They are caught in a web of coordinate oath-takers and decision-makers, each himself or herself possessed of some epistemic and legal authority and an obligation of his or her own under the oath. Where that decision-maker acts beyond his office, or fails to consider the question at hand in good faith, or does not leave behind some evidence that he or she has done so, there is no occasion for deference. Where the

[37] *Walker v. Birmingham*, 388 U.S. 307, 321 (1967).

[38] See, e.g., *Parents Involved in Community Schools v. Seattle School Dist. No. 1*, 127 S. Ct. 2738, 2798 (2007) (Stevens, J., dissenting).

[39] *Walker*, 388 U.S. at 315.

necessary conditions are met, however, judicial duty can and perhaps must accommodate deference.

This is arguably the situation faced by the Court in *Walker*. The ordinance under which Walker and the other petitioners were subjected to the contempt order no doubt had serious constitutional problems, and the Supreme Court would not hesitate to strike it down within a couple of years when the occasion presented itself.[40] But the *Walker* Court was differently situated. It faced, not the statute itself, but the decision of a coordinate oath-taker – the state court – applying its contempt powers in a case in which jurisdiction clearly lay.[41] In those circumstances, judicial duty under the oath was best satisfied not by attacking the ordinance itself, but by deferring to the epistemic and legal authority of the lower court.

No such deference would be necessary or appropriate if the coordinate oath-taker had simply acted outside its oath and office altogether, in a way that destroyed any claim to legal or epistemic authority. But absent those conditions, the path to judicial duty under the oath left room for – indeed, may have compelled – deference to the coordinate decision-maker. Thus Justice Stewart was careful to note that "this is not a case where the injunction was transparently invalid or had only a frivolous pretense to validity."[42] Professor Gudridge suggests that this insistence creates a tension with the Court's later ruling in *Shuttlesworth*.[43] But it seems perfectly consistent with the relationship between the oath and deference that I have described here – which, in Gudridge's words, requires courts to bring to bear both "considerations warranting regulation" *and* "considerations suggesting limits to regulation."[44]

The application of the collateral bar rule in *Walker* thus balanced judges' judicial duty under the oath with the need to defer to other oath-takers, seemingly acting within the bounds of their own oaths and their own legal and/or epistemic authority. It did not bless the underlying ordinance, of which the Court would make swift work in *Shuttlesworth*. But its approach

[40] See *Shuttlesworth v. Birmingham*, 394 U.S. 147 (1969).

[41] See *Walker*, 388 U.S. at 315, "Without question the state court that issued the injunction had, as a court of equity, jurisdiction over the petitioners and over the subject matter of the controversy."

[42] Id. For a rare instance of a court reversing a contempt order because it was transparently invalid, see *In re Providence Journal Co.*, 820 F.2d 1342 (1st Cir. 1986).

[43] See Gudridge, "Emergency, Legality, Sovereignty: Birmingham, 1963," pp. 90–91, 98–102.

[44] Id., 91.

might indeed be seen as advancing "the civilizing hand of law" in a system of multiple oath-takers.[45]

We could make similar observations about some of the other cases discussed by Professor Gudridge. It is consistent with, if broader than, the Court's insistence in the earlier case of *Howat v. Kansas*, in which the Court insisted on enforcing an injunction by a lower court with proper jurisdiction that "*duly*" exercised its injunctive powers, even if the reviewing court might have independently reached a different decision.[46] It is also consistent with *United States v. Shipp*, in which Justice Holmes for the Court rejected the contention of a Tennessee county sheriff that the federal courts had no jurisdiction over him in a contempt action for acquiescing in the lynching of a black prisoner, because the prisoner had presented no serious constitutional question in his habeas action.[47] *Shipp* in fact presents multiple factors that are consistent with my reading of deference and the oath. On the one hand, as Justice Holmes asserted, the question whether the Supreme Court had jurisdiction was a question that "this court, and this court alone," must decide, consistently with the Justices' oaths.[48] On the other hand, any claim to deference that Shipp himself might assert as a coordinate oath-taker surely foundered on the fact that, by acquiescing to the mob, he had acted well outside the bounds of his office and his oath. Finally, my reading fits Justice Frankfurter's concurrence in *United States v. United Mine Workers*, which upheld a contempt order against a union, in which Frankfurter argued in favor of deference to a lower court's contempt order unless it "is so obviously traveling outside its orbit as to be merely usurping judicial forms and facilities."[49]

What of *Korematsu*? Here, too, I think the case can be read as speaking to the relationship between the oath and deference. As an initial matter, there is no mystery why the Court should have reached the merits in *Korematsu* while refusing to do so in *Walker*. The case arose on a direct challenge to the law, rather than, as in *Walker*, raising matters that were collateral to the central question of the jurisdiction and authority of a lower court judge. But

[45] *Walker*, 388 U.S. at 321.

[46] *Howat v. Kansas*, 258 U.S. 181, 280–81 (1922) (emphasis added).

[47] *United States v. Shipp*, 203 U.S. 563 (1906).

[48] Id. at 573.

[49] *United States v. United Mine Workers*, 330 U.S. 258, 309 (1947) (Frankfurter, J., concurring in the judgment).

the deference paid to General DeWitt's order in *Korematsu* also speaks to the same kind of deference concerns that played so great a part in *Walker*. As in most wartime cases, General DeWitt could claim precisely the kind of legal and epistemic authority that makes judges uneasy and compels them to make room for judicial deference somewhere within the fulfillment of their oaths to decide cases in accordance with the law. The Constitution vests the political branches with primary authority to act in times of war; and combined with that legal authority is the obvious epistemic authority that military officials bring to bear in wartime cases, and which judges believe they lack.

Thus, although the Court purported to apply a rule of strict scrutiny consistent with its duty under the oath to apply the Constitution to the case at hand, its application of this test was influenced by the fact that Congress had "repos[ed] its confidence in this time of war in our military leaders,"[50] and by the epistemic insecurity caused by the fact that General DeWitt's decision to issue the exclusion order was taken "under conditions of uncertainty, when the officials do not know how the war is going to turn out."[51] Questions of the Court's own legal and epistemic authority, relative to the authority of other decision-makers, thus led it to temper its duty under the oath with a substantial degree of deference to another official who was also tasked under oath with the duty to act appropriately in a difficult situation.[52]

Knowing what we know now, we might wish otherwise. We might wish the Court had acted more skeptically toward DeWitt – or, to put it differently, that it had placed its own duty under the oath above any deference

[50] *Korematsu*, 323 U.S. at 223.

[51] Mark Tushnet, "Defending Korematsu?: Reflections on Civil Liberties in Wartime," *Wisconsin Law Review* (2003): 273, 283.

[52] To be sure, there was considerable evidence that General DeWitt acted out of racism rather than through the proper exercise of legal or epistemic authority. See Rostow, "Japanese American Cases," 489. But those improper motives may have been less than clear to his bureaucratic superiors, who may have acted in due reliance upon his stated reasons why exclusion was necessary. See Tushnet, "Defending Korematsu," 290. General DeWitt might have presented his superiors, and the Supreme Court, with "knowingly distorted information." Id. But it would be difficult for the court to second-guess that information in an uncertain time, and it might still defer to his *ex ante* assessment of the risk that necessitated the policy. See id. at 291, "The fact that policies are developed in uncertain times on the basis of information not fully available outside the decision-making bureaucracy may account for the courts' initial acquiescence in the policies, and for the subsequent critical reactions when the previously unavailable information becomes available."

to DeWitt and other oath-takers.[53] But as long as courts must balance their own duties under the oath with deference to the legal and epistemic authorities of other oath-takers such as General DeWitt, they will likely act more or less as they did in *Korematsu*, and in *Walker* for that matter. They will focus on the good faith of the coordinate decision maker who is "charged with responsibility" under an oath of his own, on whether he has "attempted to carry out [his] duties" within the bounds of his oath and his epistemic authority.[54] If he has, they will be reluctant to disturb that official's decision, even if they would have reached a different one on their own (as *Shuttlesworth* suggests); if he has acted well beyond the bounds of epistemic or legal authority, the path to doing their own duty under the oath will be clearer.[55]

III.

None of what has been said so far should be construed as an absolute defense of the Court's decisions in *Walker* and *Korematsu*. Nor should it be taken as

[53] This is one of the lessons of Professor Tushnet's article, which discusses the "social learning" that takes place after each cycle of repressive decision making during emergencies. But as Tushnet observes, courts are likely to fight the last war in such cases; although they may not be taken in by identical assurances in subsequent cases, each new emergency will present new questions that again lead the courts to defer to the epistemic and legal authority of other decision makers. That is not to say that courts have not responded to these social learning occasions at all. For a discussion of the ways in which courts in free speech cases, including those involving national security or incitements to violence or lawless action, have ramped up the level of judicial scrutiny as a prophylactic device that compensates for their propensity to overestimate the likelihood of harm in such cases, see Paul Horwitz, "Free Speech as Risk Analysis: Heuristics, Biases, and Institutions in the First Amendment," *Temple Law Review* 76 (2003): 1.

[54] Gudridge, "Emergency, Legality, Sovereignty: Birmingham, 1963," p. 114.

[55] This analysis also applies to some of the other cases discussed in the second section of Professor Gudridge's paper, which focuses on overbreadth doctrine, and for reasons similar to those offered by Gudridge. Professor Gudridge suggests that both legislative and judicial jurisdiction constitutes "an exercise of responsibility, constitutionally achieved only if legislation reproduces constitutional commitments (in some way or another) within the substance of the law made, in cases (at least) in which constitutional commitments might be plausibly understood to impinge." Id. at 112. There is an interesting unacknowledged echo here of his argument, in his article on the judicial oath, that the oath created "an obligation to account for disagreement, to demonstrate no disloyalty or dishonor, to answer the charge of 'no theory[,]' … to 'expound.'" Gudridge, "The Office of the Oath," 401. This description of the duty of an oath-taker may apply more to judges than to other officials, and it may be too broad in both cases. But the general point seems consistent with the occasions for judicial deference under the oath that I have described here: judges will be more apt to defer to an official who has made a clear good-faith

stating a fundamental point of disagreement with Professor Gudridge. To the contrary, I share his view that both cases can be read in light of their focus on the "[o]fficial good faith" of coordinate officials – whether lower courts or actors in the political branches – rather than on "due recognition … of competing concerns."[56] We could, of course, question whether the Court was too quick to assume the good faith of those officials in both cases, and thus perhaps too quick to surrender its duty under the judicial oath to see that justice was done.

Still, this is, I think, a decidedly more sympathetic account than the one offered by Professor Gudridge, let alone some of the other critics of both *Walker* and *Korematsu*. It suggests, among other things, that *Walker* cannot be viewed only as a jurispathic act whose underlying purpose was to defend the courts' own "institutional privilege of force – that is, jurisdiction."[57] *Walker* and *Korematsu* are both expressions of judicial insecurity, but they are not simply efforts to resolve that insecurity by asserting their supremacy within their jurisdiction. Rather, both cases represent an effort by judges to balance their obligations under the oath to "say what the law is"[58] with the questions of legal and epistemic authority that plague the courts, especially in a system in which coordinate judicial and political officials share the same duty under the oath. That balance may be improperly struck in particular cases, but it seems both understandable and likely that a workable effort to live under the oath in our system, given judges' shared authority and imperfect knowledge, will require them to continue attempting to strike it.

effort to state, and comply with, his own oath-bound duty to honor the Constitution. Thus, when Justice Kennedy upheld a set of procedures determining who should be confined in a state "supermax" prison, his deference to state penal officials had much to do with the array of procedural guarantees put in place by the state, which suggested a good-faith effort to safeguard the prisoners' constitutional rights. See *Wilkinson v. Austin*, 545 U.S. 209 (2005). Conversely, the dispersal ordinance at issue in *City of Chicago v. Morales*, 527 U.S. 41 (1999), failed to provide the kind of evidence that the lawmakers had engaged in a good-faith effort under their oaths to address the constitutional questions raised by the ordinance that might justify judicial deference. We can similarly see Justice O'Connor's employment of the due process device in *Hamdi v. Rumsfeld*, 542 U.S. 507 (2004), as a way of ensuring that military officials at Guantanamo Bay would subsequently incorporate a good-faith recognition of constitutional concerns into their confinement of purported enemy combatants; then, and only then, would judicial deference to the coordinate officials be justified.

56 Gudridge, "Emergency, Legality, Sovereignty: Birmingham, 1963," p. 114.

57 Cover, "Foreword," 54.

58 *Marbury v. Madison*, 5 U.S. (1 Cranch.) 137, 177 (1803).

This understanding of the relationship between the oath and deference may also contribute to our understanding of the relationship between legality and emergency. The oath itself, with its firm imposition on judges of the obligation to faithfully and impartially judge according to the Constitution, strongly suggests that judges' duties under their oaths are the same in emergencies or in ordinary time. The Constitution may itself allow the appropriate official ample authority to act in response to an emergency, but that power only extends as far as the Constitution reaches, and judges in particular (although not judges alone) are bound by oath not to stray beyond the borders of that authority.[59] In short, nothing inherent in the judicial oath, or judges' sense of their duties, permits a distinction between emergencies and normal cases.

At the same time, whether in ordinary cases or emergencies, judges acting under their oaths still have to confront difficult questions about the limits of their legal and epistemic authority. As we have seen, deference is one response to this situation. Deference might be particularly appropriate in cases that strain the limits of judges' own legal or epistemic authority – or, to approach it from the other side, when the law appears to assign primary responsibility to a more expert decision-maker.[60] In these cases, judges are most likely to limit their inquiries to the narrow matter of whether the coordinate decision-maker was acting in good faith within his authority and expertise. This understanding of the relationship between deference and the oath suggests, as Professor Gudridge argues, that law and judicial duty can *accommodate* emergencies within the conventional legal framework without demanding a radical departure from the way judges approach their duties in ordinary times.

I conclude by returning to the question with which I began – why courts so rigorously maintain "order," and how citizens should feel about this. We might acknowledge that an approach to the issues discussed above that focuses on judicial duty under the oath, rather than broader questions of justice, leaves an important gap. It treats legal interpretation as a closed system, one in which the oath-takers, whether judges or other officials, are accorded special deference in their understanding of the law while

[59] For an interesting discussion of the ways in which the Constitution "expressly brought necessity itself under the law," see Hamburger, *Law and Judicial Duty*, 335n12.

[60] See Horwitz, "Three Faces of Deference," 1093.

righteous outsiders, like Martin Luther King or Fred Korematsu, are given none at all. In that sense, whether or not the law is as jurispathic as Professor Cover once suggested, it is certainly less interested in what other *nomoi* might have to say about these questions than it is in the authority and expertise of the official circle of interpreters. The law may be more interested in authority than in moral authority. It is not clear, however, that a workable system of legal "order" resting on the oath, with or without the sometimes leavening effect of deference, can do more.

3

The Banality of Emergency: On the Time and Space of "Political Necessity"

Leonard C. Feldman

Introduction

Emergencies are sudden and dramatic. They call forth an immediate response. When a state of necessity emerges, time becomes compressed. We know this all too well from popular culture, in particular the frantic actions of Jack Bauer on Fox television's *24*. Bauer is an expert at torturing the "ticking bomb terrorist," and the urgency of his actions are reflected in his frequent (non)explanation to his bosses further up the bureaucratic ladder of the counterterrorism unit: "there's no time, I'll explain later." In a condition of necessity, *there is no time*. Jack Bauer, and Jack Bauer alone, must decide what to do in that moment of crisis. Without time, Jack Bauer is sovereign. Or, more accurately, Jack Bauer is sovereign *because there is no time*.

Emergency is closely connected in discourse and practice to the concept of necessity. When extra-legal action is taken in an emergency, the justification is necessity, and here the term brings forth at least three distinct but related meanings: the idea of *crisis or urgency* itself (the state of necessity being synonymous with a state of emergency), the idea of *indispensability* (an action is a necessity because it is the *only* available means of overcoming the crisis condition) and the idea of *inevitability* (as more than one commentator on emergency powers has states, in such a condition, agents of the state *will as a matter of course*, do "whatever it takes").[1] Tick-tock, tick-tock... Emergency and necessity: there is no time, there is only one thing to do, and such a thing will be done.

[1] On indispensability and inevitability as twin features of necessity, see Mark Neocleous, *Critique of Security* (Montreal CA: McGill-Queen's University Press, 2008), p. 34, citing HW Fowler, *Dictionary of Modern English Usage*.

I don't think this dramatized version of the ticking bomb is particularly instructive for our understanding of the politics of emergency as it is experienced in the real world. For instance, Kim Scheppele, David Luban, and others[2] have argued persuasively that the assumptions built into the ticking bomb hypothetical bear little resemblance to the context of bureaucratic complexity and epistemological uncertainty that define the space and time of the actual use of torture. But the most obvious message of the ticking bomb hypothetical – *there is no time* – has nevertheless been taken up in a particular and problematic way by contemporary normative theorists of emergency powers. Some of these scholars, such as Oren Gross, explicitly embrace the ticking bomb hypothetical as if it is a useful hypothetical for thinking about the general problem of emergency powers.[3] Others, such as Bruce Ackerman, more interested in the emergency power of detention than the use of coercive interrogation methods, do not. But they all have largely accepted the assumptions of time compression and the resulting sovereignty presented in the ticking bomb hypothetical. Having abandoned the temporal dimension to the Jack Bauers of the world, they have responded to emergency and necessity on the *spatial* dimension.

Normative theorists have focused on the space of law and debated whether necessity is and should be inside the law or outside the law. I suggest here that the emergency powers debate has made a mistake in prioritizing the spatial dimension over the temporal and (as a consequence, I argue) emphasizing sovereignty over governmentality. Where the sovereignty paradigm emphasizes a single (even "miraculous") moment of decision, governmentality emphasizes what Foucault describes as the ongoing temporal processes of managing a population. This mistake has been repeated by contemporary commentators who work on emergency powers issues in the Western canon of political philosophy as well. (In other words, both first-order normative theory and second-order canonical commentary have made this mistake.) These two conceptual moves – the focus on the spatial relationship between necessity and the legal order and the moment of the sovereign decision – can be traced back to Carl Schmitt. I want to examine

2 David Luban, "Liberalism, Torture, and the Ticking Bomb" in *The Torture Debate in America*, Ed. by Karen Greenberg (New York: Cambridge University Press, 2006), pp. 35–83; Kim Scheppele, "Hypothetical Torture in the 'War on Terrorism,'" *Journal of National Security Law and Policy* (2005).

3 See Oren Gross, "Chaos and Rules: Should Responses to Violent Crises Always Be Constitutional? *Yale Law Journal*, 112 (2003).

the ways in which Schmitt's approach has distorted the contemporary emergency powers debate.[4] Schmitt's shadow has even been cast over John Locke's influential theory of prerogative power in the current literature, and I seek to show how, understood properly, Locke's theory actually involves a more complex and nuanced analysis of the time and space of emergency that can function as a helpful corrective to the Schmittian legacy.

What are the consequences of privileging space over time? By reifying "models" of emergency and "doctrines" of necessity as either legal or extra-legal, these approaches neglect the constitutive role of political contestation in producing and traversing that boundary. Bringing back in the temporal dimension of emergency powers and emphasizing the governmentalist aspects of seemingly sovereign exceptionalism allows greater insight into how emergency politics actually proceed. Indeed, recent work has emerged, challenging the reification of emergency power models, stressing not the extraordinary nature of a "state of exception" but rather the prosaic politics of emergency.[5] As Kim Scheppele writes, "when emergency powers are used, they are almost never the sort of total emergencies that cover all or even most aspects of political life as one might imagine from the theory."[6] But before examining the prosaic politics of emergency – my examples in the second half of this chapter are the doctrine of "police emergency" and other constitutional exceptions to fourth amendment restrictions on

[4] In examining Schmitt's influence upon the contemporary debate I follow William Scheuerman, "Survey Article: Emergency Powers and Rule of Law After 9/11," *The Journal of Political Philosophy* Vol. 14, No. 1 (2006), but characterize the nature of the influence somewhat differently.

[5] This literature contests the norm/exception framework for making sense of the politics of emergency descriptively (and sometimes normatively as well). As Nomi Lazar writes, "Only from a more nuanced perspective on crisis government, receptive to different kinds of norms (rules, principles, constitutional, legal, and moral) and aware of the fluid character of political enablement and constraint can we develop a conceptual and normative framework that can guide legislators and leaders and serve as benchmarks for citizens to promote accountability for outcomes." See Nomi Claire Lazar, "Must Exceptionalism Prove the Rule? An Angle on Emergency Government in the History of Political Thought" *Politics & Society*, Vol. 34, No. 2, June 2006, p. 267. See also, Kim Scheppele, "Legal and Extra-Legal Emergencies," *Oxford Handbook of Law and Politics* Peter Meyers, *Civic War and the Corruption of the Citizen* (Chicago: University of Chicago Press, forthcoming), and David Dyzenhaus, "The State of Emergency in Legal Theory," in *Global Anti-Terrorism Law and Policy*, ed. Victor Ramraj, Michael Hor, and Kent Roach (Cambridge, UK: Cambridge University Press, 2005) and *The Constitution of Law: Legality in a Time of Emergency* (Cambridge UK: Cambridge University Press, 2006).

[6] Kim Lane Scheppele, "Legal and Extra-Legal Emergencies," in *Oxford Handbook of Law and Politics*, p. 174.

warrantless search and seizures – I want to focus critically on emergency as it appears in high theory, and in particular on the "miraculous" moment of the sovereign decision and the spatial relationship between exceptionalism and the legal order. The goal of this discussion is to suggest that the spatial/sovereignty/miracle paradigm might better be replaced with a temporal/governmentality/pastoral paradigm for the study of the politics of emergency.

There Is No Time: Sovereignty's Moment

The idea that necessity compresses time and requires an urgent decision is in some ways uncontestable. Urgency simply *is* a defining feature of an emergency.[7] But because this assumption of time compression has such an obvious taken-for-granted character, it tends to crowd out some of the other more complex aspects of political time that also define the life of an emergency. Let me return here very briefly to the issue of torture. Since *actual* torture occurred over a period of years on detainees who might or might not have had useful information by agents of the state who sought bureaucratic guidelines for an *ongoing* program of coercive interrogation, the compressed temporality of the ticking bomb hypothetical should be subject to critical scrutiny. As David Luban writes, "the ticking-bomb hypothetical ... assumes a single, ad hoc decision about whether to torture ... But in the real world of interrogations, decisions are not made one-off. The real world is a world of policies, guidelines, and directives. It is a world of *practices*, not of ad hoc emergency measures."[8]

In order to scrutinize the assumption of time compression and a singular decision, I want to move to the theoretical register. The role of time compression in legitimating extraordinary powers has a theoretical/philosophic origin as well. Carl Schmitt's version of time compression is expressed in his idea of a decision on the exception. Schmitt collapses two different moments of decision in his famous characterization of sovereignty. Logically this involves two discrete decisions occurring at different points in time – first, a decision that there exists an emergency of such magnitude that it warrants the suspension of law, and second, a decision concerning what particular

7 As Ian Zuckerman puts it "an emergency is an unanticipated, fundamental threat to the legal order that is temporary and urgent in the double sense that it requires quick action and is of limited duration." ("One Law for War and Peace? Judicial Review and Emergency Powers between the Norm and the Exception," *Constellations* 2006, p. 523.)

8 Luban, "Liberalism, Torture and the Ticking Bomb," p. 47.

measures should be taken to respond to the emergency. In discussions of "Commissarial Dictatorship" in an earlier work, Schmitt had kept these two decisions separate. Indeed, one of the features of a commissarial dictatorship is the separation of these two decisions in terms of both different moments in time and who is deciding. In the Roman system, for instance, one body (the senate via the consuls) decides on the emergency and appoints a dictator, and it is the dictator who subsequently decides what measures must be taken to resolve the crisis. However, in *Political Theology* Schmitt's definition of sovereignty brings these two moments together as if they are one momentary decision: "Sovereign is he who decides on the exception ... He decides whether there is an extreme emergency as well as what must be done to eliminate it."[9] The idea that the sovereign "decides on the exception" collapses these two decisions into one, made by a single actor.[10]

Schmitt's time compression in his definition of sovereignty can be traced to the analogy he draws between the exception and the miracle. Schmitt writes, " All significant concepts of the modern theory of the state are secularized theological concepts ... The exception in jurisprudence is analogous to the miracle in theology."[11] The exception, like the miracle, take us out of normal time – the exception is a transformative moment. What Schmitt only hints at is the way in which the "miraculous" nature of the exception must be different for a regime officially dedicated to eliminating the exception as compared to a regime in which personalistic sovereignty is embraced.

The miraculous nature of the exception arises in what Schmitt describes as the seventeenth- to eighteenth-century analogy between the sovereign and God: "To the conception of God in the seventeenth and eighteenth centuries belongs the idea of his transcendence vis-à-vis the world, just as to that period's philosophy of state belongs the notion of the transcendence of the sovereign vis-à-vis the state."[12] Just as an omnipotent God performs miracles by suspending the laws of nature, the political sovereign suspends

9 Carl Schmitt, *Political Theology: Four Chapters on the Concept of Sovereignty* trans. by George Schwab (Chicago: University of Chicago Press, 2005), pp. 5, 7. See John McCormick, "The Dilemmas of Dictatorship: Carl Schmitt and Constitutional Emergency Powers," in *Law as Politics: Carl Schmitt's Critique of Liberalism*, Ed. by David Dyzenhaus (Durham NC: Duke University Press, 1998), p. 223.

10 See McCormick, "Dilemmas."

11 Schmitt, *Political Theology*, p. 36.

12 Schmitt, *Political Theology*, p. 49.

positive laws. The argument is one of analogies and transference: from theology to "the theory of the state."[13]

The miraculous nature of the exception changes, however, when Schmitt discusses the nature of the exception in a nineteenth- and twentieth-century political context, shaped by legal positivism, deism, and liberal rationalism. In such a political context, the sovereign has been "radically pushed aside," Schmitt writes, and "the machine now runs by itself."[14]

The miraculous nature of the sovereign exception is different at this point, I believe, because the concept of personalistic sovereignty has been discredited, along with the theology of theism that stood behind it. Schmitt subtly but significantly alters the miraculous nature of the exception for the secularizing time in which he writes: "In the exception," Schmitt writes, "the power of real life breaks through the crust of a mechanism that has become torpid by repetition."[15] The exception in its eighteenth-century form was the intervention of a sovereign to suspend regular law; the nineteenth-century exception, by contrast, involves the eruption of real life into the machine of the modern state, which has become nothing more than "a huge industrial plant."[16] The exception becomes here a form of redemption. The state of exception redeems a corrupt liberal constitutional political order that had grown "torpid by repetition."[17]

Despite these differences, the miraculous nature of the exception reinforces Schmitt's overall conception of political time. The sovereign decision on the exception is a moment of either transcendence or eruption. In contrast, normal legality is defined by *repetition* – the same thing happening over and over again.[18]

Schmitt's critique of "dilatory compromises" in his work *Constitutional Theory* provides a fuller picture of his conception of political time.[19] Dilatory compromises do not resolve a deep division in a polity; they involve, rather,

[13] Schmitt, *Political Theology*, p. 36.

[14] Schmitt, *Political Theology*, p. 48.

[15] Schmitt, *Political Theology*, p. 15.

[16] Schmitt, *Political Theology*, p. 65.

[17] On this point see McCormick, "Dilemmas," p. 225. This section repeats some of my analysis in "Schmitt, Locke and the Boundaries of Liberalism," *Konturen* 1 (2008), available at: http://konturen.uoregon.edu/vol1_Feldman.html.

[18] See John McCormick, "Irrational Choice and Mortal Combat as Political Destiny: The Essential Carl Schmitt," *American Review of Political Science* (2007), p. 320.

[19] Carl Schmitt, *Constitutional Theory*, trans. by Jeffrey Seitzer (Durham NC: Duke University Press, 2007).

deferring the necessary decisions that the constitution-making power needs to make. Sometimes, according to Schmitt, this occurs through vague language; sometimes it occurs through blatantly contradictory claims within a constitutional law. Schmitt is at his most perceptive here, and his readings of the specific compromises within the Weimar Constitution manifest the energy of an engaged critic. Nevertheless, his analysis seems foreshortened by the cramped temporal possibilities allowed by his concepts: decision *or* postponement of the decision – a moment of existential choosing or endless delay. Like Schmitt's critique of dilatory compromises, his contrast between the repetitions of bureaucratic legalism and the moment of miraculous decision eliminates the possibility of a more nuanced consideration of the temporal possibilities of prosaic politics. Like the dilatory, repetition speaks to the monotony of the same until the moment of transformation (the miraculous, the exceptional) breaks through.

The Spatialized Emergency Powers Debate

While necessity in Schmitt compresses time to a moment, breaking through the repetitions of the normal, its spatiality is more complex. Indeed, having compressed the time of the exception to one miraculous moment, Schmitt emphasizes spatial metaphors, declaring the exception "a borderline concept . . . pertaining to the outermost sphere."[20] He who "decides" at this limit is situated in a paradoxical space. Schmitt writes of the sovereign, "Although he stands outside the normally valid legal system, he nevertheless belongs to it, for it is he who must decide whether the constitution needs to be suspended in its entirety."[21] Schmitt's sovereign "stands outside" the legal order but nevertheless "belongs to it" – the sovereign is simultaneously inside and outside the legal, constitutional order.[22]

Some, such as Giorgio Agamben, have pursued the paradoxical nature of this spatial relationship and turned Schmitt's account in a *deconstructive* direction.[23] Others have followed Schmitt in the assumption that time

20 Schmitt, *Political Theology*, p. 5.

21 Schmitt, *Political Theology*, p. 7.

22 For a wonderful analysis of this paradoxical space, and its representation as a mobius strip, see Tracy McNulty, "The Gap in the Law and the Border-Breaching Functionof the Exception" *Konturen*, Vol. 1 (2008), available at: http://konturen.uoregon.edu/vol1_McNulty.html

23 See Giorgio Agamben, *Homo Sacer: Sovereign Power and Bare Life*, trans by Daniel Heller-Roazen (Stanford CA: Stanford University Press, 1998), chapter 1 and Giorgio Agamben, *State*

compression defines an emergency but have taken Schmitt's spatial metaphor ("outside but belonging to") and, in essence, fractured it into distinct and discrete positions. Where Schmitt's paradoxical formulation makes the sovereignty/law relationship undecidable in two ways (is the exception inside of law or outside of law; are there two regimes or one?), the current debate resolves the paradox into a collection of distinct models of emergency. But just as Schmitt emphasizes space over time, these models are defined and disputed via a spatial metaphor of law as a container.

The contemporary debate (as well as contemporary commentary on canonical theorists writing on emergency) often splits between those who see emergency, necessity, or the exception as existing outside of law and those who see emergency, necessity, or the exception as existing (or being capable of existing) inside of law. But the debate is more complicated than that. It actually breaks down into four approaches, when the legal/extra-legal dimension is bisected by the distinction between one regime and two regimes, as expressed in the following table.[24]

Regime as:	*Necessity as:*	
	"Inside" Law	"Outside" Law
Monist	Constitutional Authoritarianism "Legal" exception – necessity as a source of expansive legal interpretation. Inherent executive powers. (Yoo, Paulsen, Posner) Key *Enabling* Institution: Presidency	Legal Traditionalism Exception is expelled from law and rejected. Normal law is sufficient for exigencies. (Cole, Tribe, Schauer) Key *Constraining* Institution: Courts
Dualist	Institutional Reformism Neo-Roman republican – separate constitutional emergency regime. (Ackerman, Rossiter) Key *Enabling and Constraining* Institution: Legislatures	Normative Extra-legalism Neo-Lockean prerogative – separate emergency action but denied constitutional form. (Gross, Tushnet) Key *Constraining* Institutions: Legislatures/Publics

of Exception, trans. by Kevin Attell (Chicago: University of Chicago Press, 2005). For discussion of the Schmitt – Agamben relationship on this point see Scheuerman, "Survey Article," pp. 68–69.

24 This table synthesizes and elaborates upon the "maps" of the emergency powers debate presents by several participants. On the distinction between monism and dualism, see John

The spatial metaphor of law as a container and this mapping of distinct models of emergency make good sense of the current normative debate about necessity and the law. However, it runs into difficulties as participants in this debate struggle to identify whether an existing real-world emergency regime or canonical theory argument counts as legal or extra-legal. When is an argument one of constitutional necessity as opposed to extra-constitutional necessity? Oren Gross and Fionnuala Ní Aoláin, from the normative extra-legalist approach, struggle to place particular theorists and practitioners in the right box. They present five rival approaches to the issue of necessity's relationship to law. These five views divide between two "constitutional" approaches and three approaches "operating outside the constitutional sphere."[25] The two constitutional approaches are as follows:

1. Necessity as a source of law
2. Necessity as a "meta-rule of constitutional construction"

The three extra-constitutional approaches are as follows:

1. Necessity as political, rendering legal issues irrelevant
2. Necessity as suspending law but not creating new law
3. Necessity as excusing illegal conduct without rendering it legal *or* suspending law

So how do we know if an argument about necessity is constitutional or extra-constitutional? Gross and Aoláin's struggle to place theorists' models of emergency in the correct box (inside or outside law) is palpable in their reading of Lockean prerogative. They write, "This reading of Locke brings the theory of prerogative power closer to that model of accommodation ... which regards the principle of necessity as an independent source of constitutional law. However, it seems that a more consistent reading of Locke suggests that the prerogative power ought to be recognized for what

Ferejohn and Pasquale Pasquino, "The Law of the Exception: A Typology of Emergency Powers," *International Journal of Constitutional Law*, Vol. 2, No. 2 (2004). On the distinction between institutional reformers and extra-legalists, see William Scheuerman, "Survey Article: Emergency Powers and Rule of Law After 9/11," *The Journal of Political Philosophy*, Vol. 14, No. 1 (2006) and Andrew Arato, "Their Creative Thinking and Ours: Ackerman's *Emergency Constitution* After *Hamdan*," *Constellations* Vol. 13, No. 4 (2006), pp. 546–572

25 Oren Gross and Fionnuala Ní Aoláin, *Law in Times of Crisis: Emergency Powers in Theory and Practice* (Cambridge UK: Cambridge University Press, 2006), p. 47.

it is, namely an extra-constitutional and extra-legal power."[26] They are not alone; the secondary literature on Lockean prerogative is focused intently on the inside/outside problematic, with some interpretations emphasizing passages where Locke seems to place the power to act outside of particular laws but within a constitutional structure and other interpretations focusing on the places where Locke seems to posit prerogative as a "natural" and extra-constitutional power whose misuse can only be countered by popular rebellion.[27]

Another example – President Lincoln – presents a similar interpretive dilemma for the spatializing ambitions of participants in the emergency powers debate such as Gross and Aoláin. On the one hand they situate Lincoln as departing from an extra-legal model of prerogative embraced by Jefferson, embracing a theory of inherent constitutional powers. Gross and Aoláin write that, "Lincoln's wartime presidency ushered in a theory of crisis government based on the concept of inherent presidential powers," such that Lincoln may be viewed as the originator of an approach to "Constitutional necessity."[28] On the other hand, they acknowledge that "other possible readings of Lincoln's claims to such powers … bring his actions closer to the Extra-Legal Measures model."[29] The key to such an alternate reading lies in Lincoln's relation to Congress and his claim that acts of "public necessity" though not (necessarily) constitutional can be given subsequent congressional ratification. The sole difference between these positions seems to be whether "necessity … in and of itself, make[s] legal that which in other circumstances would have been illegal."[30] But the requirement of ex post ratification as opposed to assertions of constitutional inherent powers is a thin distinction on which to hang the

[26] Gross and Aoláin, *Law in Times of Crisis*, p. 122. On Lincoln, see pp. 128–129.

[27] See for instance: Ross J. Corbett, "The Extraconstitutionality of Lockean Prerogative," *The Review of Politics*, Vol. 68 (2006), Clement Fatovic, "Constitutionalism and Contingency: Locke's Theory of Prerogative," *History of Political Thought* Vol. 25, No. 2 [Summer 2004], Lee Ward, "Locke on Executive Power and Liberal Constitutionalism," *Canadian Journal of Political Science*, Vol. 38, No. 3 (September 2005), David Weaver, "Leadership, Locke and the Federalist," *American Journal of Political Science*, Vol. 41, No. 2 (April 1997), pp. 420–446, and Benjamin A. Kleinerman, "Can the Prince Really Be Tamed? Executive Prerogative, Popular Apathy, and the Constitutional Frame in Locke's Second Treatise," *American Political Science Review*, Vol. 101, No. 2 (May 2007), pp. 209–222.

[28] Gross and Aoláin, *Law in Times of Crisis*, p. 48.

[29] Gross and Aoláin, *Law in Times of Crisis*, p. 128.

[30] Gross and Aoláin, *Law in Times of Crisis*, p. 131.

difference between two supposedly distinct models of necessity – the constitutional and the extra-legal. (If anything, the distinction is actually between a monistic vision of constitutional necessity and a dualist vision of constitutional necessity.)

Empirical scholars of emergency powers give us reason to doubt whether such line drawing could ever succeed. As Kim Scheppele argues, "the practice of emergencies, like the theory and the law on the subject, also hovers between the legal and the extra-legal."[31] Interpretive indeterminacy (as in the Locke and Lincoln examples) may reflect, then, a more fundamental complexity. But "hovering" may not be quite the correct word as it implies a temporally static and fundamentally spatial relationship between emergency and law. What the spatial emphasis misses is the way in which the legal or extra-legal nature of necessity is shaped by the vicissitudes of political time. I turn to these in the next section.

Prerogative's Moment(s)

So let me focus on Locke now, as he has been so influential for the contemporary theoretical debate over emergency powers. Is Locke's prerogative constitutional or extra-constitutional? Where is the line between the legal and the extra-legal and on which side of the line does Lockean prerogative fall? The reason commentators keep returning to this inside/outside debate is because, I argue, they smuggle back into Locke Carl Schmitt's sovereign moment. Having compressed political time to the decision, they miss Locke's nuanced temporal-spatial dialectic. For most, the Schmittian assumptions are implicit, but Clement Fatovic makes the interpretation of prerogative as sovereignty's miraculous moment explicit. Fatovic extends Schmitt's argument about the seventeenth- to eighteenth-century exception-miracle analogy to the work of Locke, whom Schmitt himself had dismissed as evading the exception through a naïve liberal legalism. In this way, Fatovic brilliantly builds on Schmitt while also subverting his entire critique of liberalism. Fatovic rejects Schmitt's caricatured vision of rationalist liberalism and its deistic worldview: "Far from adhering dogmatically to some kind of debilitating deistic normativism that would impair

[31] Kim Scheppele, "Legal and Extra-Legal Emergencies," *Oxford Handbook of Law and Politics*, p. 174.

the ability to recognize the exception, liberalism sometimes lapses into a treacherous form of theistic decisionism that threatens its core moral and epistemological commitments."[32] In so doing, Fatovic sets up the choice starkly: Either Schmitt is correct in claiming Locke and the other varieties of rationalist liberal thought as seeking to banish the exception in a rule-governed universe *or* Locke's prerogative-wielding executive is, in fact, the equivalent of a miracle-producing sovereign dictator. And indeed, it is with the latter that Fatovic ends up: He writes, "Like an omnipresent being, the Lockean executive keeps a watchful and benevolent eye over the turbulent affairs of men in case his intervention is required."[33] While, as I will argue, this formulation more accurately links prerogative to priestly, pastoral power, Fatovic takes a more Schmittian line: "If prerogative is analogous to the miracle, then the executive who invokes prerogative is analogous to God, if only for a moment."[34] To the extent that prerogative is analogous to the miracle, Fatovic is surely right to emphasize the moment: The executive can only be sovereign in the moment of decision. But does this Schmittian reading make sense of Locke's overall depiction of prerogative power?

To be sure, Fatovic's reading of Locke's lurking sovereign moment is reinforced by Locke's discussion of other "exceptional moments" – not those of the deployment of extra-legal executive power but those of individuals confronted with existential threats in both the state of nature and civil society. For instance, Locke argues that a person *both in the state of nature and in civil society* is justified in killing a thief:

> Thus a *thief*, whom I cannot harm, but by appeal to the law, for having stolen all that I am worth, I may kill, when he sets on me to rob me but of my horse or coat; because the law, which was made for my preservation, where it cannot interpose to secure my life from present force, which, if lost, is capable of no reparation, permits me my own defence, and the right of war, a liberty to kill the aggressor, *because the aggressor allows not time to appeal to our common judge*, nor the decision of law, for remedy in a case where the mischief may be irreparable. (§19)

In civil society it is the *absence of time*, not the absence of a common power, that allows the person to take on such a sovereign, extra-legal power. And

[32] Clement Fatovic, "The Political Theology of Prerogative: The Jurisprudential Miracle in Liberal Constitutional Thought," *Perspectives on Politics* 6, 3 (September 2008), p. 491.

[33] Fatovic, "Political Theology of Prerogative," p. 492.

[34] Fatovic, "Political Theology of Prerogative," p. 488.

this is the same time compression that leads Locke to justify executive prerogative over and against the legislature in certain conditions. For instance, at the point in his chapter on prerogative power when Locke gives his most complete definition of it, he immediately follows that definition with a justification from time compression:

> This power to act according to discretion, for the public good, without the prescription of the law, and sometimes even against it, *is* that which is called *prerogative*: for since in some governments the law-making power is not always in being, and is usually too numerous, and so too slow, for the dispatch requisite to execution; and because also it is impossible to foresee, and so by laws provide for, all accidents and necessities that may concern the public . . .; therefore there is a latitude left to the executive power. (§160)

Nevertheless, other aspects of Locke's account of prerogative work against this reading of prerogative as miraculous sovereign decision. This is so because Locke, I argue, embeds prerogative in ongoing political time as opposed to understanding it as involving singular moments of eruption or transcendence. Locke situates his discussion of prerogative in terms of two different aspects of political time: time compression in a situation of public exigency and the flux of political events. The first is an argument in favor of prerogative (as discussed earlier). The second is both an argument in favor of prerogative *and* an argument about *what happens to* prerogative.

This is a line of thought about the vicissitudes of political and social development – in a word: *contingency*.[35] Locke justifies the prerogative power to engage in redistricting, fixing the "rotten boroughs" of legislatures by describing the "things of this world" as "in so constant a flux, that nothing remains long in the same state" (§157). "People, riches, trade, power, change their stations," Locke writes, "flourishing mighty cities come to ruin, and prove in times neglected desolate corners, whilst other unfrequented places grow into populous countries, filled with wealth and inhabitants" (§157). The changeability of things in the world requires a power that has the flexibility to respond in a way that more static and rigid legislation cannot. But Locke does not rest content with an account of political contingency as something to which prerogative responds.

[35] See Ian Zuckerman, "One Law."

Prerogative power is itself in a constant state of flux, because "god-like princes" governing faithfully with the public good in mind, succeed in enlarging the domain of prerogative as a result of the people's acceptance of such rule. At this point Locke notes the ironic possibilities of political development insofar as that "the reigns of *good* princes have been always most dangerous to the liberties of their people." This is so because a good prince may be followed by a "weak and ill prince" who claims extra-legal prerogative as a "prerogative belonging to him by right of his office" (§164). Locke goes on to describe this process in detail. The successors to good princes:

> managing the government with different thoughts, would draw the actions of those good rulers into precedent, and make them the standard of their *prerogative*, as if what had been done only for the good of the people was a right in them to do, for the harm of the people, if they so pleased; it has often occasioned contest, and sometimes public disorders, before the people could recover their original right, and get that to be declared not to be *prerogative*, which truly never was so. (§166)

Notice here how Locke embeds the legal-spatial dimension of prerogative (inside or outside the law) within the temporality of contingent political developments: Prerogative's place inside or outside basic law is not fixed – those misusers of prerogative claim as a right via precedent what their predecessors had done without legal justification. But the misuse of prerogative, occurring "inside" the law, also may trigger constitutional resistance, when the people "recover their original right." Tacit acceptance becomes constitutional resistance, when the vicissitudes of political development lead us from a "god-like prince" to a "weak and ill prince" (§§165, 164).[36]

Thus, while extra-legalists like Gross tend to reify the spatial, their inspiration – Locke – actually develops a more nuanced understanding of the temporal (and the spatial as a result). Locke describes a dynamic in which prerogative power is itself always up for political contestation. Indeed, its status – whether it is "inside" the constitution or "outside" the constitution is itself a matter of ongoing political dispute.

[36] For a detailed account of this way of understanding Lockean prerogative see Leonard C. Feldman, "Judging Necessity: Democracy and Extra-legalism," *Political Theory*, Vol. 36 No. 4 (August 2008), pp. 550–577.

Prerogative and Pastoral Power

If the time of prerogative is not simply a "moment" of decision for Locke but rather a process of ongoing claiming and contestation occurring at the boundary of law, it is also the case that the prince is not well understood as a god-like performer of miracles. Lockean prerogative is embedded in a political theology, but that political theology is better understood in terms of the convergence of certain practices and not in terms of conceptual analogies. Indeed the framing of prerogative in terms of the God-like ability to perform miracles leads to a misunderstanding of the actual religious nature of Lockean prerogative – a power that is articulated not in a normless void but within the framework of natural law *and* ongoing contestation via vigilant popular review. Given these two key structuring constraints on prerogative, Foucault is actually more helpful here than Schmitt in theorizing the broad contours of the religion/politics intersection that makes prerogative intelligible. His focus on ministering as a feature of liberalism that sits at the intersection of religion and politics brings the politics of emergency back down to earth.

In his lectures "Security, Territory, Population" of 1977–1978 Foucault traces modern governmentality (the practices, techniques, and forms of knowledge deployed to manage populations) to the Christian pastorate, to what he describes as the specific forms of pastoral power. Foucault defines governmentality most broadly as a "state of government which essentially bear on the population and calls upon and employs economic knowledge as an instrument... correspond[ing] to a society controlled by apparatuses of security."[37] The Christian pastorate is, Foucault declares, "the prelude to what I have called governmentality."[38] While these lectures are more exploratory and suggestive than Foucault's books, they provoke an interesting way into thinking about the "political theology" of liberalism and prerogative power within a liberal order. This despite the fact that liberalism is not explicitly thematized here, as Foucault concentrates mostly on preliberal political rationalities preparing the way for his focus on liberalism and neoliberalism in the 1979 course on Biopolitics. As Golder argues, Foucault is describing the religious origins not of a philosophic concept but

[37] Michel Foucault, *Security, Territory, Population: Lectures at the College De France 1977–1978* (New York, Palgrave Macmillan, 2007), p. 110.

[38] Foucault, *Security*, p. 184.

of the "material practices of government," exposing "the pastoral logic of our purportedly secular political rationality."[39] Foucault asserts:

> [I]f there really is a relationship between religion and politics in modern Western societies, it may be that the essential aspect of this relationship is not found in the interplay between Church and state, but rather between the pastorate and government. In other words, in modern Europe at least, the fundamental problem is undoubtedly not the Pope and the Emperor, but rather that mixed figure, or the two figures who in our language... share one and the same name of minister. The minister, with all the ambiguity of this word, is perhaps the real problem and where the relationship between religion and politics, between government and the pastorate, is really situated.[40]

Contra Schmitt's account of the religion/politics relationship in the West, Foucault's version does not rely upon the idea of analogy between a religious category and a political one. Foucault, by contrast, emphasizes "that mixed figure" – the minister – who sits at the intersection of religion and politics. In other words, it is not so much that the sovereign is analogous to God, but rather, that sovereignty is infused with something other than sovereignty. This occurs as a consequence of the "transition from the pastoral of souls to the political government of men." Christian pastoral power involves ongoing care, surveillance and mutual responsibility. "The Christian pastorate," Foucault asserts, "is also absolutely innovative in establishing a structure, a technique of, at once, power, investigation, self-examination and the examination of others." Pastoral power also provokes resistance, what Foucault calls "counter-conduct": "Just as there have been forms of resistance to power as the exercise of political sovereignty,... have there not been forms of resistance to power as conducting?"[41]

By situating pastoral power at the root of governmentality, and, significantly, reason of state, Foucault also directs attention to a particular kind of *ethos* animating state power. As the pastoral inflects state power – sovereign power – in the sixteenth century, sovereignty becomes something more than an absolute power with no juridical limits. But Foucault's story is a bit ambiguous because while, on the one hand, he links the art of governing

39 Ben Golder, "Foucault and the Genealogy of Pastoral Power," *Radical Philosophy Review*, Vol. 10, No. 2 (2007), pp. 173, 176.

40 Foucault, *Security*, p. 192.

41 Foucault, *Security*, pp. 183, 195, 228.

back to the pastoral, he also describes a break in the seventeenth century when the art of governing comes into its own, distinct from both God's rule over nature and the pastor's guidance of his flock:

> The sovereign is required to do more than purely and simply exercise his sovereignty, and in doing more than exercise sovereignty he is called upon for something other than God's acton in relation to nature, the pastor's in relation to his flock, the father's in relation to his children, or the shepherd in relation to his sheep. In short, in relation to his sovereignty, and in relation to the pastorate, something more is demanded from him, something different, something else. This is government."[42]

The sovereign does not just rule, he also governs. From this an important consequence follows, I believe: At the formal level, because sovereignty occurs, as Schmitt reminds us, in a lawless void, it is also a normless void. By adding the dimension of history and concrete practices, Foucault reminds us that lawless sovereignty is shaped by something else – the norms and logics of governmentality as well as the pressure of resistant practices. Certain dilemmas and textual difficulties in Locke's account of prerogative can be usefully viewed through the lens of pastoral power. This is a power that appears to have no legal or constitutional basis – it is a natural power – but for Locke it is limited by a norm that can roughly be described as "community caretaking." Locke's prerogative wielding prince does not perform miracles. Fixing "rotten boroughs," tearing down a house when the neighbor's house is on fire, exercising the power of the pardon, the prince *governs*. What Locke is describing in his discussion of princely prerogative is neither a legally authorized and legally constrained office nor a normless void of sovereign exceptionalism but rather the emergence of governance as a particular set of practices, knowledge, and values.

This way of situating liberal prerogative's political theology may, of course, seem to have the effect of ennobling lawless power. But I do not think that is a necessary consequence of a more nuanced and historically grounded analysis of the norms and logics of liberal prerogative. Rather, this approach helps us to flesh out the moral and discursive terrain upon which prerogative and its contestation take place.

[42] Foucault, *Security*, p. 237.

Police Emergency and the Legal Rhetoric of Necessity

The politics of emergency in liberal democracies is much messier that the picture of "neo-sovereignty" and its miraculous (or redemptive) decisions; the politics of emergency is embedded in ongoing political struggle, infused with pastoral notions of rule, and linked less to sovereignty than to governmental interventions upon the population.[43] The pastoral dimension of emergency becomes clearer when we look at my first contemporary example – the doctrine of police emergency.

Even here, we see the influence of Schmitt, as even prosaic policing has been framed by theorists within the language of sovereignty by those who focus on a moment of decision. Giorgio Agamben, diagnosing the current U.S.-dominated international order as one governed by a "sovereign police,"[44] argues that the sovereign police on the international stage express the buried logic of sovereignty and the exception at work in regular policing itself: "If the sovereign, in fact, is the one who marks the point of indistinction between violence and right by proclaiming the state of exception and suspending the validity of the law, the police are always operating within a similar state of exception."[45] So Agamben does not seek to distinguish sovereign exceptionalism from more run-of-the-mill police emergencies. For Agamben, they reveal the same state of exception.[46]

Popular representations of the police frequently reinforce (and ennoble) the "sovereign police." The Museum of Crime and Punishment in Washington, D.C. displays this police sovereignty as a spectacle. A wall poster titled "Submission" in an exhibit filled with fetish objects – handcuffs,

[43] This is what Judith Butler has described as sovereignty occurring on the terrain of governmentality. (Judith Butler, *Precarious Life* [London: Verso, 2004], p. 61.)

[44] Giorgio Agamben, *Means Without End: Notes on Politics*, translated by Vincenzo Binetti and Cesare Casarino (Minneapolis: University of Minnesota Press, 2000). Agamben, writing at the time of the first Gulf War, was surely quite prescient here. The logic of militarized humanitarianism appears to be one of international policing, partially converting the enemy into a criminal – the enemy is no longer the respected adversary in a Westphalian system nor is he the domestic criminal covered by domestic legal protections. The confused category "unlawful enemy combatant" expresses the nature of this state of exception perfectly.

[45] Agamben, *Means Without End*, p. 103.

[46] In other places, Schmitt follows this path as well. For instance, Schmitt writes of the traces of sovereignty in the modern bureaucratic state. As McCormick writes, "Liberal denials notwithstanding, every concrete decision, whether exercised by a magistrate, police officer, social worker, judge, or the president himself according to Schmitt, entails a moment of discretion that cannot be justified rationally or derived directly from the legal order." (McCormick, "Irrational Choice and Mortal Combat," p. 318).

leather restraints, weapons ranging from billy clubs to tasers to guns. "Larger batons," the exhibit helpfully informs, "are used exclusively in large civil disturbances." The poster describes the sovereign judgment of the police in dangerous circumstances:

> When they are met with resistance, the police have to make a decision about how much force is required to control the situation, from an angry and irrational individual, to a mob armed with weapons.

The dominant atmosphere is sadism energized by sensory overload, encouraging identification with police violence (on one wall poster "you have them subdued, how do you keep them in custody?"). Affirming such a state of exception, rights have little place in the exhibit; a brief discussion of the Miranda ruling gets delegitimated through the concluding information that Miranda was later killed and his murderer let go because his killer invoked his own Miranda rights.[47] (The exhibit does not discuss the myriad ways police weaken or avoid the Miranda warning.)

Agamben's description of the "sovereign police" extends Schmitt's definition of sovereignty and the state of exception downward, to the micro-levels of discretionary decision making in police–citizen encounters. And, to be sure, there is some support for such an extension within Schmitt's own writings, when he describes the traces of sovereignty that remain, even in a legalistic system that seeks to deny the exception. Schmitt writes of the peculiar identity of the state: "There always exists the same inexplicable identity: lawgiver, executive power, police, pardoner, welfare institution ... The state acts in many disguises but always as the same invisible person."[48]

[47] This perfect pseudo-museum for neoliberal times (private, for-profit, authoritarian) encourages its subjects to make a wide-range of identifications. The exhibit begins with a peculiar interpellation: the audience member as *potential* criminal who has to make the right cost/benefit calculation to stay on the right side of the law. "Make the right choices" the voice intones around a montage of criminal justice images on flat screen TVs, "if you think you can beat the law, think again ... Is what you plan to do worth a month, a year, or the rest of your life behind bars?" From this initial point, the exhibit invites its subjects to project themselves into a variety of positions: romantic identification with the criminal (as in the exhibit on dashing bank robbers and mobsters in American history); masochistic identification with him after his arrest (including a prison cell converted to an amusement ride-style escape tunnel); sadistic identification with police officers. But the exhibit ends with a final interpellation: the museum-going subject as potential crime victim. "Don't be a victim" the last room implores, with a list of security-focused precautions.

[48] Schmitt, *Political Theology*, p. 38.

But of course the police in constitutional democracies are not quite as sovereign as Agamben or the museum suggest. Laws and bureaucratic procedures hedge in the exercise of police discretion, and nowhere is this clearer than in the limits on police searches of, and intrusions into, private spaces. Everyone knows to ask the question, "do you have a search warrant?" just as they know the text of the Miranda warning – such rights consciousness is part of the "national culture," as Justice Rehnquist noted in *Dickerson v. U.S.* (2000). This form of legal consciousness is significant both in itself and for what it means for the everyday negotiation of rights claiming in official/citizen interactions. But it is naïve to assume the existence of durable limits on police discretion simply because a particular narrative of the fourth amendment's limit on unreasonable searches and seizures has circulated so broadly within popular culture. Despite this legal consciousness various kinds of judicially approved and unapproved police searches are regularly tolerated (street corner pat downs, breathalyzer tests, airport security, invasive border inspections), and the police are adept at working around legal limitations. If the police and other officers of the state are not quite as hedged in as popular legal consciousness might indicate, nor are they quite the sovereigns operating in an anomic state of exception as Agamben would have it.

This means that rights are neither absolute trumps of sovereign power nor meaningless abstractions in the concrete experience of a "state of exception." As John Parry argues, rights need to be understood within the framework of administrative governance: "Rather than trumps against government action, rights are factors considered in the formation of policing policy and the execution of that policy."[49]

This way of thinking about rights has implications for how we think about emergency, necessity and the general issue of legal exceptions. When rights become more messily entangled in ongoing governance and policy, so too does the category of necessity. The doctrine of police emergency serves as an illustration of the complex legal space of necessity – a space that does not easily reduce to either "inside" or "outside" the law – and an illustration of the complex position of police policy vis-à-vis the law. In the doctrine of police emergency, the suspension of constitutional guarantees (against

[49] John T. Parry, "Rights and Discretion in Criminal Procedure's 'War on Terror'," *Ohio State Journal of Criminal Law* 6 (2008), p. 331.

unreasonable searches and seizures) is not accomplished by the police becoming sovereign agents and going "outside the law". Rather, the doctrine enables a shift between different kinds of law – between the criminal law police function of law enforcement and the civil law function of what the Supreme Court calls "community caretaking."

The Fourth Amendment to the U.S. Constitution prohibits in its first clause "unreasonable searches and seizures" and in its second clause requires "probably cause" for the issuance of a search warrant. The standard of reasonableness and the standard of probable cause are not identical – some warrantless searches or seizures, for instance, turn out to be reasonable, and indeed it is through the language of emergency and necessity that reasonableness comes to be redefined.

In Fourth Amendment jurisprudence, the emergency exception to warrant requirements is closely connected to a notion of the police's "community caretaking" (as opposed to law enforcement) function. A police emergency usually refers to an immediate danger to life (or perhaps property) in which case the police may be justified in entering a private space without a warrant. This police emergency implicates the police in their common law authorized function of community caretaking. In *Cady v. Dombrowski*, Justice Rehnquist writes for the majority:

> Local police officers, unlike federal officers, frequently investigate vehicle accidents in which there is no claim of criminal liability and engage in what, for want of a better term, may be described as community caretaking functions, totally divorced from the detection, investigation, or acquisition of evidence relating to the violation of a criminal statute.[50]

A search of an automobile's trunk without a warrant was reasonable, because it occurred according to the court as part of this caretaking function: "concern for the safety of the general public who might be endangered if an intruder removed a revolver from the trunk of the vehicle."[51]

We might then usefully view the police action in its caretaking function as a delegated version of "princely" prerogative power in a liberal order – discretionary power outside of law exercised for the good of the community.[52]

[50] *Cady v. Dombrowski* 37 L. Ed. 2d 706, p. 715.

[51] *Cady v. Dombrowski* 37 L. Ed. 2d 706, p. 718.

[52] See Kathleen Arnold, "Domestic War," *Polity*, Vol. 39, No. 1 (January 2007), p. 9.

Nevertheless, this police power is not sovereignty but discretionary power oriented toward a vague but nevertheless significant notion of the public good and hedged in (imperfectly) by legal constraints.

This case serves as a prosaic example of the more complex spatiality of law – it is not simply a question of "inside" versus "outside" the law, nor is it a question of one law for normal times and another law for emergencies. Rather, emergency shifts the police into the domain of civil law community care-taking, where fourth amendment protections do not apply. This emergency implicates the police in their common law authorized function of community caretaking. But emergency, or its related – though some suggest analytically distinct[53] – category of exigent circumstances, may refer to an immediate danger of a loss of evidence in a criminal case, in which case it is the police in their law enforcement role that are justified in a warrantless entry.[54] This exigent circumstances exception is usually kept distinct from the doctrine of police emergency, but it follows a similar logic – urgency demands a warrantless intrusion of a protected private space. The difference is that an exigent circumstances intrusion is an exception used by the police in their criminal law enforcement capacity not their community caretaking capacity. Thus two kinds of exceptions to the Fourth Amendment are cognized by courts under the category of police emergency – one does not so much suspend law as it does make civil (as opposed to criminal) law applicable: the police as community caretakers are then justified in engaging in what Bacigal calls an "emergency intrusion" to protect endangered life. The second kind of exception suspends law in the name of enforcing law: police as law enforcers must suspend Fourth Amendment protections to gain evidence that is at risk of being lost what Bacigal calls an "emergency search" or "intrusion for criminal investigation."[55]

The line between caretaking and law enforcement, between the civil and the criminal, is both established *and undermined* by the doctrine of

[53] John F. Decker writes that "exigent circumstances" should "be understood to cover only those situations where the police take warrantless action due to their reasonable belief that there exists a serious potential for the destruction of evidence of a crime should they take the time to procure a warrant." ("Emergency Circumstances, Police Responses, and Fourth Amendment Restrictions," *The Journal of Criminal Law and Criminology*, Vol. 89, No. 2 (Winter 1999), p. 444).

[54] Ronald J. Bacigal, "The Emergency Exception to the Fourth Amendment," *University of Richmond Law Review* 9 (1975).

[55] Bacigal, "Emergency Exception," p. 254.

police emergency. The facts of the case in *Cady v. Dumbrowski* are a prime example of the blurred boundary between the civil and the criminal. A warrantless search is justified by appeal to the community caretaking (civil) function of policing, but such a search subsequently results in the gathering of evidence that is used in a criminal prosecution.[56] Other cases follow this pattern: Police enter a home without a warrant as a result of a report of a drug overdose. While searching the person's body for identification, the police discover illegal drugs. Key to upholding such a search as reasonable is a court's finding that "the officer was not investigating criminal conduct under the pretext of exercising his community caretaking function."[57] Indeed while police emergency is articulated as a doctrine fairly consistently in relation to community-caretaking (civil) functions such as police response to a person in need of medical attention, a fire, or other current dangers to public safety, courts only have the opportunity to articulate such doctrine as a result of subsequent criminal law enforcement action, such as seizure of evidence of a crime that occurred subsequent to community-caretaking activity.

Another constitutional exception in the context of community-caretaking is worth noting. Related to the doctrine of police emergency is fourth amendment jurisprudence concerning reasonable use of force by police in circumstances of emergency or necessity. *Scott v. Harris*[58] concerns a high

[56] The blurring of the boundary between the community caretaking and law enforcement functions of police is consistent with the blurring of the boundary between the civil and the criminal in the application of new trespass laws. In another attempt to reduce fourth amendment protections, municipalities have passed "trespass exclusion" ordinances, which enable both private landowners and public authorities to banish people from wide areas of a city for periods as long as a year. In addition, these exclusion orders allow police officers to search people once they are found in violation of a previous order. Beckett and Herbert cite one former police officer who speaks enthusiastically about the utility of a trespass admonishment: "[It] gives you a year, worth of, you know, being able to shake 'em, and pat 'em down ... I mean, technically, they've trespassed, once you stop them, they can be under arrest ... So every time I stop someone who's been trespassed, then I can completely search them." These ordinances blur the boundary between the criminal and the civil because, while they are defined as civil, they authorize the police to arrest people who have violated the order to stay out of a particular area. As Beckett and Herbert write, "these exclusions are defined as civil in nature, a construction that alleviates the authorities from an obligation to guarantee due process to those excluded." In both the case of the ambiguity of the category of police emergency and in the application of trespass laws, the blurring of the boundary between the civil and the criminal works to suspend the fourth amendment. (Katherine Beckett and Steve Herbert, "Dealing With Disorder: Social Control in the Post-Industrial City," *Theoretical Criminology*, Vol. 12, No. 1 [2008], p. 11.)

[57] Decker, "Emergency Circumstances," p. 460.

[58] 127 S. Ct 1769 (2007).

speed chase in which a police officer, Scott, rammed a fleeing suspect's automobile, rendering Harris a paraplegic. Here, rather than the issue of a "reasonable search" it is an issue of a "reasonable seizure" and more specifically the use of deadly force to apprehend a fleeing subject (which in constitutional terms constitutes a "seizure"). Once again, circumstances of emergency directly shape what counts as reasonable. It is the danger posed to the public of a vehicle careening wildly down a two-lane highway that justifies extraordinary measures. Thus we might say that the police act as community-caretakers when they use deadly force to effect their seizure.

The complexity of the relationship between the public safety and criminal law functions of policing is evident here as it is in the case of judicial review of police emergency searches. What is different in this case, as opposed to the police emergency case of emergency intrusion and search, is that the Supreme Court does not subordinate the categories of criminal law in justifying emergency seizure. To the contrary, the court makes *culpability* central to the analysis of emergency ethics. Writing for the majority, Justice Scalia first describes a weighing of competing risks:

> Scott defends his actions by pointing to the paramount governmental interest in ensuring public safety, ... [I]n judging whether Scott's actions were reasonable, we must consider the risk of bodily harm that Scott's actions posed to respondent in light of the threat to the public that Scott was trying to eliminate. Although there is no obvious way to quantify the risks on either side, it is clear from the videotape that respondent posed an actual and imminent threat to the lives of any pedestrian who might have been present, to other civilian motorists... It is equally clear that Scott's actions posed a high likelihood of serious injury or death to respondent...[59]

But risk analysis, and the probabilistic-consequentialist mode of reasoning it invites is insufficient; It receives from Scalia a peculiar inflection from criminal law and traditional morality at this point:

> So how does a court go about weighing the perhaps lesser probability of injuring or killing numerous bystanders against the perhaps larger probability of injuring or killing a single person? We think it appropriate in this process to take into account not only the number of lives at risk, but also their relative culpability. It was respondent, after all,

[59] *Scott v. Harris* 127 S. Ct 1769 (2007), p. 1778.

> who intentionally placed himself and the public in danger by unlawfully engaging in the reckless flight that ultimate produced the choice between two evils that Scott confronted.[60]

By framing this as a choice of evils (the need to choose "the lesser evil"), the Court, as Parry notes, adopts the logic of necessity:

> the Court expressly linked its analysis to 'the choice between two evils,' which is the language of the necessity defense, in which otherwise illegal conduct is justified if it will avoid a greater harm. That is to say, Officer Scott's conduct was consistent with the Constitution, in part because it was necessary. Necessity in this context is not simply a defense. Rather the idea of necessity in a case like *Scott* uses notions of emergency or extremity to create or insulate state power and declare it reasonable, where it would be unauthorized and unreasonable in normal circumstances.[61]

Furthermore, the court adopts the logic of necessity but refuses the purely social-welfare logic usually involved, and opts for a choice of evils framework that is resolved by the categories of criminal guilt and innocence. Reasonableness comes to hinge upon numbers *and* culpability. This moralized consequentialism (in which the unresolvable arithmetic of risks and numbers is resolved by predetermined categories of innocence and guilt) is also a departure from prior tests of reasonableness the Supreme Court had embraced. For instance in the case of *Graham v. Connor*, the Court, to determine the constitutionality of police use of force, raised a more complex but also specific set of questions concerning the severity of the crime, the immediacy of the threat, and the distinction between fleeing arrest and resisting arrest.[62] By contrast, *Scott* presents a choice of evils framework familiar from the ticking-bomb hypothetical: a utilitarian calculus of numbers of lives at risk, salted by the assumed guilt of the recipient of discretionary state violence.

I want to suggest that it is not only that this "prosaic politics of emergency" can shed light on the more dramatic politics of emergency in a national security state conducting a "War on Terror." The relationship between

60 *Scott v. Harris*, p. 1778.

61 John T. Parry, "Rights and Discretion in Criminal Procedure's 'War on Terror'," *Ohio State Journal of Criminal Law* 6 (2008), p. 326.

62 See Rachel A. Harmon, "When is Police Violence Justified?" *Northwestern University Law Review*, Vol. 102, No. 3 (2008), p. 18.

these court cases dealing with police discretion in the context of "prosaic emergency" and the state's assertion of extraordinary powers in a declared national emergency involves multiple lines of influence: On the one hand, the broader politics of emergency post 9/11 shapes the everyday politics of police emergency, as Parry has persuasively argued.[63] On the other hand, the more dramatic assertions of supposed sovereign exceptionalism feed off of everyday emergency. In this regard one of the Office of Legal Counsel memos by Bush Administration lawyer John Yoo recently released by the Obama Administration is significant as it targets fourth amendment limits on search and seizure as well.

The October 23, 2001 opinion supports domestic counter-terrorism efforts by the military. The logic is one of necessity, here framed in the dubious terms of "self-defense." Yoo's overall contention is that "the Chief Executive is inherently vested with broad discretion to employ military force both domestically and abroad when necessary to safeguard the public welfare..."[64] War and "national emergency" are fused together in the memo in order to render the distinction between foreign and domestic executive power irrelevant. Yoo perfectly dramatizes Kathleen Arnold's point about the fusing of discretionary power in foreign affairs and "domestic wars" in a liberal prerogative state, signaling what Arnold describes as "a new reason of state embodying the welfare of the people and operating both domestically and externally." [65]

Engaging specific constitutional and legislative issues, Yoo argues that the Posse Comitatus act does not apply, because it only bars the military from engaging in domestic law enforcement activity: "Because using military force to combat terrorist acts would be for the purpose of protecting the nation's security, rather than executing the laws, domestic deployment in the current situation would not violate the PCA."[66] This stunning argument

63 Parry, "Rights and Discretion."

64 John Yoo, "Memorandum for Alberto R. Gonzales Re: Authority for Use of Military Force to Combat Terrorist Activities *Within the United States*" October 23, 2001, p. 12. Available at: http://www.usdoj.gov/olc/docs/memomilitaryforcecombatus10232001.pdf

65 Arnold, "Domestic War," p. 19. Neocleous makes a similar point about liberal prerogative in Locke and since: "In a move we will see become one of the most common tropes of security politics, the distinction between external and internal affairs is obliterated and the Executive is given the power to act according to discretion in 'emergency situation' and on the grounds of security, without the prescription of law and sometimes against law." (*Critique of Security*, p. 17).

66 Yoo, "Memorandum," p. 17.

would have the result of placing no limits on domestic deployment of the military, given the elastic nature of national security. But it resonates with the distinction in Fourth Amendment jurisprudence distinguishing between law enforcement and community care-taking functions of the police themselves.

As far as what the military deployed domestically might actually be able to do, Yoo cites some of the cases establishing exceptions to the warrant requirement (but curiously neglects to cite both the police emergency exception and the border search exception). This discussion of prosaic exceptions to the Fourth Amendment warrant requirement serves less to make an argument as it does to loosen the hold of Constitutional norms on the reader's mind, prefatory to a much more sweeping claim: "However well suited the warrant and probable cause requirements may be as applied to criminal investigations or to other law enforcement activities, they are unsuited to the demands of wartime and the military necessity to successfully prosecute a war against an enemy."[67] Although he seeks to establish that the fourth amendment *does not apply* to the domestic military operations he supports, *even if it does apply* exceptions internal to its application by the courts can achieve a similar objective.

And so Yoo returns to the prosaic politics of the fourth amendment one more time, noting that warrantless searches are often declared reasonable "even in the context of ordinary law enforcement by the police".[68] Reasonableness is, after all, shaped by emergency and the requirement of a warrant may be suspended while the Fourth Amendment still applies: "In light of the extraordinary emergency created by the September 11 [sic], and taking account also of the compelling need military commanders would no doubt have to act swiftly in particular exigent circumstances, we think that the courts – if they applied the Fourth Amendment at all – would find the challenged military conduct was 'reasonable'."[69] (Yoo concludes with the same bizarre self-defense argument he used in the infamous August 1, 2002 "torture memo".) In the same memo, then, Yoo both asserts an "external" conception of necessity – Constitutional provisions do not apply to the military operating domestically as the military operates domestically in a state of exception – and an "internal" conception – the prosaic politics of necessity

[67] Yoo, "Memorandum," p. 24.
[68] Yoo, "Memorandum," p. 35.
[69] Yoo, "Memorandum," p. 35.

provides the exception as courts apply the fourth amendment standard of reasonableness.

Conclusion

As the debates between rule of law absolutists, extra-legalists like Gross, constitutional authoritarians like Yoo, and neo-Roman reformers like Ackerman make clear, the ongoingness of emergency powers debates constantly exceeds one reified model of the insides and outsides of law. The temporal processes of politics do not simply occur "within" a particular model, but also produce such models as the provisional outcomes of agonal conflict. Necessity becomes constitutional when it is embraced by quiescent public and official institutions who claim a right of necessity; it migrates to the domain of the extra-constitutional when the pressure of resistant publics and institutions effectively marginalizes certain arguments and actions.

In a funny way the most famous of theorists of "the sovereign exception" reminds us of the everyday politics of the emergency when, in *Political Theology*, Schmitt writes, "not every extraordinary measure, not every police emergency or emergency decree, is necessarily an exception. What characterizes an exception is principally unlimited authority, which means the suspension of the entire existing order."[70] Such a distinction has largely been forgotten in the rhetorical inflation of emergency measures to "exceptional" levels – a rhetorical inflation that attempts to redeploy Schmitt's account of sovereignty in a left-critical direction. But perhaps the best thing we can take from Schmitt is not his famous definition of sovereignty centering on that "miraculous" moment of decision but rather his acknowledgment that not all emergencies implicate or call forth the kind of unitary, executive sovereignty he admires.[71] In other words, we ought to insist anew

[70] Schmitt, *Political Theology*, p. 12.

[71] We might also find other surprising resources in Schmitt's *Constitutional Theory*. As opposed to his rather unhelpful opposition between the "dilatory" postponement and the momentary decision, we might turn to his more nuanced and suggestive analysis of the different ways in which the people relate to the constitution: "prior to," "inside," and "next to." Here Schmitt does not articulate a spatial paradox as he does with his discussion of sovereignty in relation to law in *Political Theology* (outside, but belonging to). Rather he describes a complex series of relationships that involve both the temporal (the people as prior to the constitution, the people as constituent power), the spatial (the people as inside the constitution, as a constituted power), and a complex admixture of the two (the people as "alongside" or "compared with" the constitution – a relationship that implies the ongoingness of political time and a spatial complexity that defies any simple inside/outside formulation).

on this distinction, from the reverse perspective. Rather than, like Schmitt, insisting on the difference between a true state of exception and "lesser" emergencies in order to establish the redemptive and generative power of a state of exception, we would instead insist on the difference as a way to gain better insight into the prosaic (and perhaps more insidious) politics of emergency in the life of constitutional democracies.

Comment on Chapter 3

Emergencies, Body Parts and Price Gouging

J. Shahar Dillbary*

I. Introduction

The study of emergency has received much attention from political theorists such as Carl Schmitt, Michel Foucault, and Giorgio Agambden. Relying on the realms of philosophy, theology, and morality, these scholars and their contemporary counterparts have focused on whether acts of the sovereign in times of emergency lie "inside" the law (i.e., whether they are subject to scrutiny) or "outside" the law.[1] Many of those who place states' actions in emergencies outside the law, like Schmitt, analogize the power of the sovereign to the miracle in theology. "Just as an omnipotent God performs miracles by suspending the laws of nature," the argument goes, "the political sovereign suspends positive law."[2] Some analogize "legal exceptions" in times of emergency to another religious concept: the Christian pastorate. Foucault, for example, compares the sovereign's function to

* Assistant Professor, University of Alabama School of Law. B.A in Law, Bar-Ilan University, LL.B. in Economics Bar-Ilan University, LL.M. University of Chicago School of Law, J.S.D University of Chicago School of Law. This article is part of the *Sovereignty, Legality, Emergency Symposium* that took place on October 2008 at the University of Alabama School of Law.

1 Leonard Feldman, "The Banality of Emergency," published in this issue at pp. 136–164.

2 Feldman, "The Banality of Emergency," *supra* note 1 at pp. 136–164 (discussing the Schmittian approach). *See also* Clement Fatovic, "The Political Theology of Prerogative: The Jurisprudential Miracle in Liberal Constitutional Thought," *Perspectives on Politics*, Vol. 6, No. 3 (2008), p. 488. ("If prerogative is analogous to the miracle, then the executive who invokes prerogative is analogous to God, if only for a moment.") The theistic discourse can be traced back to Carl Schmitt's famous argument that "all significant concepts of the modern theory of the state are secularized theological concepts." Carl Schmitt, *Political Theology* (Chicago: University of Chicago Press, 1985), p. 38 (translated by George Schwab).

a relation between "the pastor [and] his flock."[3] Others support a middle ground. They propose the adoption of a separate body of law that would deal with emergencies.[4] Under the latter's proposal, once a declaration of emergency has been issued, this unique body of law would provide the executive with special authorities that would trump "normal law." Proponents of this approach place emergencies "outside" of "normal law" but still inside the legal framework.

This article, however, takes a different approach. Rather than resorting to theology or philosophy, it relies on the study of economics to analyze two types of emergencies. I refer to the first type of emergency as "public emergencies." Public emergencies require the sovereign to modify or suspend the entire existing order.[5] Natural disasters such as hurricanes and earthquakes as well as man-made accidents or acts of terror are but a few examples. "Private emergencies", on the other hand, do not impact the entire population. They are more limited or, as the name suggests, "private" in nature. Examples include a sailor mooring her boat to another's dock due to extreme weather,[6] or a patient in need of an organ transplant.[7] These

[3] Michel Foucault, *Security, Territory, Population: Lectures at the College De France 1977–1978* (New York: Palgrave Macmillan, 2007), pp. 192, 233. Professor Feldman describes this power as "natural" but one which is limited to "community caretaking." *Id.* at *supra* note 1, at pp. 136–164.

[4] *See, e.g.*, Bruce Ackerman, *Before the Next Attack* (New Haven: Yale University Press, 2006), pp. 47–49.

[5] This definition follows Carl Schmitt's definition of an emergency: "what characterizes an exception is principally unlimited authority, which means the suspension of the entire existing order." Carl Schmitt, *Political Theology* (Chicago: University of Chicago Press, 1985), p. 12 (translated by George Schwab).

[6] *See, e.g.*, *Ploof v. Putnam*, 81 Vt. 471 (1908).

[7] Compare *Strunk v. Strunk*, 445 S.W.2d 145 (1969), *McFall v. Shimp*, 1978 Pa. Dist. & Cnty. Dec. LEXIS 70 (Pa. C.P. 1978). Organ transplants in the United States are highly regulated. The National Organ Transplant Act of 1984 (NOTA) was promulgated in response to the shortage of donated organs. NOTA established the Organ Procurement and Transplant Network, a unified, transparent network overseeing organ transplants in the United States. Under section 274e of the NOTA it is "unlawful for any person to knowingly acquire, receive, or otherwise transfer any human organ for valuable consideration for use in human transplantation if the transfer affects interstate commerce." 42 USCS § 274e. "Valuable consideration" does not include reasonable payments associated with the procurement and implantation and other related expenses (such as travel, housing, and lost wages) incurred by the donor in connection with the donation. *Id.* At the state level, virtually every jurisdiction has adopted the Uniform Anatomical Gift Act (UAGA) of 1968. *See* http://www.nccusl.org/Update/ActSearchResults.aspx (last visited October 12, 2009). The UAGA was revised in 1987 and once again in 2006 (the latter version has been adopted by 39 states). In its current version, the UAGA is limited to donations from deceased donors as a result of gifts made before or after their deaths.

are clearly life-threatening situations. The sailor would surely die if denied access to the dock, and so would the patient absent the organ transplant. Albeit private, the state is often involved in such emergencies. A state may have the right to directly deprive (or "take") someone's property, limb, or life under its police authority; or it can authorize one individual to "take" from another. In the examples above, the state (via its courts or legislation) must decide whether the dock owner can exercise its property right to stop the sailor from mooring her boat and under what conditions, if any, one can coerce another to "give" her limb.

A preliminary question that comes immediately to mind is whether economic analysis should answer these questions at all; or whether matters of life and death should be analyzed through the prism of theology, philosophy, or morality only. What if economic analysis and deontological considerations lead to different directions? After all, economic analysis of the law has been often accused of being revolting in a moral sense. Members of the law and economics movement, to give a few examples, refer to accidents as "sunk cost." They seek to design laws that would result in an "efficient level of accidents," not ones that are designed to compensate the victim (or avoid accidents altogether). For them, babies, body parts, and sex are commodities and services; and criminals, even rapists, are actors in markets.[8] The argument made here, however, is quite modest and does not require a determination as to which rationales should govern in case of a conflict. It is simply that economic rationales should be considered in analyzing emergencies. Specifically, this article argues that emergencies are often subject to the same laws of supply and demand and do not mandate any special legal treatment. Intervention in these situations can reduce total (societal) welfare and harm the very victims of these emergencies.

The remainder of the article is organized as follows. Part II focuses on private emergencies. It investigates two different decisions in which courts were asked to compel one to undergo a medical procedure to give an organ that would save the life of another. The first, refusing to issue an injunction,

[8] *See* Richard Posner, *Economic Analysis of Law*, 7th ed. (2007), p. 216, Elisabeth M. Landes & Richard A. Posner, "The Economics of the Baby Shortage," *Journal of Legal Studies*, Vol. 7 (1978), p. 323; Dennis W. Carlton & Daniel R. Fischel, "The Regulation of Insider Trading," *Stanford Law Review*, Vol. 35 (1983), p. 857; Richard A. Epstein, "The Human and Economic Dimensions of Altruism: The Case of Organ Transplantation," *John M. Olin Law & Economics Working Paper* No. 385 (2nd Series).

premised its decision on society's "respect to the individual." The other reached the opposite conclusion based on the state's "inherent authority" as the "father of the people." This article argues that these seemingly contradictory decisions can be reconciled using economic theory. The article also investigates strategic behaviors, remedial reactions, and under what conditions, if any, courts (or regulators) should intervene in organ transactions. Part III focuses on price gouging that often follows public emergencies. It reviews a number of anti-price gouging laws, their structure, and the conditions that trigger them as well as the justifications for and against these laws. After discussing the economic role of pricing, this article demonstrates, using a number of examples, how the so-called "exorbitant prices" help decrease shortages, enable inflow of essential commodities, allocate scarce resources, reduce strategic behavior and queues, and stabilize demand. It argues that the assumption underlying anti-price gouging laws – that markets fail in times of emergency – is often erroneous; and it concludes that anti-price gouging laws reduce total welfare, interfere with evacuation and reconstruction efforts, and therefore should be repealed. Part IV provides concluding remarks.

II. Private Emergencies

The analysis of private emergencies begins with a short contour of a well-known private mechanism: *contracts*. Contracts undoubtedly enhance efficiency. Among other things, they enable parties to allocate risks, extract information, and transfer goods, thereby leading to a better resource allocation and an increase in total welfare. The following example is illustrative. Assume a seller is willing to sell for $20 a widget for which a buyer is willing to pay $40. If transaction costs are not prohibitive, the parties will agree on a price between $20 and $40. Assume the parties agree on a price of $25. By simply exchanging a product she values at only $20 for $25, the seller would make a profit of $5. The buyer would also be better off. She would pay $25 for a widget she values at $40. The result is that the widget would gravitate from the low value individual (the seller) to the higher value one (the buyer) and total (or societal) welfare would increase by $20.

Contracts are undeniably welfare enhancing; but what if the widget is a body organ? In the face of a "private emergency," should the sovereign be allowed to "take" an organ from one person and give it to another? This very question arose in *McFall v. Shimp*[9] and *Strunk v. Strunk*.[10] The plaintiff in *McFall* was a 39-year-old male who suffered from a rare disease, curable only by a bone marrow transplant from a close relative. After the defendant, the only suitable donor, refused to submit to the transplant, the plaintiff sought a preliminary injunction compelling the operation. The question before the court was whether "in order to save the life of one of its members by the only means available, may society infringe upon ones … right to his 'bodily security'?"[11] The court treated the issue as one of first impression, noting that a "diligent search has produced no authority" save an ancient 700-year-old English statute.[12] With no guiding precedents, the court refused to compel the defendant to undergo the surgery. It explained:

> Our society, contrary to many others, has as its first principle, the respect for the individual, and that society and government exist to protect the individual from being invaded and hurt by another. … In this case, the chancellor is being asked to force one member of society to undergo a medical procedure which would provide that part of that individual's body would be removed from him and given to another so that the other could live. Morally, this decision rests with defendant, and, in the view of the court, the refusal of defendant is morally indefensible. For our law to compel defendant to submit to an intrusion of his body would change every concept and principle upon which our society is founded. To do so would defeat the sanctity of the individual, and would impose a rule which would know no limits, and one could not imagine where the line would be drawn.

In *Strunk*, however, the court arrived at a different conclusion. The plaintiff in *Strunk* was the mother of two sons. The eldest, Tommy, suffered from a fatal kidney disease and the youngest, Jerry, was an incompetent ward of the state with an I.Q. comparable to that of a six-year-old. Upon discovering that Tommy's life could only be saved by a kidney transplant from Jerry, the plaintiff petitioned the court to compel the transplant. Unlike *McFall*, the *Strunk* court believed that it had an "inherent authority" to compel an individual to undergo emergency medical procedures in order to save the life of

9 *McFall*, 1978 Pa. Dist. & Cnty. Dec. LEXIS 70 (Pa. C.P. 1978).
10 *Strunk*, 445 S.W.2d 145 (1969).
11 *McFall*, at 91.
12 *Id.*

another.[13] The court noted that "with regard to the origin and source of … jurisdiction [over the persons of others], the doctrine now commonly maintained is that it represents a delegation to the chancellor of the *Crown's right as parens patriae* [father of the people] to interfere in particular cases for the benefit of such persons as are incapable of protecting themselves."[14]

How can one square *McFall* with *Strunk*? The dogmatist would argue that the two decisions are distinguishable. One involved a situation in which the "donor" was competent, while the other dealt with a donor who suffered from a "mental defect."[15] The cynical view would be that *McFall* took a utilitarian approach: preferring the life of a productive married and working adult over that of the "mentally defective" (much emphasized facts in a very short decision).[16] The political theorist, on the other hand, would argue that the two decisions represent two different philosophies (or prosaic treatments) of the "exception." Specifically, it would argue that the *Strunk* court followed a Foucauldian approach. The court description of its authority, especially the reference to the king as the "father of the people" is reminiscent of Foucault's analogy of the royal function ("to procure the common good of the multitude"[17]) to the pastoral power. "To that extent," noted Foucault, "the king's function is not substantially different from that of the pastor."[18]

To the economist, however, *McFall* and *Strunk* are two sides of the same coin. The only difference between them is that the first occurred in a low transaction cost setting (and thus did not require any intervention) while in the latter transaction costs were prohibitive. When two adults, as in *McFall*, can make a determination as to whether they are willing to sell or buy an

[13] The court found authority to supplant the defendant's (Jerry) inability to consent with its own in "a universal rule of equity that where a person is not equal to protecting himself in a particular case, the court will … afford whatever relief may be necessary to protect his interests and preserve his estates." *Strunk* at 147.

[14] *Id* (Emphasis added). The dissent was of the view that the court does not have the authority to compel the surgery (noting that "parents may be free to become martyrs themselves. But it does not follow they are free, in identical circumstances, to make martyrs of their children before they have reached the age of full and legal discretion when they can make that choice for themselves."). *Id*. at 150.

[15] This seems to be the majority's view in *Strunk*. *Id*. at 146.

[16] *Id*.

[17] Michel Foucault, *Security, Territory, Population: Lectures at the College De France 1977–1978* (New York: Palgrave Macmillan, 2007), p. 233.

[18] *Id*.

organ there is no need to intervene. As long as the parties find the transaction beneficial, they will reach an agreement. Just like the widget example, if the donee (buyer) values the organ more than the donor (seller), the parties will reach an agreement that will make both better off.[19] In *Strunk*, on the other hand, transaction costs were prohibitive. Although both parties were interested in the transaction,[20] one of the parties (Jerry) was unable to communicate his wishes (he was incompetent). In such situations, where the market fails, an intervention by the court (or regulation) can be justified. The court in these cases is asked to mimic the market and ensure that a desirable transaction takes place.[21]

But if contracts are such a great device, why could not the parties in *McFall* reach an agreement (assuming that McFall was willing and able to pay Shimp)? Sometimes there are strategic reasons for a party to channel a transaction from the market into the court system. For instance, suppose that a donee is willing to pay $10,000 for an organ that the donor is willing to sell for $5,000. Assume further that the donee believes that if the court compels the transplant the jury will set the damages (or price) at $4,000. In such a case (and assuming litigation costs are low), the donee's best strategy is to ask the court for an injunction to compel the transplant. An injunction would enable the donee to bypass the market for organs (i.e., avoid paying the contract price of $5,000–$10,000) in the same way that theft bypasses the market for ordinary goods.[22] A private transaction is superior to a court's proceedings for a variety of other reasons. An agreement ensures that both parties are better off (otherwise they would not enter into a binding

[19] The fact that one party, the donor, had an advantageous bargaining power (Shimp was the *only* suitable donor) only means that the surplus generated by the transaction will not be evenly distributed between the parties.

[20] The majority opinion in *Strunk* was predicated upon Jerry's emotional and psychological dependence on his older brother and the limited risks involved with the surgery.

[21] Contracts, it should be noted, are superior to regulatory (or court) intervention for a number of reasons. First, contracts save wasteful costs to society. Instead of relying on judges and juries and a long and costly litigation process, agreements represent a much cheaper alternative. Second, and related, a judicial determination is also likely to result in a mistake. A court (or a jury) would have to determine the damages to the "donor" in case the latter is compelled to give an organ and may either over or under compensate the donor. Finally, contracts ensure that desirable transactions take place and that inefficient ones do not.

[22] This is a paraphrase on Judge Posner's analysis of rape. *See* Richard Posner, *Economic Analysis of Law*, 7th ed. (2007), p. 216 ("Rape bypasses the market in sexual relations (marital or otherwise) in the same way that theft bypasses the markets in ordinary goods and services, and it should therefore be forbidden.").

agreement), it saves unnecessary and wasteful litigation costs thereby allowing society to better allocate its (scarce) resources and avoid the costly mistakes that a third party (judge or jury) is bound to make from time to time.

The legal system recognizes the superiority of market mechanisms over courts' intervention. Rules regarding remedies designed to deal with "emergencies," such as specific performance, injunctions, and punitive damages, can often be justified on the feasibility (and superiority) of market transactions:

> Punitive damages are necessary in some cases to make sure that people channel transactions through the market when the costs of voluntary transactions are low. We do not want a person to be able to take his neighbor's car and when the neighbor complains tell him to go sue for its value. We want to make such expropriations valueless to the expropriator and we can do this by adding a punitive exaction to the judgment for the market value of what is taken. This function of punitive damages is particularly important in areas such as defamation and sexual assault, where the tortfeasor may, if the only price of the tort is having to compensate his victim, commit the tort because he derives greater pleasure from the act than the victim incurs pain.[23]

McFall and *Strunk* are rightly decided but their legal premise seems to be lacking. These decisions have little to do with morality, "the Crown's right as parens patriae" or "respect for the individual." Rather, they can be explained by a Coasian approach and the difference in transaction costs. Simply put, when parties can negotiate, an injunction to compel an action will often interfere with the market.

III. Public Emergencies

Natural disasters and other forms of public emergencies undoubtedly pose immense challenges. In addition to the large number of casualties, survivors of the catastrophe, as well as rescue and reconstruction teams, face a hard reality. The disruption of commerce due to severely damaged or destroyed businesses and supporting infrastructure creates a real shortage in essential commodities and services that cripples rescue and repair efforts. This shortage in essentials is often accompanied by a much debated and often

[23] *Kemezy v. Peters*, 79 F.3d 33, 34–35 (1996).

condemned phenomenon: price gouging[24] – a situation where sellers offer their goods in distressed areas at what is often perceived as "unreasonable," "opportunistic," or "excessive" prices.

Many states have promulgated laws to fight and eradicate price gouging.[25] These laws are dormant in times of peace, but they enter into effect upon a declaration of a "state of emergency" or "abnormal market disruption."[26] Some statutes specify the type of events that may trigger the declaration (such as hurricanes or terror attacks), while others also refer to declarations and advisories issued by state and federal authorities.[27] The definition of price gouging also varies among states and is often vague and open-ended.[28] Many anti-price gouging laws use terms such as "unconscionable" or "unfair."[29] Some states prohibit sales at above the average price in a defined

[24] *See, e.g.*, the series of comments and responses to Judge Posner and Professor Becker's Blog (*available at* http://www.becker-posner-blog.com/archives/2005/10/) (last visited May 29, 2009).

[25] *See e.g.*, infra notes 26–32. Some anti-price gouging laws apply to a large number of commodities and services not only those which are on high demand in times of emergency but broader definitions are commonplace. *Compare e.g.*, Ind. Code 4–6-9.1–2 (defining "price gouging" as "charging a consumer an unconscionable amount for the sale of fuel") with Ark. Code Ann. § 4–88-303.

[26] *See, e.g.*, N.Y. Gen. Bus. Law § 396-r (noting that "during periods of abnormal disruption of the market … or other extraordinary adverse circumstances, some parties within the chain of distribution of consumer goods [take] unfair advantage of consumers by charging grossly excessive prices for essential consumer goods and services"); Ark. Code Ann. § 4–88-303 ("Upon the proclamation of a state of emergency resulting from a … natural or man-made disaster declared by the President of the United States or the Governor and upon the declaration of a local emergency … by the executive officer of any city or county … or during any period of time during which a red condition under the Homeland Security Advisory System has been declared by either the United States Department of Homeland Security or the Arkansas Department of Emergency Management, it is unlawful for any person … to sell or offer to sell any consumer … goods … for a price of more than ten percent (10 percent) above the price charged by that person for those goods or services immediately prior to the proclamation of emergency").

[27] *See, e.g.*, Ark. Code Ann. § 4–88-303.

[28] This of course results in high enforcement and litigation cost. *See e.g.*, The White House Paper on "The Economic Consequences of Gasoline 'Price Gouging' Legislation," June 20, 2007, *available at* http://georgewbush-whitehouse.archives.gov/cea/Price_Gouging_WP_062007.html (last visited Nov. 2, 2009) (agreeing with the FTC Chairman's conclusion that anti-price gouging laws "likely will do consumers more harm than good" and noting that "the difficulty in defining 'price gouging' would create an unnecessary regulatory regime with potentially high litigation costs and great uncertainty" that "would deter investment in new supply, increasing prices in the long run").

[29] N.Y. Gen. Bus. Law § 396-r (prohibiting "unconscionably excessive prices" which are defined as prices that are "unconscionably extreme" or prices that are charged using "unfair leverage or unconscionable means"). *See also* N.Y. Gen. Bus. Law § 396-r(3) (providing that "whether a price is unconscionably excessive is a question of law for the court"); Va. Code Ann. § 59.1–527.

period of time prior to the declaration of emergency,[30] while others are willing to tolerate price increases up to a certain percentage.[31]

The standard argument supporting anti-price gouging laws is that they prevent unscrupulous sellers of essential products – those that are most needed after a disaster – from "taking advantage" of those who are in dire distress.[32] Their goal is to impede "opportunistic" attempts by sellers "to capitalize on other people's hardship and misery."[33] "Anyone who is trying to take advantage of this situation" the argument goes, "should be investigated and prosecuted."[34] Despite the strong sentiments that price gouging generates, there now exists a consensus among economists that anti-price gouging laws do not mitigate shortages but rather exacerbate them.[35]

The assumption underlying anti-price gouging laws is that in times of emergencies *markets fail*. New York, for example, limits the application of its anti-price gouging law to situations of "abnormal disruption of the market," which it defines as "any change in the market ... resulting from stress of weather, convulsion of nature, failure or shortage of electric power or other source of energy, strike, civil disorder, war, military action, national or

30 *See, e.g.*, Fla. Stat. Ann. § 501.160.

31 *See* Ala. Code § 8–31-4 (defining an "unconscionable price" as "a price that exceeds, by an amount equal to or in excess of twenty-five percent the average price at which the same or similar commodity ... was obtainable in the affected area during the last 30 days immediately prior to the declared state of emergency and the increase in the price charged is not attributable to reasonable costs incurred in connection with the rental or sale of the commodity").

32 N.Y. Gen. Bus. Law § 396-r (1).

33 Joseph Treaster, "Hurricane Charlie: The Economics; With Storm Gone, Floridian Are Hit With Price Gouging," *New York Times*, August 18, 2004, http://query.nytimes.com/gst/fullpage.html?res=9D01E1DC113FF93BA2575BC0A9629C8B63) (last visited May 29, 2009).

34 Mark Preston, "GOP Urges Price Gouging Prob on Gas," CNN.Com, April 25, 2006, http://www.cnn.com/2006/POLITICS/04/24/gas.investigation/index.html (last visited May 29, 2009) (Citing House Speaker Dennis Hastert, R-Illinois, and Senate Majority Leader Bill Frist, R-Tennessee letter to President Bush).

35 Geoffrey Rapp, "Gouging: Terrorist Attacks, Hurricanes, and the Legal and Economic Aspects of Post Disaster Price Regulation," *Kentucky Law Journal* 94 (2005): 535; W. David Montgomery et al, "Potential Effects of Proposed Price Gouging Legislation on The Cost and Severity of Gasoline Supply Interruptions," *Journal of Competition Law & Economics* 3 (2007): 357, 359 (concluding that "imposing temporary price controls could increase the overall economic losses due to a supply interruption of the same magnitude as that followed Katrina and Rita by almost $1.9 billion"); Judge Posner and professor Becker's Blog (*available at* http://www.becker-posner-blog.com/archives/2005/10/) (last visited May 29, 2009) (referring to anti-price gouging laws as a "profound mistake"); Michael Brewer, "Planning Disaster: Price Gouging Statutes and the Shortage They Create," *Brooklyn Law Review* 72 (2007): 1101; David Skarbek, "Market Failure and Natural Disasters: A Reexamining of Anti-Gouging Laws," *Public Contract Law Journal* 37, no. 4 (2008).

local emergency. ..."[36] Market failure and abnormal situations (emergencies included), however, are not synonymous terms. One does not necessarily imply the existence of the other. A shortage simply means that at a certain price level the demand for some goods exceeds supply or, put differently, that resources are scarce.[37] This scarcity is the very subject of economic theory:

> The economist studies the disposal of scarce means. He is interested in the way different degrees of scarcity of different goods give rise to different ratios of valuation between them, and he is interested in the way in which changes in conditions of scarcity, whether coming from changes in ends or changes in means – from the demand side or the supply side – affect these ratios. Economics is the science which studies human behavior as a relationship between ends and scarce means which have alternative uses.[38]

To understand the role that price gouging serves, we must first understand the role of prices. Prices are not just a dollar value assigned to goods, they are signals. Prices are declarations of sellers' willingness to part with goods and buyers' willingness to pay. They also inform sellers of opportunities available to potential buyers in the market. In a competitive market, the price informs each seller that if she prices her product above the "market price," consumers are likely to decline her offer. It also informs the seller that if she can come up with a more efficient manufacturing or marketing process, she may be able to offer the same good for less and attract more business. Pricing above cost (such as monopoly pricing) also serves as a magnet. It informs potential entrants that rents are available and (absent

[36] *See, e.g.*, N.Y. Gen. Bus. Law § 396-r.

[37] *See* Federal Trade Commission, "Investigation of Gasoline Price Manipulation and Post Katrina Gasoline Price Increases," p. ix (http://www.ftc.gov/reports/060518PublicGasolinePricesInvestigationReportFinal.pdf) ("In the cities with the largest price increases, the sizes of the increases were consistent with the standard supply and demand competitive paradigm. Moreover, in general, the wholesalers and retailers that raised prices the most within particular cities in the weeks following the hurricanes were not firms that experienced increases in market power (stemming, for example, from the closing of rivals). Rather, they were firms that experienced the largest reductions in their own supplies and the greatest increases in their own costs." For a review of other studies reaching similar conclusions, see W. David Montgomery et al, "Potential Effects of Proposed Price Gouging Legislation on The Cost and Severity of Gasoline Supply Interruptions," *Journal of Competition Law and Economics* 3 (2007): 357, 370–374.

[38] Lionel Robbins, *An Essay on the Nature and Significance of Economic Science* (London: Macmillan and Co., Limited), 16 (http://www.mises.org/books/robbinsessay2.pdf).

barriers to entry) helps attract new entrants and revive competition. In a market in long-term equilibrium, the price may inform a seller of its competitors' cost structure.[39] To firms that attempt to conspire (in violation of antitrust laws), the price charged by members of the cartel often indicates possible deviation from a price fixing agreement. A unified price, under certain circumstances, may alert the antitrust and competition authorities that a cartel may be in operation. A price can even provide information about the product's qualities, and may serve as an indicator of high search costs.[40]

Prices are also a measure of scarcity. A high price indicates that a certain commodity is scarce, while a low price indicates abundance. Diamonds and gold are scarce, not because of their inherent attributes, but because they are hard (or just costly) to locate and harvest.[41] In contrast, air, while certainly not less useful than diamonds, is costless because it is everywhere. It is not scarce. Prices also help allocate resources, or to use the economists' jargon, achieve "allocative efficiency." Allocative efficiency ensures that scarce resources are allocated to those consumers who value them the most. It is achieved by allowing scarce commodities and services to gravitate from the low to high value user.

But how do these understandings help us analyze price gouging? In times of emergencies, commodities are often scarce. Generators, gas, and even water can be hard to find. The price of goods in these situations must rise. The price is the voice of scarcity. It announces to the world that a certain commodity is in short supply or in high demand (or both). Sellers – often an attentive audience for such cries – will likely respond. In their ears, the sound of scarcity translates to a prospect for high profits. Motivated by greed and a primal rent seeking instinct, these sellers would flock from localities in which their commodities are less scarce to distressed areas. Those who arrive first will receive a prize for their efforts – they will be able to charge high prices (and thus realize

[39] Gil Sadka, "The Economic Consequences of Accounting Fraud in Product Markets: Theory and a Case from the US Telecommunications Industry (WorldCom)," *American Law & Economics Review* 8, no. 3 (2006): 439–475.

[40] *See* J. Shahar Dilbary, "Famous Trademarks and The Rational Basis To Protect Irrational Beliefs," *George Mason Law Review* 14 (2007): 605; J. Shahar Dillbary, "Getting the Word Out: The Informational Role of Trademarks," 40 *Arizona State Law Journal* (Winter 2009), http://ssrn.com/abstract=1126857.

[41] For a different view see: Edward J. Epstein, *The Rise and Fall of Diamonds: The Shattering of a Brilliant Illusion* (1982).

large profits). But overtime, with the inflow of sellers, the commodities will become less scarce and pre-emergency prices will be restored.

The high, so-called "exorbitant," prices also achieve allocative efficiency. In times of emergency, where chaos manifests, prices help sort users into different groups according to the value they assign to the scarce resources. Those who value the essential commodities more than others will be willing to purchase the goods at higher prices (as long as their benefits from these commodities exceed the cost); and thus, should be accorded priority.

Price regulation tampers with this (efficient) market mechanism. A price cap mutes the voice of scarcity. It stops those sellers who are willing to rush into distressed areas to offer their much desired goods, from doing so. The following example is illustrative. Assume that a hurricane hits two localities. The first is directly hit, causing the price of generators to increase from $250 to $2,000.[42] The second suffered only minor damages, causing the price of generators to increase to (only) $1,000. Assume further that the sellers' cost to produce a generator is only $100 and that transportation and shipping costs between the two localities are $300. In this situation, the rent seeking seller located in the less affected area faces one of two options. She can either (a) continue to sell in the less affected locality and realize a profit of $900 (1,000 – 100); or (b) she can ship her generators to the severely impacted area and realize a profit of $1,600 (2,000 – 100 – 300). Motivated by the prospect of high profits, sellers located in the relatively unaffected area would of course sell at the distressed area.[43] If, however, an anti-price gouging law in the distressed locality prohibits price increases, those sellers will not offer their commodities to those who need them the most.

Some anti-price gouging laws, it should be noted, allow a price increase up to a certain percentage (e.g., 25 percent in Alabama)[44] or a price increase

[42] *See* Joseph Treaster, "Hurricane Charlie: The Economics; With Storm Gone, Floridian Are Hit With Price Gouging," *New York Times*, August 18, 2004, http://query.nytimes.com/gst/fullpage.html?res=9D01E1DC113FF93BA2575BC0A9629C8B63) (last visited May 29, 2009).

[43] *See, e.g.*, Abhi Raghunathan, "South Florida Shortages Fuel Black Market," *St. Petersburg Times*, October 29, 2005, 1B. ("They stand patiently in clumps at gas stations all over South Florida, lugging empty buckets, milk bottles, even pickle jars. While Hurricane Wilma has been a burden for most, it has been an opportunity for others. Kenol Pierre, 32, had just put $10 of gas in a red gas can at a service station in Miami's Little Haiti neighborhood. Some of it was for his own vehicle, and the rest was for some fast cash. 'I can sell it and get maybe $20 or $30', said Pierre, an immigrant from Haiti. 'Waiting for an hour is easy for me.' Pierre is part of a thriving black market in South Florida, where ice and water are prized commodities and gasoline the new gold.")

[44] Ala. Code § 8–31-4.

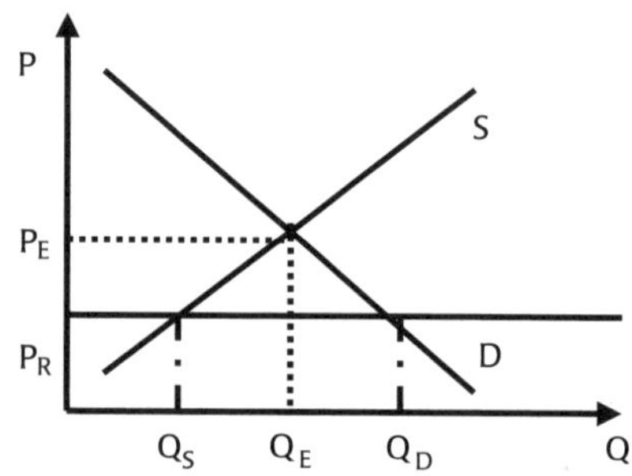

Figure 3.1 Price regulation in the market for generators.

that is due to increase costs.[45] These exceptions, however, often have little or no effect. In the above example, the seller would decline to sell her merchandise even if the price increased by 300 percent from $250 to $750 simply because she can enjoy a profit of $900 if she sells at the less distressed locality. What these laws fail to recognize is that in addition to out of pocket expenses (such as shipping costs) sellers also incur opportunity costs. If the seller in our example chooses to sell her commodities at one locality she *forgoes* the profit she could have earned at the other.[46] Price caps on essential goods thus harm the very consumers these laws seek to protect.

Moreover, if prices are artificially kept at a low level, more people will be willing to purchase generators compared to the number of generators available. In such a case, allocation of generators may become inefficient. Generators may be sold on a first come first serve basis (until supply is depleted) rather than to the highest value consumer. Assume for example that Buyer-1 is willing to pay $300 for the same generator for which Buyer-2 is willing to pay $2,000. If the price is kept at $250 per unit, Buyer-1 may receive the generator instead of Buyer-2.

But there are more pieces in this puzzle: the forces of supply and demand are often much stronger than any anti-price gouging laws. Effective price caps actually *create* shortages. This is illustrated in Figure 3.1.

[45] N.Y. Gen. Bus. Law § 396-r(3)(b)(ii) (prohibiting "unconscionably excessive prices" but allowing a seller to "rebut a prima facie case with evidence that additional costs not within the control of the [seller] were imposed on the [seller] for the goods or services").

[46] The situation is even worse if one locality declares a state of emergency that triggers its anti-price gouging laws while an adjacent locality does not.

Absent any price cap the market for generators will be in equilibrium where supply meets demand. Q_E units will be sold at price P_E. If the sellers cannot offer their merchandise at more than P_R, the quantity demanded at that price, Q_D, will exceed the number of units sellers are willing to sell at that price, Q_S ($Q_D > Q_S$). In such a situation, a "secondary" (or "black") market often develops. Ad hoc entrepreneurs will purchase the much desired goods at the regulated (low) price, only to offer them at a higher price to others.[47] To illustrate, assume that Buyer-1 in the above example purchased the generator for $250 because it was the first to arrive at the store. Buyer-2 would have been willing to pay Buyer-1 up to $2,000. If negotiation is possible, the parties will strike a deal at a price of $250–$2,000.[48] The prospect of rents generates a secondary market that results in a distributional affect, but will not eliminate desirable transactions from taking place (unless transaction costs are prohibitive). More people may try to engage in this arbitrage-like transactions, thereby increasing the demand for the already much demanded goods. They will seek to purchase goods at the regulated price in order to resell them to other consumers with a higher willingness to pay. This will likely increase transaction costs and enable tax evasion. More importantly, it will make it harder for high value customers to locate the goods they need (even at the higher price). The result is that anti-price gouging laws that are meant to eliminate "opportunistic" behavior foster one.

The so-called "exorbitant" prices have another desirable effect. They incentivize sellers to *stock* commodities that are usually not on high demand but are much desired after a hurricane warning is issued. Commodities such as generators, planks of wood, flashlights, and candles are often carried and sold only (or mainly) in times of emergency. Storing and shelving these goods, however, comes at a high (opportunity) cost. Sometimes, it is simply unprofitable to sell these goods. Price gouging, however, helps prepare for future shortages. Reverting back to the generator example, assume that it costs $100 to manufacture a generator for which consumers are willing to pay only $70 in times of tranquility but $1,500 in times of emergency.

47 *See* Abhi Raghunathan, "South Florida Shortages Fuel Black Market," *supra* note 43.

48 The secondary transaction is efficient because it "clears the market," but it is inferior to an unregulated market. Anti-price gouging laws, however, may increase transaction costs and even jeopardize this secondary market altogether. If the expected costs from penalties (a function of the fines and enforcement efforts) are high enough they may deter such transactions.

If price gouging laws prohibit price increases the seller will not carry generators. Selling a \$100 generator for \$70 is just bad business. But if price increases are allowed and the seller believes that there is a 10 percent probability that a hurricane would hit the locality, generators will be available. The expected benefit of stocking a generator would be \$140 (10% × [1,500 – 100]), \$40 more than the cost of a generator.[49]

Not only do anti-price gouging laws provide little incentives to store essentials, but they also cause the little supply available to deplete faster compared to a no-price cap regime. This is especially the case in the market for gasoline. The fear of running out of gas causes consumers to fill up their tanks more frequently and maintain a higher-than-usual level of gas in their tanks. This in turn increases the already long queues at gas stations and dries up inventories.[50] This phenomenon can be easily modeled. Assume that the average tank size contains X gallons and that in times of tranquility the average consumer fills up her tank when it reaches α capacity. For example, if $\alpha = 0.25$ and $X = 20$ gallons, the average consumer fills her gas tank when it reaches quarter capacity (or when it reaches 5 gallons). Assume further that in times of emergency, afraid that gas will not be available, consumers fuel their tanks when they reach β capacity ($\beta > \alpha$). The average level of gas in consumers' tanks thus would increase from $X(\alpha + 1)/2$ to $X(\beta + 1)/2$[51] and demand for gas would thus increase at a magnitude of $(\beta + 1)/(\alpha + 1)$. For example, if consumers pump gas when the gas level of their tank reaches a level of 3/4 instead of 1/4, the average gas level in their tanks would increase from 5/8 to 7/8, causing a 40 percent increase in the demand for gas.

In sum, price gouging is often condemned for being immoral for taking advantage of consumers in need. Economic theory, however, proves this to be wrong. Price gouging is not the problem (scarcity is) but rather a remedy.

49 Assuming the risk neutral seller can return the generator to the manufacturer if it is not sold. If, however, the seller cannot return the generator to the manufacturer, the seller's expected benefit from carrying a generator would be \$113 (10% × [1,500 – 100] + 90% × [70 – 100]), still \$13 more than the cost of a generator.

50 W. David Montgomery et al., "Potential Effects of Proposed Price Gouging Legislation on The Cost and Severity of Gasoline Supply Interruptions," *Journal of Competition Law & Economics* 3 (2007): 357, 376.

51 The average levels in consumers' tanks, assuming gas in consumers' tanks is equally distributed, is $(X + \alpha X)/2$ or $X(\alpha + 1)/2$.

IV. Conclusion

Professor Feldman reports that much of the current debate among political theorists revolves around whether emergencies lie within or outside the law.[52] This article argues that economic theory can and does provide important insights into the proper placement and scope of emergency law; and therefore should not be ignored. It focuses on the markets for body parts and other essential goods in times of emergency and it concludes that emergencies are often subject to the same laws of supply and demand that control in times of tranquility, and thus often do not mandate any legal intervention. Emergencies, private or public, do not necessarily imply a market failure and thus often do not require a unique or an "exceptional" treatment "outside the law."[53]

[52] *Supra* note 1 at pp. 136–164.
[53] *See supra* notes 1–4 and accompanying text.

4

The Racial Sovereign

Sumi Cho* and Gil Gott**

A dominant theme in post-9/11 scholarship on national security law has been the somber elaboration of necessary and rational trade-offs, or balancings, brought about by the urgently reconstituting relationship between sovereign emergency reality and civil liberty aspiration. This discourse has been critiqued as "Schmittean" for its decisionistic effects, but the core of liberal legal thinking of the period actually remains in tension with "proto-realist" writers like Carl Schmitt, who famously framed sovereignty through the notion of the exception, that is, a politico-legal dynamic that takes hold during times of emergency and calls forth sovereign suspensions of law.[1] Schmitt thought that liberal rule of law could not stand in the way of an effective sovereign and that entertaining such a fantasy could create instability in the underlying political order itself. Paradigmatic Schmittean "decisions on the exception" by sovereign holders of state power were thought to reveal a

* Professor, DePaul University College of Law; J.D., University of California at Berkeley; Ph.D. University of California at Berkeley (Ethnic Studies). I thank Austin Sarat for his conceptualization of this volume and graciousness throughout the editing process. The chapter benefit from research assistance by Mark Giangrande, Jodi Schuette, and Charlene Recio. I am grateful for comments from George Lipsitz, Addie Rolnick, and Saúl Sarabia, and the support of the African American Policy Forum.

** Associate Professor, DePaul University, International Studies; J.D., University of Illinois at Urbana-Champaign. Ph.D., University of California at Berkeley (German). I would like to thank our children Maia Cho and Quin Cho for their support and understanding during the drafting of this chapter.

1 Schmitt's influence on the post-9/11 scholarship is evident from a cursory review of the literature where he works typically as a foil to rule of law and critical conceptualizations of security and law. More recent scholarship has problematized the instrumentalization of Schmitt in the recent literature. See David Chandler, "The Revival of Carl Schmitt in International Relations: The Last Refuge of Critical Theorists?" *Millennium: Journal of International Studies* 37, no. 1 (2008): 27–48. See generally Carl Schmitt, *Political Theology: Four Chapters on the Concept of Sovereignty* (2004).

fundamental myth and potentially fatal flaw of liberal democratic constitutionalism. This perspective would, in fact, subject many forms of post-9/11 liberal legal balancing discourse to a kind of realist razor that looks to *effective* power and constraint for its insights. Or, it could push us to look more deeply at the relationship between such liberal rule of law "decisionism" and underlying questions of political economy and social order "stability."

Schmittean realism describes and endorses the order-seeking world of early twentieth-century inter-imperial rivalry, but its rejection of liberal "ultrapolitics" and faux universalism as well underlines for critical scholars the socially inflected, identity/ideology-driven basis of the liberal imperialist security state. Moreover, Schmitt's extra-legal "state of exception" as a thoroughly politicized (as rendered here: racialized and imperial) conception and symbol of modern state sovereignty has seemed especially apt as the legal establishment grapples with the current imperialist crisis in U.S. law and policy. However, critiques of capitulation to emergency-think after 9/11 as Schmittean decisionism have, perhaps, undertheorized the various possible linkages to Schmittean theory and ontology.[2] A less apparent synergy between Schmitt and the new mainstream of law and security can perhaps be found outside an elaboration of the plausibilities and limits of liberal legal management of emergency power – a project Schmitt would presumably reject. In its antipolitical self-understanding, liberal law-based discourse may instead move us both in the direction of violent "crusade" politics and toward uncritical support for a democratically disastrous state-imperial formation.

Legal liberalism discounts the Schmittean realist view of sovereignty, ironically, by engaging national security "concerns" at face value, irrespective of the long record of involuntary sacrifice fraudulently imposed upon racial minorities through declarations of emergency and threat.[3] Legal liberalism may process cases of such sovereign racial subjugation, in retrospect, as way stations on the road toward a democratically evolved

[2] See Gil Gott, "The Devil We Know: Racial Subordination and National Security Law," *Villanova Law Review* 50 (2005): 1080–83. David Chandler has exposed the misuse of Schmitt by critical theorists and provides insights for the argument about linkages between liberal and Schmittean ontologies. See Chandler, "The Revival of Carl Schmitt," 27.

[3] Critical Race scholar Derrick Bell has forwarded the notion of "racial compromise," in which disparate groups of whites achieve a compromise over their disagreements by involuntarily sacrificing the interests of racial minorities. Derrick Bell, *Race, Racism & American Law*, 5th ed. (Aspen, 2004): 40–47.

security constitutionalism,[4] or through the promise that racial subjects will be safeguarded/dispensed with generally through a situationally optimal, process-based emergency constitutionalism,[5] albeit marked for many by a deferential jurisprudence that dare not question political motivations or assessments of the security branches.[6]

In this paper, we glimpse anew at Leviathan – now in its guise as "the racial sovereign" – to analyze the changing contours of the liberal-imperial framing of sovereignty and security. We review the history of racial contingency in the legal meanings of sovereignty and security, and probe ways of placing that legal history in the context of an unfolding subordinationist/ imperialist socio-legal dynamic. We hope to use such an understanding of the racial sovereign to better grasp the underlying dialectics of contemporary "colorblind" approaches to the (r)evolving sovereignty/security regime of law and policy. Here, as elsewhere, we find that the universalist conceits of liberalism form a preserve for the unleashing and rationalization of "liberal enmity," an unexpectedly extreme and destructive culturalist rendering of the political. The irony here is that such a rendering is the kind of irrational "ultra-politics" Schmitt warned against, even as it underwrites a politics shot through with the Schmittean imperial political ontology.[7] Both lead

4 See Mark Tushnet, "Defending Korematsu?: Reflections on Civil Liberties in Wartime," *Wisconsin Law Review* (2003): 273. For a critique of Tushnet's work as "social learning"-oriented constitutionalism, see Gott, "The Devil We Know,"1080–83.

5 Bruce Ackerman is an example of a left-liberal constitutionalist who incorporates social justice concerns into his security model and acknowledges the racially pernicious effects of emergency constitutionalism. Ackerman ultimately capitulates to that unfairness in cases on the frontier of his protective system with its safeguard of a "super-majoritarian escalator" (whereby emergency powers are subject to periodic reauthorization only by an ever-increasing majority of Congress. See Bruce Ackerman, "The Emergency Constitution," *Yale Law Journal* 113 (2004): 1040. Ackerman gives as paradigmatic limit cases, i.e., cases where his emergency constitution would find its protective limit, the Japanese internment and Palestinian intifada. It is an approach that acknowledges the identity-contingent limitations of any balancing test in the face of construed threats to security, but stops short of offering any substantive constitutional protection against such abuses. See Gott, "The Devil We Know," 1090–93. In a nation in which the election of the first African American president would mean also a simultaneous emptying out of the U.S. Senate of all its African American representation, such a super-majoritarian congressional safeguard is perhaps not as reassuring as it would be in a more racially-balanced democracy.

6 See Samuel Issacharoff and Richard H. Pildes, "Between Civil Liberatianism and Executive Unilateralism: An Institutional Process Approach to Rights during Wartime," *Theoretical Inquiries in Law* 5 (2004): 5. See also Gott, "The Devil We Know,"1084–90 (discussing and critiquing various process-based approaches).

7 See Sergei Prozorov, "Liberal Enmity: The Figure and the Foe in the Political Ontology of Liberalism," *Millennium: Journal of International Studies* 35 (2006): 75–99.

to the closure of the political from the standpoint of a more fundamental, non-imperialist democracy.

I. Introduction: The Terrorist Candidate and the Racial Sovereign

The period leading up to the 2008 presidential election, at the dawning of this allegedly "post-racial" era,[8] was certainly an interesting time to be a critical race theorist and legal scholar. On October 7, after the dismal 0-for-3 nature of the only vice-presidential debate and the first two presidential debates, the McCain-Palin playbook called for diverting the focus from the cataclysmic tanking of the economy to a more ominous threat facing the voting public: the threat to national security posed by an African American candidate with an Arab-sounding name, whose alleged secret ties to domestic terrorism threatened the survival of the country. Attacks in speeches by Sarah Palin during the week of October 6, 2008 were racialized[9] (not to mention gendered) in the way they presented Obama as either a terrorist or the terrorist's "Manchurian candidate" who would target "his own country." The attacks were premised on the thread-barest of illegitimate associational guilt projections, breathtaking in atemporality, involving Bill Ayers, former leader of the Weather Underground group whose violent antiwar activities took place when Obama was in elementary school.[10] In an almost choreographed

[8] For my definition of post-racialism, see Sumi Cho, "Post-racialism," *Iowa Law Review* 94 (2009): 1589 (defining post-racialism as an ideology that reflects a belief that due to "racial progress," the state need not engage in race-based decision-making or adopt race-based remedies, and that civil society should eschew race as a central organizing principle of social action).

[9] By racialized, we mean providing racial content or meaning where none previously existed. See Michael Omi and Howard Winant, *Racial Formation in the United States: From the 1960s to the 1990s*, 2nd ed. (New York: Oxford University Press, 1994).

[10] A *Chicago Sun-Times* blogger posted the transcript of Gov. Palin's Clearwater, Florida speech on her blog, "The Scoop from Washington." Lynn Sweet, Sarah Palin slams Obama again on Ayers at Florida Rally. Transcript, http://blogs.suntimes.com/sweet/2008/10/sarah_palin_slams_obama_again.html (accessed on August 16, 2009).The relevant portion of the transcript is excerpted below:

> So, I do have to apologize, though, for being a little bit impatient, a little bit annoyed. But anyways, so one of the questions about well what do I read everyday? And my answer was sort of flippant, Well, I was reading my copy of the *New York Times* the other day, okay. (Boos.) And I knew you guys would react that way, okay. So I'm reading the *New York Times*, though, and I was really interested to read about Barack's friends from Chicago, as the New York Times (put it ?). (Applause.) Now it turns out one of his earliest supporters is a man named Bill Ayers. (Boos.) And according to the *New York Times* he was a domestic terrorist and part of a group that quote, "launched a campaign of bombings that would target the Pentagon and our U.S. Capitol." (Boos.) And then there's even more to the story.

response to such demagoguery, the audiences booed on cue, and a shout of "Kill him!" was even heard coming from somewhere in the crowd.

One takeaway message from this rather nasty turn in the campaign, at least for purposes of this discussion, derives from the automaticity of response that can be counted upon by those who orchestrate such neutral-sounding but clearly racially coded character attacks on Obama. Their racialized "calls" resonate in chillingly predictable ways with their increasingly mob-like, volatile, identity-thumping and racially homogeneous congregants: "Who is the real Barack Obama?" "What does he plan for America?" The fact that the faithful performed as expected should be the least surprising aspect of the implementation of this Rovian strategy. The ultimate "decider" or sovereign – like Jesus – cannot be racially ambiguous. As such, any candidate of color whose physical presentation departs from the tradition of homogeneity would have to overcome a presumption of "otherness" and a hard cynicism about one's readiness to rule and appropriateness for the nation's highest office.

Indeed, presidential politics in the post-civil rights era have made ample resort to racial electioneering, even in the absence of an actual African American electoral opponent. Beginning with Nixon's 1968 campaign, strategist Kevin Phillips helped devise (and later exposed) the "southern strategy," which consciously exploited white racial resentment toward civil rights reforms to transform the formerly Democratic South into a new Republican stronghold. Phillips saw that the New Deal coalition's dominance in the South could be disrupted by deploying coded anti-Black campaign rhetoric.[11] In 1980, Ronald Reagan kicked off his post-convention presidential campaign in Philadelphia, Mississippi, a site made famous through the brutal murders of three civil rights workers by Klansmen and the local refusal to prosecute the perpetrators.[12] Speaking to a predominantly

> Barack Obama says that Ayers was just someone in the neighborhood, but that's less than truthful. His own top adviser said that they were quote, "certainly friendly." In fact, Obama held one of his first meetings of his political career in Bill Ayers living room. (Boos.) And they worked together on various projects in Chicago. And, you know, these are the same guys who think that patriotism is paying higher taxes. (Boos.) Remember, that's what Joe Biden had said. And I am just so fearful that this is not a man who sees America the way that you and I see America, as the greatest source for good in this world. (Applause.) I'm afraid this is someone who sees America as imperfect enough to work with a former domestic terrorist who had targeted his own country. (Boos.)

[11] Michael Omi and Howard Winant, *Racial Formation in the United States: From the 1960s to the 1990s*, 2nd ed. (New York, 1994): 124.

[12] Omi and Winant, *Racial Formation*, 133. The relevant portion of Reagan's speech follows: "Programs like education and others should be turned back to the states and local

white crowd of supporters, Reagan pledged to return education and other functions to the states and local entities, declaring, "I believe in states' rights."[13] He vowed to change federal regulations and structures to "put us back where we belong."[14] His vice president and successor, George H. W. Bush Sr. would benefit from one of the most infamous campaign commercials ever developed by an allegedly independent advocacy group, the "National Security PAC."[15] The 1988 commercial, depicting a menacing mug shot of African American felon "Willie" Horton, played upon "every suburban mother's greatest fear" in an attempt to make the case that Governor Michael Dukakis was too "soft on crime."[16] Even Bill Clinton, the nation's "first Black President" would contribute to this tradition in his 1992 campaign by abolishing the racial caucuses to the Democratic Party. Clinton also made headlines by his carefully staged public rebuke of African American hip-hop artist Sistah Souljah, designed to enhance his appeal among "Reagan Democrats" by signaling his independence from "special interest groups."[17]

That race, racial imagery, and racially coded discourse play such a central and consistent role in presidential campaigns during the era of "formal equality," suggests the existence of a racial filter, or prerequisite of sorts, in the political culture that conditions the meaning and function of the executive branch. The racial prerequisite may be physical (candidates must be

communities with the tax sources to fund them. I believe in states' rights. I believe in people doing as much as they can at the community level and the private level." David Brooks, "Opinion Editorial: History and Calumny," *New York Times*, November 9, 2007.

13 Id.

14 The full speech is available at www.onlinemadison.com/ftp/reagan/reaganneshoba.mp3.

15 Jake Tapper, "The Willie Horton Alumni Association" (August 25, 2000), http://archive.salon.com/politics/feature/2000/08/25/horton/index.html (accessed May 27, 2009).

16 The ad was produced by GOP media consultant, Larry McCarthy, who produced the commercial as an independent advocacy group ostensibly unaffiliated with the Bush campaign. The ad succeeded in gaining approval from a first version of the commercial with the network censors, then substituted a second version of the commercial with the menacing mug shot of Willie Horton inserted prominently into the frame. Although no evidence linking the infamous Willie Horton ad to the Bush campaign was ever established, Lee Atwater, the architect of Bush's successful 1988 election, made a deathbed apology to Michael Dukakis for pledging to make "Willie Horton his running mate." Michael Oreskes, "Lee Atwater, Master of Tactics for Bush and GOP Dies at 40," *New York Times*, March 30, 1991, http://query.nytimes.com/gst/fullpage.html?res=9D0CEED91F3DF933A05750C0A967958260&sec=&spon=&pagewanted=1 (accessed on May 27, 2009).

17 Omi and Winant, *Racial Formation*, 151 (detailing Clinton's underlying message in his rebuke, that African Americans could be just as "racist" as whites and needed to be challenged just as vigorously as racist whites, thereby converting the legacy of racism to individual prejudice).

white) or ideological (insider candidates must signal adequate whiteness using race-coded language, racialized imagery, etc., while outsider candidates must signal their rejection of racial identity or adopt a "transcendent" racial identity). It is hard to avoid the conclusion that the politics around the election of U.S. presidents has been, and remains, steeped in a tradition of "racial sovereigness." Indeed, the April 15, 2009 "tea party" protests widely reported on Fox News Channel reveal that post-election, partisan political performances (taking aim at the reverse "racial sovereign" in the person of President Obama) remain deeply racialized.

We observe that this historical racial inflection of the state-executive function tracks the identity-driven ontologies and normative predilections of state security and emergency discourse. As the U.S. executive symbolizes and embodies the interests and meanings of a racially hinged sociopolitical arrangement, we may similarly historicize the state security function within a broader Anglo-imperial trajectory. Central to the "flimsy convention" by which the liberal imperial state has claimed "the capacity and duty to hold power within a historical continuum of catastrophic violence" are the arch-symbolic and highly racialized rituals of executive power and security.[18]

The professional punditry's decontextualized understanding of the 2008 campaign's racial dynamics, reflecting the profound grip social contingency may have on our ability intellectually to grapple with race in politics, recalls for us how so much of the post-9/11 scholarship on national security law has revolved around a frustrating emergency/legality binarism that seems to have little to say about the fundamental social contingencies of "sovereignty" and "security." Indeed, looking back over the past eight years or so, it is worth asking how much of our generation's contribution to grappling with the hypertrophying American security state and its imperial imbrications has been a professionally risk-averse acceptance, avoidance, or collective reification of highly suspect and contingent sovereign projections (war on terror, full spectrum domination, Islamic terrorism, homeland security, unlawful enemy combatants, "wartime" footing, ticking time bombs, weapons of mass destruction, material support for terrorism/Muslim charities, etc.).

[18] Language taken from *Max Pensky, Melancholy Dialectics: Walter Benjamin and the Play of Mourning* (1993): 77.

What by now should have earned our profound skepticism has instead insinuated itself into the very categories by which we imagine both the facts and norms of rule of law systems in late modernity. Our collective processes of legal rationalization place the discipline and profession in a, shall we say, less than antagonistic relationship with imperial formations and seldom escape a kind of mass intellectual deductionism that returns us again and again to the categorical imperatives of the modern sovereign – the great Leviathan – a self-referential ontology of order and empire. We propose originating legal engagement of sovereignty critically, paralleling the critiques of "whiteness as property,"[19] which requires being willing to foreground the exclusions and social contingencies of "liberal enmity" in the construction of security and sovereignty related law and politics.[20] These parallel areas of liberal legal construction – property and sovereignty – derive force from similar claims regarding universality of interest and formal legal rationality. Yet, both seem historically inseparable from socially exclusionary regimes and highly contingent exercises of state police power.[21]

II. The Racial Contingency of Sovereignty

"Sovereignty," as used in this chapter, refers to a form of both social identity and political organization. Generally, recognition of the socially and politically contingent nature of sovereignty works against reification of the state and its systems through sovereign deductionism. R. B. J. Walker suggests understanding sovereignty as a "spatialized answer" to the difficult political and theoretical questions inherent in the legitimation narratives and logic of the modern interstate system: exactly what, where and who are the "natural and proper" repositories of legitimate politics?[22] Sovereignty marks the modern pattern of "resolution" between universalist claims and the kinds of particularistic interests that wield such claims in the contest of political aggrandizement. Our understanding of the racial contingency of

19 Cheryl Harris' canonical critical race theory text, Whiteness as Property, revealed how whiteness has been and continues to be a legally recognized and protected property interest. Cheryl Harris, "Whiteness as Property," *Harvard Law Review* 106 (1993): 1709.

20 See Sergei Prozorov, "Liberal Enmity: The Figure of the Foe in the Political Ontology of Liberalism," *Millennium: Journal of International Studies* 35, no.1 (2006): 75–99.

21 Natsu Taylor Saito, *From Chinese Exclusion to Guantanamo Bay: Plenary Power and the Prerogative State* (University Press of Colorado, 2007).

22 R. B. J. Walker, *Inside/Outside: International Relations as Political Theory* (1993): ix.

sovereignty derives from the record of historical resolutions that gave meaning to American sovereignty and its inherent powers.[23]

Sovereignty and other foundational legal principles in the United States developed homologously with the structures of societal racial formation.[24] So, for example, how federalism would be defined, who could be a "citizen," or what is meant by "military necessity" or "national security" all "grew up" next to the question of what it meant to be white, what it meant for "America" to be white, and what it meant to lack whiteness in the United States. Courts developed the lofty but *racially contingent foundational legal principles* in a way that effectively solidified the stratifications of racial caste. These foundational legal principles transcended legal rationales or distinctions, and asked the big questions of what it meant to be a nation, what the relationship was between state and federal governments, and how private property became constructed in the United States. National sovereignty,[25]

[23] As the Supreme Court in *Chae Chan Ping* elaborated, "[t]he powers to declare war, make treaties, suppress insurrection, repel invasion, regulate foreign commerce, secure republican governments to the states, and admit subjects of other nations to citizenship, are all sovereign powers, restricted in their exercise only by the constitution itself and considerations of public policy and justice which control, more or less, the conduct of all civilized nations." *Chae Chan Ping v. U.S.*, 130 U.S. 581, 604 (1889).

[24] Omi and Winant define racial formation as "the process by which social, economic and political forces determine the content and importance of racial categories, and by which they are in turn shaped by racial meanings." Omi and Winant, *Racial Formation*, 61. Racialization refers to "the extension of racial meaning to a previously racially unclassified relationship, social practice, or group," such as the historic assignment to the category of "Negro," or "Black" to culturally distinct groups of African tribes enslaved in the United States, or the creation of the category of Asian through exclusionist immigration, property and family formation laws and policies that aggregated Chinese, Japanese, Koreans, Filipinos, and South Asians into a pan-ethnic category and identity. However, the project here is to not to reveal how the racialized subject was previously un-racialized, but the opposite. Rather than identifying the non-racialized roots of an explicitly racialized group (relationship or social practice) such as "Blacks" or "Asians," we instead seek to excavate the racial origins and meaning of the relationship between the law and foundational principles such as sovereignty in a "racial contingency" project.

[25] See *Johnson v. M'Intosh*, 21 U.S. 543, 587 (1823) (Chief Justice John Marshall declaring for the Supreme Court contrary to the established understanding of the law of nations, that "discovery gave an exclusive right to extinguish the Indian title of occupancy, either by purchase or by conquest; and gave also *a right to such a degree of sovereignty, as the circumstances of the people would allow them to exercise*.") (Emphasis added.) Chief Justice Marshall later elaborated "the circumstances of the people" as "fierce savages, whose occupation was war, and whose subsistence was drawn chiefly from the forest. To leave them in possession of their country, was to leave the country a wilderness; to govern them as a distinct people, was impossible, because they were as brave and as high spirited as they were fierce, and were ready to repel by arms every attempt on their independence." Id. at 589; *Cherokee Nation v. United States*, 30 U.S. 1, 17–18 (1831) (circumscribing indigenous sovereignty to the oxymoronic "domestic dependent nation" by rationalizing in part that "the habits and usages of the Indians" whose "appeal was to the

federalism,[26] separation of powers,[27] and plenary power[28] are all central legal principles on which the United States was founded. Each term embeds a racialized history in which race and law were mutually constructed. That these foundational legal principles originate in racial contingency and become defined and refined in the context of racial conflict reveals the historical processes by which race and law have been mutually constitutive in the United States.[29]

tomahawk," "was well understood by the statesmen who framed the Constitution of the United States, and might furnish some reason for omitting to enumerate them among the parties who might sue in the courts of the Union").

26 See Civil Rights Cases, 109 U.S. at 11 (striking the Civil Rights Act of 1875 prohibiting segregation in public accommodations and conveyances on the basis that "legislative power conferred upon Congress ... does not invest ... power to legislate upon subjects which are within the domain of state legislation"); Slaughter-House Cases, 83 United States 36, 78 (1 Wall.) (1872) (arguing that recognition of the federal government's concurrent jurisdiction for the "privileges and immunities of citizenship" under the Fourteenth Amendment would "fetter and degrade the State governments by subjecting them to the control of Congress" as well as "radically change the whole theory of the relations of the State and Federal governments to each other"); *Blyew v. United States*, 80 U.S. 581 (1 Wall.) (1872) (denying federal jurisdiction under Civil Rights Act of 1866 for murder of an African American family by whites despite state law prohibiting testimony by African Americans unless they were parties to the case); *Hall v. DeCuir*, 95 U.S. 485, 488 (1878) (striking as unconstitutional a state statute requiring equal rights and privileges on public conveyances on the grounds that such legislation "does encroach upon the exclusive power of Congress"); *Giles v. Harris*, 189 U.S. 475, 488 (1903) (upholding state refusal to enroll onto voting lists prospective African American voters on the basis that such "relief from a great political wrong ... by the people of a state and the state itself, must be given by them or by the legislative and political department of the government of the United States").

27 See Fong Yue Ting, 149 U.S. 698, 731 (1893) (stating that the judicial branch has no power to judge the "wisdom, the policy or the judgment" of Congress); *Chae Chan Ping*, 130 U.S. at 602–3 (announcing that the Supreme Court has no authority to pass judgment upon the morality of other branches of government).

28 *Chae Chan Ping*, 130 U.S. 581, 606 (1889) (declaring Congress' determination on immigration laws even where such laws explicitly discriminate by race as "conclusive upon the judiciary" insofar as Congress, not the Supreme Court, "considers the presence of foreigners of a different race in tis country, who will not assimilate with us, to be dangerous to its peace and security"); *U.S. v. Kagama* 118 U.S. 375, 384 (1886) (holding that the federal government alone has the power to enforce its laws upon the Indian tribes); *Lone Wolf v. Hitchcock*, 187 U.S. 553, 565 (1903) (holding that Congress has always exercised plenary power over the Indian tribes). See generally Natsu Taylor Saito, *From Chinese Exclusion to Guantanamo Bay: Plenary Power and the Prerogative State* (University Press of Colorado, 2007) (detailing the emergence of plenary power as a racially subordinating legal rationale that violates the rule of law, international law, and constitutional norms); see also Sarah H. Cleveland, "Powers Inherent in Sovereignty: Indians, Aliens, Territories, and the Nineteenth Century Origins of Plenary Power over Foreign Affairs," *Texas Law Review* 81, no. 1 (2002): 278 (arguing that judicially recognized powers that inhere in sovereignty have origins in both international law and "racist, illiberal ideology" and continue to exert influence over judicial decision-making).

29 For an elaboration of this analysis of the racialization of foundational legal principles, see Cho, "Post-racialism," 1609–10.

During the pre-civil rights era, courts actually played a key role in promoting America's unique form of "racial dictatorship."[30] An important judicial function in preserving the social order and system of privileges revolved around developing allegedly neutral *foundational legal principles* in a way that effectively locked in the stratifications of racial caste. These foundational legal principles were more encompassing than *mere legal rationales or doctrines* – such as "no private constitutional rights"[31] or the "equal application," doctrine,[32] and the low-hanging fruit of "make/find,"[33] "public/

[30] Omi and Winant used this term to describe the period preceding the Civil Rights movement in the United States. Omi and Winant, *Racial Formation*, 65–67 (explaining that from 1607 to 1865, people of color were excluded from the realm of politics, then briefly included during the Reconstruction experiment from 1865–77, then segregated and disenfranchised for almost the next hundred years). See also, Robert A. Williams, *Like at Loaded Weapon: The Rehnquist Court, Indian Rights, and the Legal History of Racism in America* (Minneapolis: University of Minnesota Press, 2005): xx–xxi.

[31] See Civil Rights Cases, 109 U.S. 3, 17 (1883) (finding that the Civil Rights Act of 1875 has no authority in the Constitution insofar as "the wrongful act of an individual, unsupported by any [state] authority, is simply a private wrong" and does not give rise to a civil rights violation); *United States v. Harris*, 106 U.S. 629, 640 (1883) (upholding challenge by indicted white members of lynch mob who beat four African American prisoners and killed one of them on the grounds that Ku Klux Klan Act of 1871 "is directed exclusively against the action of private persons, without reference to the laws of the State" and is therefore unwarranted by the Fourteenth Amendment); *Virginia v. Rives*, 100 U.S. 313, 318 (1880), ruling that exclusion of African Americans from juries does not violate the Fourteenth Amendment by construing such exclusion as the "action of private individuals" and not state action; *United States v. Cruikshank*, 92 U.S. 542, 554 (1875), arresting judgment and dismissing charges against white defendants including state officials for massacre of African Americans on the basis that the Fourteenth Amendment does not "add anything to the rights which one citizen has under the Constitution against another"; *James v. Bowman*, 190 U.S. 127, 136 (1903) (denuding Fifteenth Amendment of force by concluding that Section 5507 of the Revised Statutes was unconstitutional as the amendment does not contemplate "wrongful individual acts").

[32] See *Giles v. Harris*, 189 U.S. 475, 486–87 (1903), rationalizing non-relief in "grandfather clause" voting rights case by stating that "if a white man came here on the same general allegations, admitting his sympathy with the plan, but alleging some special prejudice that had kept him off the list, we hardly should think it necessary to meet him with a reasoned answer"; *Williams v. State of Mississippi*, 170 U.S. 213, 222 (1898), upholding state constitution and laws excluding African Americans from jury service through use of criteria with disparate racial impact on basis that such exclusions "reach weak and vicious white men as well as weak and vicious black men"; *Pace v. State of Alabama*, 106 U.S. 583, 585 (1882), finding no constitutional violation in antimiscegenation statute since "the punishment of each offending person, whether white or black, is the same".

[33] See *Fong Yue Ting*, 149 U.S. 698, 731 (1893), stating that the judicial branch has no power to judge the "wisdom, the policy or the judgment" of Congress; *Chae Chan Ping v. United States*, 130 U.S. 581, 602–3 (1889), "When once it is established that Congress possesses the power to pass an act, our province ends with its construction, and its application to cases as they are presented for determination."

private,"[34] or "social v. civil rights"[35] *legal distinctions*. While legal distinctions, rationales, and doctrines as well as lofty foundational legal principles all formalistically comported with the Fourteenth Amendment's explicit prohibition against racially discriminatory state action by adopting race-neutral discourse, the effect of each method of discursive disenfranchisement was to circumscribe legally the set of economic, social, and political possibilities available to racialized subjects vs. first-class, "socially-vested" citizens.

In short, during the era of dictatorship, rather than serve as counter-majoritarian checks or balances on the subordinating impulse of society, the John Jay-Vinson Courts (up to 1954) participated in a racist "call-and-response" with society that prefigured the broader, neutral-sounding principles upon which the "nation" would find its grounding. In this way, political power, social privilege, and cultural supremacy became functions of whiteness, and vice versa, all filtered consistently and broadly through law. Whites, as a social group, benefited from an amazingly efficient synergism in the mutual back-and-forth between law and society. In the pre-civil rights era, courts played a key role in enabling unreconstructed (post-Reconstruction) whiteness to develop behind high-sounding, but thoroughly racially contingent foundational principles in defining the nation and its imperatives.

For critical theorists familiar with the "whiteness as property" argument, it may not be a hard sell to extend the racial contingency insight to sovereignty, particularly if we are looking at jurisprudential developments of

34 Once the Supreme Court established a "state action" prerequisite for Fourteenth Amendment claims in Civil Rights Cases, the "no private constitutional rights" doctrine discussed previously underwrote the public/private distinction. See also *Yick Wo*, 119 U.S. at 374.

35 See *Plessy*, 163 U.S. 537, 544 (1896), upholding state segregation statute by arguing that Fourteenth Amendment "could not have been intended to … enforce social, as distinguished from political (civil), equality, or a commingling of the two races upon terms unsatisfactory to either"; *Strauder v. West Virginia*, 100 U.S. 303, 306 (1879), affirming the Fourteenth Amendment's purpose as "securing to a race recently emancipated … all the civil rights that the superior race enjoy"; *Civil Rights Cases*, 109 U.S. at 25, distinguishing between constitutional protection of the "essential [civil] rights of life, liberty, and property" compared to "mere [social] discriminations on account of race or color," such as those discriminations in the "enjoyment of accommodations in inns, public conveyances, and places of amusement"; see also *Reva Siegel*, "Why Equal Protection No Longer Protects: The Evolving Forms of Status-Enforcing State Action," *Stanford Law Review* 49 (1997) 1111, 1119–28, detailing the pre-Brown history of the Supreme Court delineation between constitutionally protected "civil" and "political" rights versus unprotected "social" rights.

the pre-civil rights era. In her now canonical work, *Whiteness as Property*, critical race scholar Cheryl Harris identified the jurisprudential tradition of enshrining whiteness as a legally recognized and protected property interest. As one example, she analyzed the language in *Plessy v. Ferguson*, revealing how the Court sought to acknowledge the reputation of being a white person (in a segregated railcar case) as a material interest worthy of judicial notice and legal protection.[36] Professor Harris' approach to understanding property law as fundamentally animated by identity-based norms, privileges, and expectations may be transposed, as we will suggest, in discussing sovereignty and security, as well as other foundational concepts of U.S. public law. The ideology of white supremacy often operated on the surface of formal discourses of law and politics, even in Supreme Court opinions. The discourse of sovereignty originates most significantly in the early nineteenth-century Marshall Court with the Native American sovereignty cases and continues through the late nineteenth-century immigration cases to the turn of the century in the "Insular cases" and beyond.

A. The Limits of Native Sovereignty: The Marshall Trilogy and Quasi-Sovereigns

The central issue in John Marshall's trilogy of cases – concerning the status of the Cherokee nation under threat from the state of Georgia and the "Indian-hater" president, Andrew Jackson – was the meaning of native and U.S. sovereignty.[37] The Marshall Court attempted, in a sense, to triangulate

[36] Cheryl Harris, "Whiteness as Property," *Harvard Law Review* 106 (1994): 1707, 1713–14.

[37] Of course, there is already a rich and established literature on indigenous sovereignty in legal scholarship to which I owe this analysis. This analysis of native sovereignty as defined through the Marshall Trilogy provides more of a summary of this literature, to set up the conversation of how race comparatively maps onto foundational legal principles like sovereignty. For a partial sampling of legal scholarship interpreting indigenous sovereignty through the Marshall Trilogy, see Ward Churchill, *Struggle for the Land: Native North American Resistance to Genocide, Ecocide and Colonization* (San Francisco: City Lights, 2nd. revised ed., 2002); Felix S. Cohen, *Handbook of Federal Indian Law* (Buffalo: William S. Hein, 1998); Vine DeLoria Jr. and Clifford Lyttle, *American Indians, American Justice* (Austin: University of Texas Press, 1983); Tim Alan Garrison, *The Legal Ideology of Removal: The Southern Judiciary and the Sovereignty of Native American Nations* (Athens, GA: University of Georgia Press, 2002); Rennard Strickland, *Fire and the Spirits: Cherokee Law from Clan to Court* (Norman: University of Oklahoma Press, 1975); David E. Wilkins, *American Indian Sovereignty and the Supreme Court, The Masking of Justice* (Austin: University of Texas Press, 1997); Robert A. Williams Jr., *The American Indian in Western Legal Thought: The Discourses of Conquest* (New York: Oxford University Press, 1990); Robert A. Williams Jr., *Like a Loaded Weapon: The Rehnquist Court, Indian Rights, and the Legal History*

a federal-state-Indian relationship in a way that would reference established international law in forwarding a minimalist notion of native sovereignty (for self-serving purposes as discussed below) and reconciling conflicting state and federal expansionist interests.[38] The complex confluences of competing interests in each case – state/federal, federal/Indian, state/Indian, and Indian/non-Indian – rendered impossible the challenge of developing a coherent and lasting model of native sovereignty.[39]

of Racism in America (Minneapolis: University of Minnesota Press, 2005). See also Milner S. Ball, "Comment, John Marshall and Indian Nations in the Beginning and Now," *John Marshall Law Review* 33 (2000): 1183; Anthony Peirson Xavier Bothwell, *Annual Survey of International & Comparative Law* 6 (2000): 175; Sarah H. Cleveland, "Powers Inherent in Sovereignty: Indians, Aliens, Territories, and the Nineteenth Century Origins of Plenary Power over Foreign Affairs," *Texas Law Review* 81 (2002): 1, 26; Robert N. Clinton, "Redressing the Legacy of Conquest: A Vision Quest for a Decolonized Federal Indian Law," *Arkansas Law Review* 46 (1993): 77; Matthew L. M. Fletcher, "The Iron Cold of the Marshall Trilogy," *North Dakota Law Review* 82 (2006): 627; Philip P. Frickey, "Marshalling Past and Present: Colonialism, Constitutionalism, and Interpretation in Federal Indian Law," *Harvard Law Review* 107 (1993): 381; Philip P. Frickey, "(Native) American Exceptionalism in Federal Public Law," *Harvard Law Review* 119 (2005): 431; Steve Newcomb, "The Evidence of Christian Nationalism in Federal Indian Law: The Doctrine of Discovery, Johnson v. McIntosh, and Plenary Power," *New York University Review of Law & Social Change* 20 (1993): 7; Judith V. Royster, "The Legacy of Allotment," *Arizona State Law Journal* 27 (1995): 1; Chief Justice Robert Yazzie, "The Cherokee Nation of Indians, et. al., v. Georgia," *Kansas Journal Law & Public Policy* 8 (1999): 159; David Wilkins, "John Quincy Adams, A Constitutional Conundrum: The Resilience of Tribal Sovereignty during American Nationalism and Expansion: 1810–1871," *Oklahoma City University Law Review* 25 (2000): 87.

38 Of course, indigenous nations and legal scholars/practitioners have been navigating the "courts of the conqueror" to seize upon the contradictions inherent to the articulation of quasi-sovereign sand "domestic dependent nation" status hailing from the Marshall Trilogy, combining the more favorable language with federal laws or canons of interpretation to provide for more favorable modern applications in the courts. See e.g., Stacy L. Leeds, "Moving toward Exclusive Tribal Autonomy over Lands and Natural Resources," *Natural Resources Journal* 46 (2006): 439 (using language from *Johnson v. M'Intosh* to extend the Non-Intercourse Act, which requires federal approval to alienate tribal trust lands to be extended to fee lands with approval by tribal governments).

39 The incoherence and dynamic nature of defining indigenous sovereignty in the courts is reflected in the recent decision in the 2004 *United States v. Lara* case, where (of all people) Justice Thomas forthrightly points out the confused nature of federal Indian law hailing from its doubtful assumption that Congress has plenary power authority over Indian affairs. See Phillip P. Frickey, "(Native) American Exceptionalism in Federal Public Law," *Harvard Law Review* 119 (2005): 470–71. Despite the incoherence of the Supreme Court's formulation of quasi-sovereignty, indigenous nations and legal scholars are developing creative and organic conceptions of tribal sovereignty that emphasizes a more vigorous, inter-subjective and communal definition. Hope M. Babcock, "A Civil-Republican Vision of 'Domestic Dependent Nations' in the Twenty-First Century: Tribal Sovereignty Re-envisioned, Reinvigorated, and Re-empowered," *Utah Law Review* (2005): 443; Wallace Coffey and Rebecca Tsosie, "Rethinking the Tribal Sovereignty Doctrine: Cultural Sovereignty and the Collective

Historically, there is little doubt as to whether native nations in North America operated as "sovereign entities," as suggested in the nearly 400 treaties that were put into force between the various indigenous nations and the United States between 1778 and 1871 – when Congress unilaterally enacted "The End of Treaty Making" legislation to capitalize on the shifting balance of force that began to clearly favor non-Indians in the late conquest era.[40] There is also little doubt that former practice under British rule recognized indigenous nations in colonies as sovereigns possessing the capacity to alienate their property to the crown through treaty. Indeed, it was well-established in Europe, and in the infancy of international law, that sovereignty and land title of the indigenous were not legally extinguished by mere colonial ambition under the so-called Doctrine of Discovery. Rather, the Doctrine of Discovery acted as a sort of "right of preemption,"[41] which mediated potential disputes among colonizers by granting to the colonizer that made the "discovery" of an indigenous nation previously unknown in Europe, a superior right to negotiate treaties with Indians over other colonizing powers.[42] Thus, the doctrine provided for the colonizer to have

Future of Indian Nations," *Stanford Law & Policy Review* 12 (2001): 191; Carole Goldberg, "Individual Rights and Tribal Revitalization," *Arizona State Law Journal* 35 (2003): 889; L. Scott Gould, "The Consent Paradigm: Tribal Sovereignty at the Millennium," *Columbia Law Review* 96 (1996): 809; Sarah Krakoff, "A Narrative of Sovereignty: Illuminating the Paradox of the Domestic Dependent Nation," *Oregon Law Review* 83 (2004): 1109; Sarah Krakoff, "The Vices and Virtues of Sovereignty," *Connecticut Law Review* 38 (2006): 797; Robert B. Porter, "Decolonizing Indigenous Governance: Observations on Restoring Greater Faith and Legitimacy in the Government of the Seneca Nation," *Kansas Journal of Law and Public Policy* 8 (1999): 97; Robert B. Porter, "Strengthening Tribal Sovereignty Through Government Reform: What Are the Issues," *Kansas Journal of Law and Public Policy* 7 (1997): 72; John Randolph Prince, "Indian Country: A Different Model of Sovereignty," *Gonzaga Law Review.* 33 (1997–98): 103; Angela R. Riley, "(Tribal) Sovereignty and Illiberalism," *California Law Review.* 95 (2007): 799; Angela R. Riley, "Tribal Sovereignty in a Post-9/11 World," *North Dakota Law Review* 82 (2006): 953; Rebecca Anita Tsosie, "What Does It Mean to 'Build a Nation'? Re-Imagining Indigenous Political Identity in an Era of Self-Determination," *Asian-Pacific Law & Policy Journal* 7 (2006): 38; Blake A. Watson, "The Thrust and Parry of Federal Indian Law," *Dayton Law Review* 23 (1998): 437.

40 One scholar puts the number of treaties signed between 1778 and 1871 at 370. See Glenn T. Morris, "International Law and Politics," in *Native Americans and the Law: Contemporary and Historical Perspectives on American Indian Rights, Freedoms, and Sovereignty*, ed. John R. Wunder, 333 (1996). End of Treaty Making statute.

41 Francis Paul Prucha, *American Indian Treaties: The History of a Political Anomaly* (Berkeley: University of California Press, 1997): 227.

42 Vine Deloria Jr. and Clifford M. Lytle, *American Indians, American Justice* (Austin: University of Texas Press, 1983), analyzing Chief Justice Marshall's articulation of the "doctrine of discovery" as a corrupted interpretation of the original principle as set forth by Spanish theologian,

exclusive rights to negotiate land cessions; but, as practiced in Europe, it did *not* divest or extinguish indigenous title. It merely permitted extinguishment of indigenous title if the indigenous nation agreed to it, by virtue of treaty with the first-in-line European power.

In the early history of the United States, and consistent with this practice across the Atlantic, no less than the author of the Declaration of Independence, Thomas Jefferson, in conceptualizing the new nation's relationships, acknowledged that Indians have "full, undivided, and independent sovereignty as long as they choose to keep it."[43] The principles behind this early acknowledgment and practice of recognizing native sovereignty in the new nation were both pragmatic and efficient (from the non-Indian perspective). Given the military balance of power in favor of indigenous nations, the British Crown and the early U.S. government understood that it was much less costly to secure voluntary agreements for land cessions from Indians through treaty than to engage military hostilities to acquire indigenous land by conquest alone.[44]

However, by the 1820s and 1830s when the Marshall Trilogy cases were decided, this underlying "interest convergence" to respect native sovereignty, emerging international law, and established European practice because it was in the U.S. interests – so long as the military balance of power did not strongly favor the United States – began to dissolve as state governments

Francisco de Vittoria, 4; Nell Jessup Newton, "Federal Power Over Indians: Its Sources, Scope and Limitations," *University of Pennsylvania Law Review* 132 (1984): 195, 248 (pointing out Chief Justice Taney's misstatement of the doctrine in Dred Scott as well as Chief Justice Marshall's misconception in M'Intosh).

43 Francis Paul Prucha, *American Indian Treaties*, 227.

44 Ward Churchill, "Social Justice Movements and LatCrit Community: The Law Stood Squarely on Its Head: U.S. Legal Doctrine, Indigenous Self-Determination and the Question of World Order," *Oregon Law Review* 81(2002): 670–72, tracing initial treatment of indigenous nations by colonists as sovereigns possessing full ownership rights due to powerful Indian peoples outnumbering European Settlers and the accompanying change in legal relations after the "demographic/military balance in the west had begun to shift decisively in [the United States'] favor. Cleveland, "Powers Inherent in Sovereignty," 26, commenting that "[t]he absence of any express federal power to regulate internal Indian affairs is not surprising given that, when the Constitution was drafted, Indian tribes were highly autonomous and viewed as a serious external threat to the security of the new nation"; Vine DeLoria Jr., "Self-Determination and the Concept of Sovereignty," in *Native American Sovereignty*, ed. John R. Wunder, 22 (New York: Garland Press, 1996), observing that Indian communities were accorded a "European version of sovereignty" as long as they held "sufficient territory and military strength" to determine the outcome of colonial conflicts.

and white settlers viewed Indian country with expansionist designs. In the context of these cases, the particular historical fact of Cherokee land holdings in some of the richest farmland in the state, and the subsequent discovery of gold there, gave compelling imperial-economic force to the state of Georgia's calls for Indian removal to west of the Mississippi.[45]

The historical backdrop of expansionist desire in a white settler state and shifting military power between the United States and native nations created the dramatic tension that called upon the very best, intellectually and politically, that John Marshall could summon to conjure an illusion of legality and legitimacy in the clear light of a brutal "taking." The difficult task confronting Justice Marshall, from *Johnson v. M'Intosh* through *Worcester v. Georgia*, was certainly not explaining the taking itself, which could have been achieved without significantly jeopardizing the credibility and authority of the Supreme Court that he so sought to enhance according to prevailing white supremacist norms of the day. The difficulty for Marshall inhered in the paradox of needing to grant enough native sovereignty to validate treaties in which Indian tribes ceded land title to the new American nation, yet not too much native sovereignty to grant Indians the ability to enforce said treaties or to independently challenge the transgressions against native sovereignty exercised by the state or federal governments.[46] Marshall's already difficult task was made even more so by the outright defiance of the state of Georgia, which challenged the authority of the Supreme Court more than once throughout the course of this string of cases. Thus, Marshall's objective was not only to cast a "now you see it, now you don't"[47] sort of native sovereignty, but also to satisfy and legally ground the settler state's expansionist (acknowledging native sovereignty to uphold cession) *and* subordinationist (denying native sovereignty to uphold subordination) ambitions. In doing so, however, Marshall had to further subordinate state sovereignty to federal sovereignty and did so, in part, by rolling out a newly refabricated interpretation of native sovereignty.

45 Sidney L. Harring, *Crow Dog's Case: American Indian Sovereignty, Tribal Law, and the United States Law in the Nineteenth Century* (Cambridge, U.K.: Cambridge University Press, 1994): 27.

46 Churchill, "Social Justice Movements and LatCrit Community," 677–78 (pointing out how Justice Marshall granted indigenous nations "with a sufficient measure of sovereignty to alienate their territory by treaty when and wherever the U.S. desired they do so, but never with enough to refuse").

47 See John Randolph Prince, "Indian Country: A Different Model of Sovereignty," *Gonzaga Law Review* 33 (1997–98): 103, 115 (incorporating a heading in his article entitled, "First Nation Sovereignty: *Now You See It, Now You Don't*") (emphasis added).

In the first trilogy case, *Johnson v. M'Intosh*, decided in 1823, the Supreme Court was confronted with a land dispute between two white men that had origins in one man claiming that his title to the property in question, based on a public sale under British supervision from the Piankeshaw nation, was superior to that of another, whose title came from a sale by designated federal land officers of the United States.[48] Thus, the Supreme Court was called upon to determine what legal effect, if any, should be given to the Piankeshaw cession, and whether it was superior to the U.S. cession. In order to do so, the Supreme Court would have to confront the question of whether the Piankeshaw possessed sufficient sovereignty as a nation to be able to make the disputed cession. Even though no indigenous person was a party to this action involving two white men, the stakes could not have been higher for native nations, as the right to hold and cede title to indigenous property was at issue. In his *M'Intosh* opinion, Chief Justice Marshall held that the Piankeshaw title could not be sustained.

In so doing, Marshall used, or rather twisted, international law to divest indigenous nations of their preeminent sovereignty vis-a-vis the U.S. federal and state governments. Relying upon various distortions of the Doctrine of Discovery and its related Rights of Conquest, Justice Marshall proved quite capable at fulfilling the hegemony-preserving task at hand. He reviewed and faithfully reconstructed the Doctrine of Discovery used by European crowns to regulate the business of colonization: "The exclusion of all other Europeans, necessarily gave to the nation making the discovery the sole right of acquiring the soil from the natives. ..." But in the next breath, Marshall proceeded to fabricate, out of whole cloth and without citation, the "fundamental principle":

> They [indigenous people] were admitted to be the rightful occupants of the soil, with a legal as well as just claim to retain possession of it ...; but their rights to complete sovereignty, as independent nations, were necessarily diminished, and their power to dispose of the soil at their own will, to whomsoever they please, was denied by the original fundamental principle, that discovery gave exclusive title to those who made it.[49]

Somehow, with the deftness and brutality that one experiences now as sinister, Justice Marshall's legal sleight of hand stated, but then restated the

[48] *Johnson v. M'Intosh*, 21 U.S. 523 (1823).
[49] Id. at 574.

Doctrine of Discovery, and in the process, "diminished" native sovereignty to "dispose of the soil ... to whomsoever they please" by mischaracterizing the meaning of legal right that inured to the discoverer.

Perhaps realizing the (hegemonically) unsatisfying nature of his restatement and misstatement of the discovery doctrine, Marshall then turns to a second argument, asking whether the "American states rejected or adopted this principle" that it is the exclusive right of the discoverer to "appropriate the lands occupied by the Indians."[50] Continuing in a grand declaration-absent-citation register, Justice Marshall opines:

> The United States, then, have unequivocally acceded to that great and broad rule by which its civilized inhabitants now hold this country. They maintain, as all others have maintained, that discovery gave an exclusive right to extinguish the Indian title of occupancy, either by purchase or by conquest; and gave also *a right to such a degree of sovereignty, as the circumstances of the people would allow them to exercise*.[51]

Just as the opinion seems to have exhausted the overworked Doctrine of Discovery and related Rights of Conquest, the Supreme Court proceeds to some of its most controversial "color-commentary" on the history of legal title from the British crown to the present day (at the time). In what some would overlook as mere *dicta*, Justice Marshall provides a kind of "cleanup" argument to rectify the foregoing distortion. To understand the necessity of the cleanup argument and why it should not be made harmless by categorization as dicta, we need to grasp the full flimsiness of the Marshall's arguments.

One of Justice Marshall's key arguments involved his (mis)interpretation of the Doctrines of Discovery. As stated previously, Marshall's reliance on the discovery doctrines and incipient international law to ground his *M'Intosh* opinion is problematic for its studied combination of accurate and inaccurate statements of the doctrine – the most egregious of which is Marshall's

50 Id. Territorium res nullius was the more precise principle hailing from the Doctrine of Discovery that Justice Marshall deployed to divest indigenous title on the grounds that territory was "uninhabited territory" that might then be claimed by the first to "discover" it. Territorium res nullius, combined with the ancient doctrine of "Norman Yoke," derived from British legal philosophy, provided that, like Lockean notions of property, an owner was required to build upon, cultivate, or otherwise transform their property from a "state of wilderness" or forfeit title to it. In such a case, the land in question would be considered "vacant" and available to whomever would be willing to mix the land with one's labor. Churchill, "Social Justice Movements and LatCrit Community," 665–70.

51 *Johnson v. M'Intosh*, 21 U.S. at 587 (emphasis added).

wholesale conversion of native rights to alienate their property, despite the cited doctrine and established practice and law among European crowns to the contrary. More fundamentally though, as suggested in his judicial notice of European supremacy ("the character and religion of its inhabitants afforded an apology for considering them as a people over whom the superior genius of Europe might claim an ascendancy"), the Doctrines of Discovery drew cultural force from assumed European Christian supremacy and beliefs that the world could be divided rationally among competing colonial powers.

Justice Marshall relies on a second key concept of international law – the rights of conquest rationale, or "the British made me do it." Here, Marshall opines that "[i]t is not for the Courts of this country to question the validity of this title, or to sustain one which is incompatible with it." He suggests that conquest is equally available as a route to indigenous title as purchase. However, under the Rights of Conquest, understood to be a subset of the Doctrine of Discovery, appropriating indigenous land by conquest could only occur under very limited circumstances through "just war," where: (1) the indigenous population initiates unprovoked attack upon representatives or subjects of the "discovery" power; (2) the indigenous arbitrarily refuse trade with discoverers' representatives; or (3) indigenous refuse to allow Christian missionaries of discoverers among them.[52] If any of these conditions were met, just war could ensue in accordance with the "law of nations," with the discoverer entitled to extinguish indigenous title as "compensation" for the costs of waging war. The case for title by conquest is extremely difficult to make. And as an historical matter, the British favored acquiring title by purchase, a policy adopted by the United States in 1787 NW Ordinance, in which Congress foreswore war and title by conquest with native nations in favor of negotiating treaties in the "utmost good faith."[53]

Perhaps recognizing that both arguments based on the law of nations might be subject to critique by European crowns and jurists who would recognize the Supreme Court's misapplications, Justice Marshall resorts to a sheer power, or "might makes right," argument. In *M'Intosh*, he concludes that "conquest gives a title which the Courts of the conqueror cannot deny." The truncation of judicial review as a direct function of

[52] Churchill, "Social Justice Movements and LatCrit Community," 680–81.

[53] Id. at 52.

imperial political theology certainly leaves the "rule of law" in a state of suspension.

However "extravagant the pretension of converting the discovery of an inhabited country into conquest may appear," if a country has "been acquired[,] … it becomes the law of the land, and cannot be questioned." However "opposed to natural right, and to the usages of civilized nations," if "indispensable to that system under which the country has been settled and adapted to the actual condition of the two people [,] … [title by conquest] cannot be rejected by Courts of justice." The Supreme Court's seeming "inevitability" defense rings hollow because only the court can prevent this inevitability from occurring, as it has a clear choice of which land title it chooses to acknowledge, and of which form of native sovereignty it elects to recognize.

Given the limited persuasiveness of the Supreme Court's previously stated rationales, the seeming dicta of *M'Intosh* takes on more force, and operates as the catch-all argument that gives epistemic force to the otherwise reasoned legal argument. In short, the court must "resort to some new and different rule" other than the rule of law that would ordinarily prevail among conqueror and conquered, which is "better adapted to the "actual state of things." The punch line to this extended soliloquy on native sovereignty and Euro-British colonial history, is that indigenous people are too "fierce," too "savage," too "uncivilized," too "forest" and "wilderness," to be included within the circle of the law's protection. They do not meet the *anthropological threshold or minimum* necessary to be viewed as worthy of legal subjecthood. As such, their sovereignty, in a Western sense, cannot coexist with that of "civilized nations." Insofar as incorporation of the fierce savage is impossible without jeopardizing [white] "families to the perpetual hazard of being massacred,"[54] native sovereignty must be scaled to match the "actual state of things." In this way, the court defines and limits the concept of sovereignty through the constructed inferior racial identity of the Indian-other.

After setting up sovereignty's racial logic, Justice Marshall added to the monstrosity in a subsequent 1831 case, *Cherokee Nations v. Georgia*. In this case, the Cherokee nation sought to enjoin the state of Georgia's

[54] *M'Intosh*, 590.

increasing encroachment on its self-governance by appealing to Article 3 of the Constitution, which permits "foreign states" to bring suit against states of the Union, and the seemingly jurisdictional/procedural question again returned Marshall to the substantively important question of native sovereignty. In deciding against native sovereignty that would permit the Cherokees to sue the state of Georgia in federal court, the Supreme Court expressed its skepticism about whether "those tribes that reside within the acknowledged boundaries of the U.S. can, with strict accuracy, be denominated foreign nations. They may, more correctly, perhaps, be denominated domestic dependent nations," a tension-filled, if not incoherent concept that converted the legal equality assumed by the hundreds of treaties entered into by the United States and native nations into a hierarchical and subjugationist relationship of ward/guardian. To arrive at this conclusion, which cancelled out Cherokee claims to sufficient sovereignty to sue on their own behalf, Marshall considered the founders' "original intent" as to whether Indian nations qualified as foreign nation under Article III of the Constitution:

> the habits and usages of the Indians, in their intercourse with their white neighbors, ought not be entirely disregarded. At the time the Constitution was framed, the idea of appealing to an American court of justice for an assertion of right or redress of wrong,[sic] had perhaps never entered the mind of an Indian or his tribe. Their appeal was to the tomahawk, or to the government. This was well understood by the statesmen who framed the Constitution of the United States, and might furnish some reason for omitting to enumerate them among the parties who might sue in the courts of the Union.[55]

The Marshall Trilogy is rounded out by a third case, *Worcester v. Georgia*, decided in 1832. Although commented upon as a highly revered opinion, reflecting Marshall's magnanimity toward Indians, the case continues to run unabated with judicial notice of Indian savagery. Although this case, more than any other in the trilogy, sought to emphasize the "nation" aspect of the domestic dependent nation construct announced in *Cherokee Nation*, it did so by appealing to the imagery of Indian savagery as initially developed in the first two cases. Indeed, the savagery necessitated the

[55] Williams Jr., *Like a Loaded Weapon*, 62 citing to and analyzing *Cherokee Nation* case.

degree of sovereignty afforded by the Supreme Court, as the inherently "fierce and warlike" character of Indians rendered them incommensurable others who gave the English Crown no choice but to recognize "their right to self-government." In *Worcester*, the Supreme Court perfected its balancing act of "now you see it/now you don't" Indian sovereignty by expanding its application of the Doctrine of Discovery to include a necessity argument – premised upon inherent racial incommensurability – to warrant self-governance within the colonial governmentality. Moreover, the "fierce and warlike" nature of Indians necessitated that only the Crown would have sovereign supremacy over them, a sovereignty that was then ceded after the Revolutionary War to the U.S. federal government. The Marshall Trilogy, over the years, refined and defined the court's Doctrine of Discovery as an effective colonial governmentality that could reserve to the federal government its supremacy over both the states and Indian domestic dependent nations. By ceding some acknowledgment of native sovereignty in terms of right to self-government, the Supreme Court lost nothing, as the federal government would still prevail over Indians in the established ward/guardian relationship. Moreover, recalcitrant states like Georgia would be legally subjected to the federal interest in controlling Indian affairs.

By granting to indigenous nations only a racially and culturally contingent quasi-sovereignty, vis-à-vis the states of the Union, while also remaining in a "state of pupilage," vis-à-vis the federal government, the Marshall Trilogy achieved the difficult task that lay before Justice Marshall. The "domestic dependent nation" construction brilliantly granted just enough sovereignty to indigenous nations to quiet title to U.S. lands gained through the hundreds of treaties with native nations prior to 1871, yet not enough sovereignty to allow for indigenous nations, like the Cherokee, to vindicate their property rights and sovereign powers in the "courts of the Conqueror."[56] Moreover, the triangulation of Indian-state-federal powers allowed the federal government to assert its sovereign authority and supremacy over states, as well as Indians, in determining what would happen to valuable lands and natural resources within the contested territories.

[56] Nell Jessup Newton "Indian Claims in the Courts of the Conqueror," *American University Law Review* 41 (1992): 753 (retrieving Justice Marshall's apt phrase from *Johnson v. M' Intosh*).

B. Chinese Immigration/Deportation: Plenary Power and the "Credible White Witness"

Late nineteenth-century immigration and deportation cases involving Chinese and Japanese immigrants further illustrate the racial contingency of sovereignty as articulated by the plenary power doctrine.[57] The first federal immigration statutes in the United States were racially explicit and exclusionary, as well as gendered, classed, and sexed. Beginning with the 1875 Page Law, Congress sought to prohibit convicts and prostitutes from entering the United States. However, the prohibition against prostitutes was not general, but specific to Chinese prostitutes. Immigration laws and policies accommodated employer preferences for single, able-bodied, migratory men from China unencumbered by families. And, as Eithne Luibhéid has pointed out in *Entry Denied: Controlling Sexuality at the Border*, immigration agents tended to presume that all Chinese women immigrating to the United States were prostitutes, thereby threatening the hegemony of the hetero-patriarchal model of family-based immigration.[58]

Within seven years of the Page Law, Congress passed the Chinese Exclusion Act of 1882, which prohibited Chinese laborers from immigrating, and renewed it ten years later in the Geary Act of 1892. The 1882 Act was challenged by Chae Chan Ping, a laborer who had lived in the United States for over a decade and had returned to China to visit his family. He had made sure he had the requisite reentry certificate that was required at the time, but, prior to his return, Congress passed legislation barring the reentry of lawful Chinese residents who had gone overseas, even if they had obtained the previously required certificate.

Chae Chan Ping challenged his barring, alleging a due process claim and a violation of the Burlingame Treaty of 1868 between the United States and China, which guaranteed free migration between the two countries. The Supreme Court upheld the law and denied Chae Chan Ping's claim, dispensing with the treaty by implementing a novel "last in time" rule to grant the subsequent statute priority. The constitutional claim was rejected by invoking

57 Plenary power doctrine has its origins not only in Chinese immigration and deportation cases, but also in native sovereignty cases and the Insular cases. For a sample of some of the plenary power scholarship in these other contexts, see Saito, *From Chinese Exclusion to Guantanamo Bay*. Cleveland, "Powers Inherent in Sovereignty: Indians, 26; Newton, "Federal Power Over Indians: 195, 248.

58 Eithne Luibhéid, *Entry Denied: Controlling Sexuality at the Border* (Minneapolis: University of Minnesota Press, 2002).

the federal government's sovereign prerogative over national security and its territorial borders, or, as Justice Field put it, "[t]he power of exclusion of foreigners being an incident of sovereignty belonging to the government of the United States as a part of those sovereign powers delegated by the constitution, the right to its exercise at any time when, in the judgment of the government, the interests of the country require it, cannot be granted away or restrained on behalf of any one."[59] Even if the Supreme Court believes congressional decision making is explicitly racial, involving "foreigners of a different race ... who will not assimilate with us," and who are considered "dangerous to its peace and security," Congress's determination is "conclusive upon the judiciary," due to this early articulation of plenary power.[60]

Three years after *Chae Chan Ping* was decided, the Supreme Court had steadier footing in its developing plenary power doctrine to exclude an unmarried, Japanese woman suspected of becoming a "public charge" in the 1892 case, *Nishimura Ekiu v. U.S.* The problematics of an immigration agent's racial, gender, and class assumptions – that the Japanese immigrant woman would become a public charge warranting exclusion – are obscured by the necessity of a nation to exercise its powers inherent in sovereignty to "self-preservation." To hear the Supreme Court and Congress tell it, Chinese and Japanese women posed such a threat to the nation's self-preservation that the court had to abdicate its assigned judicial function of constitutional review for a model favoring an unrestrained and unilateral Congress or executive. Writing for the Supreme Court, Justice Gray acknowledged that "every sovereign nation has the power, as inherent in sovereignty, and essential to self-preservation, to forbid the entrance of foreigners within its dominions. ..."

But perhaps the most revealing case on the racialization of plenary power was decided one year later in 1893, in *Fong Yue Ting v. U.S.* The Geary Act, enacted one year prior, required every Chinese laborer to carry a "certificate of residence," or pass card of sorts, to prove, upon request, one's lawful resident status post–exclusion. Being caught without one would result in deportation, unless the unfortunate laborer is able to convince a judge that he is here legally, a claim that would have to be supported by "at least one credible white witness." Individuals and organizations within

59 *Chae Chan Ping v. U.S.*, 130 U.S. 581, 609 (1889).
60 Id.

the considerable Chinese community in San Francisco sought to challenge the registration requirement. As late as one month prior to the deadline, less than one percent of San Francisco's estimated Chinese labor population had registered under the Geary Act. Nationwide, only 13.5 percent of Chinese complied with the Geary Act, leaving about 85,000 subject to deportation. Two of those refusing were Fong Yue Ting and Wong Quong, as part of the resistance organized by the Chinese Six Companies. They were arrested and ordered deported, along with a third laborer, Lee Joe, who had tried to register, but was denied a certificate because his witnesses were Chinese, not white.[61]

The *Fong Yue Ting* Court upheld the dismissal of the writ of habeus corpus by invoking a political/judicial distinction before applying the logic of plenary power: "[I]t behooves the court to be careful that it does not undertake to pass upon political questions, the final decision of which has been committed by the constitution to the other departments of the government."[62] Plenary power also provided the distinction for the outcome in *Yick Wo v. Hopkins*, where the Fourteenth Amendment was applied to Chinese immigrants, even though they were not citizens, to strike a municipal ordinance applied with a racially "uneven hand." Writing for the majority, Justice Gray found *Yick Wo* inapposite because "[t]he question there was of the power of a state over aliens continuing to reside within its jurisdiction, not of the power of the United States to put an end to their residence in the country." Gray's reasoning suggests that both substance and source matter, with plenary power acting as constitutional trump card.

Although there was no "state action," in that Congress enacted the explicit discrimination against the Chinese, dissenting opinions took notice of the Fourteenth Amendment analogy to the case at hand. Justice Brewer's dissenting opinion cited to the due process and equal protection language from *Yick Wo v. Hopkins*, taking particular notice that the Fourteenth Amendment "is not confined to the protection of citizens": "[t]hese provisions are universal in their application to all persons within the territorial jurisdiction, without regard to any differences of race, of color, or of nationality; and the equal protection of the laws is a pledge of the protection of equal laws." Reasoning

[61] Lucy Salyer, *Laws Harsh as Tigers': Enforcement of the Chinese Exclusion Laws* (Berkeley: University of California Press, 1995), 47–48.

[62] *Fong Yue Ting*, 149 U.S. 698, 712 (1893).

by analogy, Justice Brewer argued that "[i]f the use of the word 'person' in the Fourteenth Amendment protects all individuals lawfully within the State, the use of the same word, 'person,' in the Fifth must be equally comprehensive, and secures to all persons lawfully within the territory of the United States the protection named therein." Justice Field also cited to *Yick Wo* in his dissenting opinion, pointing out that "[t]he fundamental rights to life, liberty, and the pursuit of happiness, ... are secured by those maxims of constitutional law which are the monuments showing the victorious progress of the race in securing to man the blessings of civilization under the reign of just and equal laws." Rounding out the dissenters, Justice Fuller provided the harshest critique of the Gray majority, suggesting that any "plenary power"-type precedent borrowed from Great Britain or European crowns may be historically accurate, but constitutionally lacking:

> It may be admitted that the power has been exercised by the various Governments of Europe. Spain expelled the Moors; England, in the reign of Edward I., banished 15,000 Jews; 149 U.S., in 1685, by revoking the edict of Nantes, which gave religious liberty to Protestants in France, drove out the Huguenots. Nor does such severity of European Governments belong only to the distant post. Within three years, Russia has banished many thousands of Jews, and apparently intends the expulsion of the whole race – an act of barbarity which has aroused the indignation of all Christendom. Such was the feeling in this country that, friendly as our relations with Russia had always been, President Harrison felt compelled to call the attention of Congress to it in his message in 1891 as a fit subject for national remonstrance. Indeed, all the instances mentioned have been condemned for their barbarity and cruelty, and no power to perpetrate such barbarity is to be implied from the nature of our Government, and certainly is not found in any delegated powers under the Constitution.

Justice Fuller objected to the majority's abdication of its constitutional review powers on the basis of an asserted plenary power: "The United States [government] is one of limited and delegated powers. It takes nothing from the usages or the former action of European Governments, nor does it take any power by any supposed inherent sovereignty. There is a great deal of confusion in the use of the word 'sovereignty.'"

Plenary power emerges as a legal doctrine at the turn of the nineteenth century, at a moment when the Supreme Court must determine whether to apply the constitutional norms of equal protection and due process to Chinese immigrants, who sought relief from explicitly racist and exclusionist federal immigration and deportation laws. Rather than apply the obvious equal protection and due process protections in the Fifth Amendment, as urged by the *Fong Yue Ting* dissenters, the court instead relies upon the new foundational principle of "plenary power" to resolve the racial conflict and sidestep racial justice for Chinese immigrants. This pattern of the court relying upon plenary power as judicial abdication does not end (or for that matter, start) with Chinese immigration and exclusion .

C. Insular Cases and Imperialism: Applying the Constitution (or Not) in the "Territories"

At the turn of the nineteenth century, a debate within the U.S. body politic centered around whether the United States should emulate European nations to become an imperial power. This debate intensified following the Spanish-American War and the 1898 Treaty of Paris, ending that conflict by transferring Spain's interests in its former colonies to the United States, including Puerto Rico, Cuba, the Philippines, and Guam. The question of U.S. imperialism dominated the U.S. presidential election of 1900 between Republican President William McKinley, a staunch advocate for imperialism, and Democratic challenger William Jennings Bryan, a critic of McKinley's imperialist policies. The question of whether the new territories were, or could be, part of the United States also played out in legal academe and, soon enough, in the courts.

The Insular Cases defined the relationship between the United States and its territories or colonies. The most famous of these cases, decided in 1901 before the Supreme Court, concerned whether a tax imposed on crates of oranges shipped from Puerto Rico to New York could be subject to levy under the Foraker Act, which imposed duties upon goods from Puerto Rico up to 15 percent of duties imposed on foreign goods. The tax would apply only if Puerto Rico were determined to be separate from the United States, as the Uniformity Clause of the Constitution provided similar treatment among the states of the United States, none of which were subject to the Foraker Act tax. In *Downes v. Bidwell*, this seemingly mundane question began a heated debate within the court about the application of the Constitution to the newly acquired territories – a debate that would play out over the next two decades in a series of cases. The Insular Cases are significant to this inquiry because they reflect the manipulation of the concept of sovereignty based on both racial and cultural characteristics.[63]

In *Downes*, the Supreme Court determined that, with respect to the Foraker Act, Puerto Rico was not a part of the United States, and therefore, the Uniformity Clause of the Constitution would not apply. The case occasioned five separate opinions written by the Justices. Both Justice Brown's opinion for the court in *Downes* and the concurrence by Justice White, the latter of which would become the dominant framing of the now-entrenched functional doctrine of extraterritoriality, are infused with the odious imperial paternalism and Anglo-centric common sense of the day. Brown took the opportunity to warn about the danger to the imperial project of automatic inclusion under the Constitution of "alien races":

> A false step at this time might be fatal to the development of what Chief Justice Marshall called the American empire. Choice in some cases, the natural gravitation of small bodies towards large ones in others, the result of a successful war in still others, may bring about conditions which would render the annexation of distant possessions desirable.

[63] The conversation in legal scholarship on the Insular Cases, once subdued, is now very lively. For a sample of this literature, see essays by various legal scholars in *Foreign in a Domestic Sense: Puerto Rico, American Expansion, and the Constitution*, Christina Duffy Burnett and Burke Marshall, eds. (Durham: Duke University Press, 2001); James Edward Kerr, *The Insular Cases: The Role of the Judiciary in American Expansionism* (Port Washington, NY: Kennikat Press, 1982); Gary Lawson and Guy Seidman, *The Constitution of Empire: Territorial Expansion and American Legal History* (New Haven, CN: Yale University Press, 2004); Pedro A. Malavet, *America's Colony: The Political and Cultural Conflict between the United States and Puerto Rico* (New York: New York University Press, 2004); Jorge Trias Monge, *Puerto Rico: The Trials of the Oldest Colony in the World* (New Haven: Yale University Press, 1997); Bartholemew H. Sparrow, *The Insular Cases and the Emergence of American Empire* (Lawrence: University of Kansas Press, 2006); Juan R. Torruella, *The Supreme Court and Puerto Rico: The Doctrine of Separate and Unequal* (La Editorial Universidad de Puerto Rico, 1985); Jose A. Cabranes, "Puerto Rico: Colonialism as Constitutional Doctrine," *Harvard Law Review* 100 (1986): 450; Sanford V. Levinson, "Why the Canon Should be Expanded to Include the Insular Cases and the Saga of American Expansionism," *Constitutional Commentary* 17 (2000): 241; Pedro Malavet, "From *Downes v. Bidwell* to *Boumediene v. Bush*" (SSRN, 2009); Efren Rivera Ramos, "The Legal Construction of Identity: The Judicial and Social Legacy of American Colonialism: The Insular Cases (1901–1922)," *Revista Juridica Universidad de Puerto Rico* 65 (1996): 225; Ediberto Roman, "The Alien-Citizen Paradox and Other Consequences of U.S. Colonialism," *Florida State University Law Review* 26 (1998): 1; Carlos R. Soltero, "The Supreme Court Should Overrule the Territorial Incorporation Doctrine and End One Hundred Years of Judicially Condoned Colonialism," *Chicano-Latino Law Review* 22 (2001): 1; Gabriel A. Terras, "The United States and Puerto Rico and the Territorial Incorporation Doctrine: Reaching a Century of Constitutional Authoritarianism," *John Marshall Law Review* 31 (1997): 55.

> If those possessions are inhabited by alien races, differing from us in religion, customs, laws, methods of taxation, and modes of thought, the administration of government and justice, according to Anglo-Saxon principles, may for a time be impossible; and the question at once arises whether large concessions ought not to be made for a time, that ultimately our own theories may be carried out, and the blessings of a free government under the Constitution extended to them. We decline to hold that there is anything in the Constitution to forbid such action.[64]

Justice White shapes his analysis in a way that recalls Marshall's Indian trilogy, not only in its lengthy passages citing Justice Marshall's conquest/incorporation language from *Johnson v. M'Intosh*, but also with its unincorporated territories notion reminiscent of domestic dependent nations.[65] Justice White coins a new usage in his *Downes* concurrence: "unincorporated territories" – an in-between category that places a constitutional veneer over the imperial project with "guaranties of certain fundamental personal rights declared in the Constitution" to be provided by the U.S. government to "non-citizen inhabitants."[66]

White's concurrence, like Brown's opinion, throws up the specter of non-assimilable savages and alien races in framing the impulse and significance of the functional approach. Henceforth, territorial possessions of the United States could be, as a matter of political, military, or administrative expediency, treated as either incorporated or unincorporated territories, and full membership rights and constitutional protections would only be awarded to those in territories qualifying for incorporation as a matter of civilizational and racial standing. The incorporated/unincorporated distinction served to constitutionalize, in neutral terms, the race-based decision making that served to deny application of the Constitution to the "alien races."

[64] *Downes*, at 286–87.

[65] The quoted language includes in part:

> The title by conquest is acquired and maintained by force. The conqueror prescribes it limits. ... Most usually [the conquered] are incorporated with the victorious nation, and become subjects or citizens of the government with which they are connected. The new and the old members of the society mingle with each other; the distinction between them is gradually lost, and they make one people.
>
> When this conquest is complete, and the conquered inhabitants can be blended with the conquerors, or safely governed as a distinct people. ...

Downes v. Bidwell, 182 U.S. at 282 (quoting *Johnson v. M'Intosh*, 21 U.S. at 543, 589).

[66] *Boumediene v. Bush*, 553 U.S. at 28 (2008)(quoting from Balzac v. Puerto Rico).

The parallel between the Insular Cases and the Marshall Trilogy became even clearer after another Insular Case had been decided in *DeLima v. Bidwell*. In *DeLima*, the Supreme Court was considering yet another tax for a shipment of sugar from Puerto Rico to the United States. But the *DeLima* facts differed from *Downes* insofar as the challenge to the duties occurred after the 1898 Treaty of Paris, but under the Dingely Act that preceded the Foraker Act, and assessed levies from goods shipped from "foreign countries." Thus, the question the Supreme Court had to decide, after determining in *Downes* that Puerto Rico was not part of the United States for purposes of applying the Constitution, was whether it was foreign. Curiously, the Supreme Court struck down the tax assessed under the Dingley Act, concluding that Puerto Rico was not a foreign country. So, like the Cherokee nation's "domestic dependent nation" status, Puerto Rico also existed in the liminal sovereign space of being neither domestic (per *Downes*) nor foreign (per *DeLima*). Justice White described this liminality most aptly:

> In an international sense Porto Rico [*sic*] was not a foreign country, since it was subject to the sovereignty of and was owned by the United States, [but] it was *foreign to the United States in a domestic sense*, because the island had not been incorporated into the United States, but was merely appurtenant thereto as a possession.[67]

Filipinos would fare even worse on the racial gradation scale than residents of the other U.S. insular territories. The Taft Commission, headed by William Howard Taft, and charged with gathering data to assist in the colonial administration of the territory, had a dim view of the residents of the Philippine Islands:

> It is universally conceded that the Negritos of to-day are the disappearing remnants of a people which once populated the entire archipelago. They are, physically, weaklings of low stature, with black skin, closely-curling hair, flat noses, thick lips, and large, clumsy feet. In the matter of intelligence they stand at or near the bottom of the human series, and they are believed to be incapable of any considerable degree of civilization or advancement.[68]

[67] *Downes v. Bidwell*, 182 U.S. (J. White, concurring, at 342).

[68] Mark S. Weiner, "Teutonic Constitutionalism," in *Foreign in a Domestic Sense: Puerto Rico, American Expansion, and the Constitution*, ed. Christina Duffy Burnett and Burke Marshall, 66 (Durham/London: Duke University Press, 2001).

As historian Ronald Takaki pointed out about the popular imagery of the Chinese, a "negroization" process drew physical, biological, and cultural similarities between Africans and Asians to exclude them from the body politic and realm of first-class citizenship.

Eligibility for statehood, like nationhood, turned, once again, upon a territory's residents meeting the anthropological minimum established by the racialized, imperial logic of the day. In her book, *From Chinese Exclusion to Guantanamo Bay: Plenary Power and the Prerogative State*, Professor Saito argues persuasively that this denial of relief on the basis that courts are unable to undertake constitutional review of matters deemed to involve inherent powers of the sovereign is not at all arbitrary or aberrant, but instead follows a consistent pattern against "relatively powerless Others."[69] In this way, sovereign power – be it nationhood, statehood, or plenary power – is utterly racial in origin and development. Race and sovereignty, as illustrated by the legal history affecting indigenous people, immigrant Asians, and insular territory residents, are mutually constitutive. The racial contingency of sovereignty analysis is but one example of this mutual constitutivity in U.S. law and its fundamental legal principles – neutral in appearance, but always already racialized.

III. Security and Race

Having tracked the concept of sovereignty in U.S. law through the racialized structure and ideology that breathed life and meaning into it, we suggest pursuing a similar inquiry into the structure and history of national security in law. Thus, we would not approach security as a sort of self-standing, a priori category of modern political or ethical life. We favor, instead, a rather unrelenting engagement with the structural, cultural, institutional, and discursive groundings of security, historicizing and highlighting the contingency and political corrosiveness of its force in law and beyond. There is, for example, only problematic recourse to an "already there" national community or a unified, determinate set of interests capable of sustaining the discursive payload assigned national security in culture and law. Nonetheless, sovereign deductionism, the assumption of national/

[69] Saito, *From Chinese Exclusion to Guantanamo Bay*, 14.

state security as a priori norm category in law, not as a socially contingent "fact condition" external to it, takes as many forms as there are strands of post-9/11 legal scholarship. Such scholarship is, in fact, engaged powerfully, perhaps even primarily, when taken as a whole, in "cultural"[70] work that bears the historical resonances of imperial racial, class, and gendered contingency.

The growing body of scholarship on U.S. national security law simply has not contemplated the framing of inquiry in critical/anti-imperial terms.[71] Is it the common sense of the moment that legal liberalism, or liberal democracy, for that matter, can neither critique nor seek to problematize analytically the imperial projects that precipitate and condition any variety of constitutional crises that scholars have been describing and parsing? Must we accept securitization processes as legal facts, so to speak, which must remain "mysterious" yet controlling for law?[72] Certainly, since 9/11, the common sense seems to have been pointing us generally in the direction of a clashing-civilizations thesis, with attendant exclusions, subordinations, and "free passes" to those fighting to defend "our way of life and freedom." There is much to discuss: abuses of the "war on terrorism" from Guantanamo Bay to Abu Ghraib, the socially pernicious National Security Entry/Exit Registration System (NSEERS) program, current Immigration and Customs Enforcement (ICE) raids terrifying Latino communities, FBI "infiltration" of mosques throughout the United States and the targeting of Muslim charities for terrorism prosecutions, etc. We offer here but a brief sketch of this latest round of creative-destructive security discourse from the perspective of anti-imperial race critique.

70 See Peter J. Katzenstein, "Introduction: Alternative Perspectives in National Security," in *The Culture of National Security: Norms and Identity in World Politics* 2, ed. Peter J. Katzenstein (Irvington, NY: Columbia University Press, 1996).

71 Thinking perhaps along the general lines of Duncan Kennedy's essay "Iraq: The Case for Losing," (referring to the case for losing the Iraq War), *Brooklyn Journal of International Law* 31 (2006): 1. The invocation by scholars of international humanitarian and human rights law and culture necessarily sounds in anti-unilateralism, though these same legal regimes have been implicated in neoliberal globalization and western "rule of law" imperialisms.

72 Securitization refers to an understanding of security discourse as a form of politics, specifically the attempt to place certain questions outside the realm of political contestation. Securitization as a critical concept denies to security discourse anything like the privilege of an objective or even subjective engagement with actual risk and instead analyzes security invocation as a form of speech act. See generally Copenhagen School works such as Barry Buzan, Ole Waever and Jaap de Wilde, *Security: A New Framework for Analysis* (Boulder: Lynne Rienner, 1997).

The Japanese internment provides the crucial historical racial backdrop for present-day U.S. security law and policy discussions. Yet the focus in much of the scholarship on the parameters of war powers balancing returns us to the familiar disciplinary binary represented in the *Curtiss-Wright* and *Youngstown* cases.[73] We find that the battle over disciplinary precedents continues to privilege the narrowed optic of cases that historically articulate the mechanics and processes of state power projection at the expense of a critical legal genealogy of national security rationales and institutions.[74] The balancing optic, paradigmatically captured in Justice Jackson's *Youngstown* concurrence with its imagery of ebbs and "zones of twilight" (along with the possibility of the executive actually personifying federal sovereignty), has little to do with the lessons of the internment's jurisprudence and, not at all coincidentally, sheds little light on political branch overreach and aggression despite Jackson's suggestion that some power may actually be denied the government. In thinking about national security law from the perspective of the internment a wholly different image is called to mind: the machine. Jerry Kang's critical history of the Supreme Court's internment jurisprudence places the promise of court-led balancing into a different light altogether when he concludes the court "was a full participant in the internment machinery."[75]

The effects of September 11 on many Muslims, Arabs, and South Asians have been socially disastrous, and the racialization of "the terrorist threat" has meant that no one from these communities is beyond the reach of reaction. Thoroughly mapping the role of law in these disasters is an unfolding critical project, much of which is being undertaken by community organizations or advocates on behalf of the affected communities. Two recently adjudicated cases, the Supreme Court's *Boumediene* decision and the criminal trial of Muhammad Salah in a Chicago federal court illustrate the complexities involved. *Boumediene* represents the first time the Supreme Court has ever ruled a joint executive/congressional action during wartime unconstitutional, or extended habeas corpus protection to

73 *United States v. Curtiss-Wright Export Corp.* 209 U.S. 304 (1936); *Youngstown Sheet & Tube Co. v. Sawyer*, 343 U.S. 579 (1952).

74 These issues were addressed in the earlier article, Gott, "A Tale of New Precedents."

75 Jerry Kang, "Denying Prejudice: Internment, Redress, and Denial," *UCLA Law Review* 51 (2004): 933, 963.

noncitizens and nationals held as enemy prisoners outside the territorial United States. However, *Boumediene* is remarkable as well for the way in which the opinion misreads the racialized precedents of U.S. imperial law. The *Salah* trial is a stunning case of firsts as well, most notably marking the first time that what appears to have been a known coerced confession has ever been admitted in a U.S. court. The *Salah* case has, as coda, a not guilty jury verdict (on the terrorism charge), but Salah's and his codefendant's excessive prison sentences on lesser charges, and the more recent Muslim charity verdicts, suggest an ongoing racialization of the federal criminal law of national security.

To place the criminal cases and *Boumediene* in context, we turn briefly to a memo written by Jay Bybee back in February of 2002 – not one of the infamous torture memos released in 2009, but a memo on the status of the Taliban under Article 4 of the Third Geneva Convention of 1949. The Taliban memo made less of a splash than the torture memos, but conveyed nonetheless the basis behind denial of legal subjecthood and humanity that drives a political culture of torture. Bybee's memo, which claimed to rely on facts supplied by the Department of Defense, is seeded liberally with stock Orientalist anthropology, from its musing about the significance of black Taliban turbans and tribal flags to the referencing of the Taliban as a "feudal" or "tribal" organization, a ragtag militia on a gun-slinging frontier right out of *Lawrence of Arabia*, not organized and not modern enough to warrant inclusion under Article 4 of the Convention. Bybee suggests the Taliban's adherence to Islamic law cannot be reconciled with adherence to international legal principles, arguing without irony that the Taliban "have killed for racial or religious purposes" and committed a host of other disqualifying outrages: "massacres," "raping," "pillaging," and "various other atrocities."

Bybee's Taliban memo, though as weak on legal logic as the later torture memos, represents nonetheless a quite consequential cultural logic reminiscent of the sort nineteenth-century British liberalism adopted in its engagement with empire. Per the Bybee memo, the failure of the Taliban to evince an adequate level of civilization, of modernization, and of the requisite acceptance of liberal standards leads to its exclusion from the legal regime of war and humanitarianism. As Professor Mehta showed, too, for British India, the universal values of liberalism are made to hinge on an anthropological determination of sorts.[76] Liberal decency, social mutuality, recognitional reciprocity, juridical subjecthood, and self-government are reserved for those who place themselves in the position of declaring and describing the civilizational divide from the standpoint of a normatively superior unity (progress, rationality, civility); attack dogs, torture, abandonment, and juridical exclusion are what is coming to those deemed through the imperial encounter too strange to be assimilated to that unity. Liberal crusade politics, indeed.

The *Boumediene* and *Salah* cases represent two distinct moments in the socio-legal process of what we approach as an imperialist-racial formation of enemy civilization peoples, comprising especially Arabs and Muslims. Recently, much scholarly light has been cast on the status of Arabs and Muslims in the United States, much of it strengthening a racial formation analysis. In our opinion, this inquiry requires analysis of the systemic determinants and ideological legitimating structure related to the group subordination in question (how might it be tied to material historical determinants of U.S. social dialectics?), state action toward "social construction" of racial otherness, essentialization of an ethnically diverse group into a bloc and, of course, actual subordination of the group. The analysis here takes seriously the claims of writers like Steven Salaita that "anti-Arab racism" may be expressed in the United States "because anti-Arab racism better enables the American government to intervene in Arab nations."[77] Salaita ties anti-Arab racism to what he terms "imperial adventurism," suggesting the world historical dimension within which this expression of cultural "othering" occurs.

Boumediene is significant constitutionally for its rejection of the extreme view that foreign nationals subjected to U.S. action abroad should be denied all constitutional rights, including habeas corpus, and for its adoption of a more pragmatic or "functional" approach.[78] The case has also been

[76] Uday Singh Mehta, *Liberalism and Empire: A Study in Nineteenth Century Liberal Thought* (Chicago: University of Chicago Press, 1999). Mehta adopts a less structural approach to liberalism than perhaps his research would support, arguing that the imperial impulse may indeed have originated from within liberalism, but that it is not an inevitable consequence of liberalism.

[77] Steven Salaita, *Anti-Arab Racism in the USA* (Pluto, 2006), 109. Salaita uses the term *anti-Arab racism* as a general category, which stands in close relationship with other racist manifestations such as Islamophobia. Salaita, Anti-Arab Racism, 6–15.

[78] See Gerald L. Neuman, "The Extraterritorial Constitution After *Boumediene v. Bush, Southern California Law Review* 82 (2009): 259. Neuman assesses the case as "having fundamental

understood, symbolically, as a legal rebuff to political branch overreach in attempting to militarize justice pursuant to the war on terror. However, it is the decision's superficial treatment of the racialized history of imperial extraterritoriality precedent that may be most telling. The opinion of the Supreme Court in *Boumediene* traces a century and a half of history regarding extraterritorial application of the U.S. Constitution in a few pages, after which it endorses the approach taken by Justice White in a concurring opinion at the turn of the last century in the Insular Cases. Nothing is mentioned in the opinion about the imperial-racist dimension of the Insular Cases, despite much recent scholarship emphasizing this aspect. Pedro Malavet captures the Supreme Court's moves in the following terms:

> The court reasserted a rule of plenary power over territorial citizens while barely acknowledging those citizens' existence and without recognizing the duration of the occupation of the current United States territories. The majority may have cast new doubt on the applicability of fundamental rights guaranteed by the Bill of Rights to the territorial citizens. Then, without any sense of irony, the court discussed the Philippines and its "transition to independence," rearticulating in the process the doctrine of the Insular Cases as an *old* and *well-established* rule to be flexibly applied to *temporary and transitional* situations. The majority then places what is currently happening in Guantánamo Bay in the category of these temporary situations.[79]

It is perhaps no surprise that behind such a historically simplified rendering of the Insular Cases and their doctrine of constitutional extraterritoriality (the functional approach), the *Boumediene* decision offers little hope of a constitutionalism conditioned by considerations other than those that can be characterized as political branch expediency in management of imperial possessions and relations. The opinion in *Boumediene* is based in part on *Downes v. Bidwell* – as described above, one of the more bluntly racialized Supreme Court texts and one that openly incorporated a judicial concern for maintenance of a racially stratified empire into its logic – with no mention of the case's problematic pedigree.

conceptual importance for U.S. constitutionalism" for its adoption of the functional approach, yet notes that the decision left ambiguous much about the Court's understanding of that approach. Neuman, "The Extraterritorial Constitution," 268–74.

79 Pedro Malavet, "From *Downes v. Bidwell* to *Boumediene v. Bush*" (SSRN, 2009): 50–51 (emphasis in original).

Indeed, the *Boumediene* opinion, in reiterating the *Downes* Court's now relegitimated concern about the "uncertainty and instability" that would result from extending constitutional protections to the territories (articulated as a concern for displacement of existing legal systems), quotes directly from some of the *Downes* opinion's troubling racialized language: "It is obvious that in the annexation of outlying and distant possessions grave questions will arise from differences of race, habits, laws and customs of the people, and from differences of soil, climate and production. . . ."[80] The *Boumediene* opinion left out the rest of that statement, however: "which may require action on the part of Congress that would be quite unnecessary in the annexation of contiguous territory inhabited only by people of the same race, or by scattered bodies of native Indians."[81]

This is the constitutional logic and precedent that informs the approach in *Boudmediene*. What can one say about this? Malavet understands the *Boumediene* decision from the perspective of the *still* "unincorporated," but territorially possessed, peoples first encountered in the *Downes* era. Importantly, he ties the cases together through the imperialist projects they each underwrite: "The rationalization of avoiding 'overburdening' the different 'cultures' acquired as spoils of the Spanish-American War today gives way to the needs of the so-called war on terror. . . . [The federal government is] given almost unfettered authority to deal with large groups of persons who, often in spite of their U.S. citizenship, are to be treated as lesser citizens and ultimately as lesser human beings."[82] Crucial similarities (amidst important differences) between the two periods inhere in the race-imperial politics and world order that conditions each.

In the *Insular Cases*, the Supreme Court's opinions rather forthrightly link the imperial/white supremacist project to the need for a functional approach to constitutional extraterritoriality. In *Boumediene*, the court's adoption of the old racist functionalist jurisprudence seems at once aware of the problematic precedential genealogy involved, but generally accepting of the Insular era's view of governmental discretion over imperial possessions and relations. In both cases, the court seems to have located its jurisprudence at a pivotal point of racial ideology and imperial imperative.

80 *Boumediene v. Bush*, 553 U.S. at 27 (2008).
81 *Downes v. Bidwell*, 182 U.S. 244, 282 (1901).
82 Malavet, "From Downes v. Bidwell," 5.

For the Insular era court, infusing *Downes* with the politically resonant racist ideology of the day, while setting up a system of exploiting the new imperial possessions at arms length, found a convergence point for competing kinds of racist nationalism – one domestic in focus and driven by working class white concerns, and one imperial in thrust serving the interests of commerce, shipping, and banking. By comparison, the Supreme Court in *Boumediene* adopts a decontextualized "colorblind" read of the functional doctrine's history, in preserving a minimal level of legal due process for detainees at Guantanamo, while defaulting to wide latitude otherwise for executive and/or congressional action in managing imperial territories and relations.

Interestingly, the history of extraterritoriality doctrine tracks through the nineteenth-century "race case" of *Dred Scott v. Sandford*, "notorious" as the case that declared black slaves could not be citizens of the United States. Dred Scott was actually also a territoriality case of first impression, holding that the Constitution applied fully in U.S. territories. This meant that slave owners' due process rights had to be respected throughout the United States and its territories, and, combined with the denial of citizenship rights to slaves, that racial, *not territorial*, status would determine the question of rights extension under expansionist conditions. Thus was *Dred Scott* reversed on the extraterritoriality question by the holding in *Downes*. The *Boumediene* opinion mentions this longer history of extraterritoriality doctrine, referring to *Dred Scott* as "notable (and notorious)" precedent in this regard, but skirts the question of how to make sense of the trajectory from *Dred Scott*, through the Insular Cases, and to the present day.

The avoidance by the Insular Court of *Dred Scott* on the extraterritoriality question should be analyzed as a moment in law's *evolving* relationship with imperial expansion and race, and in no way a rejection of the scandal of *Dred Scott*.[83] *Boumediene* evinces a "flattened description" of extraterritoriality precedent, giving a "sanitized account of the motivations for the Insular Cases doctrine" and "underplaying the racial element in U.S. colonialism."[84] All this is crucial to the Supreme Court's divining from that troubled history a precedential common thread that shows no sense of bearing constitutional witness to the catastrophes of U.S. territoriality law: "the

[83] This seems to have been part of the "spin" at the time the Insular Cases were decided. Id. at 33.
[84] Neuman, "The Extraterritorial Constitution," 270.

idea that questions of extraterritoriality turn on objective factors and practical concerns, not formalism."[85]

The trial of Muhammad Salah, litigated around the time of *Boumediene*, shows the creep of anti-Muslim, anti-Arab securitization into criminal law. A parallel move can be observed in "terrorist tort litigation" and, taken together, these kinds of "domestic" cases show how the war on terrorism has extended the processes of legal securitization. Securitization, a process whereby security discourse and law expand beyond traditional categories, or even threaten to over-ride the operation of legal process (as in the case of state-sanctioned torture), may be the dominant mode of racialization affecting Arabs and Muslims in the United States.

The *Salah* trial, the Muslim charities terrorism conspiracy cases, and recent terrorist tort litigation are remarkable for their novel uses of evidence (coerced interrogation of defendant allowed), their use of an anonymous foreign governmental agent as witness in a civil litigation, their presentations by plaintiff attorneys of highly prejudicial images and descriptions of violent attacks and religion to prove intent. We understand these cases alongside the Supreme Court's return to Insular Case jurisprudence in its *Boumediene* decision, as part of a surging securitization of law most directly affecting Muslims and Arabs. While *Boumediene* operates in the analysis at the level of grand constitutional narrative, and thus can best be understood for the ways it strips territoriality law of its most disturbing "plot entanglements" while rationalizing detention, the criminal and civil cases reflect a rather more assertive form of securitization with specific linkage to U.S. imperialism's investment in the Palestine-Israel conflict.

Salah's case revolves around his arrest and imprisonment by Israel Defense Forces soldiers in the early 1990s.[86] Shin Bet, Israel's security agency, interrogated Salah incommunicado for months – over the strong contemporaneous objections of U.S. State Department personnel in Israel and the United States – resulting in the production of a rather implausible 50-plus page handwritten confession. Salah has maintained the confession

[85] *Boumediene v. Bush*, 553 U.S. at 34 (2008).

[86] This section relies on the descriptions of the Salah case provided in a two part article written by his lawyers. See Michael E. Deutsch and Erica Thompson, "Secrets and Lies: The Persecution of Muhammad Salah (Part I)," *Journal of Palestine Studies* 37, no. 1 (2008): 38–58; Michael E. Deutsch and Erica Thompson, "Secrets and Lies: The Prosecution of Muhammad Salah (Part II)," *Journal of Palestine Studies* 38, no. 1 (2008): 25–53.

was false and coerced, extracted through use of torture and other coercive interrogation methods known to be commonly used by Shin Bet at the time. Anonymous Shin Bet agents who testified at Salah's trial denied Salah's claims, and it is likely the jury verdict hinged in large part on which version the jury believed. Salah, a U.S. citizen and grocer in Chicago, had been prominently profiled in the media as a secret, U.S.-based military commander of Hamas, both at the time of his detention in Israel through government leaks to the media about his interrogation, and again more than a decade later at the time of his indictment through Attorney General John Ashcroft's nationally televised press briefing.

In the U.S. indictment, Salah was charged with racketeering, material support for terrorism, and an obstruction of justice charge (the latter based on Salah's responses to interrogatories in the *Boim* tort terrorism litigation). The government dropped the material support charge on the eve of trial, and the jury acquitted on the racketeering/terrorism charge. As Salah's lawyers wrote after the trial, Salah's conviction and eventual sentencing on the obstruction charge were unofficially reported by several jurors to have resulted from *jury compromise*, a typically pro-prosecution decision dynamic whereby an otherwise acquitted defendant is found guilty on a lesser charge, but by less than the standard of jury unanimity lawfully required. Moreover, the acquittals did not preclude the judge from using defendant's conduct related to the acquitted charges in sentencing on the lesser compromise conviction. Indeed, the government argued precisely that in pushing the judge to apply "terrorism enhancement" to the sentencing decision on the obstruction charge.[87]

The *Salah* case seems to fall squarely into a category of politicized prosecution that is increasingly prominent in the federal record after 9/11. Justice Department data on terrorism-related prosecutions, convictions, and sentencing strongly suggest a pattern of "technical" or "disingenuous" prosecutions.[88] Individual motivations of investigators and prosecutors in such cases may include a range of concerns including "budgetary pressures, political

[87] See Deutsch and Thompson, "Secrets and Lies (Part II)," 48–49. Deutsch and Thompson point out that the twenty-one-month sentence Salah received for, in effect, objecting to overreaching and intrusive interrogatories in a civil suit, was excessive. The defense had not been allowed to put on evidence that would have explained Salah's objection to the Boim interrogatories as political intimidation. Id.

[88] These concepts are developed by Todd Lochner, "Sound and Fury: Pretextual Prosecution and Department of Justice Antiterrorism Efforts," *Law and Policy* 30, no. 2 (2008): 168–93. Lochner's

imperatives, and reputational interests," each pushing to "make technical and disingenuous prosecutions more likely to occur."[89] Even more specifically, we might include such prosecutions as those motivated by a racial animus (a form of disingenuous prosecution), or in which the defendant may be deemed technically in violation of the law, while engaged in behavior that was not the intended target of the criminal statute (an example of technical prosecution).[90]

Muhammad Salah's situation has many markings of such a prosecution. Exactly which form of prosecutorial "discretion" was at work is difficult to pinpoint, but for purposes of the analysis here, we suggest understanding this and other such politically and culturally charged antiterrorism prosecutions from the perspective of the political imperatives at work and the effects on target actors. These prosecutions show the government engaged in various forms of extreme case-making tactics, amounting to what Salah's lawyers refer to as a "military court sitting in the city of Chicago."[91] Salah's attorneys describe the "conflicting narratives" that drove the prosecution and defense theories of the case: even though the prosecution "claimed not to take sides in the Palestinian-Israeli struggle [,]... [f]or the prosecution, Hamas was a ruthless Islamic fundamentalist terrorist operation driven by hatred of the Jewish people and committed to the destruction of Israel and the derailment of the peace process.... For the defense, Hamas was a legitimate part of the Palestinian national movement for self-determination...." The prosecution sought to deny that Hamas could engage in charitable or humanitarian work apart from terrorism, and the defense argued the

analysis, relying on Justice Department data provided though the Transactional Records Access Clearinghouse, suggests that these types of prosecution may be occurring in the context of antiterrorism prosecution rather than so-called pretextual prosecutions of the sort the government used to "bring down" Al Capone. Pretextual prosecutions are often defended, in fact, through invocation of the Capone prosecution. Lochner defines technical prosecutions generally as "cases in which prosecutors employ a direct means that fails to achieve the law's overarching purpose" and "defendant meets the technical requirements for violating a given law but engaged in behavior that legislators probably did not have in mind when creating that law." Lochner, "Sound and Fury," 174. Disingenuous prosecutions are "cases in which prosecutors employ an indirect means that fails to achieve the law's overarching purpose. ... It would be disingenuous to try a defendant for an immigration offense, ostensibly because that defendant had some relation to terrorism, but in actuality because the prosecutor was motivated by racial animus." Id at 175.

89 Id. at 187.

90 Id. at 174–75.

91 Deutsch and Thompson, "Secrets and Lies (Part I)," 38–58.

importance of social services provided through Hamas for Palestinians under severe conditions of occupation and depredation.[92]

Investigative journalist Amy Waldman, writing in *Atlantic Monthly*, views the prosecutions from the perspective of the war effort: "Abroad, the government has pursued a doctrine of preemptive war. At home, it has pursued a strategy of what might be called preemptive prosecution. The criminal-justice system, the Justice Department said in a recent white paper on counterterrorism, now 'operates effectively as an element of national power.' … This preemptive strategy represents a major moral and legal change in the American approach to justice. Its premise is that terrorism – implicitly, *Islamic* terrorism – represents a singular, unprecedented threat to American safety and society."[93]

Importantly, Waldman's survey of the cases maps how Islam has been integrated into the structure of proving terrorist intent in U.S. courts:

> Jurors have been schooled in the difference between fatwa (religious edict), and *fatah* (conquest). They have had tutorials in the history of Islam, from the angel Gabriel's revelation of the Koran to the Prophet Muhammad to the rise of Osama bin Laden. They have learned about the meaning of *bida*, or innovation; the authentic chain of transmission for a hadith; and the virgins awaiting a martyr in paradise.
>
> Such a thorough judicial disquisition of a religion has no modern parallel in America. Unless religious beliefs bear directly on guilt – the use of the illegal drug peyote in religious rituals, for example – they are generally barred from trials as prejudicial. Why have the rules changed? Because, as Aziz Huq, a lawyer at New York University's Brennan Center for Justice, puts it, in recent times no other religion has been "so intimately linked in the public mind to violence." Since 9/11, judges have given lawyers wide latitude to bring religion into the courtroom.[94]

We are back to Bybee's Taliban memo.

Putting Islam "on trial" in this way may serve a number of functions with regard to the various, and sometimes competing, impulses of imperial racism. A sweeping demonization of Islam marks the political culture to

[92] Id. at 41.

[93] Amy Waldman, "Prophetic Justice," *The Atlantic*, October 2006, http://www.theatlantic.com/doc/200610/waldman-islam (retrieved on May 28, 2009).

[94] Id.

such an extent that Obama's Muslim father and "secret Muslim identity" became serious concerns for large numbers of voters in the 2008 election. This enemy culture engages the dynamics of liberal enmity in a manner quite functional to the geopolitical aspirations of America's would-be Lawrences of Arabia. The trials, taken as a whole, appear as so many performative groundings of such enmity, and indeed, function as assertions of sovereign control (counterterrorism justice as "national power") over a form of insecurity that appears quite beyond sovereign power's reach.

Salah and other antiterrorism prosecutions targeting support for Palestinians are positioned both as denials of political autonomy for Palestinian supporters in the United States, and as functional to the project of ongoing denial of political autonomy to Palestinians in the occupied territories. Deutsch and Thompson, Salah's lawyers, observed the close cooperation in the case between Shin Bet and prosecution. This cooperation – as the defense argued, in effect, a governmental joint venture – worked to prevent Salah from accessing exculpatory evidence, especially with regard to Shin Bet's use of torture and other coercive techniques in extracting the crucial 1993 confession.[95] Juries, like the one in *Salah* or the first Holy Land Foundation trial in Dallas, may not buy "the line" the prosecution sells in such cases, but the legal lines that result resonate strongly with both cultural processes of enmity and the imperial investments in resource control and status quo maintenance of the territorial questions in Palestine.

The particular imperial racial project hypothesized in this section is redolent of what some international relations scholars see as a deepening securitization of western societies, while we would add that the project evinces both ideological and structural dimensions of a second macro-level social process: Muslim and Arab racialization. The processes are intertwined in what may be understood as a transitional event in U.S. racial formation. This evolving formation harkens back in ways to the racialization of Asians in the United States, a group whose status was succinctly stated in U.S. naturalization law as "aliens ineligible to citizenship." The national and racial dimensions of Asian exclusion are mirrored in recent forms of anti-Muslim/anti-Arab alienation and Othering. However, whereas Asian exclusion and racialization fit generally with the ways Asians were incorporated into mid-late nineteenth and early twentieth-century structures of

[95] Deutsch and Thompson, "Secrets and Lies (Part II)," 35–38.

U.S. labor and commerce, Muslims' and Arabs' statuses should perhaps be thought through theoretically in terms of contemporary structures of resource control and globalization, but certainly not just as ideological fantasms of unmoored liberal enmity.

IV. Conclusion

In reflecting on the most recent episodes in the long history of race and the exercises of sovereign power, we may be informed by the work of early racial formation theorist Harry Chang, as recently précised by Bob Wing. This work, from the 1970s, proposes a dialectical approach to race that does not lose sight of structural-capitalist dimensions of racial formation. While this latest chapter of U.S. national closure has been increasingly viewed as a new form of racism or xenophobia, Chang's racial formation theory suggests the necessity of tying this instance of racialized subordination, dialectically, to the broader imperial project of U.S. led globalization. We have used the term *imperial racism* to refer to this evolving dimension of racial formation.

In response to Schmitt's sovereign realism, Walter Benjamin posited a permanent "state of exception," understood as the legal and political articulation of subaltern social relations in modernity. From this kind of critical perspective, we may see U.S. sovereignty, in part, as the self-referencing logos of a series of racial projects for control of land, labor, and resources, through which sovereign power over life and death is exercised and legitimized in conjunction with the territorialized line-drawing of racial Othering. The defining move in a critical unraveling of the national security balancing puzzle, therefore, may be to place a laser-like focus on the kinds of subordinationist projects that sovereign line-drawing and its legal forms underwrite.

Ideas of emergency, exigency, and exception should not be theorized abstractly, but understood historically and socially. Scholars of Indian law have cautioned similarly, that to read the Marshall Trilogy "straight" with its mystifying back-and-forth ("now you see it, now you don't" native sovereignty) obfuscates, rather than clarifies, the nature of native sovereignty in the early nineteenth century because it occludes the profound historical significance of Indian removal. The discourse of emergency and sovereign imposition outside the Rule of Law has always been functional and operationalized in the shadow of outsider group construction. Emergency, exceptions, and plenary power flow deductively, tropes of epoch-defining systems of social subordination. Injuries bound up with those abuses of power are what we wish to "balance away," akin to the way "collateral damage" allows us to skim over the deep contradictions of our modern "wars for peace" and "humanitarian violence." In rethinking the questions of sovereignty, emergency and legality, perhaps the fundamental question to ask ourselves is how our models of emergency constitutionalism relate to the ontology of order under empire. To perceive security interests as always already racialized and imperial moves us in another direction, one that problematizes the fascistic trap door in the foundation of modern imperial state power with its violence-legitimating discourses of security and exclusion.

As Benjamin suggested, we begin to conceive of something like the creation of a real state of emergency by rejecting the binary closures of security/legality, and recognizing the historical and structural dimensions of racial sovereignty.

Comment on Chapter 4

Toward a Nonracial Sovereign

Debra Lyn Bassett*

Professors Cho and Gott's article, "The Racial Sovereign," makes a powerful argument that both sovereignty and national security are racially contingent and racially subordinating concepts. In this brief commentary, I would like to offer some thoughts that both complement and supplement their work.

I. Complements: Of Theorists, Philosophers, and Commentators

As Professor Angela Harris has observed, "Race ... has long been central to the exercise of sovereign power in the United States."[1] In "The Racial Sovereign," Professors Cho and Gott trace the sovereign's historic use of the emergency power to subjugate Native Americans, African-Americans, Asian-Americans, and its current extension to Arab-Americans, Muslims, and Latino/as.[2] Although their paper is well supported, it could be complemented by the works of additional commentators – some less conventional, but others who, in fact, are planted firmly in the traditional binary framing of sovereignty and emergency that Professors Cho and Gott seek to reject. In some instances the commentator's additional support is express, while in other instances it requires inferential links, but the support is there nevertheless.

* Justice Marshall F. McComb, Professor of Law, Southwestern Law School. E-mail: dbassett@swlaw.edu. Many thanks to Professor Austin Sarat for his invitation to participate in the Sovereignty, Legality, and Emergency Symposium, and to Dean Ken Randall and Dean Bryant Garth for their encouragement and research support.

[1] Angela P. Harris, "Introduction," *Florida Law Review* 55 (2003): 319, 330.

[2] Sumi Cho and Gil Gott, "The Racial Sovereign," Draft of 10/17/08 [hereinafter Cho and Gott Draft].

Historically, a particularly prominent theorist and philosopher in the traditional study of sovereignty and emergency is Michel Foucault, who expressly discussed race and the sovereign in his work.

A. Foucault

Michel Foucault, perhaps the most prominent French philosopher of the 1970s and 1980s, discussed race and the sovereign in an express and direct manner that both parallels and encompasses Professors Cho and Gott's work – a somewhat surprising commonality of viewpoints that might not ordinarily be expected of a French philosopher and a critical race scholar. However, a brief overview of some of Foucault's work illustrates the point.

Foucault notes the centrality of power to sovereignty,[3] but argues that rather than deriving powers from sovereignty, we should shift our focus to power itself – and specifically to a theory of domination.[4] "[R]elations of domination provide the access road that leads to the analysis of power. ..."[5] Foucault discusses war as the permanent basis of all institutions of power, stating, "The war that is going on beneath order and peace, the war that undermines our society and divides it in a binary mode is, basically, a race war."[6]

Race and racism are a pervasive force in Foucault's work. Foucault asserts that "the famous dazzling effect of power ... is not something that petrifies, solidifies, and immobilizes the entire social body, and thus keeps it in order; it is in fact a divisive light that illuminates one side of the social body but leaves the other side in shadow or casts it into darkness."[7] To Foucault, war is at the base of power because war requires physical confrontation and matters of life and death.[8]

3 Michel Foucault, *"Society Must Be Defended": Lectures at the College de France 1975–1976* (New York: Picador, 1997): 36 (noting that the theory of sovereignty "is bound up with" power).

4 Id. at 45.

5 Id. at 46; see also id. "Rather than looking at the three prerequisites of law, unity, and subject – which make sovereignty both the source of power and the basis of institutions – I think that we have to adopt the threefold point of view of the techniques, the heterogeneity of techniques, and the subjugation-effects that make technologies of domination the real fabric of both power relations and the great apparatuses of power. ... [W]e should be studying domination and not sovereignty. ..."

6 Id. at 59–60.

7 Id. at 70.

8 Id. at 240, 262. When it is simply a matter of eliminating the adversary in economic terms, or of taking away his privileges, there is no need for racism. Once it is a matter of coming to terms

In sum, Foucault tells us that war is the basis of a sovereign's power, and that even when not at war in a literal sense,

> the war continues to rage within the mechanisms of power, or at least to constitute the secret motor of institutions, laws, and order. Beneath the omissions, the illusions, and the lies of those who would have us believe in the necessities of nature or the functional requirements of order, we have to rediscover war: war is the cipher of peace. It divides the entire social body, and it does so on a permanent basis; it puts all of us on one side or the other. And it is not enough to rediscover this war as an explanatory principle; it has to be reactivated. We have to force it out of the silent, larval forms in which it goes on without anyone realizing it. . . .[9]

Thus, Foucault, like Professors Cho and Gott, sees a racial (and racist) sovereign. War, which is at the center of the sovereign's power, drives that racism – which is always there, even if muted – to the surface. Accordingly, both Foucault and Professors Cho and Gott create parallel analyses by calling for a recognition of the racial sovereign, and both also call for a redirection or refocusing on dominance and subordination in attempting to understand sovereignty and power. These calls are step one of a two-step process: step one seeks acknowledgment and focus, whereas step two asks what can be done. Shifting to step two brings us to contemporary American commentators.

B. American Legal Commentators

In discussing contemporary commentators in the traditional discourse concerning sovereignty and emergency, it helps to focus on three of the works most often cited, those by Mark Tushnet,[10] Bruce Ackerman,[11] and an article

with the thought of a one-to-one encounter with the adversary, and with the need to fight him physically, to risk one's own life and to try to kill him, there is a need for racism. Id. at 262. This approach, of course, bears strong similarity to Professors Cho and Gott's assertions. See Cho and Gott Draft, supra n. 2, at 19 ("Sovereignty seems to be nothing more than a name we give to a racially subordinating system by which power over life and death is exercised and legitimized for certain 'othered' people.").

9 Foucault, supra n. 3, at 268.

10 Mark Tushnet, "Defending Korematsu?: Reflections on Civil Liberties in Wartime," *Wisconsin Law Review* (2003): 273.

11 Bruce Ackerman, "The Emergency Constitution," *Yale Law Journal* 113 (2004): 1029.

co-authored by Samuel Issacharoff and Richard Pildes.[12] Although these three works approach issues of sovereignty and emergency from different perspectives and offer different conclusions, all three expressly acknowledge the racial component that has tainted the exercise of sovereignty in an emergency context. Professor Tushnet notes our tendency to respond to "perceived threats with a persistent creation of an Other."[13] Professor Ackerman notes the "problems of ethnic, religious, and racial profiling" in the emergency context,[14] and our tendency to identify a "demonology" in which "segments of the population [are marked out] as peculiarly appropriate targets for emergency measures."[15] Professors Issacharoff and Pildes note that "[t]he evidence offered for General DeWitt's decision [to intern Japanese-Americans during World War II] rested on ethnic stereotyping and fear, not genuine fact."[16] The sovereign's use of a racialized "other" in an emergency context – and the acknowledgment of this racial reaction by these three prominent commentators and many others – creates the profile of a nearly intractable, momentous structural racial issue for the United States, and contrasts sharply with the modest proposals for reform. Ultimately, the solutions are an acute disappointment.

Professor Tushnet takes the self-described "optimistic view" that we are learning from our past mistakes to "ratchet down our reaction to what we perceive to be a threat each time we observe what we think in retrospect were exaggerated reactions to threats."[17] He suggests that we should take comfort from the fact that "nothing on the scale of the Japanese internment has yet been proposed during the current [so-called War on Terror] situation."[18]

Professors Issacharoff and Pildes seem to suggest that our governmental system works better in emergencies than is given credit, with the courts

[12] Samuel Issacharoff and Richard H. Pildes, "Between Civil Libertarianism and Executive Unilateralism: An Institutional Process Approach to Rights during Wartime," *Theoretical Inquiries in Law* 5 (2004): 1.

[13] Tushnet, supra n. 10, at 298.

[14] Ackerman, supra n. 11, at 1075.

[15] Id. at 1049.

[16] Issacharoff and Pildes, supra n. 12, at 20.

[17] Tushnet, supra n. 10, at 295.

[18] Id.; see also Gary Gerstle, "Pluralism and the War on Terror," *Dissent* 50(2) (2003): 31–38 (comparing post 9/11 developments to the treatment of German Americans in World War I, southern and eastern Europeans after World War I, and Japanese Americans in World War II). Professor Ackerman, however, describes Professor Tushnet's approach as "a remarkably complacent view of this cycle." Ackerman, supra n. 11, at 1042.

accepting executive decisions authorized or supported by Congress, but willing to find executive abuse of its emergency powers when Congress has been disapproving of the executive's actions.[19]

Professor Ackerman offers a more specific and ambitious proposal involving the passage of legislation for dealing with an emergency resulting from an actual attack.[20] One of the most distinctive provisions of this legislative proposal is a "supermajoritarian escalator," whereby the legislature could approve the executive's call for a state of emergency, but only for a brief time – Professor Ackerman suggests two or three months.[21] At the end of this period, a continuation of the state of emergency would require supermajoritarian approval at increasing levels: sixty percent for the first two-month extension; 70 percent for the next two-month extension; 80 percent for a subsequent two-month extension.[22] Although Professor Ackerman acknowledges – to a greater degree than the works of the other two commentators – the often racial component of the sovereign's exercise of the emergency power, his ultimate proposal falls disappointingly short: he calls for "financial compensation to all innocents who have been swept into preventive detention."[23]

I do not want to shortchange or underestimate the significance of the compensation component of Professor Ackerman's proposal, because such compensation serves both a deterrent purpose and a reparations purpose. However, compensation serves both purposes in only a limited manner. Deterrence is of a limited nature because compensation will not prevent overinclusiveness in the use of detention, and the reparations purpose is of a limited nature because most of the consequences of detention are not compensable – the innocent's unjustified loss of liberty; the forced separation from the people and activities that give life meaning; the frustration of suffering a complete loss of individual control over one's circumstances; the

[19] Issacharoff and Pildes, supra n. 12, at 25. [T]he courts have, in practice, neither abdicated that role entirely nor defined their role aggressively; instead, courts have only sought to ensure vigilance over the institutional tendency to concentrate power in the hands of the executive and its military. If Congress endorses or perhaps even acquiesces in that concentration, the courts have accepted that judgment. If Congress has resisted, the courts have found the executive to have gone beyond even its wartime powers (Id.).

[20] Ackerman, supra n. 11, at 1059 (distinguishing an actual attack from merely a "clear and present danger").

[21] Id. at 1047.

[22] Id.

[23] Id. at 1062.

embarrassment and shame of being identified, albeit wrongly, as a danger to society; and the shattering loss of faith that accompanies a wrongful accusation and detention. Compensation is certainly superior to mere release without comment or with only the barest of apologies. However, Professor Ackerman's proposal, as was true also of Professors Tushnet, Issacharoff, and Pildes' proposals, ultimately treats the racial component as an unfortunate reality that is inherent to emergency situations.

In essence, these commentators all reach the same dismal conclusion. There is recognition and exposure of potential issues with the sovereign's exercise of the emergency power only after the fact; preventive measures and guidance are conspicuously absent. Apparently we are left merely to hope that the sovereign (and the sovereign's advisors) will exercise the emergency power wisely.

I would posit that a faulty foundation is to blame for this unsatisfactory outcome – specifically, that too much credence is being ascribed to the philosophical-theoretical notion of sovereignty. Carl Schmitt's famous contribution, "Sovereign is he who decides on the exception,"[24] frames the issue as the sovereign in the abstract, with too little attention paid to the actual exercise of sovereignty. In other words, abstract hypothetical emergencies are the underlying justification for emergency powers.

In the philosophical-theoretical sense, the argument always lurks that an emergency, by definition, pulls the sovereign outside the parameters of legal norms or guidance. However, Schmitt himself suggested a narrow meaning of the emergency exception:

> The exception … can at best be characterized as a case of extreme peril, a danger to the existence of the state, or the like. … The precise details of an emergency cannot be anticipated, nor can one spell out what may take place in such a case, especially when it is truly a matter of an extreme emergency and of how it is to be eliminated. The precondition as well as the content of jurisdictional competence in such a case must necessarily be unlimited. … The most guidance the constitution can provide is to indicate who can act in such a case. … [The sovereign] decides whether there is an extreme emergency as well as what must be done to eliminate it. Although he stands outside the normally valid legal system, he nevertheless belongs to it, for it is

[24] Carl Schmitt, *Political Theology: Four Chapters on the Concept of Sovereignty* (Chicago: University of Chicago Press, 1985): 5.

> he who must decide whether the constitution needs to be suspended in its entirety.[25]

The theory of the sovereign's emergency power – much like the spiraling hypothetical in a philosophy or law school classroom – is largely an abstraction rather than a practical reality. Yet we use the spiraling hypothetical to justify the sovereign's broad emergency power, which in turn, permits the sovereign to exercise broad emergency powers even when such powers are unnecessary to the specific situation at hand.

In every so-called emergency over the past 100 years, the sovereign had choices. Indeed, even in the two major instances in which attacks occurred on U.S. soil – Pearl Harbor and 9/11 – the available choices were wide-ranging, and in neither instance was there an actual need to operate outside of existing legal norms. Unfortunately, however, the sovereign has repeatedly made a racialized choice, and thereby has taken the politically expedient path of playing to ignorance and racism. Theories based on broad conceptions of sovereignty and emergency are a poor match as justifications for real-world scenarios, perhaps because broad powers can be both tempting and blinding – and certainly post hoc rationalizations (as well as post hoc recriminations) are woefully insufficient remedies.

II. Supplements: Of Emergencies, Race, and Criteria

To the extent that sovereignty is a synonym for power,[26] that power often has been, and continues often to be, employed in a racialized manner in the emergency context. But such racialized sovereign power, while the most offensive use of the emergency power, is not the only use of the emergency power – and to that extent, perhaps Professors Cho and Gott's racial argument is overinclusive.

[25] Id. at 6–7; see also Austin Sarat and Conor Clarke, "Beyond Discretion: Prosecution, the Logic of Sovereignty, and the Limits of Law," *Law & Social Inquiry* 33 (2008): 387, 408 (noting that, "For Schmitt, the exceptions that define sovereignty become most apparent in situations of emergency or extreme peril, where legal norms fail to prescribe the appropriate action. … Because norms cannot adequately encompass exceptional cases – like emergencies – the decision that a real exception exists cannot therefore be entirely derived from norms.").

[26] See *Webster's New World Dictionary*, Second College Edition (New York: Simon and Schuster, 1982): 1363 (defining sovereign as "supreme in power, rank, or authority"); see also *Black's Law Dictionary*, Fifth Edition (St. Paul: West Publishing, 1979): 1252, defining sovereignty as "[t]he supreme, absolute, and uncontrollable power by which any citizen is governed and is the person or body of persons in the state to whom there is politically no superior."

The sovereign emergency power includes, and U.S. presidents have invoked such power to accomplish, among other things, calling reservists to active duty;[27] sending military troops overseas;[28] rationing food, gasoline, and commodities;[29] and seizing and controlling coal mines.[30] President Roosevelt declared a state of emergency during the banking crisis;[31] President Nixon did the same during the post office strike.[32] In each of these instances, neither the crises that led to the use of sovereign emergency power, nor the sovereign's response, was obviously racialized. Accordingly, although the most egregious and offensive use of the sovereign emergency power has involved some form of racialization, it may be an overstatement to paint the sovereign emergency power with an exclusively racial brush.

The understandable disappointment reflected in Professors Cho and Gott's observation that "[s]overeignty seems to be nothing more than a name we give to a racially subordinating system by which power over life and death is exercised and legitimized for certain 'othered' people"[33] makes perfect sense in light of prominent commentators' unsatisfactory response to the repeated racialization of the sovereign's emergency power. And indeed, the repeated use of the sovereign power to subjugate minority populations is an historical fact. However, I think that perhaps Professors Cho and Gott's argument reaches just a bit too far.

Professors Cho, Gott, Ackerman, Tushnet, Issacharoff, and Pildes all agree that race has been a component of some prominent invocations of the sovereign's emergency power, and all agree that this racial component has been employed in an overbroad manner that has resulted in the detention of tremendous numbers of entirely innocent individuals. And while Professors Cho and Gott's "racial sovereign" characterization may overstate the issue by brushing over other, nonracial, exercises of the sovereign

27 See Special Committee on National Emergencies and Delegated Emergency Powers, *A Recommended National Emergencies Act*, S. Rep. No. 93–1170, at 2 (1974), reprinted in Senate Committee on Government Operations and the Special Committee on National Emergencies and Delegated Emergency Powers, The National Emergencies Act (Public Law 94–412): Source Book: Legislative History, Texts, and Other Documents 19, 20 (Comm. Print 1976) [hereinafter Source Book].

28 Id.

29 Id.

30 See id.; see also *United States v. United Mine Workers of America*, 330 U.S. 258 (1947).

31 See Source Book, supra n. 28, at 119.

32 See id. at 120.

33 Cho and Gott Draft, supra n. 2, at 19.

emergency power, arguably Professors Ackerman, Tushnet, Issacharoff, and Pildes do not go far enough, and thereby understate the issue.

Not every national security situation involving the potential for a response based on race, ethnicity, or national origin has been acted upon in the same manner as the Japanese-American internments during World War II and the so-called War on Terror detentions of today. During World War II, President Franklin D. Roosevelt signed Executive Order 9066,[34] which granted power to the military to exclude people from specified areas. Although the Executive Order itself made no mention of race, the order was implemented with a distinctly racial cast. Pursuant to Executive Order 9066, the military declared the entire West Coast a designated military area – but enforced that declaration primarily against those of Japanese ancestry. Approximately 120,000 persons of Japanese ancestry, including 70,000 who were U.S. citizens, were confined to U.S. internment camps.[35] During World War II, of course, the United States was at war not only with Japan, but also with Germany and Italy. Contrary to conventional wisdom, individuals of German and Italian ancestry also were interned or relocated during World War II, but in far fewer numbers – nearly 11,000 of German descent and 2,000 of Italian descent.[36] Thus, neither the numbers nor the circumstances of the German and Italian internments paralleled the Japanese internment experience.[37]

34 Exec. Order No. 9066, 7 Fed. Reg. 1407 (February 25, 1942).

35 Eric K. Yamamoto, Margaret Chon, Carol L. Izumi, Jerry Kang, and Frank H. Wu, *Race, Rights and Reparation: Law and the Japanese American Internment* (Waltham, MA: Aspen Publishers, 2001): xxiii, 101.

36 Evelyn Nieves, "Past Recalled for Japanese-Americans," *New York Times*, September 27, 2001, p. A26 (in addition to more than 120,000 of Japanese ancestry, the U.S. government also interned "nearly 11,000 Germans and German-Americans and 2,000 Italians" during World War II); see Timothy J. Holian, The German-Americans and World War II: An Ethnic Experience (Jackson, TN: Grove/Atlantic Press, 1998): 1 (noting the "arrest and internment of over 10,000 members of America's German community as dangerous enemy aliens and enemy sympathizers, a fact denied by numerous commentators, historians, and scholars. ..."); see id. at 3, "[A]ccording to Immigration and Naturalization Service records, 10,905 German legal resident aliens and German-Americans were taken in under the enemy alien program." See generally Stephen Fox, *Uncivil Liberties: Italian Americans Under Siege during World War II* (Universal Publishers, 2000) (discussing the internment and relocation of Italians and Germans, including American citizens, in the United States during World War II).

37 But see Holian, supra n. 36, at 3, "Contrary to popular versions of the story, many German legal resident aliens, and some German-Americans, were not afforded the protections granted Americans under the Constitution, nor even under existing standards for enemy alien detainees."

The distinction between the West Coast Japanese-descent internments and the German- and Italian-descent internments during World War II, of course, was that there were simply so many individuals of German and Italian descent living in the United States during World War II that, purely as a practical matter, they simply could not all be subjected to mass internment.[38] Similarly, the West Coast Japanese-descent internments did not extend to Hawaii, despite the Pearl Harbor bombing and the significant Japanese-descent population, because the very large numbers of individuals of Japanese ancestry residing in the relatively small and geographically isolated state of Hawaii posed a practical prohibition to race-wide internment.[39]

My point is twofold. First, historically, the sovereign has repeatedly used race to identify the "enemy" in an emergency context, based on unfounded assumptions and implemented under circumstances that were overbroad, unfair, and discriminatory.[40] The basic theme is always the same. "The government's justification for [the internment of those of Japanese descent during World War II, for example] was simple and chilling: the ancestry of Japanese Americans made them likely to side with Japan during World War II."[41] The use of racially based detention and internment has achieved three things at once: (1) stigmatizing racially identifiable "others" as dangerous and treasonous; (2) heightening the perception that whiteness identifies "real" Americans; and (3) affirming that whiteness is power in a most literal sense, by creating and implementing a system of white dominance based on a form of racial subjugation.[42]

38 Fox, supra n. 36, at 228, "[T]here were simply too many of the European aliens and their extended families scattered across the nation to make a policy of relocation practically feasible. The several hundred thousand Germans and Italians living in the United States, plus their immediate descendants, represented as many as 11,000,000 potential relocatees."; see also Eugene V. Rostow, "The Japanese-American Cases – A Disaster," *Yale Law Journal* 54 (1945): 497, 508 (same).

39 Fox, supra n. 36, at 161 noting that the government "had not removed the Japanese from Hawaii, despite the obvious threat to American security there, because the Japanese made up 37 percent of Hawaii's population."

40 See Patricia J. Williams, *Seeing a Color-Blind Future: The Paradox of Race* (New York: Farrar, Straus & Giroux, 1997): 6, "[T]he habits of racial thought in Western society ... encapsulate some of the greatest mistakes in human history."

41 Alfred C. Yen, "Praising with Faint Damnation – the Troubling Rehabilitation of Korematsu," *Boston College Law Review* 40 (1998): 1.

42 See Cheryl I. Harris, "Whiteness as Property," in *Critical Race Theory*, eds. Kimberle Crenshaw et al. (New York: New Press, 1995): 276, 287, "Whiteness is an aspect of racial identity surely, but it is much more; it remains a concept based on relations of power, a social construct predicated on white dominance and black subjugation."

In addition to being both simplistic[43] and offensive, such an approach has been completely ineffective. Using race as a proxy for patriotism and loyalty employs a grossly overbroad criterion that history has repeatedly shown to be utterly useless. In particular, despite the internments during World War II of individuals of Japanese, German, and Italian ancestry – totaling more than 130,000 people – no act of espionage or sabotage was ever attributed to any U.S. citizen of such heritage.[44]

Second, and following from the first, relying on race as an indicator of U.S. patriotism and loyalty is absurd, particularly when the anti-patriotism barometer is set specifically at a non-white presumption. The most devastating recent acts of U.S. disloyalty – spying for the Soviet Union, the Oklahoma City bombing, and the anthrax scare – were all perpetrated by whites. But we didn't round up and intern all whites, all male whites, or all dark-haired male whites, in response. In short, we have used other, more discriminating (in the narrowing sense), methods in the past to distinguish a smaller number of individuals for detention or internment.

These observations justify an outright prohibition on the use of race as a criterion for any form of mass detention, internment, or relocation ordered pursuant to the sovereign emergency power – which, after all, is simply an extension of our ostensibly colorblind Constitution to the emergency situation. As a matter of political expediency, racially based detention makes the government look like it is doing something; race is often an "easy" identifier as contrasted with other investigative methods that require information beyond a person's physical appearance and surname; and racially based detention tends to be greeted with widespread public approval. But a racial criterion not only plays into fears – it confirms them. By employing a racial focus, the government sends the message that indeed this racialized enemy cannot be trusted and is to be feared, thus affirming racist fears in the general population, and contributing to

[43] Fox, supra n. 36, at 172 describing the "theme of racism" that has been the government's general response as both "[s]o powerful" and "so simplistic."

[44] U.S. Commission on Wartime Relocation and Internment of Civilians, *Personal Justice Denied: Report of the Commission on Wartime Relocation and Internment of Civilians* (Seattle: University of Washington Press, 1997): 3, stating that there was no act of espionage or sabotage attributed to any U.S. citizen of Japanese ancestry at any point during World War II; see also Fox, supra n. 36, at 193 (noting that despite the arrests of thousands of Germans and Italians in the U.S. during World War II, "the courts never convicted a single alien of an act of sabotage during the war.").

paranoia and acts of disassociation toward, and acts of violence against, the racialized "enemy."[45]

Our country has made progress – we elected Barack Obama as president of the United States. Electing a black man to the presidency was unimaginable only a short time ago. However, the undercurrent of racism is never far from the surface. Even during President Obama's presidential campaign, there were individuals who expressly articulated concerns about voting for a black man, as well as individuals who feared that despite Obama's lead in the polls, there could be substantial numbers who ultimately would not vote for him on Election Day for racial reasons. As Professor Williams has so eloquently stated, "While I do want to underscore that I embrace color-blindness as a legitimate hope for the future, I worry that we tend to enshrine the notion with a kind of utopianism whose naivete will ensure its elusiveness.... [I]t is a dangerous if comprehensible temptation to imagine inclusiveness by imagining away any obstacles."[46]

It is far too human to overreact in the face of an emergency. It can be hard to be the voice of reason and calm in a sea of fear and panic; the repeated historical precedent for a racially based reaction suggests that individual mettle is insufficient to overcome the pressures and emotions that accompany emergency. Written directives incorporated into the National Emergencies Act and mandating the use of nonracial criteria as the basis for any mass detention thereby requires a more thoughtful and more rational discussion, and more specific and justifiable detention criteria. This is precisely what it means to be a nation of laws, not men.[47] And perhaps, in the aftermath, we will find that such measures have aided those exercising the sovereign power to move away from the racial sovereign and toward a nonracial sovereign.

[45] See generally Gil Gott, "The Devil We Know: Racial Subordination and National Security Law," *Villanova Law Review* 50 (2005): 1073.

[46] Williams, supra n. 40, at 4–6.

[47] See *Joint Anti-Fascist Refugee Committee v. McGrath*, 341 U.S. 123, 177 (1951). Douglas, J., concurring, "It is not enough to know that the men applying the standard are honorable and devoted men. This is a government of laws not of men."

5

Should Constitutional Democracies Redefine Emergencies and the Legal Regimes Suitable for Them?

Michel Rosenfeld*

Introduction

Since the 9/11 2001 terrorist attacks on the United States, several Western constitutional democracies have resorted extraordinary emergency powers resulting in significant and, in many cases, seemingly excessive, curtailments of civil liberties. Traditional theory and practice drew a sharp divide between states of normalcy and states of emergency – usually in times of foreign or civil war – where the life of the polity was believed to be under threat. Global terror and the reaction against it involving the so-called "war on terror" raise serious challenges to this traditional approach.

Looking at these new challenges, I will argue that the traditional approach is inadequate to deal with the new dangers and challenges that confront the contemporary constitutional democracy, whether these stem from global or local terror in possession of increasingly devastating weapons, or from the spread of fundamentalist religion, or else from mass migrations or other massive social or economic dislocations due to globalization. I will advance the thesis that a more appropriate legal regime to deal with contemporary problems can be devised on the basis of a tripartite division distinguishing between conditions of emergency, conditions of stress, and conditions of normalcy. Focus on conditions of stress will reveal that in confronting certain contemporary threats, such as global terror and politically organized fundamentalist religion, the reinforcement of fundamental rights rather than their restriction in the pursuit of greater security may be best poised in many instances to safeguard and reinforce constitutional democracy.

* Justice Sydney L. Robins, Professor of Human Rights, Benjamin N. Cardozo School of Law, New York City.

Times of stress are neither ordinary times nor times of crisis. In the context of a crisis, be it military, economic, social, or natural, the head of government may be entitled to proclaim exceptional powers and to suspend constitutional rights, including political rights. In an acute crisis, the polity is singularly focused on survival and all other political concerns and objectives recede into the background.[1] In contrast, in ordinary times, the polity can readily absorb the full impact of the give and take of everyday politics, and political rights as well as other constitutional rights ought to be protected to their fullest possible extent.

Times of stress differ from those of crisis primarily in terms of the severity, intensity, and duration of the respective threats involved. The line between the two may be difficult to draw, but a less severe, less intense, and more durable threat is likely to give rise to times of stress whereas a severe, intense, concentrated threat, of relatively shorter duration, is likely to provoke a crisis. For example, a foreign military invasion or a widespread domestic insurrection is likely to provoke a crisis. On the other hand, the aftermath of the terrorist attacks such as those against New York City on September 11, 2001, Madrid on March 11, 2004, or London on July 7, 2005, which may involve threats, perceived threats, launching a "war on terror" fought mainly in far away countries, arrest and detention of potential terrorists, but no further terrorist attack on the United States, Spain, or the United Kingdom as of the time of this writing, has produced times of stress rather than times of crisis.[2]

Should rights in times of stress fall somewhere between rights in times of crisis and those in ordinary times? Should rights in times of stress be the same as those prevalent in ordinary times, but be protected to a lesser extent than the latter? Should there be any special civil or political rights for times of stress?

1 The grant and duration of exceptional emergency powers are problematic not in relation to their proper use as means to combat threats to the life of the polity, but in relation to the potential for abuse in the invocation or prolongation of such powers. See Bruce Ackerman, "The Emergency Constitution," *Yale Law Journal* 113 (2004): 1029, 1040.

2 It is important, for example, to distinguish the long-term aftermath from the immediate impact and short-term consequences of the September 11 attacks. Indeed, the day of the attacks, which resulted in around 3,000 deaths, and subsequent days in which the American nation had to cope with the shock of the sudden and unexpected attacks and with the prospect of the imminence of further such attacks can be characterized fairly as a time of crisis. The long period of disquiet that followed those first few weeks, however, is better described as one of stress than of crisis.

What links the approach to rights and the conception of constitutional democracy advanced here is that they are both dynamic and functional. Their paramount task is to cope with the evolving and shifting tensions between identity and difference – or unity and diversity – that confronts all pluralistic polities, that is polities in which the citizenry embraces diverse and often competing or conflicting conceptions of the good.[3] In other words, pluralistic polities – and all contemporary constitutional democracies are pluralistic in the sense understood here – must constantly strive to cope with conflicts between the need to maintain or promote sufficient unity, on the one hand, and the need to accommodate broad enough diversity to allow for optimal coexistence among adherents of different and often divergent conceptions of the good, on the other.

To allow for a systematic examination of the nature, role, and place, of political rights within a pluralistic conception of constitutional democracy, I will proceed as follows. Part I will articulate the broad outlines of the conceptual framework within which the inquiry into civil and political rights will be carried out. It will focus on the theoretical underpinnings of the pluralist conception of constitutional democracy by stressing the distinction between pluralism-in-fact and pluralism-as-norm; explore the proper role of the political in a pluralist polity in which the citizenry both divides and coheres along the cleavage between self and other; place constitutional democracy within a pluralist perspective; assess the relevance of the distinction between negative and positive political rights within that perspective; and, attempt a more systematic differentiation between ordinary conditions, times of stress, and times of crisis within the confines of the pluralist vision. Part II will explore the nature, function, and derivation of civil and political rights in a pluralist democracy. Emphasis will be placed both on how constitutional democracy itself may imply political rights that are not explicitly constitutionally protected and on the political dimension of protected constitutional rights that are not political in the narrow sense. Finally, Part III will concentrate on civil and political rights in times of stress through examination of issues arising out of the war on terror, the limits of tolerance, militant democracy, and the prospects of peaceful and constitutionally sanctioned secession.

3 See Michel Rosenfeld, *Just Interpretations: Law between Ethics and Politics* (Berkeley: University of California Press, 1998), 201–2 (describing such polities as being "pluralistic-in-fact" as distinguished from espousing pluralism as a normative goal or aspiration).

I. A Pluralist Conceptual Framework for Civil and Political Rights

A. Comprehensive Pluralism and the Competition among Conceptions of the Good

As a systematic approach, pluralism, or what I refer to as "comprehensive pluralism,"[4] holds that in societies that are pluralistic-in-fact, the good consists in promoting pluralism as the norm.[5] In a nutshell, comprehensive pluralism maintains that in a polity that is pluralist-in-fact, it is good to protect and promote as many competing conceptions of the good as possible, and that justice is inextricably connected to pursuit of the pluralist good. From the pluralist standpoint, no religion is inherently superior to, or "truer" than, any other, and no ideology, culture, or lifestyle is prima facie better than any other.[6] Moreover, pluralist justice is concerned with eradicating institutional entrenchment and advantages of certain conceptions of the good at the expense of others and with opening up as much space as possible to encompass equitably as many of the existing conceptions of the good within the polity as practically feasible without compromising the normative aims of pluralism.

Before pursing the pluralist approach to rights any further, it is necessary to deal with two anticipated objections. The first is that comprehensive pluralism's conception of justice sketched above does not ultimately differ in substance from Rawls', and in particular from his conception of political justice.[7] The second is that comprehensive pluralism is yet another conception of the good among many and that to privilege it with respect to political justice is as arbitrary as choosing one religious or secular conception over others. More generally, at a more abstract level, these two objections represent two sides of the same overall critique: either comprehensive pluralism is but one more monistic theory or it collapses into relativism.[8]

4 See id. at 200–201.

5 See id. at 200. The discussion that follows is based on the more extensive one provided in the book.

6 Cf. Will Kymlicka, *Multicultural Citizenship: A Liberal Theory of Minority Rights* (New York: Oxford University Press, 1995), 18–19 (distinguishing between ethno-cultural differences and "life-style" differences such as those associated with feminist or gay perspectives).

7 See John Rawls, *Political Liberalism* (New York: Columbia University Press, 1993).

8 Monism' is "roughly defined as the view that there is a single conception of the good that is correct and that all value preferences are to be judged in terms of that conception." In contrast, 'relativism' is "the view that all value preferences are ultimately purely subjective and

Rawls' liberalism (as all liberalism) is monistic in that it embraces an individualistic perspective that privileges individual liberty and equality over collective values and objectives. Consistent with this, Rawls' conception of justice, whether political or comprehensive, cannot achieve neutrality with respect to the good as it is necessarily privileges liberal values and outlooks over illiberal ones. Furthermore, whereas Rawlsian liberalism embraces pluralism and tolerance, it is confined to limited pluralism – that is, those values and outlooks that are not incompatible with liberal individualism.[9] In contrast, comprehensive pluralism is pluralistic all the way, and thus does not privilege individualist perspectives over collective ones or vice versa. But, if that is so, does not comprehensive pluralism ultimately collapse into mere relavisism? For if it does, it is self-contradictory. Indeed, if all conceptions of the good are merely subjective, and if there can be no justice independent from the good, then pluralism is no more justified than antipluralism, nor is tolerance more legitimate than intolerance.

Comprehensive pluralism can only escape from the trap of monism and relativism if it is understood dynamically as operating dialectically. Moreover, this understanding is crucial for purposes of articulating the pluralist conception of political justice and of rights, including those that ought to prevail in times of stress.

In the broadest terms, the dynamic that animates comprehensive pluralism consists in the unfolding of two concurrent processes that can be conceptualized as two successive moments within a single logic. The first logical moment comprises the equalization through leveling of all existing conceptions of the good within the polity. This first moment is the negative one. At any given time in the institutions and life of a polity, certain conceptions of the good predominate over others. For example, a polity's constitution may privilege secular outlooks over religious ones, or the polity's institutional life may favor certain religions and harm the interests of others. Accordingly, the first negative moment consists in a systematic eradication of all entrenchment or project of entrenchment of any existing

so contextually bound to the conception of the good from which they emerge that it would be meaningless to gauge them from the standpoint of any other perspective." Rosenfeld, *Just Interpretations*, 206.

9 This amounts to another way of stating that Rawlsian justice is only compatible with "reasonable" comprehensive views.

conception of the good.[10] Taken to its logical conclusion, moreover, this negative process would expel all conceptions of the good from the polity, thus completely undermining the very basis for pluralism. In other words, complete equality among all conceptions of the good can only be achieved through total suppression of each. For this reason, for the logic of pluralism to make sense, its negative moment must be supplemented by a positive one.

The positive moment requires launching a process of reintegration for all conceptions of the good leveled during the negative moment. This process of reintegration must be according to the precepts of comprehensive pluralism: the polity must accommodate as many existing conceptions of the good as possible for admission consistent with equal admission and equal opportunity for each to flourish. Accordingly, not all conceptions can be readmitted, and even those that are, cannot be readmitted on their own terms. For example, a conception of the good, such as that of a crusading religion bent on converting by force or killing the infidel may have to be excluded altogether.[11] Other conceptions, such as certain religious ones may be readmitted, but on condition of reigning in certain of their precepts, such as the duty to engage in certain overly intrusive forms of proselytism.

From the standpoint of comprehensive pluralism, every actual institutional arrangement is subject to critical assessment in terms of the dialectic framed by the tension between the two moments identified above. In actual polities, at no time are all conceptions of the good equally leveled, and at all times proponents of certain conceptions are likely to have plausible arguments for better and fuller inclusion of their viewpoint within the life of the polity. Consistent with this, comprehensive pluralism can be viewed as fighting at once on two fronts: on the one hand, it seeks to eradicate privilege among conceptions of the good; on the other, it seeks greater inclusion of, consistent with mutual coexistence among, existing competing conceptions.

If these two fronts are considered separately, then comprehensive pluralism would seem to collapse into relativism with respect to the first and into

[10] The justification for this negative moment depends on the presupposition that there is no conception of the good the entrenchment of which would be compatible with the equal entrenchment of all other conceptions of the good.

[11] Whether such a religion may in any way be readmitted would depend on whether any of its beliefs, customs, and practices could be effectively segregated from its crusading aims. If yes, then only its crusading aspects would have to be suppressed; if not, the religion altogether would have to.

monism with respect to the second. Indeed, in its leveling mode, comprehensive pluralism treats all conceptions of the good as equivalent regardless of their actual normative content. On the other hand, in its positive moment, comprehensive pluralism deals with claims to recognition by previously leveled conceptions of the good exclusively in terms of its own normative criteria.[12]

Understood dialectically, however, comprehensive pluralism is only relativistic in its struggle against privilege and hegemony among conceptions of the good; and it is only monistic in its endeavor to be both fair and as inclusive as possible with respect to granting space within the polity to competing conceptions of the good. Ultimately, comprehensive pluralism depends for its survival on the availability of conceptions of the good that differ from its own views. Liberalism, in contrast, does not depend on illiberal worldviews for its vindication, though it can afford limited tolerance toward the latter.

Comprehensive pluralism is a conception of the good, but it differs from all others in being both open toward, and dependent on, other conceptions of the good. Within the perspective of comprehensive pluralism, moreover, pluralist norms play a regulative role geared to implementation of the dialectical logic of equalization and accommodation of competing conceptions of the good. In their regulative capacity, pluralist norms constitute second-order norms as opposed to the norms espoused by other conceptions of the good, which can be characterized as first-order norms. Furthermore, as regulative, pluralism's second-order norms are hierarchically superior to first-order norms. Accordingly, when implementation of the dictates of a first-order norm would thwart the *regulative* mission of second-order norms, the former would have to yield to the latter. In other words, first-order norms must only yield when they hinder the regulative function of second-order norms. For example, tolerance is a second-order norm, but its regulative operation does not require excluding or significantly restricting all intolerant perspectives. Thus, an intolerant religion practiced by a self-contained group that has little contact with outsiders, but is at peace with them, would be unlikely to thwart the polity's institutional implementation of appropriate norms of tolerance. In contrast, an intolerant religion

[12] In this sense, though its criteria differ from those of liberalism, comprehensive pluralism's inclusiveness seems monistic much like liberal tolerance is.

that proselytizes aggressively and seeks to impose its precepts on everyone within the polity would clearly interfere with the smooth implementation of pluralist tolerance.

B. Constitutional Framework and Pluralist Politics

From the standpoint of the institutional structure of the pluralist polity, pluralism's second-order norms determine the constitutional framework, provide a substantive normative criterion for assessing or designing a working constitutional order, and circumscribe the normative space for constitutional politics. In terms of actual constitutional essentials, pluralist constitutionalism shares much in common with its liberal counterpart: they both require limitation and division of powers, adherence to the rule of law, and protection of fundamental rights.[13] The differences between the two, some of which will be addressed in greater detail below, are most apparent when focusing on details or limits. For example, as already mentioned, pluralist tolerance is different from liberal tolerance, and hence the scope of pluralist freedom of expression rights is likely to differ from that of its liberal counterpart. Similarity, the mutual relationship between individual and group rights is bound to differ as pluralism does not share liberalism's bias toward individualism.

In the pluralist context, constitutional politics relates to the operation of second-order norms on the polity's institutional design and its deployment. This boils down to two principal tasks: (1) Constitutional design through application of the relevant second-order norms to the particular circumstances of the polity involved; and (2) determining which subjects ought to be entrusted to the realm of constitutional politics, and which to the realm of ordinary politics.[14]

[13] See Michel Rosenfeld, "Modern Constitutionalism as Interplay Between Identity and Diversity," in *Constitutionalism, Identity, Difference and Legitimacy: Theoretical Perspectives*, ed. Michel Rosenfeld, 3 (Durham: Duke University Press, 1994).

[14] The distinction between constitutional and ordinary politics is one drawn by Bruce Ackerman to distinguish between politics motivated by the good of the polity as a whole and politics motivated by narrow self-interests. See Bruce Ackerman, *We The People: Foundations* (Cambridge, MA: Belknap Press of Harvard University Press, 1991), 12–13, 261–62, 265. In contrast to Ackerman, I use this distinction to underscore the difference between what the second-order norms of comprehensive pluralism require be inscribed in the institutional design of the polity or protected from majoritarian politics and what ought to be left to infra-constitutional political competition subjected to majoritarian decision-making processes. In other words, in my

Which subject should be entrusted to constitutional politics and protection, and which to ordinary majoritarian politics, cannot in many cases be determined from a mere consideration of the dictates of pluralism's second-order norms. Such determinations may depend on the range of conceptions of the good represented within the polity or on choices among a range of plausible interpretations of the implications of the relevant second-order norms. What ought to be included and what excluded from the realm of the constitution is itself a matter of constitutional politics framed by the constraints of the second-order norms of pluralism. Consistent with this, the polity must guarantee political rights of participation in the constitutional politics pursued to settle on which subjects to constitutionalize and which to leave to parliamentary politics.

C. Political Rights and the Struggle between Self and Other

Comprehensive pluralism calls for political rights relating to constitutional politics and to ordinary politics. Before dwelling any further on whether or how they differ and on what they may actually consist of, however, it is necessary briefly to examine how the realm of political relationships (both constitutional and ordinary) is circumscribed from the standpoint of comprehensive pluralism. In the context of competition among a plurality of distinct conceptions of the good, proponents of the same conception can regard their common beliefs, practices, customs, and objectives as those of a coherent *self* competing against those who do not share these and who with varying degrees of vehemence actually oppose them. The latter, in turn, constitute the *other* that stands against the self identified above. Viewed thus, moreover, political relations are the external relations between a self and another that share a common historical trajectory within a particular geographic space.[15]

Self and other are understood here in a fluid, relationational sense. For example, Catholics and Protestants in Northern Ireland relate as self and other; so do French speaking Quebecois and Anglophone Canadians;

conception, it is the dictates of the second-order norms, not the perceptions and intentions of political actors that inform the distinction between constitutional and ordinary politics.

15 Legal relations are also external relations among selves and others, and as such constitute a subset of political relationships. For a discussion of the similarities and differences between legal and political relations, see Rosenfeld, *Just Interpretations*, 76–78.

Democrats and Republicans, in the United States; and ethnic Hungarians and the rest of the population in Romania. Not only do these examples refer to splits along different divides (respectively religious, linguistic, ideological and ethnic) but also the individuals and groups involved can belong at once to different political selves and others and the boundaries between self and other can shift so that former others can become members of the same collective self and vice versa. Thus, for example, individuals who belong respectively to the Democratic and Republican Party in the United States are bound to relate as self to other in a presidential election, but they group themselves as a single self in relation to the kind of Islamic fundamentalism that stood behind the attacks of September 11, 2001. For her part, a Catholic Swiss citizen from a French speaking canton belongs to many intersecting selves confronting an equal number of intersecting others. Our citizen as part of a collective self may be opposed to different others in the context of her country's politics. Thus, she may be a Catholic as opposed to Protestants, a French speaker as opposed to German, Italian and Romanch speakers, a French speaking Catholic as opposed to French speaking Protestants, a citizen of her own canton as opposed to other cantons, a Swiss citizen as opposed to citizens of the European Union, and a feminist as opposed to anti-feminists within her own country. These multiple selves and others overlap and one's political opponents in one setting may be part of one's collective self in another. Thus, French and German speaking feminists may unite in the struggle for women's equality but divide over cultural and linguistic policy.

Relationships of self as against other can also occur within a single group. Take, for example, the case of Catholic gays. Whereas the Catholic Church rejects homosexuality, it purports to exclude the lifestyle involved, but not the person engaged in it. According to Catholicism, the homosexual is a sinner, but so are all humans and the Church is compassionate, and makes room for eventual repentance and redemption of all sinners. Does that make a Catholic gay an insider or an outsider? It may depend on the degree of alienation experienced by the gay person or group involved. More generally, self and other and different conceptions of the good need not be impermeable to one another. Issues such as that of women or gay priests in religions where the priesthood traditionally has been the exclusive preserve of heterosexual men, have been divisive, and have in certain cases cast the feminists or gays involved as others within their own religious community.

In other cases, however, the religion involved has adjusted and accepted women or gays as priests. In the latter cases, certain conceptions of the good have evolved, and have blended with, or incorporated, aspects of other such conceptions.

In spite of the complexity and fluidity of the relationships between self and other, and between conceptions of the good, pluralist political rights can be boiled down to the following. These rights are meant to regulate the external relationships between self and other (or more precisely, others, for though at some level all that is not self is other, in political terms, different others may pose different threats or challenges, for example, a particular religion may face different threats from other religions than from secular ideologies) in such a way as to equalize and accommodate as much as possible the position of self and other within the polity consistent with adherence to the second-order norms of comprehensive pluralism. Because in any complex and diverse society there are many overlapping and shifting selves and others, the political order and political rights must allow for a proper balance between unity and diversity. A polity cannot survive as such within the context of constitutional democracy unless all its constituents can identify at some level as belonging to a single political self. In some sense, all those who belong to the polity must combine into a self that stands against all those who do not belong to it and who, for this purpose, constitute the other. The bond of identity involved at the polity-wide level may be profound and deeply lasting, as in the case of a culturally, ethically and religiously homogeneous group that has shared the same geographic space over a long period of history. Or, the bond in question may be relatively shallow and fragile, as in the case of a number of disparate groups with different traditions coming together to organize into a single polity for purely external reasons, such as to better be able to defend themselves against a common enemy, or to better compete in global markets.

All individuals and groups within the polity must invest something of themselves into the polity-wide self in order to forge a common identity. At the same time, all those within the polity must protect against allowing the common polity-wide self to unduly threaten or eradicate their more particular identity as a self among others within the polity. To best achieve this may require the grant of both positive and negative political rights: positive rights to participate at the constitutional and infra-constitutional level in the politics of the polity as a whole; and, negative rights to shield at least certain aspects of communal (whether religious or not) life and individual life from inter-group politics.

From the standpoint of the dialectic between self and other that animates the politics of the pluralist polity, there is an important distinction between policies that impact on the very identity of self or other and policies that apportion benefits and burdens among the two. In other words, there are policies that threaten the very survival or integrity of a conception of the good, and others that merely somewhat advance or hinder the implementation of its societal project without affecting it at its core. There is no bright line between identity-related policies and benefit/burden related ones, but in most cases the distinction is workable, and ideally, identity-related politics should be relegated to the constitutional level, and benefits/burden-related politics to the infra-constitutional one.

D. Pluralism and the Distinction between Ordinary Times, Times of Crisis and Times of Stress

The distinction between ordinary times, times of crisis, and times of stress briefly sketched at the outset can be further elaborated consistent with the pluralist conception of politics as the ongoing confrontation between self and other. In ordinary times, conflicts between self and other do not threaten the unity of the polity and find resolution, or at least confinement, within the existing constitutional, institutional, and political framework. Thus, in spite of the fact that a number of struggles relating to identity and to the apportionment of benefits and burdens throughout the polity split the citizenry into a multiplicity of selves pitted against numerous others, the common self that binds all citizens to the unity of the polity remains glued together and shows no danger of unraveling. For such overall common identity to remain secure, no significant group must feel so alienated or excluded from the political life of the polity as to seriously consider abandoning adhesion to the self that binds together the citizenry as a whole. For all groups concerned firmly to adhere to the indivisibility of the polity, the conception of the good of each must be sufficiently integrated and accommodated within the polity that they can generally accept the resolution of identity and benefit/burden conflicts within the existing constitutional and political order as capable of meeting the requisite minimum degree of justice and fairness. In ordinary times, neither self nor other are fully satisfied with their fate and are likely to struggle continuously to ameliorate their respective position. Neither of them, however, is likely to become so dissatisfied with his or her status or with the existing institutional framework for processing conflicts as to want to withdraw from the polity.

Times of crisis, in contrast, occur when the common identity or the very life of the polity are in imminent peril. The cause of the peril may be external, as in the case of a foreign war, or internal, as in the case of civil war or violent secession. In times of crisis, the conception of the good of self or other is so little integrated or accommodated within the polity that all possible institutional resolutions of the conflict between self and other will strike one or both of them as deeply unsatisfactory and unjust.

As already pointed out, times of stress stand halfway between ordinary times and times of crisis. In times of stress, there is less extensive and less successful accommodation and integration of significantly represented conceptions of the good. Self and other are less likely than in ordinary times to consider institutional process of conflict resolution to be just or fair. The identity or unity of the common self that is supposed to bind together the citizenry is not disintegrating, but it is destabilized and under various pressures. Whereas violent secession creates a crisis, a push for peaceful secession is likely to put the polity under stress. Whereas the threat to overthrow of a democratically elected government seems bound to result in a crisis, the increasing popularity of a non-democratic party within a democracy is likely to cause stress. Whereas a conventional war may cause a crisis, terrorism and the war on terror seems more likely to create stress. Indeed, unlike a military invasion, terrorist acts are likely to be sporadic and widespread causing more psychological than physical harm. Having terrorists hidden within the polity's population would undoubtedly be unnerving and can easily lead to reactions and overreactions, undue suppression of fundamental rights or exacerbation of ethnic or racial prejudice such that certain selves and the conceptions of the good they endorse may become increasingly unhinged. At some point erosion of accommodation of certain conceptions of the good may place increasing strain on the working unity of the polity's citizenry.

Further inquiry into the effect of conditions of stress on political rights will be postponed till Part III below, in order to focus on the role of civil and political rights in contemporary constitutional democracies.

II. Pluralism and the Derivation of Civil and Political Rights

Liberalism, republicanism, and communitarianism are all compatible with varying degrees of limited pluralism. In essence, liberalism posits individual self-determination and self-fulfilment as paramount; republicanism, self-government and civic virtue; and communitarianism, communal goals and group-based solidarity.[16] As we shall see, within a pluralist perspective, there is room for limited liberalism, republicanism and communitarianism, as all three play a subordinate though indispensable role in the elaboration of pluralist politics and rights. Furthermore, within a pluralist perspective, the determination of political rights is less categorical than relational and hence highly context-dependent.

A. Pluralism and Limited Liberalism Republicanism and Communitarianism

Comprehensive pluralism encompasses limited liberalism, republicanism and communitarianism in as much as it recognizes that individual self-realization, self-government, and communal solidarity and communal self-determination have a legitimate place within a pluralist polity.[17] Moreover, liberalism, republicanism and communitarianism play both a mutually antagonistic and a complementary role when viewed from the dialectical standpoint of comprehensive pluralism. Indeed, the struggle between self and other within a pluralistic perspective is neither a purely individualistic one nor an exclusively communal one, particularly if communities are conceived as homogeneous, self-enclosed, organic units. Self-realization may be *within* or *through* one's community, or even outside of the latter. Whether the self be the individual within a community or a subgroup within a larger group, there is likely to be a conflict between self-realization and group-wide solidarity. Whereas liberalism privileges the individual over the group and communitarianism conversely primes the group over the individual, pluralism favors neither. Instead, pluralism seeks to overcome conflicts involving individual versus group, subgroup versus group, and one group versus another, by subjecting the antagonistic first-order

[16] For a more extended discussion of liberalism, republicanism, and communitarianism in relation to comprehensive pluralism, see id. at 213–234.

[17] This draws upon and expands on, my discussion of these issues in id. at 216–24.

norms competing for vindication to the edicts emanating from second-order norms. Furthermore, within a pluralistic perspective, liberalism and communitarianism are complementary as well as antagonistic in as much as the vices of an overly individualistic political order can be mitigated by greater communal emphasis and vice versa.

For its part, republican self-government is not justified for its own sake within a pluralist perspective, but rather for purposes of establishing a political course that maximizes inclusion of competing conceptions of the good consistent with the dictates of second-order norms. This means that every member of the polity – be it an individual or a communal member – must to some degree refrain from the pursuit of self-realization to join with others to manage mutual tensions and to foster mutual accommodation. Unlike republican self-government in its Rousseauean incarnation,[18] pluralist self-government doesn't require suppressing all interests for the common good. It only requires working together to implement mutual restraints that will allow for the proliferation of a plurality of modes of self-realization. Accordingly, whereas pluralist self-government is in tension with individual and communal self-realization, it complements these in the sense that it does not allow either to become dominant or one-sided. Conversely, polity-wide pluralist self-government is not supposed to impose a single society-wide common good, but rather to set the stage for coexistence among a plurality of competing conceptions of the good. And consistent with this, both the pursuit of individual self-realization and of communal solidarity serve to confine the realm of self-government and to place many societal endeavors beyond its reach.

A well ordered pluralist polity requires sustaining a dynamic tension between liberal, republican and communitarian tendencies to produce an equilibrium for purposes of accommodating as broad a spectrum of diverse conceptions of the good as possible consistent with adherence to pluralist norms. Approximation of the requisite equilibrium depends on the deployment of an array of political rights, both negative and positive, of certain rights of freedom *from* politics, and on the imposition of certain duties of political participation. Moreover, the nature and scope of the rights and

[18] See Jean-Jacques Rousseau, *The Social Contract*, ed. Charles Frankel, 14–16, 26 n. 2 (New York: Hafner, 1947), in order to partake in self-government in accordance with the general will, the citizen must subordinate self-interest to civic virtue.

duties in question are predominantly relational and contextual. These rights and duties are relational in the sense that they are the rights of a particular self against a particular other in relation to an identifiable intersubjective domain. For example, an aboriginal minority may have a right to freedom from subjection to the politics of the non-aboriginal majority within the polity in relation to intra-aboriginal affairs and in relation to regulation of aboriginal lands. On the other hand, aboriginal individuals may have different rights and duties vis a vis one another with respect to their intersubjective dealings within the same domain. Also consistent with these sets of relations, from the standpoint of the particular polity involved as a whole, intra-aboriginal affairs are beyond politics, whereas these same affairs are most likely political when considered from within the aboriginal community.[19]

Pluralist political rights are contextual in as much as the optimal inclusion of diverse conceptions of the good depends on the nature of the conceptions involved and on the particular circumstances at stake. For example, in a polity comprising several ethnic groups, each living within its own distinct geographic location, federalism, and the political rights it entails may be clearly called for. In contrast, if these same ethnic groups were not split along geographical lines, federalism would most likely be of little use in dealing with inter-ethnic group affairs. Moreover, where federalism is not a viable option, the optimal form of political organization and the particular array of political rights which it would require would depend on the actual contending conceptions of the good and on the degree of antagonism among their respective proponents. For example, where ethnic differences are sharp and intense, it might be preferable to discourage ethnic-based political parties, and to shape political rights in ways that minimize rather than exacerbate ethnic tensions. On the other hand, where ethnic tensions are not that intense, but where the interests of certain ethnic minorities tend to get lost in the shuffle, some degree of ethnic-based political representation may well further the aims of pluralism.

[19] In theory at least, it would be possible for intra-aboriginal dealings not to be political, i.e., not to involve external relationships, but only moral. This would be the case if all involved acted pursuant to internalized moral or religious imperatives rather than on the basis of political objectives.

B. Relational and Contextual Pluralist Political Rights in Action: The Example of Free Speech

The relational and contextual nature of legitimate political rights within a pluralist perspective not only entails that particular political rights may be appropriate in some contexts but not in others, but also that depending on the particular context involved, the same rights may be political or non-political. A good example of such a right is the right to free speech, which will be examined below. Indeed, a functioning democracy is inconceivable in the absence of free speech rights, yet not all conceptions or uses of free speech are in any meaningful sense political.

Certain rights, like the right to vote, are always political and from the standpoint of pluralism are indispensable in all contexts. In the presence of pluralism-in-fact, there are bound to be conflicts between proponents of different first-order objectives that cannot be resolved by appeal to second-order norms. At least in some of these cases, reliance on democratic majorities provides the best alternative and call for enforcement of the right to vote.

Other rights, such as the right to privacy with respect to a person's intimate relations are inherently not political though the determination of whether or not to afford them, or to what extent to recognize them, is political. In other words, persons do not usually use their right to choose with whom to engage in an intimate relationship for political purposes. Accordingly, in almost all conceivable circumstances, the right to privacy with respect to intimate associations is a civil right not a political one.

Free speech rights, in contrast, are sometimes political rights, and at other times nonpolitical or only incidentally political. Clearly, democracy cannot function without political will-formation or without open and wide-ranging discussion of political alternatives. On the other hand, freedom of artistic expression or freedom to communicate one's feelings may, but need not, be political, and often is not.[20] For example, an abstract painting may

[20] See Michel Rosenfeld, "The Philosophy of Free Speech in the United States" in *Mensch und Staat*, ed. Peter Hänni, 437 (Freiburg: Universitätsverl. Freiburg Schweiz, 2003), distinguishing four distinct justifications for the free speech: (1) free speech contributes to discovery of the truth; (2) it is a necessary condition of democracy; (3) free self-expression is indispensable for purposes of achieving individual autonomy; and (4) free speech promotes human dignity. Only justification (2) is distinctly political, and the respective domains carved out by each of theses justifications vary in scope, with some being more expansive than others though there is a significant amount of overlap among them.

either be intended by the artist who created it nor understood by the viewing public as conveying a political message.[21] Consistent with this, moreover, freedom to exhibit abstract art need not be protected speech is as much as freedom of speech it construed as a political right. Or, more precisely, abstract art need not be protected under a positive political right, but it may have to be protected by a negative political right – that is, be protected from intrusions coming from politics at large in order to be free to engage in the politics of art – or as a civil right.

Not only is freedom of speech in a democracy bound to be in part a political right, but also, in certain circumstances, political rights may imply at least a limited free speech right even where such right is afforded no protection as a civil right. This latter case is well illustrated by the Australian High Court's decision in *Australian Capital Television v. The Commonwealth of Australia*.[22] Australian law prohibited broadcasting paid political advertisements and otherwise restricted political discussion on the airwaves as elections were nearing. The High Court upheld a challenge against this law notwithstanding that Australia lacks a bill of rights, on the grounds that freedom to propagate and discuss political views prior to an election can be derived from the Australian Constitution's guarantee of a system of representative government. In other words, without freedom to exchange political views, there cannot be genuine representative government and hence a right to free speech is an inextricable part of a more broadly encompassing right to democratic self-government.

More generally, political rights cannot be captured by formal definitions or categorical classifications. Whether a right is political depends on its relation to politics and to the political. Moreover, within the perspective of comprehensive pluralism, all external relationships are directly or indirectly political.[23] Accordingly, a proper carving out of political rights

[21] This does not mean that abstract art lacks political significance, or more broadly, that any bright line can be drawn between political and non-political expression.

[22] (1992) 177 CLR 106.

[23] Legal relationships are also external and yet are distinct from political ones. Legal rights and duties are distinguishable from their political counterparts, but there is a strong connection between law and politics as law can be characterized as frozen or suspended politics. For further discussion, see Rosenfeld, *Just Interpretations*, 74–83. In a democracy laws are the product of parliamentary politics, and are subject to subsequent amendment or repeal through further parliamentary politics. Notwithstanding these strong connections, legal rights and duties remain distinct from their political counterparts even if the former depends for their existence on the latter.

requires submission of first-order pursuits to the constraints imposed by second-order norms supplemented by mutual accommodation of competing objectives equally compatible with second-order norms – through democratic politics, including majoritarian decision making – with a view to maximizing inclusiveness of diverse conceptions of the good.

III. Pluralist Civil and Political Rights in Times of Stress

As noted in I.D above, in ordinary times self and other (or more precisely selves and others) disagree and compete with one another, but they reach sufficient accommodation to prevent erosion or fragmentation of the overarching binding self that envelops the polity as a whole. Consistent with that, in ordinary times, citizens can enjoy the full panoply of civil and political rights derived from pluralism's second-order norms, and applied to the actual plurality of competing agendas issued from different conceptions of the good and related to different political perspectives.[24] In contrast, in times of crisis, the overarching polity-wide self is threatened with destruction, either from within or from without, and consequently all other objectives may have to be suspended to provide undivided attention to the fight for survival. In an acute crisis, civil and political rights may have to be temporarily suspended. What is more, even from the standpoint of comprehensive pluralism, the pursuit of pluralism may itself have to be provisionally abandoned till the crisis is overcome. This may sound paradoxical, but remains consistent with the logic of pluralism. Indeed, averting destruction of the space reserved for interaction among a plurality of perspectives must take priority over any actual attempt to foster accommodation within that space.

Times of stress cover the broad spectrum between ordinary times and times of emergency, that is between times where the unity of the polity seems entirely secure and times of struggle devoted to repelling mortal threats

[24] Different political agendas may be tied to different conceptions of the good, e.g., promoting religion in public schools tied to religious ideologies versus campaigning for secular public education tied to humanistic non-religious perspectives. Different political agendas, however, may also be linked to the same conception of the good when self and other disagree over the best means to the same end. For example, two liberals may differ over whether welfare entitlements promote or stifle individual pursuit of self-realization.

posed by an internal or external enemy. Accordingly, it would seem that civil and political rights in times of stress should fall somewhere between the full protection called in ordinary times and the full suspension that may be warranted in an acute crisis.

Upon closer examination, however, it does not necessarily follow that because times of stress are sandwiched between ordinary times and those of crisis that political rights in conditions of stress should be more restricted than those in ordinary times. On the contrary, arguably when the unity of the polity begins to crack but is in no imminent danger of collapse, it would seem better to reinforce rather than weaken political rights. Indeed, when self and other begin to evolve from adversaries committed to cannons of civility and rules of fair play toward downright enemies, pluralist democracy and the political rights that sustain it would seem to need reinforcement not constriction.[25]

Whatever the logic behind civil and political rights in times of stress, the shift from ordinary times to times of stress generates its own dialectic, which defies the dictates of any straightforward logic. For example, conditions of stress seem to call for militant democracy – that is, a democracy that leaves no room for antidemocratic political parties. Militant democracy, in turn, shrinks the scope of political rights by refusing to extend them to those who seek to use democratic means toward nondemocratic ends. By the same token, however, militant democracy affords greater rights – or similar rights bearing greater weight – to all political operatives who pursue democratic ends, by eliminating or severely handicapping some of their fiercest competitors. On balance, does military democracy increase political rights? Decrease them? Or, change their nature?

To get a better handle on the dialectic at work in shifts from ordinary times to those of stress and from the latter to times of crisis, it is useful to focus on the following exemplary subjects frequently linked to conditions of stress: hate speech and militant democracy; the war on terror; and, pacted secession.

25 See Chanel Mouffe, "The Limits of Liberal Pluralism: Towards an Agonistic Multipolar World Order," in *Militant Democracy*, ed. Andras Sajo, 69, 70 (Utrecht: Eleven International, 2004), distinguishing "agonism" or relation among adversaries from "antagonism" or relation among enemies and arguing that the goal of democratic politics should be to transform antagonism in to agonism.

A. Hate Speech and Militant Democracy

Hate speech – for example, expressing highly offensive, insulting, and demeaning views regarding certain racial ethnic or religious groups – certainly runs counter to the spirit of pluralism's second-order-norms. And, so do antidemocratic political parties bent on using the democratic process to destroy democracy. It does not follow, however, that hate speech and antidemocratic political parties must be banned from the political arena because they contravene pluralist morals. As in the case of crusading religions discussed above,[26] inconsistency with second-order norms is not grounds for suspension. Only interference with the *implementation* of second-order norms is.[27] In other words, the key distinction is between first-order norms that are *inconsistent* and those that are *incompatible* with second-order norms. Moreover, consistent with this distinction, there may be, from the standpoint of comprehensive pluralism, normative or strategic reasons for tolerating antidemocratic parties or hate speech. For example, an antidemocratic party may provide the means for adherents of a particular religion to pursue their conceptions of the good, which, as long as it did not trample on similar pursuits by proponents of other conceptions, would remain in conformity with pluralist morals. Tolerance of hate speech, on the other hand, may be arguably warranted from a strategic standpoint in as much as suppression of such speech might eventually strengthen rather than weaken its proponents.[28]

There are many plausible arguments for and against toleration of hate speech or antidemocratic political parties, but the only relevant ones, for present purposes, are those that revolve around the distinction between ordinary times and times of stress. Banning hate speech and insisting on militant democracy seem much more justified in times of stress than in ordinary ones. This is perhaps best illustrated by the different ways in which

[26] See supra, at 246–247.

[27] Otherwise, pluralism itself would disintegrate as acceptable first-order norms would have to be collapsible into second-order norms. Pluralism ultimately depends on maintaining a dialectical tension between first and second-order norms.

[28] This rationale has played a prominent role in the U.S. broad tolerance for hate speech. In the United States, hate speech is constitutionally protected so long as it does not incite to violence whereas in most of the rest of the world, hate speech that incites to racial, ethnic or religious hatred can be constitutionally banned, see Michel Rosenfeld, "Hate Speech in Constitutional Jurisprudence: A Comparative Analysis," *Cardozo Law Review* 24 (2003): 1523.

the United States and Germany treat Neo-Nazi speech. As made manifest by the *Skokie* cases,[29] the United States can afford to tolerate Neo-Nazi propaganda because of its minimal effect on its intended audience or on the affairs of the polity. In contrast, in Germany because of the Nazi past and of the fear that the Nazi monster may one day be reawakened, Neo-Nazi hate speech does loom as a potential threat to the unity and integrity of the polity.[30]

More generally, the distinction between ordinary times and times of stress may account for different responses to what Karl Popper has termed the "paradox of tolerance."[31] According to this paradox, tolerance of the intolerant may pave the way for the latter to come into power and eventually put an end to tolerance. Popper argues that, accordingly, to preserve tolerance one must be intolerant of the intolerant. Based on the distinction between ordinary times and those of stress, however, it is plausible to argue that from a strategic standpoint it is preferable to tolerate the intolerant so long as the fabric of the pluralist polity is not threatened.[32] Indeed, in the context of the American *Skokie* cases, for example, the legal struggle over whether or not to permit a march by a small group of Neo-Nazi had a much greater impact than the march itself, which eventually took place with barely any notice.[33] Under these circumstances, suppression of the march would have had greater negative consequences for the American polity than did the isolated utterance of Nazi propaganda largely ignored by the American public.

[29] *Collin v. Smith*, 447 F. Supp. 676 (N.D. Ill.), *aff'd*, 578 F.2d 1197 (7th Cir.), *cert. denied*, 439 U.S. 916 (1978); *Village of Skokie* v. *National Socialist Party*, 69 Ill. 2d 605, 373 N.E. 2d 21 (1978).

[30] Eric Stein, "History Against Free Speech: The New German Law Against the 'Auschwitz' and Other 'Lies,'" *Michigan Law Review* 85 (1986): 277, 279–80; Note, *Striking a Difficult Balance: Combatting the Threat of Neo-Nazism in Germany While Preserving Individual Liberties* (suggesting that Article 194(2) of the Penal Code could be used to combat neo-Nazi hate speech and propaganda); "New German Law Restricting Cyberspace," *New York Times*, July 5, 1997, summary republished by EduCom, July 6, 1997.

[31] See Karl Popper, *The Open Society and Its Enemies* (London: Routledge & Kegan Paul, 1966), 265–66 n. 4.

[32] There are of course other arguments in favor of tolerance of the intolerant. For example, consistent with a Millian belief on the eventual triumph of reason through uninhibited public discourse, refutation of the arguments of the intolerant is much more likely to be successful than attempts at suppression. See John Stuart Mill, "On Liberty," ch. 2, PP1, 19–32, in *The Philosophy of John Stuart Mill*, ed. Marshall Cohen, 205, 223–37 (New York: The Modern Library, 1961). For present purposes, however, these other arguments need not be addressed.

[33] Rosenfeld, "Hate Speech in Constitutional Jurisprudence," 1538.

In times of stress, however, tolerance of the intolerant may pave the way to times of crisis. For example, had Nazi ideology been ruthlessly suppressed during the 1920s and 1930s, perhaps the Nazis would not have come to power democratically only to destroy tolerance and democracy. In post World War Two Germany, it is the memory of the Nazi nightmare and the fear of its possible return that create conditions of stress with respect to Nazi propaganda and Neo-Nazi political activity.[34]

Intolerance of the intolerant undoubtedly shrinks the scope of tolerance, and when intolerant political speech is involved, the result is a reduction of the scope of political rights. On the other hand, as the jurisprudence under the German Basic law exemplifies, intolerance of the intolerant may also bolster other rights, including rights with a distinct political dimension.[35] Thus, one reason offered by the German Constitutional Court in justification of its finding intolerance of pro-Nazi expression to be constitutional was that such intolerance was necessary to uphold the dignity of the postwar Jewish population in Germany.[36] Because of their historical experience, tolerance of Neo-Nazi views in postwar Germany would cause the Jewish community to feel excluded from the communal and political life of the contemporary German polity.[37]

In short, unlike in the United States, in Germany Neo-Nazi propaganda created conditions of stress by threatening to drive out German Jews from the over-arching self that binds the German polity together. To counter this threat, the German Constitutional Court prescribed a reduction in the scope of political speech to reinforce basic dignity rights which are also indispensable to a sense of belonging to the polity and to meaningful and effective political participation within it.

There are obvious analogies between curbing hate speech and embracing militant democracy.[38] In an ordinary democracy, all political parties that abide by the rules of the game are allowed to compete for power whatever their ideology. In contrast, in a militant democracy, political parties that

34 As this example indicates, conditions of stress may be confined to particular areas of a polity's life or they may be pervasive throughout all areas within the polity.

35 Edward J. Eberle, "Public Discourse in Contemporary Germany," *Case Western Reserve Law Review* 47 (1997): 797, 824 n. 115, 833–41.

36 Id. at 893 (citing Auschwitz Lie, 90 BVerfGE 241 [1994]).

37 Id.

38 See Kent Roach, "Anti-Terrorism and Militant Democracy," in "Militant Democracy ..." ed. Andras Sajo, 69, 70 (Utrecht: Eleven International, 2004), 171, 183.

pursue antidemocratic ends through democratic means can be constitutionally banned.[39] Furthermore, it is also evident that adherence to militant democracy is likely to be more compelling in times of stress than in ordinary times.

There are also, however, significant disanalogies between the two cases. Pure hate speech – that is, insulting and demeaning expression against a particular group – possesses no genuine social value, and can hence be altogether banned consistent with comprehensive pluralism. If such hate speech is not banned in ordinary times, it is only for purely strategic (political) reasons. In contrast, the antidemocratic agenda of a political party may encompass norms and values entitled to all least partial protection under the dictates of comprehensive pluralism. In addition, upon closer examination, militant democracy taken to its logical extreme seems to rest on an internal contradiction. Ideally, in a democracy, all political views and agendas should be vetted and discussed and eventually submitted to the operative democratic decision-making processes in force within the polity. Moreover, within this ideal scheme, each political party should project a particular agenda distinct from all the other agendas issuing from the competing conceptions of the good vying for vindication within the polity. For each political party to remain true to its unique agenda, however, it would be necessary for it to curb internal heterodoxy or dissent. In other words, to foster optimal inter-party competition and thus best contribute to the ideal of democracy by giving each political position its own voice, political parties may have to be internally nondemocratic or even internally autocratic.

Aiming thus for representation for all political views implicitly or explicitly embraced within the polity requires militancy with respect to process – or *process-based militant democracy*. In contrast, what is customarily referred to as "militant democracy," which calls for suppression of

[39] Eberle, "Public Discourse in Contemporary Germany," 825 n. 119 (quoting *Klass Case*, 30 BVerfGE 1, 19–20 (1970), translated in Donald P. Kommers, The Constitutional Jurisprudence of the Federal Republic of Germany [1989], 230) (citation omitted):

> Constitutional provisions must not be interpreted in isolation but rather in a manner consistent with the Basic Law's fundamental principles and its system of values. ... In the context of this case it is especially significant that the Constitution ... has decided in favor of 'militant democracy' that does not submit to abuse of basic rights or an attack on the liberal order of the state. Enemies of the Constitution must not be allowed to endanger, impair, or destroy the existence of the state while claiming protection of rights granted by the Basic Law.

political parties with antidemocratic agendas, involves militancy regarding outcomes – or *outcome-based militant democracy*. In either case, militant democracy requires reliance on antidemocratic devices. Moreover, if one posits that there is bound to be an eventually unavoidable link between democratic means and ends and between antidemocratic means and ends, then process-based and outcome-based militant democracy seem to be at logger heads.

Both representation of all views, which calls for process-based militancy, and exclusion of antidemocratic political parties, which calls for outcome-based militancy, seem much more compelling in times of stress than in ordinary times. Indeed, in times of stress, various viewpoints are, or seem, threatened with exclusion, and the unity of the polity is sufficiently frayed to make possible an eventual takeover by antidemocratic forces. No such pressures are present in ordinary times, which allows for greater fluidity in the articulation of political positions and for greater tolerance of political parties with antidemocratic objectives. Accordingly, in ordinary times, neither process-based nor outcome-based militancy loom as necessary or desirable.

In times of stress, perceived threats to the unity of the polity are not only likely to be associated with antidemocratic political parties, but also with illiberal ones. Illiberal parties need not be antidemocratic. For example, a religious fundamentalist party that has the support of a majority of the electorate of a polity can remain essentially democratic both internally and externally, and yet systematically spread illiberalism. Even from the standpoint of militant democracy, however, illiberal is not synonymous with antidemocratic, and hence prohibition of illiberal parties in times of stress would not be justified as suppression of antidemocratic ones would be. Even if suppression of the latter is justified in times of stress, suppression of illiberal parties poses vexing problems that go to the heart of pluralism and democracy. This is well illustrated by the case of *Refah Partisi v. Turkey*.[40] In a divided decision, the European Court of Human Rights held that the dissolution of the Islamic Party Refah, the largest party in Turkey's parliament, ordered by the Turkish Constitutional Court was not contrary to the European Convention on Human Rights. The Turkish Court had acted because it found Refah to be a "center of activities" contrary to the principle of secularism enshrined in the Turkish Constitution. Although

40 *Refah Partisi* v. *Turkey*, 35 Eur. Ct. H.R. 3 (2002).

Refah's means and ends were both democratic in nature, the European Court's majority found that Refah's advocacy of women wearing headscarves in public places and adherence to the Koran would, if successful, lead to an impermissible surrender of the people's democratic rights to religious authorities who even if backed by large majorities, would implement illiberal policies discriminatory on the basis of sex and of religion. For the European Court's dissenting judges, however, dissolution for mere advocacy of peaceful and legal changes – through constitutional amendment, if necessary – by a political party that is democratic with respect to means and ends and that declares its adherence to the requirement of secularism imposed by the Turkish Constitution, is an unwarranted, overly drastic and disproportionate result.

From the standpoint of pluralism, unlike from that of liberalism, illiberal ideals need not be automatically excluded from the arena of democratic politics. Furthermore, from the standpoint of conditions of stress, if retreat from radical secularism were genuinely likely eventually to culminate in dissolution of the Turkish polity, then suppression of *Refah* would be justified. It could even be defended on grounds of militant democracy, but it would result in less democracy and less pluralism.[41]

On the other hand, if discord over secularism created conditions of stress in contemporary Turkey, but moving away from radical secularism would not risk the break up of the polity, but merely a realignment that may or may not live up to the prescriptions of the European Convention of Human Rights, then suppression of Refah would not be justified. In that case the risk of greater stress would not justify significantly curbing democracy and pluralism in the absence of actual erosion of the rights protected by the Convention.

What the preceding discussion of the *Refah* case illustrates is that conditions of stress do not necessarily call for militant democracy or an increase or decrease in democratic rights or in the reach of pluralism. Instead, the right solution requires a proper readjustment and balancing of competing rights and objectives depending on the particular circumstances involved, and on how far from, or near to, conditions of crisis, existing conditions of stress happen to be.

[41] It could still be consistent with comprehensive pluralism depending how close the conditions of stress happened to be in relation to conditions of crisis.

B. The War on Terror

If the issues surrounding militant democracy invite comparisons between conditions of stress and ordinary conditions, the issues raised by the war on terror require focus on the comparison between conditions of stress and states of crisis. Terrorism, as noted above, can provoke a state of crisis, such as seemed to be the case in the immediate aftermath of the attacks of September 11 in the United States, of March 11 in Madrid, and of July 7, 2007 in London. In the long run, however, as also already emphasized, the war terror, whether it be that against Al Quaeda, or those against ETA in Spain or the IRA in Northern Ireland, is more likely to produce times of stress than to sustain a state of crisis.

At first sight, the war on terror seems much more likely to affect civil rights, the rights of criminal defendants and those of detainees held without charges for long indefinite periods of time than political rights. Upon closer consideration, however, the war on terror is also likely to have some effects on certain political rights, such as, for example, the right freely to associate into pursuit of a common political project. Indeed, the war on terror may, at least prima facie, justify infiltration of certain political groups and thus adversely affect their ability to compete effectively in the political arena. Moreover, to the extent that a political party is suspected of acting in concert with, or of pursuing the agenda of, terrorists, such as was the case with the Batasuna party linked to ETA in Spain,[42] the war on terror may give rise to genuine militant democracy concerns comparable to those raised by political parties that use democratic means to achieve antidemocratic ends.

The most significant nexus between the war on terror and the political, however, concerns the boundary between a state of crisis and conditions of stress. The more the war on terror is like a veritable war, the more emergency powers may be justified with the consequent diminution of civil and political rights. On the other hand, the more the war on terror approximates combating and prosecuting crimes, the greater is the justification for those institutions that are customarily deployed in times of stress rather than for preservation of a state of crisis.[43]

[42] See Victor Ferreres Comella, "The New Regulations of Political Parties in Spain, and the Decision to Outlaw Batasuna" in "Militant Democracy ...". ed. Andras Sajo, 69, 70 (Utrecht: Eleven International, 2004), 133.

[43] Ordinary crime does not trigger conditions of stress so long as it does not threaten to drive a wedge in the polity's collective self. Even intermittent terrorist activity, in contrast, seems likely to render that collective self more vulnerable.

So long as the war on terror unfolds under conditions of stress, two kinds of constraints that may be suspended in states of emergency remain in force: rights-based constraints and democracy-based constraints. For example, it may be justified in times of crisis, but not in times of stress, to suspend *habeas corpus* rights.[44] Furthermore, whereas ordinary parliamentary democratic politics may be suspended during a state of emergency,[45] no such suspension could be justified in times of stress.

The war on terror does not justify suspension of fundamental rights, but it does allow for recalibration of the scope of such rights to account for greater concerns regarding the polity's security and well-being. This can be accomplished through judicial deployment of ordinary balancing approaches and proportionality analysis.[46] In the context of the war on terror, the weight of the fundamental rights at stake would remain the same as that ascribed to them in ordinary times. The weight accorded to security concerns and to protection of the polity's identity, however, would be greater in the war on terror than during ordinary times. Thus, in the *Hamdi* case that arose out of the United States war against Al Quaeda and the Taliban in Afghanistan, the greater weight given to the state's security interests in the midst of the war on terror resulted in significantly less extensive procedural rights for a detainee claiming that he was mistakenly arrested as an enemy combatant in Afghanistan than for an ordinary domestic criminal suspect, including one believed to be a serial killer. Even if the presumed enemy combatant poses no greater threat to life than the suspected serial killer, granting the former somewhat lesser procedural rights than the latter may well be justified under a judicial balancing approach. Ordinary criminals and even serial killers do not appear to pose polity-wide threats, or to strike against the very collective identity of the citizenry. Arguably, the threat that would be terrorists pose against the felt unity and cohesiveness of the polity may alone justify according greater weight to the polity's security interests and hence legitimate some constriction of fundamental rights.

44 See, e.g., US Const. Art I, § 9, cl. 2, allowing for such suspension.

45 See, e.g., French Const. Art 16 giving the president virtually complete power monopoly during state of emergency.

46 See, e.g., *Hamdi* v. *Rumsfeld*, 124 S. Ct. 2633 (2004), U.S. Supreme Court plurality opinion used balancing test to determine validity of continued detention without charges of war on terror prisoner; *Beit Sourik Village Council v. The Government of Israel*, HCJ 4764/04 (2004), Israel Supreme Court use of proportionality analysis to determine legality of separation barrier designed to protect Israeli civilians from would-be Palestinian suicide bombers.

Terrorists, such as those who struck New York on September 11, 2001 or Madrid on March 11, 2004, or ETA or the IRA, are not likely to pose a danger of destroying a polity the way a foreign war or a full fledged civil war might. Nevertheless, terrorism, by its very unexpected and seemingly senseless and random nature, creates fears and anxieties that affect a polity's self-confidence and self-image. These changes in turn, are likely to bring about conditions of stress. Under such conditions, moreover, and in connection with waging the war on terror, collective security and identity reinforcement may justify curtailing the scope of certain rights both civil and political. And with respect to political rights, whereas the war on terror may call for suppression of certain political parties, such as Batistuna as discussed above,[47] just as does adherence to militant democracy, the respective reasons involved are different. In the case of militant democracy, the principal fear is that democracy could be compromised; in that of the war on terror, that security will be threatened and the collective self-image of the polity destabilized.[48]

In short, to the extent that the war on terror unfolds, under conditions of stress, it does not require abolition of political rights or creation of new ones. What it calls for, is proportionate readjustment that is likely to lead to some shrinking of the scope of certain civil and political rights. Which rights, and how much shrinking, will depend on the particular circumstances involved.

C. Pacted Secession

Attempts at unilateral secession, such as those that led to civil war in the United States in the 1860s, invariably create conditions of crisis. Efforts to achieve a pacted secession, in contrast, are likely to arise under, and/or

[47] See supra, at [266].

[48] This latter point is vividly illustrated by the *Batistuna* case. In relation to the self-image of post–Franco Spain, where the identity of the polity depends on a delicate balance between a sense of national unity and accommodation of the diversity represented by autonomous regions such as Cataluña and the Basque region, Basque terrorism and separatism seem to pose a much greater identity-based threat than a security one. Indeed, such terrorism risks to upset the delicate balance between unity and diversity, thus raising the possibility of repressive unity such as that imposed by Franco, or that of a civil war between those that would yearn for a return to authoritarian rule to preserve Spain's unity, those who would preserve the status quo, and those who would seek secession of certain autonomous regions.

produce, conditions of stress, but may well avoid falling into conditions of crisis. This may seem at first paradoxical or even contradictory, given that the distinction between conditions of stress and of crisis has been cast throughout the present analysis in terms of the difference between more remote and more immediate or more imminent threats to the unity and coherence of the polity. Under further analysis, and from the perspective of comprehensive pluralism, however, no real contradiction is involved as the unity or coherence of any particular polity is not an ultimate good. Instead, a working polity that does not actually face any plausible threat of dissolution possesses a viable framework that allows for a sufficient degree of integration among the various selves and others that share the same political space. More specifically, the framework in question must provide for a well balanced array of nodes of identification and differentiation – that is, through federalism, political party democracy, minority rights – to allow all the selves and others involved to engage in dynamic and peaceful interaction while cohering together through identification with the common overall self that binds the polity together without unduly sacrificing adherence to more particular or local selves.

Existing nation-states do not necessarily provide the best suited framework for the achievement of the optimal balance between identification and differentiation within a viable political space. Sometimes, such optimal equilibrium may require integration of other selves within a larger political space, such as that provided by a transnational polity. For example, it is quite plausible that differences between Flemish-speaking and French speaking Belgians might better be addressed within the larger framework of the European Union than within the narrower bounds of the Belgian polity. On the other hand, at other times, such optimal equilibrium is unlikely to be achieved without disentangling selves and others that are in such constant confrontation as threatens the unity and well-being of their common nation-state. For example, approximating the requite balance between identification and differentiation was arguably better achieved by splitting the former Czchekoslovak nation-state into the Czcheck Republic and the Republic of Slovakia.

Dissolution and reconstitution of polities to achieve better integration of identification and differentiation is thus not per se contrary to the edicts of comprehensive pluralism. *Involuntary* dissolution (from the standpoint of all or of some groups within the polity) is certain to provoke a crisis if it seems imminent and conditions of stress if it seems plausible but more remote. On the other hand, a successfully concluded secession pact should produce neither crisis nor stress. Finally, the *prospect* of a pacted secession would most likely take place under conditions of stress in as much as it would indicate a willingness to negotiate a peaceful pacted secession coupled with uncertainty about the outcome of such negotiations which, if they were to fail, could eventually culminate in a unilateral secession or civil war.

The prospect of pacted secession was considered by the Canadian Supreme Court in *Reference re Secession of Quebec*.[49] The key question before the court was whether Quebec was legally entitled to secede unilaterally from Canada. The court answered in the negative, but added that if a clear majority in Quebec wanted to secede, the remaining provinces had an obligation to negotiate with Quebec in good faith in order to determine whether an agreement could be reached on a pacted secession. The court specified that considerations of democracy and federalism, among others, required that negotiations regarding secession be as serious and solemn as deliberations concerning adoption of a proposed constitutional amendment. Ultimately, these negotiations would be political in nature.

The court indicated that the outcome of political process of negotiation at stake was uncertain, and refused to speculate over what ought to follow should negotiations toward pacted secession fail. In terms of politics, negotiations with a view to pacted secession ought to be constitutional politics. Moreover, given the tension created within the Canadian polity by Quebec's separatist movement, these negotiations would seem bound to take place under conditions of stress.

As constitutional politics intended to redesign relationships between self and other within and across polities, a pacted secession, such as that contemplated by the Canadian Supreme Court, deals with subject-related conflicts rather than with those regarding mere benefit or burden allocations. Accordingly, consistent with comprehensive pluralism, such pacted secession should draw directly on the second-order norms that define the pluralist ethos. In short, in as much as they arise in conditions of stress, pacted secessions require both enhanced consideration of the other by the self and intensification of the role of self-government. In other words, pacted secession under stress requires greater valorization and protection of the

[49] *Supreme Court Review* 2 (1998): 217.

identity rights of self and other and an increased self-restraint to preserve self-government from accrued temptations to govern for self-realization to the exclusion of the other who seeks secession or from whom secession is sought.

In the last analysis, all the cases examined above, those of hate speech and militant democracy, of the war on terror, and of pacted secession, indicate that there is a common task under various conditions of stress. That task is to strengthen or prevent further weakening of the bonds between the multiple selves and others that in spite of the various layer of differentiation that separate them continue to cohere as a unified whole within the bounds of relevant polity. What precisely needs to be done in any particular case depends on the circumstances. In some cases, it requires strengthening certain rights, or strengthening some and weakening others. In other cases, it may require constricting the scope of certain rights to readjust proportionately the interplay between identity and difference. In yet other cases, it requires great self-restraint and self-control to prevent outright exclusion of an other that has seemingly become too distant. In any event, conditions of stress do not call for any wholesale rejection or reinvention of the civil and political rights suited for ordinary times. In most cases, conditions of stress merely require refinement and readjustment.

Conclusion

Within the ambit of comprehensive pluralism, civil and political rights are meant to stir external dealings between self and other so as to strive to a maximum possible degree of overall unity combined with accommodation of the most extensive possible diversity. In ordinary times, civil and political rights must encourage vigorous self-government, foster or protect communal solidarity and carve out a space for individual and collective self-realization. In times of crisis, the threat to unity is so grave that the polity may have to suspend its pursuit of diversity and temporarily cease recognition or enforcement of civil and political rights. In the course of a genuine struggle for survival, what unifies, or can unify, the polity as a whole must trump what does, or could further, divide it.

What is required in times of stress is less obvious because the prime objective at such times may either be a return to ordinary times or avoidance at all cost to deteriorate inexorably towards times of crisis, or both. To the extent that the focus is on return to ordinary times, the emphasis should be on reinforcement of civil and political rights, or of the most important ones even if that can only be done at the expense of others. Thus, if democracy is threatened, recourse to militant democracy, which intensifies commitment to democracy but somewhat restricts its scope, may be the best weapon to ward off such threat. On the other hand, if the task is to prevent at all costs falling into conditions of crisis, the primary concern should be to defuse clashes between self and other. And that may require increasing or decreasing the scope of civil and political rights or adjusting their weight. Thus, in the war on terror, limiting certain civil and political rights may inoculate against eventually having to suspend them altogether in the face of a crisis. Furthermore, in the case of pacted secession, the goal is to narrow the range of differences within a polity, by reassigning increasingly incompatible differences to different polities.

In the end, pluralism does not furnish a list of civil and political rights for each of the three different times discussed throughout. Instead, it provides a logic and a dialectic that allow for a determination of the particular civil and political rights that are best suited for given circumstances. In this context, the civil and political rights suited for times of stress are not that different than those suited for other times. Nevertheless, in times of stress, the same rights are likely to be more or less extensive and more or less intense, depending on whether the most urgent need is to strengthen bonds between self and other or defuse conflict between them. Furthermore, in light of the preceding analysis, legal regimes and the constitutional frameworks that circumscribe them would undoubtedly benefit if they drew clear distinctions between traditional emergency conditions and conditions of stress. Indeed, that distinction is very likely to strengthen the grip of constitutional democracy in an age of pluralism.

Comment on Chapter 5

James Leonard*

"Things fall apart; the centre cannot hold."[1]

I. Introduction

Yeats' *Second Coming* is the classic statement of anxiety in the midst of stressful times. To him, the unsettling event was the seeming collapse of Western Civilization after World War I and the uncertainty of what would follow.[2] Nearly a century has passed since Yeats' "rough beast" slouched toward Bethlehem to be born and little has changed. The old certainties have vanished while the twenty-first century witnesses clashes among peoples who are startlingly different from each other. Sometimes the differences are irreconcilable. Sometimes they lead to violent clashes or social disintegration. Usually they inject insecurity into our lives. Michel Rosenfeld's contribution to this symposium poses the question of how societies should manage the fact of diversity while reacting to threats – internal and external, real and perceived. His solution is to recognize a condition of "stressful times," located between ordinary times and crisis, where the sovereign's reactions are restrained by the need to protect the pluralistic character of the polity. While his proposal is sound in many respects, I believe that in many cases liberalism will yield the same results; Rosenfeld's scheme, moreover, underestimates the positive role that assimilation can play in a diverse society that is under stress.

* The author wishes to thank Bill Brewbaker for his insightful criticism of an earlier draft of this comment.

1 W. B. Yeats, "The Second Coming," line 3.

2 Harold Bloom, *Yeats* (Oxford: Oxford University Press, 1970), 318.

Rosenfeld argues that a modern constitutional democracy must develop appropriate political rights and institutions to protect its constituents, who collectively hold a welter of comprehensive philosophies and identities. By political rights, he means those rights that are necessary or indispensable for citizens to run their polity or receive its benefits. Political rights are distinct from civil, social and economic rights, though the latter may become ancillary to former. Rosenfeld also aims to protect such schemes to the maximum extent feasible when a polity is under threat. Thus he constructs a tripartite scheme to judge the curtailment of political rights based on the level of threat to the polity. In ordinary times (let us analogize these to Homeland Security Code Green), existing mechanisms are sufficient to resolve the usual tensions among groups of citizens without either destroying the common identity necessary to sustain the polity or threatening group identities. In times of crisis (Code Red), when the polity itself is genuinely threatened, all rights must bend to the needs of self-preservation. Between these conditions lies the middle ground of stress (Code Orange). Here the situation is murkier, and the arguments for preserving the political rights needed to accommodate diversity are, in fact, greater than under either Code Green or Red.

More generally, Professor Rosenfeld's paper attempts to extend his theory of comprehensive pluralism, set out in his 1995 book *Just Interpretations*, to the question of emergencies.[3] The essence of comprehensive pluralism is the preservation of difference within a modern pluralistic society on fair terms. This philosophy views the goal of modern constitutional democracy as the preservation of pluralism through constitutional mechanisms that strike a proper balance between majoritarian and counter-majoritarian institutions. His baseline approach is a two-step, Hegelian sort of dialectic by which all competing conceptions of the good are: 1) banished and then 2) readmitted to the polity with equal standing. The idea is to accommodate as many competing concepts of the good as possible but – here's the catch – each must be "consistent with *equal* admission and *equal* opportunity for others to flourish." For example, a complacent mainstream church is consistent with comprehensive pluralism but not one practicing aggressive proselytism.

[3] Michel Rosenfeld, *Just Interpretations: Law between Ethics and Politics* (Berkeley: University of California Press, 1998).

Yet two questions must be answered before Rosenfeld's take on emergencies can be accepted. First, is the concept of an intermediate state of "stress" unique to comprehensive pluralism or can it be achieved under competing philosophies such as liberalism or communitarianism? Second comes the question of normative justification. Rosenfeld appears to accept pluralism as an obvious good, or at least an inevitable aspect of modern life. But why should this be so? Why should assimilation not be an available option to deal with internal and external threats? I'll address the first question in Part II and the latter in Part III.

II. The Concept of Stressful Times

Rosenfeld's scheme for preserving the character of diverse societies under threat makes a valuable analytical contribution. Creating a middle ground between normalcy and war opens political theory to thoughtful responses to threats unburdened by the all-or-nothing traditional view. Emergency powers have traditionally been viewed as an exception to normal legal regimes. John Locke, for example, recognized that the executive retains a prerogative to act for the public good when not authorized by positive law or even in spite of it.[4] Responses to invasion or insurrection under this view are treated as necessary exceptions to the law itself, to be tolerated until the all clear is sounded. Rosenfeld shares the traditional view that imminent threats to the integrity of the polity require decisive responses that may devalue political rights.

An intermediate concept of stressful times short of a crisis offers an alternative to the all-or-nothing Lockean dichotomy between peace and war or insurrection. Some – though hardly all – American citizens may find Professor Rosenfeld's concept of stressful times appealing. Since the events of September 11th, 2001, and the subsequent invasions of Iraq and Afghanistan, the Bush Administration has routinely described the United States as locked in a state of war on terror. Such statements are literally true regarding the conduct of military operations in those nations; it is equally obvious that the United States remains the target of dangerous terrorist

[4] John Locke, *The Second Treatise of Government*, 160–61; See also Oren Gross and Fionnuala Ní Aoláin, *Law in Times of Crisis: Emergency Powers in Theory and Practice* (Cambridge: Cambridge University Press, 2006), 119–30.

activity at home and abroad. Daily life in the United States, however, lacks the feel of a country on a war-time footing. There are persistent news reports on the fluctuating situation in the theaters of war and saddening casualty lists but no shortages of goods much less ration cards, no conscription, no German submarines prowling our coasts, and no Red Army encircling Berlin. Today's threat is different. An ideological enemy wishes to sow terror by attacking landmarks such as the World Trade Center and, given the opportunity, would gleefully nuke New York.

Reasonable minds can disagree on the question of whether current threats to our polity are equal to or greater than those posed by a conventional war such as World War II. Just imagine the personal and systemic devastation of a nuclear detonation in a major financial center or a national capital. But we must be careful here not to beg the question since a conclusion of imminent danger tells us nothing about how a constitutional democracy should react to times of stress. If the current situation is indeed more dire than World War II or the Cuban Missile Crisis, then we live in a moment of crisis when the polity itself is threatened and political rights must bend. Stressful times, in contrast, may be painful but pose no immediate threat to our institutions. Thus the dichotomy between stress and crisis may be a useful way of evaluating sovereign responses to emergencies.

But is there only one philosophical path to a graded response to stressful conditions? Rosenfeld acknowledges that other modern political theories, such as communitarianism or liberalism are compatible with some aspects of comprehensive pluralism. To my mind, there is no apparent bar to other political theories developing a middle ground between peace, when criminal law reacts to threats, and times of true crisis when the executive may exercise extraordinary powers. The easy case is communitarianism. A communitarian polity could simply adopt a stress-oriented approach as matter of community will; its members would then be obliged to acquiesce to defend the polity's solidarity. Likewise liberalism, with its orientation toward protecting individuals from the state, can produce a calibrated scheme. Bruce Ackerman, for example has recently reacted to the perceived abuses to civil rights in the post 9/11 war on terror by calling for an intermediate "emergency constitution" of short duration.[5]

5 Bruce Ackerman, *Before the Next Attack: Preserving Civil Liberties in an Age of Terrorism* (New Haven: Yale University Press, 2006). Although Ackerman is generally considered to belong

There is an argument that even liberalism's icon, Rawls, might be comfortable with Rosenfeld's distinction between stressful times and crisis. (Before proceeding, let me make clear that this comment does not make an affirmative argument for a Rawlsian approach to emergencies; the point, rather, is that a Rawlsian approach *might* resemble Rosenfeld's in some respects.) Rawls' political liberalism, granted, focuses on the basic structure of society "over time from one generation to the next."[6] His work does not focus on emergencies and takes a dim view of war in most circumstances.[7] Rawls' emphasis is on elaborating a fair system of social cooperation among free and equal citizens in a well ordered society.[8] At first glance this formulation hardly describes a society weathering a threat. Nonetheless a measured approach to times of stress might be compatible with the Rawlsian mindset.

Basic civil rights sit at the apex of the Rawlsian world. Rawls' first principle of justice, which is explicitly prior to his second principle limiting social and economic inequalities, holds that "each person has an indefeasible claim to a fully adequate scheme of equal basic liberties for all."[9] In part they serve to protect members of pluralistic societies from the brutal application of state power needed to establish a single comprehensive moral philosophy.[10] In greater part, basic equal liberties are necessary to create the social conditions necessary for each person to exercise his or her moral capacities to have a sense of justice and to formulate a conception of the good.[11]

Although he does not discuss emergencies generally, Rawls' reluctance to deviate from basic civil rights can be seen in his discussion of the clear and present danger doctrine of American free speech jurisprudence. [12] He regards political speech as inherently dangerous and criticizes the doctrine for excluding from the public square ideas that should be decided by

to liberalism, see, e.g., Bruce Ackerman, *Social Justice in the Liberal State* (New Haven: Yale University Press, 1980), one scholar regards Ackerman's work on emergency powers as an expression of Roman civic republicanism. See Leonard C. Feldman, *The Banality of Emergency*, p. 137.

6 John Rawls, *Justice as Fairness: A Restatement* (Cambridge, MA: Belknap Press, 2001), 5.

7 John Rawls, *The Law of Peoples* (Cambridge, MA: Harvard University Press, 1999).

8 Rawls, *Justice as Fairness*, 5.

9 Id. at 42.

10 Id. at 43.

11 Id. at 43.

12 John Rawls, *Political Liberalism* (New York: Columbia University Press, 1993), 348–56.

democratic institutions precisely because they are dangerous. Rawls permits restrictions on political speech only for a "constitutional crisis of the requisite kind," that is, when democratic institutions may become dysfunctional or other basic liberties are threatened.[13] Emergencies threatening serious political on economic injury on even a state of war do not necessarily justify curtailment of basic rights.[14]

One can perceive an overlap between Rosenfeld's concept of stress and Rawls' threshold for annulling speech rights. Rawls' distinction between a "constitutional crisis of the requisite kind" and serious threats to the political or economic well-being strikes me as approximating Rosenfeld's line between stress and crisis. The correspondence isn't perfect. If anything, Rawls may be the more reluctant to bend civil liberties to emergency conditions. As I observe below, Rosenfeld is willing to balance certain rights with the sovereign's need to manage the war on terror. Rawls, in contrast, has never seen a war involving the United States that would justify the constriction of political speech.[15] Despite differences of degree, however, both men are deeply mistrustful of claims that emergencies justify nullification of rights.

In sum, liberalism seems capable of developing a concept of stressful times that coincides to some extent with Rosenfeld's scheme. The two systems share a sense that skepticism about relaxing rights except in the direst circumstances. Their normative goals, which I contrast in the next section, are quite different.

III. Pluralism in Times of Stress

Difference is a hallmark of western constitutional democracies. Countries such as the United States are home to diverse races, ethnic groups and religions as well as social and political philosophies. Such variations often create social instability or discriminatory environments. The American response to this social evolution has been to create legal protections against discrimination of the basis of one's minority status or membership in an historically disadvantaged group. Beginning in Sixties, the

[13] Id. at 355.
[14] Id. at 355.
[15] Id. at 355.

American federal government enacted a series of statutory rules against discrimination on the basis of race, gender, religion, color and national origin (e.g., the Civil Rights Act of 1964), age (the Age Discrimination in Employment Act) and disability (e.g., the Americans with Disabilities Act). Protection of minority status is also found in basic constitutional rights such as the freedoms of expression, religion or association as well as the due process mandate. Under the American model, such protections appear as individual rights enforceable by individuals as opposed to the protection of groups qua groups. Other nations have taken the latter approach. The Canadian system, for example, protects the French culture of Quebec largely though a system of language rules[16] while Belgium permits strict language restrictions within the Flemish and French speaking areas of the country.[17]

Rosenfeld rightly notes that the challenge during times of stress is to react to threats without undermining the careful arrangements that a democratic society has made to accommodate its diverse constituencies. It is not difficult to find examples of state action during periods of stress with the potential to undermine the balance of a pluralistic society. Profiling passengers of Middle Eastern origin at international airports tends to create a sense of insecurity or alienation for groups of persons whose baggage is subjected to extended hand searches. Disparaging sound-bites about "fundamentalist Islam" served up by pandering politicians are likely to have a similar effect. Nor is the challenge limited to the war on terror. Many recent immigrants to the United States, who have learned English as a second language, react defensively to the English-Only Movement's demands that other languages yield in public, such as government hearings and schools.

No one of normal sensibilities can deny the discouraging effects of such measures in a diverse society. Yet Rosenfeld's paper invites two further questions about a comprehensive pluralist approach to periods of stress. First, taking his argument for pluralism at face value, to what degree does Rosenfeld's proposal increase protections beyond those already offered by individually centered schemes such as Rawlsian liberalism? The follow up inquiry is whether the normative arguments for maximizing protections of

16 Québec, *Charter of the French Language* (1977).

17 See Belgium, *Constitution.*, art 2, which divides the country into three language based regions (Flemish, French and German) plus a bilingual Brussels..

pluralism in stressful times are as strong as Rosenfeld suggests and whether assimilation is sometimes a more appropriate response.

A. Comprehensive Pluralism vs. Rawlsian Liberalism

Let us assume for purposes of comparison that comprehensive pluralism's goal of creating safe spaces for the range of differences in a typical modern democracy is superior to other norms. One can reasonably ask, as a practical matter, how much does comprehensive pluralism add to the protections that might emerge from an application of Rawlsian principles to times of stress? To focus the inquiry, let's examine three examples used by Rosenfeld to illustrate possible liberal approaches to stressful times: hate speech restrictions, militant democracy and the war on terror.

Hate Speech

Rosenfeld defines hate speech conventionally as "expressing highly offensive, insulting and demeaning views regarding certain racial, ethnic or religious groups." Although he does not specify a social context for his analysis of hate speech, he apparently has in mind the stressful social upheavals associated with wide-scale immigration or demographic change. Rosenfeld argues that, since "pure" hate speech has no "genuine social value," it may be banned in ordinary times though it may also be tolerated for strategic reasons. A *fortiori* hate speech may be banned in times of stress. Germany's ban on expressions of Nazi ideology, for example, is an appropriate response to the stress caused by the memory of World War II and the possibility that National Socialism might re-emerge.

Can we achieve a tolerably similar result under a Rawlsian scheme? Maybe. While Rawls was concerned with fair basic social structures over time, one can make an argument that bans on hate speech might be permitted in a Rawlsian world. The argument runs roughly as follows. Rawls' first principle of justice guaranties a scheme of equal basic liberties that is compatible with the "same scheme of liberties for all."[18] Such rights are essential to the exercise of the individual's moral capacities to have a sense of justice and to formulate a concept of the good. Rawls also numbers among the "primary goods" of a democratic society "the social bases of self-respect"

[18] Rawls, *Justice as Fairness*, 42.

needed to allow persons to have a "sense of worth as persons and ... advance their ends with self-confidence."[19]

A Rawlsian might look at this stated relationship among equal liberties, self-respect and moral capacities then conclude that hate speech defeats self-worth and contributes nothing to any conceivable concept of good. The conclusion would seem to apply in ordinary as well as stressful times. Indeed, Will Kymlicka has used similar logic in arguing for multi-cultural accommodations with the framework of liberalism.[20] Further, it is not far-fetched to argue that Rawls' hypothetical interlocutors would approve of hate speech restrictions, at least for times of stress, so long these issues were allowed to slip under the veil of ignorance.

There are problems with this argument. Foremost is Rawls' view that fulfilment of basic equal liberties takes priority over attempts to correct social or economic inequalities[21] and his insistence against trade-offs of basic liberties to gain greater equality.[22] One can also counter, by analogy to Rawls' critique of the clear and present danger doctrine, that speech codes are prone to suppress necessary public discussion of a "dangerous" issue that should be resolved by democratic institutions.[23] Since Rawls did not discuss hate speech rules directly, it's difficult to know how he would have worked out the issue. If hate speech bans are acceptable under a Rawlsian scheme, then Rosenfeld's scheme would seem to duplicate the results albeit for different normative reasons. But if T. M. Scanlon is right that hate speech codes are hard to square with Rawlsian fundamentals,[24] then we must still ask whether Rosenfeld's more aggressive pluralistic norms are worth the intrusions into individual autonomy (see below).

Militant Democracy

Rosenfeld's comprehensive pluralism is also indulgent of militant democracy in times of stress. Referring to Karl Popper's "paradox of tolerance," he notes that there are times when a polity must repress the intolerant in order to preserve tolerance in society. During times of peace, societies may

[19] Id. at 59.

[20] Will Kymlicka, *Multicultural Citizenship: A Liberal Theory of Minority Rights* (Oxford: Clarendon Press, 1995).

[21] Rawls, *Justice as Fairness*, 46.

[22] Id. at 47.

[23] Cf. John Rawls, *Political Liberalism*, 349–50.

[24] T. M. Scanlon, "Adjusting Rights and Balancing Values," *Fordham Law Review* 72 (2004): 1485.

choose to endure the slings and arrows of intolerance for strategic reasons since the integrity of the polity is not threatened. During stressful times, Rosenfeld reasons, the presence of intolerant elements may provoke a crisis; hence the arguments for controlling the intolerant are much stronger in stressful circumstances. By way of example, Rosenfeld argues that control of Nazi ideology in Germany during the Twenties and Thirties might have spared us of World War II and that post-War suppression upheld the dignity of the surviving Jewish population.

Rawlsian liberalism, again, might lend itself to the same result. Justice Jackson famously said that the Constitution is not a suicide pact;[25] the same can be said of the Rawlsian social contract. Rawls conceived of society as a "fair system of cooperation." This concept is distinct from socially coordinated activity. Rather, it requires that collaboration proceed under rules that are based on reciprocity or mutuality and are reasonably acceptable to all involved.[26] It is inconceivable that an intolerant sovereign could fit within a Rawlsian framework since it would both destroy the necessary reciprocity of cooperation and would not maintain the basic rights which each persons needs to develop a sense of the good.

Whether a Rawlsian scheme would run the risk of intolerant elements within a liberal society is a more difficult question. One can make an argument that a Rawlsian analysis permits some restriction on anti-democratic forces in times of stress. Rawls stated that none of the basic rights were absolute: the priority of one right can be limited for the sake of another.[27] He further argued that the priority of a particular liberty depended on it's power to protect the moral capacity of each person to develop a sense of justice and a conception of the good.[28] While Rawls is generally hostile to content restrictions on speech[29] he recognizes that certain restraints of speech, such as rules against defaming private person, have no effect upon public reason while others, such as incitements to lawlessness, subvert democratic processes.

It strikes me as a possible (though hardly a required) reading of Rawls that anti-democratic expressions during times of stress, especially when crisis

25 *Terminiello v. Chicago*, 337 U.S. 1, 37 (1949).

26 John Rawls, *Justice as Fairness*, 6.

27 Id. at 111.

28 Id. at 113.

29 Id. at 111.

is looming, might be controlled on grounds that they interfere with the development of democratic institutions and threaten the development of moral capacity. In his discussion of the clear and present danger doctrine, Rawls holds open the possibility that speech rights may be curtailed when expression threatens other basic liberties.[30] Hence, as with rules against hate speech, a Rawlsian result might resemble that of comprehensive pluralism. The normative ambitions would again be different.

The War on Terror

Unlike situations involving hate speech or anti-democratic forces, which straddle the line between ordinary and stressful conditions, Rosenfeld locates the war on terror near the boundary between times of stress and crisis. He concedes that, the more the war on terror resembles a hot war, the greater the sovereign's need to curtail basic civil and political rights. The proper approach, Rosenfeld argues, is to balance existing rights against the sovereign's need to maintain security and to reinforce the polity's collective self image against the fears and anxieties caused by terrorist acts. Hence procedural rights of Guantanamo detainees might be limited as in *Hamdi*. In some cases political parties associated with violent separatist movements, such as Batistuna in the Basque regions of Spain might be banned to protect the delicately balanced national identity.

I am more skeptical about Rawlsian liberalism making the sorts of concessions that Rosenfeld contemplates here. Certainly a polity ordered on Rawlsian principles has a compelling interest in protecting itself from the effects of a prolonged war on terror and the disruptions that terrorism brings to the individualized pursuits of citizens and the development of each's moral powers. But Rawls' already noted comments in *Political Liberalism*, that no war so far has threatened the stability of the United States constitutional system sufficiently to justify restraints of political speech, makes it doubtful that he would contemplate the compromising of an essential right such as habeas corpus. Perhaps here the normative difference between the Rosenfeld and the Rawlsian liberal makes a real difference. Liberalism's dedication to individualism requires it to regard a single curtailment of rights as significant. A comprehensive pluralist, on the other hand, might

30 Rawls, *Political Liberalism*, 356.

regard the adjustment of rights as an acceptable price for maintaining a climate friendly to difference in spite of threats to the polity.

B. Pluralism as a Norm in Times of Stress

There will thus be situations in which liberalism will not achieve the same results as pluralism. The foregoing examples reflect a potential convergence of liberal and pluralistic interests that sometimes can be served by the same devices. In other cases, convergence will be frustrated by liberalism's individual orientation. Laws prohibiting aggressive religious proselytizing, for example, might be acceptable under comprehensive pluralism but would be unlikely to survive a Rawlsian screening. Likewise constitutional structures allocating public offices according to ethnic criteria may be acceptable in a pluralist regime but would likely violate Rawls' Second Principle of Justice requiring that offices be "open to all under conditions of fair equality of opportunity."

For those situations where pluralism lends itself to a distinct approach, we must now ask whether its norms provide the most appropriate guidance under conditions of stress. The following passage in Rosenfeld's paper is key to evaluating his approach:

> [I]t does not necessarily follow that because times of stress are sandwiched between ordinary times and those of crisis that political rights in conditions of stress should be more restricted than those in ordinary times. On the contrary, arguably when the unity of the polity begins to crack but is in no imminent danger of collapse, it would seem better reinforce rather than to weaken political rights.

At first glance this statement is sensible. No enlightened ruler wants to discard a carefully structured social system lightly. But Rosenfeld is not a neutral observer; he refers to the political rights that undergird a pluralist state. Hence we must press the question: why are pluralist norms preferable to others in confronting stressful times? The question has two aspects.

First, there is the attractiveness of the norm itself. Why, even in ordinary times, would we want to maintain a system based on pluralist norms rather than shifting to another perspective? Needless to say a thorough evaluation of comprehensive pluralism and its competitors exceeds the limitations of this forum. So, I'll limit myself to general comments about the assumptions that underlie pluralism and the trade-offs involved in following its path in times of emergency.

Rosenfeld, if I read his paper correctly, believes that diversity within a modern, western society is inevitable and thus requires protection. As such he concurs with Rawls' observation that modern society is pluralistic in fact.[31] Nor is he an everything-goes-multi-cultural-relativist. Under his dialectical process for clearing away social elements and readmitting them after being screened for compatibility within a pluralistic milieu, not all groups or comprehensive moral ideas will survive. The chief advantage of this philosophy is the creation of harmonious social spaces where it is safe for the various elements of society to be different.

Pluralism nevertheless comes at a cost, most obviously the loss of individual orientation that is characteristic of liberalism. Individuals and private associations would lose some prerogatives that might be deemed incompatible with a particular pluralistic community such as aggressive religious proselytizing or undifferentiated citizenship. There is not much to say about this trade-off that hasn't already been said already in the context of communitarian or multiculturalist proposals: the more one moves toward an equality model that includes collective rights, the fewer one's regrets over the loss of liberty-driven interests.

I wish to focus on a different cost (though a pluralist would hardly call it such): the power of the sovereign to encourage assimilation. Although the idea is presently out of fashion among elites and the academy,[32] adoption and even imposition of a prescribed national identity has been an important element in the formation of many nations. National identity, as reflected by compliance with certain beliefs or practices, is a powerful tool in creating a sense of solidarity and allegiance among citizens that is useful when a polity is threatened. In *The Discovery of France*, Graham Robb traces the evolution of the French nation after the Revolution from an agglomeration of peoples only 11 percent of whom spoke "pure French" to the present where the ability to speak this language is a test of Frenchness.[33] Such an evolution would have been unlikely under

[31] Rawls, *Justice as Fairness*, 3.

[32] Samuel P. Huntington, *Who Are We? The Challenges to America's National Identity* (New York: Simon & Schuster, 2004), 143, 327.

[33] Graham Robb, *The Discovery of France: A Historical Geography from the Revolution to the First World War* (New York: W. W. Norton, 2007), 52.

pluralist precepts. The American experience has been similar. Until the Sixties, immigrants were expected to learn English and other adapt to the American mores such as the Protestant work ethic and the renunciation of past allegiances.[34]

Let me be clear that I am not arguing that every society should adopt a program of assimilation out of some nostalgic impulse. Reasonable persons can conclude, for example, that a federal structure empowering territorially concentrated cultural or language minorities is a rational pluralistic solution to the challenges of difference. Spain, Belgium and Canada have taken this approach. I do suggest that some polities may find that selective assimilation is a useful way of dealing with difference in ordinary times and with threats in times of stress, especially when stressful conditions are created by the fact of difference itself.

Take the example of mass migrations and radical demographic change, a situation that Rosenfeld correctly treats as stressful. Newcomers are typically divided from old line citizens by language and sometimes by ethnicity, religion and persisting allegiance to their native lands. There's little one can do to change ethnicity while attempts at forced religious conversion are unthinkable. Sovereign authorities can, however, encourage assimilation by gentler means. Traditional civil rights laws prohibiting intentional discrimination in employment and services may bring old and new citizens together in the public realm. At the same time, the sovereign can also take positive steps to move newcomers toward mainstream norms such as requirements that one learn and use an official language in public settings,[35] compulsory education under a curriculum that teaches core national values, or renunciation of foreign citizenship. Such actions would no doubt challenge certain notions of identity and encroach upon pluralism's mandate to accommodate the maximum number of concepts of the good. (It might also be in tension with the Rawlsian mandate to protect individualized conceptions of good).

Certain stresses created by the war on terror might also be addressed by encouraging greater assimilation. Threats against a polity arising in a remote area of the world, such as the Middle East, may be complicated by

[34] Huntington, *Who Are We?*, 182–99.

[35] For a contrary view, cf. Cristina M. Rodríguez, "Language and Participation," *California Law Review* 94 (2006): 687.

the presence of a domestic population with religious or ethnic ties to that region. One striking fact about the 2005 London transport bombings was that three of four suicide bombers were of Pakistani origin but also native born Britons.[36] Subsequent polling revealed a high degree of social alienation among British Muslims.[37] Separation of Muslims from the larger British society is no doubt a complex phenomenon influenced by British support for American policy in the Middle East and the War in Iraq, economic disadvantage, prolonged detention of Muslims by security forces, continuing ties with home countries, patronizing treatment by government officials and so forth.[38] Commentators have also observed that Islamic practices such as veiling the female face are difficult to reconcile with secular western views.[39] In light of these substantial challenges it seems reasonable to preserve the option of promoting reconciliation through assimilation. Nudging Muslim children toward ethnically and religiously diverse schools, for example, might provide valuable exposure to civic concepts that are not emphasized in faith schools or madrasas and thereby lessen the social separation that contributes to radicalization.

IV. Conclusion

Michel Rosenfeld's pluralistic approach to periods of stress is partially successful. Everyone, even those who are uncomfortable with the philosophy of comprehensive pluralism, can credit him with envisioning an intermediate state of danger that permits measured responses rather than the disregard for ordinary law often required by a full blown crisis. Advocates of social pluralism should be grateful that less immediate threats need not undo carefully constructed institutions that protect difference. Rawlsian liberals may be relieved that the pluralist approach will sometimes resemble their own.

36 Alan Cowell and Don Van Natta Jr, "Bombings in London: London Bombings; 4 From Britain Carried Out Terror Blasts, Police Say," *New York Times*, July 13, 2005; Lizette Alvarez, "Bombings in London: The Fourth Bomber; New Muslim at 15, Terror Suspect at 19," *New York Times*, July 18, 2005.

37 See, e.g., Timothy Garton Ash, "What Young British Muslims Say Can Be Shocking – Some of It Is also True," *The Guardian*, Aug. 10, 2006, http://www.guardian.co.uk/commentisfree/2006/aug/10/comment.rac (accessed on December 17, 2008).

38 Wendy Kristianasen, "Britain's Multiculturalism Falters," *Le Monde Diplomatique*, Nov. 2006, http://mondediplo.com/2006/11/02ukmuslims (accessed on December 17, 2008).

39 Huntington, *Who Are We?*, 188–189.

Pluralism, however, cannot relieve every point of stress. There will be times when only a strong sense of national identity will bolster a society's framework and defenses. We should be hesitant to let that option go. Perhaps Yeats' falconer has more power than he realized to keep the falcon from widening its gyre.

Index